For the Record

Volume 1

Intimate profiles of hit-making recording artists: Jimmy Gilmer
and the Fireballs, Gary "U.S." Bonds, the Tokens, the Angels,
Peter and Gordon, the Beau Brummels, Sam the Sham and the Pharaohs,
the Lovin' Spoonful, Gary Puckett and the Union Gap,
Country Joe and the Fish, and Iron Butterfly

Marti Smiley Childs
and Jeff March

For the Record, **Volume 1**

Intimate profiles of hit-making recording artists:
Jimmy Gilmer and the Fireballs, Gary "U.S." Bonds, the Tokens,
the Angels, Peter and Gordon, the Beau Brummels,
Sam the Sham and the Pharaohs, the Lovin' Spoonful,
Gary Puckett and the Union Gap,
Country Joe and the Fish, and Iron Butterfly

Third Edition

Originally titled *Echoes of the Sixties*

P.O. Box 171
Collierville, TN 38017

ISBN-13: 978-1-937317-55-3

Printed in the United States of America

 "Baby Boomers" know this, but for those who may not, the symbol (at left) seen throughout this book represents a 45 rpm adaptor, used to convert the large center hole of 45 rpm singles for play on turntables with small-diameter spindles designed for 33 1/3 rpm.

Table of Contents

Acknowledgments

We would not have been able to create this book without the enthusiastic cooperation of the performers about whom we wrote, as well as their family members, producers, managers and musical colleagues, and others with whom we spoke. We offer our gratitude to all of them listed here.

THE FIREBALLS
Eric Budd
Jimmy Gilmer
Dawn Lark
Stan Lark
Jerry MacNeish
Chuck Tharp
George Tomsco
Dan Trammell

GARY "U.S." BONDS
Gary Anderson
Donnie Brooks

THE TOKENS
Donnie Brooks
Mitch Margo
Phil Margo
Hank Medress
Jay Siegel

THE ANGELS
Peggy Santiglia Davison
Barbara Allbut Brown
Kenny Schreiber
Phyllis "Jiggs" Allbut
  Sirico

PETER AND GORDON
Peter Asher
Kathy Holland
Gordon Waller

**THE BEAU
BRUMMELS**
Ron Elliott
Ron Meagher
Declan Mulligan
John Petersen
Catherine Valentino
Sal Valentino

**SAM THE SHAM AND
THE PHARAOHS**
Paul "Butch" Gibson
Denise Martin

Jean Martin
Jerry Patterson
Ann Samudio
Domingo "Sam" Samudio
Ray Stinnett

**THE LOVIN'
SPOONFUL**
Steve Boone
Joe Butler
John Sebastian
Jerry Yester

**GARY PUCKETT AND
THE UNION GAP**
Dwight Bement
Donnie Brooks
Kerry Chater
Jim Dotson
Gary Puckett
Paul Wheatbread
Gary Withem

**COUNTRY JOE AND
THE FISH**
Bruce Barthol
David Bennett Cohen
Barbara Joy Langer
Barry Melton

IRON BUTTERFLY
Erik Braunn
Ron Bushy
Lee Dorman
Doug Ingle

PHOTOGRAPHY
Richard Bermack
Gary J. Bernas
Joel Brodsky
Annetta Brown
Josh Budd
Ron Bushy
Lynn Gillespie Chater
David Bennett Cohen

Henry Diltz
Amanda Domingues
Expressly Portraits
Charles Gage
Mary Frances Abernathy
  Gibson
Dick Gilfether
Chuck Goehrig
Dawn Lark
Marsha March
Natalie Martel
Jean Martin
Ron Meagher
Jane Medress
Tanya G. Mulligan
Mickey O'Keefe
Photofest Archives
Tina Quirino
Christine Santelli
Catherine Sebastian
Jon Seong
Scott Shea
Ken Shuper
Tim Stahl
Joan Tharp
Georgeann Albrecht
  Trammell
Paul Vakselis
John Vincent
Franco Vogt
Chris Walter, Photofeatures
Clyde Williston
Penny Withem

MUSIC CHART DATA
Joel Whitburn's Record
Research Inc.

**ART DIRECTION/
GRAPHIC DESIGN**
Marti Smiley Childs,
Book-Prep.com

Preface

As the 1960s draw ever more distant in our recollective rear-view mirror, the overwhelming influence of those watershed years in redefining American culture becomes ever more apparent. The 30 million Americans who called themselves children of the '60s, people who were born between 1946 and 1956 and lived their formative years during that decade, found a common bond in the events, sights, and sounds of that remarkable era of change.

Ushered in under the stalwart leadership of Dwight Eisenhower, the 1960s soon took an abrupt idealistic turn skyward as charismatic John Kennedy unfolded his vision of the New Frontier that included a promise to land an American astronaut on the moon by the end of the decade. We had no idea how wild the ride would be through that jubilant, chaotic, angry decade, a blur of sights and sounds through which we hung on for dear life. And pop music provided the soundtrack that reflected the shifting political and sociological climate of the era.

The decade dawned in innocence, with the pop charts dominated by doo-wop and innocuous puppy love ballads by teen idols Frankie Avalon, Brenda Lee, Fabian, Dion and the Belmonts, and others of the bouffant-hair set. The first indication of the potency of pop came in the early part of the decade, when the twist dance craze heralded a string of dance-inciting hits by Chubby Checker, Dee Dee Sharp, the Dovells, Gary "U.S." Bonds, Little Eva, and Joey Dee and his Starliters — the stomp, the hucklebuck, the watusi, the fly, the limbo, the slop, the pony, the mashed potato, and other dances that were not only immensely popular among teenagers, but captivated adults as well.

While dancers were gyrating, however, the groundwork for profound societal changes was under way. Sit-ins began February 1, 1960, in Greensboro, North Carolina, in protest of the treatment of four Black college students who were refused service at a lunch counter in a Woolworth's store. At the University of Mississippi, 3,000 troops quelled an October 1962 riot that was provoked by the admission of James Meredith as the first Black student at the campus. The following August, 200,000 civil rights demonstrators gathered in Washington, D.C., where the Rev. Martin Luther King delivered his stirring "I Have a Dream" speech.

Meanwhile, international tensions were building between the United States and communist nations. On May 1, 1960, the Soviet Union shot down an American U-2 reconnaissance plane over Russia. The United States severed relations in January 1961 with Soviet ally Cuba after that island nation commandeered American business properties in Cuba, and three months later an American-engineered military attempt to overthrow Cuban premier Fidel Castro failed. Halfway around the world, American military personnel had been dispatched in South Vietnam since the mid-'50s as advisers to help train South Vietnamese troops for combat with communist North Vietnam. But America's posture in the conflict changed in February 1962, when President John Kennedy authorized American military "advisers" to return fire if attacked by enemy troops. The discovery of a buildup of Soviet missiles in Cuba aimed toward the United States led to an American naval and air blockade that brought the two nations separated by only 90 miles to the brink of war in October 1962.

Despite the immensity of the consequences that would follow, mainstream America paid little heed to the growing intensity of the civil rights movement and the escalation of the Vietnam conflict. Hit recordings by the Beach Boys, Jan and Dean, Dick Dale and the Del-Tones, the Fireballs, and the Angels reflected the preoccupation of American kids with surfing, cars, and dating. The undercurrents of folk music that the Tokens rode with "The Lion Sleeps Tonight" in early 1962 surfaced prominently in 1963, when the college-based, hand-clapping "hootenanny" fad thrust the Kingston Trio, the New Christy Minstrels, the Rooftop Singers, and Peter, Paul, and Mary into the top 20. Even though their success at the time was based more on musical than on lyrical content, the folk-flavored hits of the early '60s — particularly those by Peter, Paul, and Mary — helped elevate the social consciousness of pop music and the acceptance of acoustic folk music artists such as Pete Seeger, Joan Baez, and Bob Dylan. Peter, Paul, and Mary first popularized the music of Dylan, whose composition "Blowin' in the Wind" became an anthem for the civil rights movement and whose influence on pop music became monumental.

The assassination of President Kennedy in Dallas on November 22, 1963, rocked America to its foundations. U.S. involvement in Vietnam, which had begun with 700 military advisers in 1956, had increased to 15,000 troops by the time of Kennedy's death. In those confused times, American kids were ripe for a change. And in those closing days of 1963, disc jockeys at a few radio stations complied by spinning a record called "From Me to You" by an English band calling itself the Beatles. After the Beatles' "I Want to Hold Your Hand" captured the No. 1 position on the *Billboard* Hot 100, where it remained for seven weeks in February and March 1964, American kids embraced everyone and everything British. Peter and Gordon, Chad and Jeremy, the Moody Blues, the Rolling

Stones, Marianne Faithfull, Herman's Hermits, Dusty Springfield, Gerry and the Pacemakers, the Animals, Petula Clark, the Dave Clark Five, the Kinks, Cilla Black, Billy J. Kramer with the Dakotas, and other British performers catapulted onto the American charts — and into the repertoire of American bands. British influences were infused successfully by a number of American bands, including the Beau Brummels and the Sir Douglas Quintet. And because the Beatles played so well to television audiences, a number of bands including Sam the Sham and the Pharaohs, Paul Revere and the Raiders and, later, Gary Puckett and the Union Gap achieved prominence not only on the basis of their musical talents but also by virtue of their visual appeal through their costumed personas.

Midway through the decade, the nation found itself deep in turmoil. American involvement in the Vietnam War increased dramatically after passage of the Tonkin Resolution in August 1964 led to President Lyndon Johnson's authorization of bombing raids over North Vietnam. In August 1965 the impoverished Watts section of Los Angeles erupted in flames as racially fueled rioting spread throughout the city. Antiwar protests that had begun on college campuses spread to the streets as well. And when folksinger Bob Dylan shocked acoustic folk aficionados by appearing on stage backed by an amplified blues-rock band in 1965, he energized popular music as a tool of social protest. Barry McGuire's "The Eve of Destruction," Donovan's "Universal Soldier," Buffalo Springfield's "For What It's Worth," the Byrds' "Chimes of Freedom," and other songs protesting war and discrimination altered the vernacular of pop music, defined the genre of folk-rock perfected by the Lovin' Spoonful, the Mamas and the Papas, the Turtles, and other bands, and helped galvanize the youth movement.

As the Vietnam war dragged on and escalated despite public outcry, many young people began seeking respite in the escapism offered by hallucinogenic drugs — inspired by the vivid musical imagery present in post-1965 Beatles albums and by the preachings of psychologist Timothy Leary, who after experimenting with hallucinogenic drugs urged his followers to "tune in, turn on, and drop out." Intertwined with the peace movement, the "hippie" bohemian counterculture that flowered in San Francisco's Haight-Ashbury district in 1966 and 1967 gave rise to "psychedelic" music, heavily laden with drug references and mind-numbing acoustic feedback. A scant five years after adolescent boys with crew cuts and girls with ponytails were digging Bobby Rydell, the Four Seasons, and the Shirelles, many of them had grown long, shaggy hair, distanced themselves from their family's values, and embraced the wildly soaring and often dark and brooding music of Jefferson Airplane, Iron Butterfly, Cream, Steppenwolf, Country Joe and the Fish, the Doors, Big Brother and the Holding Company, Spirit, and the Jimi Hendrix Experience, all of whom remained popular through the end of the decade.

Since those days, echoes of the '60s resound strong in contemporary culture. We hear the echoes on oldies radio stations, in motion pictures, in television commercials. Oldies remain the touchpoint for a generation of adults who call themselves children of the '60s. The music lives on. But what of the artists who recorded the anguished, the important, the cherished songs of those years?

We now have updated and reissued all four of our biographical books about recording artists under the *For the Record* title. *For the Record, Volume 1,* which updates and expands upon our original 1999 book *Echoes of the Sixties,* reveals what each of these artists did with their lives following the end of their reign on the pop music charts. Many of the artists of the '60s remained in the recording industry, moving into production, talent management, background singing, commercial jingle recording, concert booking, or executive positions. But many others moved on to other fields, taking advantage of new opportunities and discovering new abilities. This book shares the aspirations, trials, triumphs, and life's lessons learned by the musical pied pipers of a remarkable decade.

Authenticated, authorized biographies

For the Record, Volume 1 is the product of five guiding principles:

- We obtained information about all artists we profiled from conversations we had with the performers themselves (and with family members of some of the deceased performers);

- We collaborated with the performers, who reviewed and authenticated our manuscripts;

- All performers profiled were soloists or members of vocal groups or bands whose recordings scored on the national pop music singles and/ or album charts during the late 1950s and '60s;

- We placed an emphasis on achievement, celebrating the personal and professional triumphs of performers within and outside the music industry following the 1960s;

- We intentionally selected artists who are representative of the widely divergent musical styles that distinguished the 1960s from all the other decades of the 20th century — musical diversity encompassing and influenced by rockabilly, rhythm and blues, surf music, jazz, folk standards, calypso, pop ballads, the British Invasion, novelty tunes, folk-rock, art rock, psychedelia, and country music.

Each of the 11 chapters is devoted to a vocal group, soloist, or band, introduced through an opening essay recalling their attainment of fame during the 1960s. The sequence of the chapters parallels the chronological order in which each of the performers first achieved national renown. Following the opening essay in each chapter, biographical epilogues tell the stories of what has become of each of the performers in the decades since. While several bands underwent personnel changes, we concentrated on the individuals who were present during the principal hit-making years of each ensemble during the 1960s. Although we contacted each surviving member of each band, some declined to participate in the project, and we excluded others who never left the spotlight. But 42 artists agreed to speak with us. These epilogues explore the personal and professional choices they made once the music faded and the concert arenas emptied. Through deeply personal and revealing conversations with each of these artists, we have created illuminating profiles of the musical composers and performers who influenced the styles, thoughts, and attitudes of a generation of Americans and helped in many ways to shape the course of history.

The collective goal of these performers was to gain a recording contract, to perpetuate their music in vinyl grooves *for the record.* And our goal in writing this book was to explore the paths they followed in pursuing their dreams — professional as well as personal — and to document that *for the record.*

We're pleased to introduce you to 42 individuals whose songs are as familiar as old friends, but who you never really knew — until now. These singers and musicians share their joy, their pain, their insights, and their dreams. Through their stories, we learn something about ourselves. This book is written for those of you who want to know more about the artists you hear on the oldies radio channels and audio streams. And it's written as well for those of you who grew up with the music of that unforgettable era and in whose souls still resound the echoes of the '60s.

— Marti Smiley Childs and Jeff March

Letter from Dick Clark

September 9, 1997

Thank you so much for sending along your sample of "Echoes of the '60s", Jeff and Marti. The depth of detail is extraordinary. Anyone who is into the inner-workings of music should find it fascinating.

I wish you much good luck with it. Thanks for sending it along.

Sincerely,

Dick Clark

Dick Clark

DC/as

Jeff March
Marti Childs
EDITPROS
P.O. Box 1981
Davis, CA 95617-1981

As we began writing manuscripts in 1997 for our first book, *Echoes of the Sixties*, the predecessor of *For the Record, Volume 1*, we received encouragement from Dick Clark (Note: The EditPros P.O. Box shown is no longer in use).

The Fireballs in 1958, at their first photo session. L-R: George Tomsco (lead guitar), Chuck Tharp (vocals), Eric Budd (drums), Stan Lark (bass), and Dan Trammell (rhythm guitar). Photo by: Clyde Williston.

Sugar Shack

The Fireballs

Featuring vocalists Chuck Tharp and Jimmy Gilmer

Although the hit-making era of the Fireballs spanned only nine years, the band that first glimmered at the close of the innocent '50s weathered one of the most tumultuous periods in musical and cultural history that smothered the careers of many other artists. Formed in 1958, the band consisting of lead guitarist George Tomsco, singer-guitarist Chuck Tharp, drummer Eric Budd, rhythm guitarist Dan Trammell, and bass guitarist Stan Lark drew a measure of inspiration by recording in the same New Mexico studio in which the legendary Buddy Holly and the Crickets cut their hits.

The Fireballs, who first achieved renown with a cluster of guitar-driven instrumentals in a style also advocated by Duane Eddy, Jørgen Ingmann, Ernie Freeman, Link Wray, and the Ventures, were chameleon-like in their ability to change style in step with the times. The musical charts in 1963 were populated by hits from an eclectic assemblage of artists, including Japanese vocalist Kyu Sakamoto, the Singing Nun from Belgium, doo-woppers-turned-surfers Jan & Dean, crooner Steve Lawrence, the folksinging Kingston Trio and Peter, Paul, and Mary, balladeer Bobby Vinton, and 13-year-old Little Stevie Wonder, who made his stunning debut with the chart-topping "Fingertips, Part II." But the record that remained the longest time in the No. 1 position that year — five weeks — came from a group that hadn't scored a hit for two years: the Fireballs.

The Fireballs, all from the tiny town of Raton, New Mexico, initially came to the national forefront in 1959 through the production genius of Norman Petty, whose studio in the New Mexico town of Clovis produced hit recordings for Buddy Holly, Roy Orbison, Jimmy Bowen, Buddy Knox, and the String-A-Longs. Acting as the Fireballs' manager, Petty began sending their tapes to record companies, including Kapp Records. In early 1959, when *Gunsmoke* was the highest-rated prime-time television program, Domenico Modugno's "Nel Blu Dipinto di Blu (Volare)" captured top honors in the first-ever Grammy awards, and

Alaska became the 49th state, "Fireball" released by Kapp landed on local charts in the Southwest. And the Fireballs took to the road.

Touring was anything but glamorous. "I wouldn't want to go through again what we did those years," said George. "During our first tour we sold tools out of our tool box to buy hamburgers. Sometimes our meals were crackers and water. We usually had no money for motels, so we slept in our cars. We spent the summer of 1959 on the road in the Midwest with no air conditioning in our cars. We had no way to clean up or get our laundry done. We'd pull into service stations and they'd look at us and ask, 'You boys following the harvest?' That burning desire to be in the music business kept us going."

Danny Trammell found touring particularly disheartening. "We lived on peanuts. I remember one time we wanted to take a disc jockey out to dinner but we didn't have enough money to order hamburgers for everybody. The disc jockey got fed but I didn't. We were popular but we didn't have any money," Trammell sardonically observed.

As the camaraderie among the boys strengthened on the road, they took on nicknames they gave each other. George was called "Shirsk." Stan was called "Dumbo." And Danny was "Trampy." Some days on tour were more uncomfortable than others. Dan remembers one in particular. "On the way to a tour date we were driving by a bunch of plum trees. We pulled over on the side of the road, picked up a bunch of plums and put them in our T-shirts. As we drove on down the road we ate all those plums. Let me tell you what, when we were on stage playing at about 9 that night, I looked at Stan and his fingers were strumming his bass guitar but he was not moving otherwise. And I looked back at poor Eric and he had this pained look on his face. Well, in about 10 more minutes, I realized what they were going through. Man, we all had the runs. We were suffering on stage. I don't know how many intermissions we had to have that night," he laughed.

Life on the road gave the Fireballs grander experiences as well. At a Massachusetts performance in which the band appeared on the bill with the Everly Brothers, Eric Budd found himself sitting in the dressing room with Don and Phil Everly. "They sang 'Bye Bye Love' to me back there. Two years earlier I listened to that song every morning on the radio, and here I was backstage with them. To this day, I hear an Everly Brothers song and I stop what I'm doing to listen. They were just two damn swell guys. They didn't have a big head and they had time to talk. I was as impressed with them as individuals as I was with their harmonizing and musicianship."

Eric also spoke fondly of "country gentleman" Sonny James, with whom the Fireballs toured for a month. "We were his backup band on a Midwest tour. He was a fabulous gentleman. When Sonny James was on the stage, the bar was closed. He was a very religious person and his contract specified that no alcoholic beverages could be served when he was performing. I remember traveling down the road with everyone asleep except Sonny James, who was sitting in the back seat with his guitar, softly singing religious songs." During that tour with Sonny James in the early fall of 1959, the Fireballs experienced their first change in personnel when Dan Trammell left the group due to asthma.

To their discredit, producers at Kapp Records became ambivalent about the band's potential and thought little of a new song called "Curious," which George had written in 1959. So Petty approached Norman Wienstroer, executive with a new record company called Top Rank International, where he sold "Curious" within an hour. Wienstroer signed the band in part because "Curious" reminded him of a coastal resort town in England he had recently visited. With the blessing of George and Norm Petty, Top Rank renamed the song after the town — "Torquay." Released under its new title, the rhythmic instrumental single became the first record by the Fireballs to make the national charts when it premiered on the *Billboard* Hot 100 on September 28, 1959. The Ventures, the Challengers, and the British band the Scorpions also recorded and released versions of the song as singles or EP (four-song) 45s. The Fireballs' "Torquay" reached No. 39 on the Hot 100, remained on the chart for 13 weeks, and solidified the popularity of the group.

On January 11, 1960, just three months after "Torquay" made the charts, another driving instrumental called "Bulldog" brought the Fireballs back into the top 40 as Top Rank prepared to release the group's first album. George Tomsco wrote the lively instrumental song, and producer Norman Petty added just enough reverb to Tomsco's clean guitar licks. The tune had the energy of a surf music instrumental, but with a hint of southwestern seasoning. Petty, who also served as the Fireballs' manager, wrote "Nearly Sunrise," the flip side instrumental. "Bulldog," on the Top Rank International label, reached No. 24 and remained on the chart for 12 weeks. The hitmaking trajectory of the Fireballs wasn't always smooth. The band's 45 rpm Top Rank single "Vaquero (Cowboy)" made the *Billboard* Hot 100 on August 29, but just barely, spending its only week on the chart at No. 99. The melodic guitar-driven instrumental was a tribute to the ranch hands of the West. George Tomsco and record producer Norman Petty wrote the song.

But the band was soon to undergo the second of three personnel changes within two years. Chuck Tharp, who had filled in on rhythm guitar after Danny's departure, himself left the group in August of 1960. Eric Budd was first to hear about his resignation, and played a hand in hiring his replacement. "During a break I had gone back to Raton and while we were there Chuck told me he was tired and was going to quit," recalled Eric, whose own departure for military service would follow in late 1961, when drummer Doug Roberts would join the band. "Years later Chuck told us he was just joking about quitting, but at the time I thought he was serious. So we went back to Clovis, and he told everyone he was going to quit." The band and Petty took him at his word.

With indications that Top Rank appeared headed for its eventual closure, the Fireballs signed in the spring of 1961 with Morty Croft's Warwick Records. The Fireballs' first single release on that label was a sizable hit, "Quite a Party." The band's fourth single to make the national charts, "Quite a Party" premiered on the *Billboard* Hot 100 on June 26, 1961. George Tomsco wrote the swingin' instrumental with a pulsating drumbeat. The flip side of the single was "Gunshot," another Tomsco composition. "Quite a Party" reached No. 27 and remained on the chart for 10 weeks.

As Chuck Tharp went to work on a ranch before enlisting in the U.S. Army, the Fireballs began searching for a new singer to take on the road on their next tour, which had already been booked. The band members and Petty thought of a young singer from Amarillo: Jimmy Gilmer.

The Jimmy Gilmer Combo, in which Jimmy sang and played rhythm guitar, had developed a following in the Texas panhandle and eventually made contact with Norman Petty. Gilmer gave credit to his drummer, Gary Swafford, who began doing session work for Petty and played with the Norman Petty Trio in the late '50s. Swafford introduced Jimmy to Norman. Although Jimmy wrote few songs, one of his compositions called "Look Alive" appealed to Petty, who recorded Gilmer and arranged for the song's release on the Decca label in 1958. "'Look Alive' was big in Amarillo, but that was about it," Gilmer said.

Unable to build success for his group beyond the Amarillo region, Gilmer had decided to abandon his musical ambitions and return to his college engineering studies in the fall of 1960 when Norm Petty phoned to ask if he'd be interested in joining the Fireballs to fill a vacancy created by the departure of singer-guitarist Chuck Tharp. "That offer was exciting because the Fireballs were going to be touring and I hadn't really done any of that," said Gilmer. The Fireballs had previously met Gilmer at Petty's studio, and they knew they'd get along together. Just like that, he joined the band.

After rehearsing for a few weeks with Jimmy, the Fireballs toured extensively throughout the Midwest, backing numerous other acts in performances. "We played for people like Donnie Brooks, the Kalin Twins, and others who had hit records at the time." Those were lean years during which the Fireballs continued to release records without significant chart success. Even so, that transitional period provided some time for creative experimentation. In the summer of 1960, the Fireballs set to work on *Blue Fire,* which may have been one of the first concept albums ever recorded, observed Jerry MacNeish, who later would play bass with the band and who served as historian for the Fireballs. All songs on the album, including "Blacksmith Blues," St. Louis Blues," and "Blues in the Night," contained either the word "blue" or "blues." However, with the collapse of Top Rank Records the album remained in the vault for more than three decades until 1993, when it was released by Ace Records.

The Fireballs had a short tenure with the Warwick label, the financial foundation of which became wobbly. As that label filed for bankruptcy in 1962, Jimmy Gilmer and the Fireballs signed with Dot Records, for which Pat Boone, Dorsey Burnette, Sonny James, and the Four Lads also recorded.

The return of the Fireballs to the charts in 1963 came through a friendship with Keith McCormack of Plainview, Texas, whose band the String-A-Longs had scored an international hit with "Wheels" in early 1961. "Keith was a friend of mine and he always had really neat songs," said Jimmy. "I sat down with him one time when we were looking for some new material to record and one of his songs happened to be 'Sugar Shack.' When we tested 'Sugar Shack' in our live performances, people wanted to hear it again."

The Fireballs recorded "Sugar Shack" during the next break in their tour schedule, but the final production didn't turn out as they had expected. All the band members worked on the song arrangement, but Petty added the song's distinguishing flute-like electronic flourish by connecting a Hammond Solovox tone generator to a Hammond B3 organ after the Fireballs had gone back on the road. "I remember Norman sent us a test pressing, and I thought he had ruined the damn record," said Gilmer. "I was very upset and I tried to stop it, but it was too late. It had already gone to pressing. Of course, had I stopped it, I probably wouldn't be where I am today," Gilmer acknowledged in 1997.

Jimmy Gilmer and the Fireballs rewarded Dot Records for signing the group by turning "Sugar Shack" into a No. 1, million-selling hit, after premiering on the *Billboard* Hot 100 on September 21, 1963. Only three weeks after its debut on the chart, "Sugar Shack" knocked Bobby Vinton's "Blue Velvet" from the No. 1 slot on October 12. "Sugar Shack" remained No. 1 for five consecutive weeks, earning distinction as *Billboard's* No. 1 record of 1963 for holding the top spot longer than any other hit that year. "Deep Purple" by Nino Tempo and April Stevens finally dislodged it. Gilmer's crisp vocals and the signature Solovox kept "Sugar Shack" in the national top 40 for 13 weeks. On November 29 of that year, RIAA awarded it a gold record for 500,000 copies sold. Dot released a follow-up with seemingly equal hit potential, "Daisy Petal Pickin,'" which premiered on the Hot 100 on December 14, 1963. Keith McCormack, Juanita Jordan, and Glynn Thames wrote the song about a guy who is plucking daisy petals to see if the girl who interests him loves him — or loves him not. The group's resurgence was unfortunately timed, however, coinciding with the emergence of a phenomenon: the British pop music "Invasion" of 1964. The Fireballs' "Daisy Petal Pickin'" managed to reach No. 15 and remained on the chart for 11 weeks. Enchanted with mop-top hair and Liverpool accents, however, American kids deserted many of their American pop music heroes during that crazed year and a few to follow. "Ain't Gonna Tell Anybody," a bouncy tune by Jimmy Gilmer and the Fireballs, premiered on the Hot 100 on March 14, 1964, amid heavy competition. It was the seventh chart record for the Fireballs, and the third with Jimmy Gilmer in the lead singer role. Ken Davis wrote the song with Juanita Jordan, who co-wrote "Daisy Petal Pickin' — the group's previous chart record. "Ain't Gonna Tell Anybody," which Norman Petty produced for the Dot label, remained on the chart for seven weeks during which it reached no higher than No. 53. The fortunes of Jimmy Gilmer and the Fireballs declined.

By the late '60s, British acts lost their franchise on the American pop music charts. Accepted musical styles became as varied as the "do-your-own-thing" clothing and hair styles through which young people expressed themselves. By 1968, pop music had begun to flex its political muscle, the drug culture was prominent, Otis Redding had come and gone, and the Doors, Cream, Jimi Hendrix, and Big Brother and the Holding Company were wreaking profound changes on how Americans defined music. In a psychedelia-tinged year in which Steppenwolf soared

Jimmy Gilmer and the Fireballs in 1964. From left: Stan Lark, Doug Roberts, George Tomsco, and Jimmy Gilmer.

on a "Magic Carpet Ride," the Beatles encouraged "Revolution," and the Chambers Brothers emphatically declared that "Time Has Come Today," the Fireballs scorched their way back onto the charts with their rendition of Tom Paxton's "Bottle of Wine," which premiered on the *Billboard* Hot 100 chart on December 30, 1967, ending a dry spell during which the band had not appeared on the charts for more than three years. "Bottle of Wine" was a rollicking top-10 hit with a sobering message of its own, condemning the ruination to which excessive use of alcohol can lead. The release, which remained on the *Billboard* chart for 14 weeks, marked the Fireballs' shift to the ATCO label (an abbreviation for Atlantic Corporation). "Goin' Away," the Fireballs' follow-up to "Bottle of Wine," premiered on the Hot 100 chart on April 13, 1968. George Tomsco and his wife at the time, Barbara Tomsco, wrote the song, and Norman Petty produced the session. The record reached No. 79 and remained on the chart for four weeks. "Come On, React," the Fireballs' 10th chart single, premiered on the Hot 100 chart on November 2, 1968. The song was written by guitarist Steve Dodge, who had played bass with the Jimmy Gilmer Combo before Jimmy joined the Fireballs. Norman Petty produced the "Come On, React" session. The record topped out at No. 63 and remained on the chart for eight weeks.

"Long Green," the Fireballs' 11th and final chart single, premiered on the *Billboard* Hot 100 chart on February 22, 1969. Kingsmen drummer Lynn Easton wrote "Long Green," which the Kingsmen also recorded. Easton also wrote the Kingsmen tunes "Annie Fanny" and "Jolly Green Giant." The Fireballs' version of "Long Green" peaked at No. 73 and remained on the chart for seven weeks. Although "Bottle of Wine" was the last significant hit for the Fireballs, that song remained on the *Billboard* Hot 100 for three and a half months in early 1968, leaving behind a powerful statement as the group exited the charts. Even though decades have passed since the group last scored a hit, the afterglow of the Fireballs still burns warmly.

The Fireballs in the late 1990s. Clockwise from left: keyboard player
Ron Cardenas, bassist Stan Lark, guitarist George Tomsco, and drummer
Dan Aguilar.

THE FIREBALLS

U.S. HIT SINGLES ON THE NATIONAL CHARTS

Debut	Peak	Gold	Title	Label
9/29/59	39		Torquay	Top Rank
1/11/60	24		Bulldog	Top Rank
8/29/60	99		Vaquero (Cowboy)	Top Rank
6/26/61	27		Quite a Party	Warwick
9/21/63	1	▲	Sugar Shack*	Dot
12/14/63	15		Daisy Petal Pickin'*	Dot
3/14/64	53		Ain't Gonna Tell Anybody*	Dot
12/30/67	9		Bottle of Wine	ATCO
4/13/68	79		Goin' Away	ATCO
11/2/68	63		Come On, React!	ATCO
2/22/69	73		Long Green	ATCO

* Jimmy Gilmer and the Fireballs

▲ symbol: RIAA certified gold record (Recording Industry Association of America)

Billboard's pop singles chart data is courtesy of Joel Whitburn's Record Research Inc., Menomonee Falls, Wisconsin.

Epilogue: George Tomsco

Lead guitarist

For three days the Fireballs had been killing time in Clovis, New Mexico. George Tomsco and the four other Fireballs had driven 235 miles from their hometown, Raton, in the state's mountainous northeastern region, to audition and to buy some recording studio time to cut their first record. They were trying to stretch the $200 they had pooled for the journey and the session. They had arrived in town on a Sunday, the last day of August 1958, only to learn that the Norman Petty Recording Studios were fully booked the first two days of the week.

When Wednesday finally arrived, they set up their gear in a studio in the late afternoon in preparation for their night session. George unpacked his brand-new Fender Stratocaster guitar and plugged it into his brand-new Fender Tremolux amplifier. As evening approached, they went to a local diner for burgers, then drove back on Seventh Street to the studio. Parked at the door was a pink Cadillac. George and the boys went inside. Through the double-paned glass separating the reception area from the studio, George saw a stranger plucking on his brand-new guitar. George angrily marched into the control room.

"Hey, who's that playing my guitar? George demanded. "I don't know that guy, and I never said he could touch my guitar."

George Tomsco in the Norman Petty Recording Studio in Clovis, New Mexico, in the 1990s. Photo by Dawn Lark.

Norman Petty, the recording studio owner, smiled. "That's Buddy Holly," he replied. The pink Cadillac belonged to Holly, who with his band the Crickets had spent the previous two days in what would be one of his last recording sessions. Petty produced the sessions and guided the brilliant career of Holly, who only five months later died along with pop stars Ritchie Valens and J.P. Richardson — the "Big Bopper" — in a plane crash during a concert tour in Iowa.

The demise of Holly, Valens, and Richardson coincided with the emergence of the Fireballs, a group whose pursuit of stardom began a year earlier in a PTA talent show in Raton, a small town nearly 6,700 feet above sea level along the old Santa Fe Trail off U.S. 85 near the Colorado border, where most folks earned their living in ranching or coal mining. George's father, Albert, had been a coal miner before he and his brother opened a service station in Raton in 1945, at the close of World War II. They also operated a local taxicab service. George's mother, Mary, who worked at home, battled ill health much of her life. Albert and Mary hoped that George would take an interest in business, put on a coat and tie, and go to work for a bank or other institution. George had something else in mind.

George, born April 24, 1940, was 5 years old when the lively music of the Harmonicats caught his ear. During the waning years of the big-band era, he also liked the smooth harmonies of the Mills Brothers, the Andrews Sisters, and the McGuire Sisters, and country standards by Lefty Frizzell, Jimmie Rodgers, and Carl Smith. By age 9, George briefly took guitar lessons, but became bored and put his notes and his guitar away in a closet. There they remained until George heard Les Paul and Mary Ford's electrifying recording of "The World Is Waiting for the Sunrise" in 1951. At about that same time, a couple of local guitar-playing brothers performing in an assembly at George's elementary school played "Guitar Boogie," a tune that had been recorded by Arthur Smith. "It was so cool. It was rock and roll, but nobody knew that yet," smiled George, who retrieved his guitar and the notes that his teacher had written. In the short time he took lessons George hadn't learned to read music, but he was able to read the chord diagrams that his teacher had drawn.

With his Gibson "cutaway" acoustic guitar equipped with an electric pickup, George began rehearsing with his accordion-playing sister, Alberta. In 1952 they played their first professional gig — a Saturday night dance at the Yankee Dance Hall in Yankee, New Mexico, about 10 miles up the canyon from Raton. "I made two bucks and I loved it," laughed George. Alberta, who already was playing regularly with a country music band, asked George to fill in. That experience led George to decide he wanted to be more than an accompanist. He wanted to play lead.

George's vision sharpened the day in 1956 when a friend invited him listen to a couple of new records he had just bought: "Rock Around the Clock" by Bill Haley and his Comets and "Mystery Train" by Elvis Presley. "I could not believe my ears. We sat there all afternoon and listened to those records over and over," said George. Gradually, radio stations began playing the new rock and roll music, and George tuned in to songs by Chuck Berry, Little Richard, the Moonglows, and other bright new stars of the day.

George paired with a school acquaintance of his, Chuck Tharp, who had a good singing voice. They persuaded friends of theirs, rhythm guitarist Dan Trammell, drummer Eric Budd, and country music bass guitarist Stan Lark, to join them in starting a rock and roll band. They began rehearsing in December 1957 and made their first appearance together in late January 1958 at a talent contest sponsored by the Raton PTA. Contest rules allowed them to perform only one song, so it had to be a good one. They chose the hottest record in the country at the time: Jerry Lee Lewis' "Great Balls of Fire." And they decided to call themselves the Fireballs. Their rocking performance captured the first-place trophy, and that was all the encouragement they needed. They rehearsed songs by Johnny Cash and Carl Perkins, and learned to play the hot new "Tequila" by the Champs as well as "Guitar Boogie" that had first caught George's ear as a sixth grader.

Although the band performed vocals as well as instrumentals, Chuck was the sole singer. "When we started out we had only one microphone," George explained. As the Fireballs began to work steadily at the Yankee Dance Hall and other nightspots in the region, George sold his Harley-Davidson motorcycle in order to buy his first solid-body Fender Stratocaster electric guitar and a new Tremolux amplifier. Pat Chavez, the high school band director, took notice of the group. He had a record lathe that he used for recording the high school band, and in the spring of 1958 he invited the boys to cut a record for the fun of it. They watched the cutter churning up curly black ringlets as it etched grooves in the smooth lacquer disc. But the Fireballs had no record contract, and no hopes of getting one.

Come June, the band dissolved as George graduated and, at the urging of his parents, enrolled in the New Mexico Institute of Mining Technologies in Socorro, along the Rio Grande about 40 miles from the

Trinity site, where the first atomic bomb was detonated. "I really didn't want to go to college," George admitted. "I wanted to pursue music, but I didn't know how to do it." His fate appeared sealed, however, when he won a "working scholarship" that he would use to subsidize his education by working half days and attending school half days.

George's job through the school was interesting enough — setting up equipment for experiments measuring patterns of explosives. But even though he was studying about mining and doing work related to the field, music remained on his mind. And in his dreams. One dream was particularly prophetic. He awoke in his dorm room in the middle of one night with a melody in his head. "It was a song that literally came to me in a dream," George said. "I reached under my bunk and got my guitar out, and figured out how to play that tune that I was hearing," said George, who still didn't know how to read or write music. "I had to play it and remember how to play it. I stayed up a couple of hours that night just playing that song over and over again." He called the song "Fireball."

The next day, George's dream prompted him to dig through his belongings and pull out his copy of the homemade acetate disc he and his buddies had recorded a few months earlier. He was playing the record when a fellow student from Clovis named Chuck Townsend overheard it and walked into George's room. "Man, that's pretty good music," said Chuck. Who is that?" George replied, "That's our little band up in Raton." Surprised, Chuck said, "You guys sound good. You should go and record over at Norm Petty's studio in Clovis where Buddy Holly records." George called his fellow Fireballs and together they decided they wanted to make a record at Petty's recording studio. George phoned Petty, who asked to hear a tape. Too embarrassed to admit he didn't have a tape recorder, George persisted, "No. We would rather play for you in person." Petty relented, and told George and the boys to drop by on a Sunday afternoon two weeks later.

George hung up the phone, promptly quit his job, and withdrew from school. "I'm going into the music business," he proudly announced. Realizing the need for material, George and Chuck Tharp set to work and together improvised an up-tempo vocal tune they called "I Don't Know." Down to Clovis they went with Stan, Eric, and Dan, taking with them a repertoire of two original songs: "I Don't Know" and "Fireball," the song that came from a dream.

At the audition, Petty listened. And then he agreed to record them, charging his usual fee for studio time: $75 per side. He had previously booked sessions for Buddy Holly and the Crickets for Monday and Tuesday, but studio time was available Wednesday afternoon. On Sunday afternoon, the boys had the $150 to cover the cost of recording their two songs. Come Wednesday afternoon, meals and motel bills eroded the Fireballs' funds to $95. Petty agreed to let them cut both songs for $75 in advance, with the remaining half of the money to be paid later.

That left the boys $20 for gas to get home in the two cars they had driven. They managed because a fill-up cost about $5 in those days. Back home the next weekend, they played a gig at a little dance hall in Springer, not far from Raton. "We made $80, sent $75 of that to Norman the very next week, and we split $5 among the five guys," George laughed. Desperate as those times were, they boys were propelled by the exuberance of youth. They were on their way.

Throughout the next four decades, the soul of the Fireballs remained aglow in George, through the band's successes and struggles, through their greatest popularity, their decline, and their re-emergence on the pop charts. George was the spark who ignited the Fireballs, and who reluctantly snuffed out the Fireballs as well.

Still touring two years after the Fireballs' 1968 monster hit, "Bottle of Wine," George found the live performances less satisfying, the demands of the road more tiring. In 1970 the group members decided to take a three-month break, and that gave them time to think about what they wanted to do. "I wanted to write and record, Jimmy wanted to go into publishing, Doug wanted to get into the nightclub business, and Stan wanted to just keep playing and making money. Stan and I were probably the closest in hoping to continue on as we had been," said George.

When drummer Doug Roberts left the Fireballs in 1970 he sold insurance while pursuing his dream of owning a club, but found nightclub management more difficult than he anticipated. Roberts died in November 1981, after a long illness. Without Doug and Jimmy, George and Stan set about rebuilding the Fireballs in 1971 and recruited a new lead singer, "Sugar Shack" composer Keith McCormack of the String-A-Longs whose 1961 hit "Wheels" was produced by Norman Petty. The reconstituted Fireballs, by then a trio, became the house band in a club in Springfield, Missouri, where they remained for two years. When the band was hired in 1973 for another steady gig in Kansas City, Keith decided to remain in Springfield, where he planned to start his own band. Then in 1974 Stan returned to Raton to run a nightclub. And George was alone.

Still, George was unwilling to abandon the Fireballs. He recruited some musicians in Kansas City and kept the band active for another decade. But George, by then based in Independence, Missouri, began to develop additional interests. In 1979 he began composing and recording jingles for Kansas City advertising agencies, a lucrative sideline. When interest in country music and line dancing surged in the early '80s, George went along and changed the name of the Fireballs to George Tomsco and the Sugar Canyon Band. But it all soured in 1984. "I got tired of beating my head against the wall. I was tired of music, and I set my guitar down," George recounted.

George Tomsco at the studios of Raton, New Mexico, radio station KRTN, in January 2026 for one of his "Fireball Friday" on-air chats with the station's hosts. Photo by Annetta Brown.

After 25 years as a professional musician, he enrolled in courses in investments and the insurance business, passed his exams, and became an agent for an insurance and investment firm. "I really liked what I learned, but I just wasn't a good salesman," George admitted. "I began looking for an excuse to get back into the music business."

George found that excuse one day in 1989 when he received a phone call in his Kansas City office asking if he could get as many Fireballs as possible to appear at a Clovis Music Festival. Without hesitation, George left the insurance business behind and moved back to New Mexico. With Eric Budd, Chuck Tharp, and Jerry MacNeish substituting on bass because of Stan's initial unavailability, George resurrected the Fireballs in Clovis. "It was a lot of fun," George told us in November 1997. The band had gone through many changes but continued working for many years after that, appearing at oldies shows, casinos, private parties, and one-nighters in clubs with George, Stan, drummer Dan Aguilar, and keyboardist-guitarist Ron Cardenas, all from Raton.

George ultimately returned to Raton, his hometown. "Raton has not changed a whole lot since 1959," smiled George, back at the "old homestead," the childhood home in which he and his sister, Alberta, grew up. "That house was the birthplace of the Fireballs," George said fondly. When their parents died, they left the property to George and Alberta. George bought out Alberta's share, and he began working on the home, which had fallen into disrepair. Down the road, the Yankee Dance Hall was still standing, but had been vacant for years. George recorded some new tracks in 2003 for an album that also included some vintage Fireballs tracks. The independent Deep Eddy Records label of Austin, Texas, released and distributed the 15-song CD, titled *HarLeeGuitar.* Although he gradually stepped away from performing by the time he reached his mid-80s, George remained actively involved in various community activities, and into 2026 continued his long-running weekly guest appearances on the "Fireball Friday" morning segment on Raton radio station KRTN, streamed live through the station's Facebook page.

Married but childless, George once again lived close to his sister Alberta, the mother of five children. "My sister and I have a very close relationship," said George affectionately. "We live near each other and there's nothing we wouldn't do for each other. That's a blessing I have. George viewed his life in terms of what he said that God has done for him. "I'm really starting to be conscious about my fellowship with Him," said George. "He's blessed my life and blessed me in music in a lot of ways. You don't realize the dimension of what God is and will do for you in your life until sometime later on, down the road. The most important thing in my life right now is Jesus Christ and my fellowship with God through Christ. He's given me music, and even though I don't read music, I've written a lot of songs. And that's a gift."

Epilogue: Stan Lark

Bassist

July 27, 1940 – August 4, 2021

Among the dozen musicians who called themselves Fireballs, only two maintained their association with the band throughout its recording history: lead guitarist George Tomsco and bassist Stan Lark.

The parity is fitting and poignant. Lark, like Tomsco, was born and raised in the small northern New Mexico town of Raton. Their kinship developed in 1951 when both were in elementary school. As they were growing up they periodically played in the same country music combo together, and Stan played an integral role in the formation of the Fireballs in 1957. Stan was there when singer-guitarist Jimmy Gilmer replaced Chuck Tharp in 1960, and he remained after Jimmy and drummer Doug Roberts left in 1970.

After taking a 16-year hiatus from performing, he returned to the stage in 1989 with the Fireballs, and continued to perform with the group intermittently until 2016. And like George, after living in a half-dozen states in the 1970s and '80s, Stan returned to Raton in the latter part of his life. He thought back to the days when he used to ride his horse from

Stan Lark (standing, second from left) with family members. Front row, left to right: Shibil, Brittany, Chelsea with dog Sophy, and Barbi. Back row: Christy, Stan, Dawn, Justin, and Shannon. Photo by John Vincent.

his parents' ranch to George's home. As late as the 1990s, Stan's mother continued to live in the house in which Stan grew up, and George took up residence in his parents' house.

"George has been one of my closest friends since I was in sixth grade," Stan said with admiration. "George and I are on all the Fireballs recordings. He and I are the only two who are on everything that's been released." And, after enduring a devastating personal loss and surviving a near-fatal accident, Stan said he learned something important about life: enjoy it. And he did.

Stan, the first of 11 children in his family, was born July 27, 1940. His parents were ranchers, but his father, Richard "Floyd" Lark, was also a teacher, owned school buses and was a performing musician. "He had to do all of that to feed 11 children," Stan laughed. Floyd had been a saxophonist who led a jazz sextet in Denver during the 1930s and '40s, and he encouraged his children's interest in music as well. One of Stan's four brothers played violin and another played cello. Three of Stan's six sisters played piano, as did Stan's mother. Floyd, the choir director at the church the family attended, wanted Stan to become a concert pianist. "But of course, I am not," smiled Stan, who took piano lessons from age 4 until he turned 12, when his piano teacher died. By that time young Stan was tired of piano, and jumped at the chance to play upright bass when the school orchestra needed a player.

Stan took to the bass easily. For five years he and his cellist and violinist brothers, also members of the orchestra, were honored by selection in the New Mexico all-state competition. Within a year of joining the orchestra Stan turned professional, playing a style of music quite distinct from classical. "I had an aunt who played honky tonk piano and a cousin who played lead guitar in a country music group called the Night Riders, and by the time I was entering the eighth grade when I was 14 years old, they had convinced my parents to let me go and play country music at dances with them." During the four years Stan sang and played with the Night Riders, his buddy George Tomsco, with whom he had been in the school choral group, was playing with another country band. When George first decided to form a rock and roll band he unhesitatingly sought Stan.

The decision to join the Fireballs took Stan far from the course he had been pursuing. As a high school student, Stan was interested in a career in petroleum engineering, in which he demonstrated a spark of ingenuity that earned recognition. He had won several scholarships and had already enrolled at New Mexico State University in Las Cruces when he and the other Fireballs first recorded at Norman Petty's studio in Clovis. "When I finished recording in the studio, I was supposed to go straight to New Mexico State, but I didn't, even though everything was already paid for." Stan's father, who had several academic degrees, was terribly upset. But Stan made the decision to follow his passion, and rather than sit in a classroom he went on the road with the Fireballs. "My life would have been very different had I stayed in school, but I don't regret anything," Stan said resolutely.

After the Fireballs began regularly playing the ballroom circuit in the Midwest in the summer of 1959, they moved to Minneapolis. It was there in 1960 that the Fireballs first met singer Donnie Brooks, who was on the road promoting his rising recording "Mission Bell." Brooks had been invited to stay in the home in which the Fireballs were living as guests. Wishing to strike up a friendship, Brooks asked the Fireballs to join him in fishing. The Fireballs declined, saying they wanted to rest for an upcoming concert appearance. Brooks still went fishing, alone, but interpreted the Fireballs' unwillingness to accompany him as aloofness. A big-hearted guy with a mischievous sense of humor, Brooks had disappeared by the time the Fireballs returned from their concert. But they had a surprise waiting for them when they turned in for the night.

"When we got into bed we found out he had short-sheeted us and wrapped these dead fish in paper and put them in our beds," laughed Stan. Attached to one fish Brooks had left a note: "Screw you, Fireballs. 'Mission Bell' is now No. 1." The next time Brooks and the Fireballs met on the road, they all shared a good laugh about the "fish incident." The Fireballs remained good friends through the years with Brooks, who became a prominent producer of oldies shows from the mid-1960s into the early 2000s.

The band worked regularly on tour with the Champs, Sonny James, Jimmy Bowen, and Bobby Vee from 1959 into the early '60s. Despite numerous personnel changes the band underwent through the '60s, Stan remained with the Fireballs for 16 years, beyond the time the band severed its relationship with Norm Petty in 1969 and began working with producer Glen Pace in North Hollywood, California.

By 1972 the Fireballs, with Keith McCormack singing lead, were based in Kansas City. "We were doing harmonies like the Eagles, but we weren't going anyplace. I got tired of looking up and seeing the same drunk falling off the same barstool every night. I was closer to George

Stan Lark performing with the Fireballs in 1992. Photo by Gary J. Bernas.

than to my own family because we grew up together. But it just burned out for me, and I decided I wanted to do something different."

Stan left the Fireballs in 1974 and returned to Raton, where he bought a nightclub, the Carriage House. There, Stan formed a six-piece country music house band that he called Willow Springs, after the original name of the town of Raton. Five years later, Stan sold the club but kept the band, which he took on the road. But on Nov. 13, 1979, the road almost did him in. On an icy stretch of Interstate 25 about 40 miles northeast of Albuquerque, Stan was a passenger in a Jaguar XKE that veered and smashed into a bridge abutment at highway speed. Stan's head was split open in the crash, but he fared better than his wife, who suffered massive injuries including four spinal fractures. She remained unconscious in intensive care for 21 days, and after regaining consciousness underwent physical therapy to learn to walk again.

As soon as he was able, Stan picked up where he left off and returned to the stage with Willow Springs. Seeking to get off the road and remain steadily in one area, the band headed west to Las Vegas, Nevada, where lounges abound. "I had three kids in the band who had degrees in music. That was one of the times that I was really pleased with the music I was doing. It was an incredible group, and we did very well. We got some really nice write-ups and the band was named Entertainer of the Year for the Nevada circuit. Unfortunately," Stan added, "we took only two weeks off in nearly two years playing the show club circuit, and the band fell apart."

Stan decided to leave music and chose a radically different professional field: the mining business. He had developed an interest in geology in high school and, had he stayed in school at the University of New Mexico, planned to study engineering and geology in preparation for a career in the petroleum industry. Even during his time with the Fireballs, Stan continued his education through correspondence courses. Over time, he earned an associate of arts degree in architectural design and engineering from North American School of Drafting in California. After Willow Springs dissolved, Stan enrolled in mining engineering and chemistry courses at the University of Nevada, Las Vegas. In 1981, the same year his 14-year marriage ended in divorce, Stan began a new phase of his life as a lab technician for a mine in the small Southern Nevada desert outpost of Pahrump. Over a four-year period he advanced to lab supervisor at mines in Nevada, Oregon, and Colorado. By 1985 he was elevated to vice president at Knox Research, which operated laboratories that conducted research and development in precious metals. He remained a mining executive until the spring of 1997, when he resigned to set up shop as an independent consultant.

Although his years in the mining industry brought Stan professional satisfaction and achievement, he endured an agonizing personal tragedy that spanned a decade. In 1982 Stan's eldest son, Bobby, received a transfusion of contaminated blood. "It took 10 years to get him, but it got him," Stan said quietly. "Bobby had a double master's from Texas Tech and had everything in the world going for him. He was 6-foot-6 and trim at 280 pounds, but dwindled down to about 90 pounds. I eventually had to carry him everyplace."

Following Bobby's death in 1992, the bonds strengthened between Stan and his old friend George Tomsco, who asked Stan to join Chuck Tharp's country music group, called Phoenix. Sensing he needed that diversion, he agreed. During his second appearance with Chuck's band at the Portales Country Club in Portales, New Mexico, Stan spotted another old friend. "Hey, Dawn," he called. A vibrant woman wheeled around and lit up in a wide grin when she saw Stan. Dawn had been a drink server in Stan's nightclub in Raton. Stan had thought about Dawn from time to time, but had no idea where she was. The two hadn't seen each other in 15 years. Like Stan, Dawn had been married and divorced. Dawn was raising her four children: daughter Brittany, born in 1989; son Shibil, born in 1984; daughter Chelsea, born in 1982; and son Justin, who was born in 1976, when Dawn worked at Stan's Carriage House in Raton. When Stan and Dawn married in 1994, Stan's two daughters from his first marriage were already grown. They were daughter Shannon, born in 1969 when Stan was touring on the strength of "Bottle of Wine," and Christy, born in 1974 when Stan owned the Carriage House.

"Dawn has been my best friend for a long time," Stan told us. "She used to babysit the girls when I had the nightclub. When they were little, her son Justin and my daughter Christy used to sleep in the same bed. They would never admit that, though," laughed Stan. Of their chance meeting, Stan said, "It's just one of those things that's worked out very well. We have a beautiful home about six miles outside of town. We

Dawn and Stan Lark. Photo by
Paul Vakselis, courtesy of Dawn Lark.

live right next to a state park and we have deer and turkeys and bears in our yard. And our rottweiler." Although Dawn grew up on a ranch in the Oklahoma panhandle, her family also owned a ranch about 35 miles from Raton.

Stan once again found himself the father of three school-age children. And he became involved in an emerging business that developed a technology to detoxify tailings from played-out gold mines. The process, which alters the chemical composition of the tailings and prevents them from leaching toxic compounds into surrounding soil, earned the approval of the federal Environmental Protection Agency. Once made inert through the chemical process, the tailings can be used in the manufacture of road surface material or building blocks. "I had been a chemist on the other side developing ways to extract metals from ore, so this is my way of giving something back," Stan explained. He worked with a nuclear physicist to design the equipment and physical plant to put the process to practical application.

Despite his immersion in mining, chemistry, new technologies, and EPA regulations, Stan left room in his life for music. George Tomsco counted on him for occasional appearances with the Fireballs, including the annual Buddy Holly Days program in Lubbock, and Norman and Vi Petty Days in Clovis. That was rooted in Stan's simple but essential theory about life. "Enjoy it," he said simply. "I've learned you can't take anything for granted. A lot of people for whatever reason are dealt hands that aren't too wonderful and they have to live with them. But I believe that people have the potential to be anything that they want to be. Life can get frustrating at times, and sometimes it gets so incredibly good that it's hard to believe. Even after losing a son, I still feel that way. There are things you wish never happened, but it also makes you realize how good and wonderful life can be and be thankful that you have it."

Stan said that even if he had been given the opportunity, he wouldn't have altered the course of his life. "There are some things that I'm not really proud of, but I don't know if I would change them because then I wouldn't be where I am right now. And right now, I'm exactly where I want to be."

Stan, unfortunately, developed metastatic bone cancer from which he died on August 4, 2021, eight days after his 81st birthday. He and his wife, Dawn, had been married since 1994.

Epilogue: Eric Budd

Drummer

October 23, 1938 – October 7, 2022

The subscribers on Eric Budd's newspaper route knew when their paper was going to land on their porch. They'd hear the whistling first. As a boy, Eric was always whistling country music tunes, and when he delivered papers on his route in Raton, New Mexico, residents could hear him coming. As a kid in the late '40s and early '50s, Eric liked the music of Webb Pierce, Faron Young, Jim Reeves, Slim Whitman, and Hank Thompson. And he became proficient at whistling their songs. "I still can't carry a tune in a wet paper sack, but I've always been able to whistle on key," Eric said with a wide grin. He and fellow Fireball George Tomsco had been friends ever since both were toddlers. "I've known George since we were neighbors back when he was about 3 and I was 4. We grew up together and went to school together. He used to go to grade school dragging a guitar with him, even though he didn't have a case for it."

Eric's musical development didn't proceed past whistling until the fifth grade, when he began playing the tonette, a simple wind instrument

Eric Budd in the 1990s. Photo by Josh Budd.

with eight finger holes and a thumb hole. Eric, born October 23, 1938, was the youngest in a family of three boys. They lived with their parents, Tom and Irma Budd, on the family's ranch on Johnson Mesa, 20 miles from Raton. "But after the war, they closed the schools out there, so we moved into town and my father became a cabinet maker and carpenter," Eric said. "My mom raised three boys, which was a fulltime job."

Eric's oldest brother, Nelson, played the violin for a while, so Eric decided to try that in sixth grade. Eric might have become a violinist were it not for a class scheduling error when he entered junior high school. "I got my schedule mixed up and ended up in the band class instead of orchestra class. So there I was carrying my violin into a band class. I very discreetly laid it down and hid it behind a partition, and walked over to the drums that were set up. And that's how I started playing drums. I just watched what the other kids did and stayed after class to practice. We played the regular Sousa marches, and the first time I had a chance to sit down to a trap set that a friend had, I was very lost, because I could play only march songs."

But Eric was intrigued, and soon bought an old set of trap drums. "It consisted of a bass drum, snare and two little cymbals about the size of pie pans," Eric laughed. Even though he was a student in band class, he was largely self-taught in drumming technique. He received an important tip at a dance sponsored by the Raton Chamber of Commerce. "For one dance, the chamber hired a New York group called the Tony Pastor Orchestra, an eight-piece rhythm band. Their drummer had a big drum set and I sat behind him all during their concert. After their performance I asked him why he didn't swing his whole arm and he told me you have to develop your speed and power with your wrist. A lot of drummers are just elbow thumpers who bang from their elbow down. I remembered what he had told me, and I taught myself to use my wrists to get my speed."

Eric had practiced with other local musicians, but had no professional experience before George Tomsco, Chuck Tharp, and Stan Lark persuaded him and rhythm guitarist Danny Trammell to perform with them in a talent contest sponsored by the local PTA. They wanted to start a rock and roll band. Even though Eric grew up on country music and Sousa marches, he had developed a liking to the new rock and roll music. "I'd wake up to this radio station from Trinidad, Colorado, that played 'Bye Bye Love' by the Everly Brothers every morning, and I became an Everly Brothers fan from day one." As the date of the PTA contest neared, Eric and his friends had time to learn only one song: "Great Balls of Fire," a hit by Jerry Lee Lewis. "I'm pretty sure it was George's cousin Ed Tomsco who suggested reversing the two words to suggest the name Fireballs," said Eric. At that time, Chuck was a high school sophomore, and George, Stan, and Dan Trammell were seniors. Eric had already graduated from high school and was working for Elco Metal Products, the company for which he remained an employee through adulthood. Eric had followed the footsteps of his brother Nelson, two and a half years his senior. Eric was working as a frame welder, a skill he had learned on the job.

Although he had begun taking engineering drafting courses at Raton Instruction Center, a junior college, Eric admitted when we spoke with him that his ambitions were less than academic. "I wanted to chase girls and have fun," he grinned. "I had no goals. I did eventually work as a draftsman and I'm mechanically minded — probably more gifted at that than I am in music," said Eric, who went on to work for the company's steel door manufacturing operation in Harper, Kansas. There, Eric was an engineer in the hardware department of the firm, since renamed Elco Manufacturing Co. "I do maintenance work and I do some machinist work. I run a lathe, I work on dies, and I make parts for machines that break down. I was interested in mechanics even when I was younger. That's what came easy to me."

But at age 20 Eric unhesitatingly interrupted his early career with Elco when stardom beckoned in the spring of 1959, after the group's first single "Fireball" captured some attention. Eric paid a local automobile pinstriping artist to paint "Fireballs" on his bass drum. "And then we took off on a gamble on a tour of Minnesota. George had heard about this booking agent in Minneapolis. We called and they said, 'Send a demo so we can hear what you sound like.' We said, 'Heck, we'll just come up and audition for ya.' So we all quit our jobs, loaded up two old junk cars with our clothes and instruments and away we went. We auditioned for him and he said, 'I like your sound. Do you have a place to stay?' He made arrangements for us to live in a house with an older couple and got us a booking about two days later in some lakeshore ballroom." During a break in performances, the five band members drove back to Clovis, New Mexico, to record some more tracks, including "Torquay." Then the Fireballs returned to Minnesota, awaiting greater success that would follow.

Eric remained with the Fireballs until November 1961, when he was drafted into the U.S. Army. After basic training at Fort Ord in California, he was transferred the following spring to Fort Bliss near El Paso before shipping out in September 1962 for Korea. There, he spent 13 months as launcher crew chief in a Hawk surface-to-air missile unit that was not involved in conflict. But he did encounter a conflict upon his arrival home. After Eric's discharge in October 1963 he met with George Tomsco and Jimmy Gilmer about rejoining the Fireballs, who were then riding high with "Sugar Shack." The group was touring, doing one-nighters throughout the country. But that no longer appealed to Eric. "I had been living out of a suitcase and a shaving kit for four years, and I decided I wanted something else." He parted company with the Fireballs for good.

Eric bummed around Albuquerque for a month, hoping to hook up with a music group offering steady work at a club. Two months later, he was still searching. "From October 1963 to February 1964 I just goofed off and lived off my soldier's retirement. By February I was hungry," Eric said. That's when he decided to phone his old boss at Elco, the company he had left nearly five years earlier. The company had an opening that it had just filled. But Eric's former boss asked, "When could you come?" Eric replied, "I'm on may way to Raton now." Eric's boss asked, "Are you going to stay a while?" Eric said he would. His boss replied, "Be here on Monday."

Eric did stay at Elco for a while, until 1970, when an Albuquerque lumber company hired him to set up a "stick shop" — a fabrication facility for metal door frames used in commercial buildings. He worked there for five years, until Elco closed its Raton shop due to labor relations difficulties. That time, Elco phoned Eric. "They wanted to know if I would be interested in going to Kansas with them and setting up a new plant there. I thought about it for about five minutes, and here I am." In addition to the facility in Harper, Kansas, the firm built another manufacturing plant in 1973 in Burns Flat, Oklahoma. When sales slippage forced the company to close its Kansas plant, Eric and several other employees transferred to the Oklahoma location, where Eric remained for eight years until returning to Harper when Elco reopened its plant there. While in Oklahoma, he met Jeanette, whom he married on Valentine's Day 1980. The next year his son Josh was born, followed two years later by the birth of his son Jesse. In high school Jesse played tuba and Josh played trombone.

Eric and his family enjoyed life in Harper, population 1,400, out on the flat Kansas prairie. "We're 45 miles southwest of Wichita, close to the Oklahoma border. We live in a double-wide mobile home on some land we bought. We're in tornado alley. I've seen them go by and heard the sirens blowing," he said matter-of-factly. "We've gone down into the shelter, but we haven't ever had any damage."

Eric enjoyed the simple life, and said his greatest preoccupation was watching his boys grow. Despite growing up in Denver Broncos country seven miles south of the Colorado border, Eric became, along with his son Jesse, a devoted Dallas Cowboys fan. Out in the garage, Eric and his son Josh tinkered with an older model Chevy pickup they bought.

For a while he had his drums set up in the garage. It was the same Slingerland Gene Krupa model drums he'd bought in Trinidad, Colorado, in 1958. He'd go out and play them from time to time, and he'd think back to the time that he met drumming greats Gene Krupa and Cozy Cole at the Metropole Cafe in New York. When the weather began to deteriorate the 40-year-old drums by 1997, however, he packed them up in their cases, where they remained.

Eric stayed in touch with his oldest brother, John, who retired after a military career in both the Army and the Navy as a machinist. And he was close to his brother Nelson, who spent 22 years in the Air Force before joining the civil service work force in Albuquerque.

Eric continued to enjoy country music, as his neighbors knew. They heard him whistling while he worked.

On October 7, 2022 — two weeks before what would have been his 84th birthday — Eric James Budd died in Conway Springs, near his longtime home in Harper, Kansas. His wife, Jeanette, had died four years earlier. Eric left behind two grown and married daughters, two married sons, and one of his brothers, Nelson Budd. He had 10 grandchildren and one great-grandson.

Epilogue: Dan Trammell

Rhythm guitarist

For two days, Dan Trammell had been riding in a cramped bus traveling from North Dakota to his parents' home in Raton, New Mexico. After riding steadily for 48 hours, with only a brief stop in Denver to change buses, Dan stiffly stood as the bus rolled to a stop and he stepped off as the air brakes released a sigh. Drawing in a deep breath of the crisp air that fall morning in 1959, Dan picked up the two heavy suitcases out of which he had lived during the previous three months. Because his parents had no telephone, he hadn't let them know he was coming home. He began walking.

As his house came into view, Dan saw his father, Joe Trammell, sawing lumber in the garage.

"Dad, I'm home," Dan announced as he approached.

"I knew you would be home today," replied his father without looking up from his work.

Dan replied, "There's no way you knew I'd be home."

"Dan, I had a dream last night," said Joe. "The Lord gave me a dream that you would be home at 12 o'clock today." Dan looked at the clock. Not only were the hour and minute hands on the 12, but so was the second hand. His father continued, "I've been praying to the Lord to jerk you out of that band. Now tell me how He did it."

Dan said he'd been having trouble breathing in the humid air and that he'd had an asthma attack while on tour in the Midwest playing rhythm guitar with the Fireballs. His health difficulties caught the attention of singer Sonny James, with whom the Fireballs were touring. James urged Trammell to quit the tour, and paid for his bus ticket home. Dan's father said, "I wondered how the Lord was going to get your attention. You know you don't have asthma. You were raised to play in a

Dan Trammell in the 1990s. Photo by Georgeann Albrecht Trammell.

church, and this rock and roll is not edifying your Heavenly Father. So if you return to this band, I'm through praying for you and you'll just have to deal with the Lord any way you can."

While the Fireballs continued to tour that fall and appeared on national television, Dan went to work for a construction company, where he took a lot of ribbing from the other guys on the job. "Hey Fireball, how about autographing my shovel for me?" they'd jeer. When the Fireballs finished their tour with Chuck Tharp playing rhythm guitar in Dan's place, they returned to Raton hoping that Dan would rejoin them on the circuit out of Minneapolis. "Danny, we need you, we want you. You're one of us, you started with us and we want to finish with you," Fireballs founder George Tomsco told him. "I could not make them understand that it was a higher power that determined I couldn't go," said Dan. Even though he left early in the recording career of the Fireballs, his remarkable musicianship helped define the distinctive sound of the band. Dan Trammell played rhythm guitar like no one else.

Known as Danny through most of his youth, Trammell was born July 20, 1940, and grew up in the mountains of northern New Mexico with his younger brother, Johnny, his father, Joe, and his mother, Agnes. They lived in a remote settlement called Black Lake, 25 miles from Taos through Palo Flechado Pass at the 9,100-foot level. "We didn't have electricity half the time and we had no running water. We got our water from a well," said Dan. His father, the son of a minister, was a minister as well. "My daddy had such a way with the Lord that I have never seen anyone come close. He was the kind of person who refused to take an offering, and as a result, I grew up in a very poor family," Dan said. He had very little spending money, and what little he was able to obtain through odd jobs he gave to his parents. He earned $5 per month hauling spring water to his school. "There was no running water and the school had outdoor toilets," recalled Dan. "Kids would leave the door open, so when you went you had to wipe the snow off the seat first. Back then, you could buy a pair of cowboy boots for $2.50 and a pair of blue jeans cost a couple of bucks. We kept ourselves clothed just on that $5 a month."

Danny got his first taste of music at age 8 when his father, who had been a fiddle player in his own youth, pulled out an old guitar and showed him how to tune it and play a few chords. But Joe demonstrated an unconventional tuning method. "It was the way Spanish people tune a guitar, by octaves. He taught me to play chords in C, F, and G, but I picked up the rhythm on my own. You can't teach anybody rhythm

— you're either born with it or you don't have it," said Dan. Since his church couldn't afford an organ or piano, Danny played guitar at services. "If you could sing in C, D, or F, that was fine. If you couldn't, I couldn't find your key," he laughed. Dan realized he needed to learn more, and tantalized by a mail order offer he heard on the radio, began saving for a guitar instruction book offered for $2.95 by a mail order house in Clint, Texas. "I don't know how long it took me to save $2.95, but I eventually set it aside, sent it to them, and in the mail I got a guitar book that taught how to play using pictures. I can't read a note of music to this day, but I can sure tear up a guitar," laughed Danny, whose inspired playing propelled the Fireballs' recordings of "Fireball," "Torquay," and "Bulldog."

When Dan entered his junior year in high school, his family came out of the wilderness and moved 85 miles to Raton, where his father established a nondenominational church. There, Dan resumed playing hymns in church with the Kay electric guitar and Magnatone amplifier he'd bought with money he earned working as a janitor at the J.J. Newberry department store and on the bottling line at the local Coca Cola bottling plant. Dan kept to himself in school. In addition to his ministry, Joe operated a second-hand store in Raton called the Bargain House. "My friends nicknamed me Bargain House. It shamed me a little bit. I didn't have the money to buy the best of clothes. Whatever money I got, I gave to my parents. I treasured them."

But as quietly as Dan went about his playing in church, George Tomsco heard about his musical talent. "Ol' George found out that I played a little rhythm guitar, and he asked me to come and jam with him," Dan recalled. "I can't play no rock and roll," Dan told George. "Man, if my daddy found out, he'd kill me." George reassured him, "We're just going to jam." Dan cautiously agreed. He snuck his guitar out of the house and slipped over to George's house. "George was awesome. He could pick when he was a teenager. There was nothing he couldn't do on a Fender guitar. I was so taken in. He was just great! And I didn't know Stan Lark, Chuck Tharp, and Eric Budd were going to be there. We knew each other in high school but I didn't know that they played instruments." At that first impromptu session, they learned to play "Great Balls of Fire," which led them to their decision to enter the local PTA talent contest. The prospect made Eric shiver.

"Oh my God," Danny said. "I can't tell my dad I'm going to play for the PTA." Dan managed to get out of the house with his guitar the day of the PTA concert, without realizing that was only the beginning.

"After we played for the PTA, darn if they didn't want us to play for the prom. Well, we played for the prom and all of the other schools wanted us to play for their proms. I finally had to come clean." Eric cautiously approached his father and said, "Look Dad, I've got a problem." His father replied, "Yeah, I know you've got a problem. I don't like the music you're playing. It doesn't edify the Almighty. But you're at the age where you're going to do what you want to do, and I'm going to have to let you do it."

Despite his growing interest in music, Danny took no music courses in school. His time in high school was aimless. "I never knew what I wanted to be. All I knew was I had to finish high school," Dan said. So when George set up the first recording session at Norman Petty's studio in Clovis, New Mexico, that was fine with Dan, who had no other particular plans. To avoid picking up the rumble of passing traffic, Petty preferred recording after dark. "Back then everybody had glass-pack mufflers and gunned it down the street. So I remember recording all night long and sleeping the next day," said Trammell. He heaped praise on Norman Petty. "Norman was not only a great pianist, he was also a genius in imagining and creating different sounds." At one recording session Petty told Trammell to unplug his electric guitar, and he close-miked the instrument. "I couldn't even hear myself playing, but the microphone was picking up the sound." The result was an ethereal "whack-whack" palpitation that gave the Fireballs a sound like no other band.

On the road, the oppressive humidity of the Midwest summer of 1959 was hard on Dan, but he pressed on until the night on tour with Sonny James in North Dakota when he experienced a severe asthma attack. "I remember finishing the show, but when I woke up in the hospital I don't remember how I ever got there," said Dan, who had no previous episodes of asthma. "I remember them giving me adrenaline shots. I don't know if the doctor even got paid because we didn't have any money at the time. Sometime I'm going to ask George and Stan if the doctor ever got paid." After his release from the hospital, Dan was resolute about continuing on the tour. A few days later, Sonny James called Dan aside. "I've got to tell you something," Sonny said. "I've been watching you on and off stage. Son, you're losing your health, and I'm going to buy your ticket home." When Dan objected, Sonny calmly replied, "At your age, you don't have the brains to think about your health. All you're thinking about is music." Dan finally agreed to accept Sonny's offer. "I loaned Chuck my guitar and Sonny James bought my bus ticket home to Raton." After one more recording session in Clovis, Dan walked away from the Fireballs for the last time.

After working in construction for a brief time, Dan landed a job in the signal department of the Santa Fe Railroad, climbing poles, installing glass insulators and wires. And he chased storms throughout the prairie states, repairing and rewiring lines fallen by wind-driven rains and tornadoes. After a year and a half on the job Dan met his first wife, Mary, with whom he had three children: Debbie, born in 1965; Joanie, born in 1968; and David, born in 1972. Through those years, Dan was content to live in quiet anonymity. "I concentrated on giving my life to the Lord. I never told anyone that I used to be a Fireball. I just worked on the railroad," he said.

Dan had remained with the railroad until 1962, when his father-in-law at the time invited Dan to join him in his retail tire business in Tyler, Texas, about 95 miles east of Dallas. Dan was initially reluctant, considering the salary, benefits, and opportunities his job in the railroad brought him. But he didn't like all the traveling associated with his job, and he was still feeling wounded after losing seniority through a consolidation of the railroad's Eastern and Western divisions. So he ultimately accepted the offer from his father-in-law and began work as a tire changer at Tyler Tire Exchange of Tyler, Texas.

"My daddy-in-law and I got along fabulously," said Dan, who dutifully dismounted and mounted tires, balanced wheels, and did other automotive work in the shop. After six months Dan's father-in-law told him that he had uncovered cash inequities and management problems at his other shop in Longview, about 40 miles to the east. He asked Dan to take over management of the Longview store. Reminding his father-in-law that he had been working in the tire business for only six months, Dan flatly stated, "I'm not a manager." His father-in-law replied, "I'll make you a deal. You go to Longview and run that store. If you succeed, we'll leave it open. If you don't succeed, we'll close it." Feeling responsible for saving the jobs of the employees in the Longview store, Dan reluctantly agreed. On his first day in the Longview location, he told the employees that they needed to work together as a team to keep the store open. In only one month the store far surpassed sales recorded under the previous manager.

After nearly 20 years, Dan's marriage to Mary dissolved over fundamental philosophical differences that arose. "Young people get married because they're in lust, not in love," he explained simply. Not long after his divorce in 1980, Dan's working relationship with his father-in-law ended as well. For 20 years, Dan had been looking forward to the day when he would inherit the business. But instead, his father-in-law sold the business in 1982 to a friend, V.C. Tharp. With no other plans, Dan remained with the business, named Texas Tire Exchange, and Tharp promptly paid him a substantial raise and increased his benefits. Dan worked for Tharp for the next 10 years, all the while setting money aside. And in 1992, when Tharp decided to sell the tire business, Dan bought it, subsequently paid off his debt, and built it into an even more successful business.

"But all goes back to a man who prayed for me," said Dan, referring to his father, who died in 1985 at the age of 79. "I gave up my popularity, and I gave up a life of glamour and a road tour, but I've since been terrifically rewarded professionally and spiritually, and that's where I'm at right now, as I'm getting ready to retire."

In 1981 he met and married Georgeann Albrecht, who worked with him for many years at Texas Tire Exchange. The couple remained together until her passing at age 76 in October 2020. Through the years Dan occasionally received small royalty checks for Fireballs recordings on which he played. And he sent each check to his mother, Agnes. "I have not kept a royalty check yet," said Dan. "I've always figured my mom had to put up with my sorry tail."

The guitar that Dan played with the Fireballs was broken and discarded, a casualty of road life, but he played on occasion for family members, friends, and for himself. "Although George and Stan kept their youth pretty well, I'm an ol' coot," he laughs. "The problem with an old musician is you still sound good, but you don't look real good on stage."

Dan remained resolute that he took the right road that day he accepted the ticket from Sonny James and boarded the bus in North Dakota. "I never had a doubt. I never looked back," he asserted. "I feel very fortunate to be where I'm at. I always give the Almighty credit, for without him we cannot do anything. The nicest thing about the boys is that they never did hold it against me when I quit. There's a bond there that will never break among me and George, Stan, Eric, and Chuck. They're still my heroes — all of them."

Epilogue: Chuck Tharp

Singer-guitarist

February 3, 1941 – March 17, 2006

Chuck Tharp spent his life doing things that most guys can only imagine, surviving dangers that most guys can't possibly imagine. As a young man, he earned his living in a saddle, "gentling" untrained horses, and herding cattle on open range. After two U.S. Army tours of duty with ground forces in Vietnam, he enlisted in the Navy and became a radar operator aboard an aircraft that was shredded by enemy fire over the Gulf of Tonkin, leaving him with paralyzing injuries from which he eventually recovered. He studied marine biology in college, became a music publishing administrator, worked as a staff songwriter in Nashville, became a fast-draw pistol champion, and performed not only with the Fireballs, but with jazz-flavored and country music bands as well. And later in life Chuck Tharp experienced a new passion: settling down in suburbia.

From the time of his childhood, Chuck was always on the move. He was only 2 years old when his father, Jim, died, and his mother, Willie, subsequently married Eugene, who earned his living as a cowboy. Chuck was born February 3, 1941, along the banks of the Rio Grande in the southwest Texas settlement of Ysleta. When Chuck was still an infant,

Chuck Tharp in the 1990s. Photo by Joan Tharp.

his folks moved to Anthony, New Mexico, then up the road to a town named Hatch, and on to Modesto, California, where Chuck started grade school. "Since my Dad was a cowboy we went where the work was," said Chuck. They remained in California only until Eugene took a job at an open-pit copper mine near Silver City, New Mexico. "Daddy worked as a brakeman on the train that carried ore from the bottom of the mine. During a rain, he was killed when his foot slipped and the train ran over him. From that point, Momma raised us all."

After completing third grade, Chuck moved with his mother, his sister, and his five brothers back to Hatch, where they remained until Chuck was 12 years old. Then they moved to Seguin, Texas, before settling in Waco. "I went to seven schools in one year. Like my Dad, all the boys in my family became ranch cowboys. I was in the saddle by the time I was 13 and drawing a man's wage. We took care of horses and cattle, rode fence, and did brandings and ropings."

During his high school years, Chuck moved with his family to Raton, New Mexico, where he found work at the 130,000-acre CS Ranch near Cimarron, about 40 miles southwest of Raton along the route of the old Santa Fe Trail. He sandwiched school between work, and he roomed with other cowboys in bunkhouses. "I'd get up an hour before sunup and ride out to the pasture, round up the catch horses, and drive them back into the corral so the cowboys could pick up their mount for the day. After that, I'd have breakfast and I'd go to school. After school, I'd go back to work until sundown. During the summer I worked sunup to sundown. "I tell ya, though, I enjoyed that life. I regretted giving it up." Still, it wasn't a hard choice. "Back then I was making $125 a month as a cowboy, but shoot, I'd make that much money in a couple of hours playing a gig with the Fireballs."

Chuck had first shown interest in music at age 3, when he entertained the neighbors by singing "The Old Lamp-Lighter" and other popular songs of the 1940s. Chuck's mother and stepfather both played guitar and sang, and his brothers and sister sang as well. Chuck, who developed a liking for country music artists, taught himself to play guitar and bass. He studied music at Raton High School, and his acquaintances in the school choir included guitarist George Tomsco and bassist Stan Lark. They started practicing after school with drummer Eric Budd and rhythm guitarist Danny Trammell and together formed the Fireballs, which began playing dates throughout the region.

The band members briefly went their separate ways following high school graduation in June 1958. Chuck became assistant manager of a record store in Las Vegas, Nevada, where his mother had moved while he was in high school. When George phoned in August 1958 and said, "Get your butt back here, we're going to make a record," Chuck packed his bags and spent every dime he had to take the bus to New Mexico to audition at Norman Petty's studio.

Six months after the initial recording session that yielded the regional hit "Fireball," Petty brought the band into the studio to record several more songs, including "Torquay" and "Cry Baby," which Top Rank Records released while the group was on the road in the Midwest. "We woke up in Minneapolis one morning and 'Cry Baby' was on the radio, and that was the side picked by the radio station in that area. But *Billboard* magazine picked 'Torquay,' so 'Torquay' became the hit side of the record because *Billboard* was the bible of the industry," Chuck explained. The momentum continued with the Fireballs' next release, the instrumental "Bulldog." But before the Fireballs scored their next top 40 hit, "Quite a Party," Chuck left the group — unintentionally, he said.

"It's a long story," he drawled. "It started out as a joke and wound up being serious. We were in between gigs and we were recording all night and sleeping all day. When we took a break and went to Raton for a couple of days in August 1960, everybody was acting bored. So I decided I'd spruce things up a bit and I said, 'Guys, I've got a flash for ya. I'm quitting the band.' They looked at me like I had just gone nuts. I was just kickin' up a little dust and havin' fun. Unfortunately, George called Norman that night and before I knew it, I had been replaced by Jimmy Gilmer. So I went and cowboyed for a couple of years, and then I went to meet Uncle Sam."

Along with his brother Gene, Chuck enlisted in the Army in 1961 and shipped out for Vietnam. He was stationed at fire support bases in the Golden Triangle and the A Shau Valley. "I was a grunt, and I did a lot of assignments with the [Green] Beret," said Chuck who, after promotion to sergeant, was named a squad leader. "I took my people out into the bush. Our mission generally was to make contact with the enemy, inflict as much damage as we could, and get the hell out." Chuck was in line to come home after a year there, but elected to remain. "I had 12 really good guys, and I decided to extend because they were like my family," said Chuck, whose men called him "Pop" because he was the oldest among them.

After his tour of duty ended and he was discharged in 1966, Chuck met and married a woman named Roma, with whom he had three daughters. Chuck took at job as a yard clerk with the Southern Pacific Railroad in Santa Cruz, California, a coastal resort town about 70 miles south of San Francisco. The railroad handled shipments of lettuce and other produce from the nearby Salinas Valley. At the same time, Chuck enrolled at Hartnell College in Salinas, then at California State University, Hayward, where he studied marine biology. With the arrival of a new baby, Chuck found it increasingly difficult to make a 7:30 a.m. class and dropped out of school, two classes short of his degree. All the while, he worked for the railroad, checking rolling stock in the yards. "I was so bored, but I didn't have the confidence to play music anymore," said Chuck. "The only other thing I liked was the military, so I went and joined the Navy."

That was in the fall of 1967. Chuck requested assignment to an antisubmarine squadron, believing that the Gulf of Tonkin was too shallow for submarines. Chuck's unit was attached to the U.S.S. Kearsarge, and as he reported for duty in San Diego his greeting wasn't quite as he expected. "Welcome aboard," he was told. "We leave for Vietnam in 90 days." For the next year, he roamed the Tonkin Gulf and skirted the Vietnamese coast as a radar operator aboard a Grumman S2 Tracker aircraft. "We would watch for anything moving south along the roads or in the water, and we'd call in gunfire from ships. They hung 250-pound Bullpup missiles on us. There wasn't a plane slow enough for us to bomb with those things, but they weren't going to throw them away, so they hung them on us," said Chuck. His job was to line up targets on his radar scope, then to call for fire when his aircraft was within three miles of the target. "We made an easy target," he said.

In 1968, Tharp's plane was ripped by enemy fire. "As we blew up two barges we went in too close to the beach, and we had to pull out over the jungle. We knew there were guns in there, and they got us." When a shower of 50-caliber bullets tore through the fuselage, Tharp was thrown through the air and landed in the console of the co-pilot, who had been killed. Tharp suffered severe spinal injuries, for which he was hospitalized, unable to walk, in a Veterans Administration hospital in Vancouver, Washington, where he remained for 18 months. "The VA didn't know exactly what my injury was or how to treat it. So I said, 'Aw hell, check me out of here.' My mother took care of me at her house, and my brothers would come over and carry me into the bath." Finally Chuck agreed to see a chiropractor. "He took an X-ray and said my spine looked like a snake." The chiropractor told Chuck, "I can fix it, but it's going to hurt like hell." It did hurt like hell. And he did fix it.

He put his back to the test when he regained interest in quick-draw pistol firing — pulling his Colt single-action pistol from his holster and firing at a target as quickly as possible, a skill he had learned during his Fireballs days. "I entered a fast draw competition, and in my first contest, I won first place," Chuck said proudly. "I even went to nationals and wound up in second place there."

Chuck, then single following his divorce from Roma in February 1970, enrolled in a community college in Vancouver with no particular goal in mind. "Come summertime in 1971 I flipped a coin. I was going to either buy a Harley and go visit a bunch of friends, or I was going to start a band," Chuck said. "Two out of three spins later, I decided to start a band."

Chuck contacted some musicians he had met in a music appreciation class at Cal State Hayward and with them formed a seven-piece jazz-oriented rock group called Open Road, with which Chuck sang and played bass. The band went on the road, playing clubs in nine states before arriving in Las Vegas, where the group eventually broke up in 1972. Open Road must have made an impression, because Chuck was immediately hired as a director of publishing for Hollywood-based Oak Records. He found the corporate environment stifling and was irritated that some of his song recommendations — including "Midnight Train to Georgia" and "Neither One of Us (Wants to Be the First to Say Goodbye)" — were ignored. "Hell, if you ain't going to listen to me, you don't need me," Chuck told them as he quit.

By then married to his second wife, Lanie, he went to Nashville on the strength of a song he co-wrote called "Sweet Country Woman," which had become a hit for Johnny Duncan. Tharp worked in Nashville from 1974 to 1976 with Frank and Nancy Music, owned in part by Frank and Nancy Sinatra and managed by producer-arranger Billy Strange. Because Chuck always felt like an outsider in Nashville, he wanted to return to California. During a trip to the Bay Area to visit his brother Gene, Chuck and his third wife decided to move to San Jose, where they bought a house in 1976. Chuck returned to performing as a solo act. Accompanied only by guitar, he booked himself into local clubs singing pop tunes by James Taylor, Billy Joel, and Neil Diamond. "I was bringing home $800–900 per week and back then that was damn good money," said Chuck. "I had a lot of fun doing that."

He was content in that role until 1989, when George Tomsco called to ask about putting the Fireballs back together. "Once a Fireball, always a Fireball," declared Chuck, by then divorced from his third wife. "I told George, 'Hell yeah,' I threw everything into the car and I left California." Back in New Mexico, Chuck reunited with George, drummer Eric Budd, and Jerry MacNeish on bass and began touring through the Southwest and Midwest, their old stomping grounds. Chuck remained with the reconstituted

Chuck Tharp in May 1998.

Fireballs until April 1997, when an old friend asked him to join a country band called Cold Country. Chuck was tired of living on the road, and agreed. In Cold Country, Chuck alternated playing rhythm and bass, and sang lead. The band played tunes by popular country artists as well as new compositions by Chuck. And he had a great time. "I'm better at country singing than I am at most anything," he declared.

Chuck always remained close to his brothers and sister. "My oldest half-brother, Sandy Linker, was a heck of a cowboy but a lousy singer," ribbed Chuck. Jimmy Tharp, next oldest, played steel guitar and sang. Jimmy, who died in 1998, performed with a number of prominent artists, including country swing greats Spade Cooley and Bob Wills. Chuck's sister Dorothy, who sang but played no instruments, died in 1997. Chuck's brother Marty, who played guitar and bass and sang well, traveled with a singing ministry. His brother Gene, who played guitar and sang, had a productive career in the computer industry until his death in 1995, when the private plane he was flying crashed in a snowstorm between Colorado Springs and Denver. Chuck's mother also died in 1995. Chuck's youngest half-brother, Bo, whose real name was Eugene Bostic Thwaits, wasn't musical.

Chuck's fourth wife, Belinda, went by Jo An or Jo. Likewise, Tharp always was known as Chuck but his legal name was Charly. "I didn't know my name had that unusual spelling until I applied for a passport in 1995," said Tharp. "I had to get my birth certificate and I looked at it and said, 'Hello?' I called my mom and asked, 'Momma, why did you give my name Charly that unusual spelling?' She said, 'I don't remember spelling it that way.' But then I decided I kind of like it," Chuck said.

Chuck readily admitted that he wasn't perfect. "I've done a lot of things wrong in my life, but I'm most proud of all of my kids." The first was his daughter Jamie, born in 1964, followed by daughters Shellie (1966), Christie (1968), Joey (1970), and Sulin (pronounced Sue-leen) (1978). He also had several step-children.

Chuck and Jo bought a house in Clovis, on a block on which they knew all their neighbors. "In San Jose I had only one good friend across the street, and I never even learned the names of any other neighbors. In Clovis, we have cookouts with everyone on the block. It's just great. A couple of my friends come over with guitars and we'll sit around and entertain the neighbors." Along with Jo, Chuck lived with his stepdaughter Gina and stepson Sean.

"I love to play music," Chuck said. "I'll do that until I'm too old to do it, which I hope never happens."

Following a battle with cancer, Charly "Chuck" Lee Tharp died of heart failure at age 65 on March 17, 2006, at Plains Regional Medical Center in Clovis, New Mexico — the town where the Fireballs and Buddy Holly had recorded their hits. He left behind his wife, Belinda "Jo An" Tharp; daughters, Jamie Weren, Shellie Marrero, Christie Bower, and Sulin Quaresma; stepdaughters Rachel Springer and Gina Massengill; stepson Sean Massengill; and a brother, Marty Tharp. He was guided in life by a simple philosophy: "Try not to hurt anybody. I've always tried to be as good to people as I can," Chuck told us. "I've always figured I don't care what I've heard about them or what anybody's said, they get at least two shots with me. But they don't get the third shot."

Epilogue: Jimmy Gilmer

Singer and guitarist

September 15, 1940 – September 7, 2024

Jimmy Gilmer in the mid-1960s.

Nine years before radio stations across the nation turned Jimmy Gilmer into a household name with the 1963 hit "Sugar Shack," Gilmer was on the radio, but with a different identity: K5CCQ. At age 14, Jimmy was licensed as a ham radio operator, and had interest in becoming an electrical engineer — even though he had only the vaguest notion of what electrical engineers did. Although he periodically used voice transmission, he communicated mostly through his hands using the dots and dashes of Morse code, in which he had to become proficient to pass the difficult general-class amateur license test. "I was smarter then than I am now," Gilmer joked about the advanced electronic theory portion of the exam. Because pulsed code transmissions typically cover far greater distances than the amplitude modulation used for voice, Jimmy applied his Morse skills in competitions in which the objective was logging as many contacts with other distant ham operators as possible within a defined time period. "I got to where I was pretty dad-gum good," said Gilmer in his soft Texas accent.

Gilmer's speech pattern belied his origin, one of many paradoxes in his life. Despite widely held perceptions, Gilmer was not a native Texan, but rather was born in Chicago and spent his toddler years in Wichita, Kansas. Even though he came from the windy city, he intensely disliked the stiff prairie winds that blew regularly through Amarillo, where he grew up. Despite stories to the contrary, he was not a pianist and never studied at a music conservatory. He strongly disagreed with insertion of the electronically generated flute-like sounds in "Sugar Shack," which he initially thought ruined the song. And although he was never attracted to country music, he wound up managing the careers of a couple of country music artists.

Jimmy Gilmer might well have become an engineer were it not for the lure of the new rock and roll music in the late '50s. "Elvis came to

Amarillo around 1956, and *Life* magazine took photographs showing girls in the audience reaching up for him." Gilmer was in the audience at that appearance and remembers the excitement Elvis generated. Inspired, Gilmer got a guitar, taught himself to play, and in his senior year formed a band composed of fellow high school students. After graduating from Amarillo High School in 1958, Gilmer enrolled at Amarillo Junior College, but the evening club dates that his band played began to compromise his performance in his 8 a.m. trigonometry class. "And my engineering ambitions started to fade away," he said.

Jimmy, who was born James Axley Gilmer Jr. on September 15, 1940, remembered frequent family sing-alongs with songs like "You Are My Sunshine" and "Birmingham Jail." Jimmy's father, who was from Oklahoma, worked in sales and credit management for Phillips Petroleum Co. in Chicago and Wichita before being named to manage a new division that opened in Amarillo. For relaxation, Jimmy's father sang in choirs, glee clubs, and barbershop quartets. Jimmy did take some private piano lessons for a couple of years beginning at age 8, but disliked the instrument and quit playing. Music meant little to him until the advent of rock and roll. And rock and roll led to his 10-year tenure with the Fireballs.

During that time, the band sputtered as well as sparked. After the success of "Sugar Shack" and "Daisy Petal Pickin'" in early 1964, the popularity of the Fireballs and many other American groups withered as British acts overran the pop charts. After a top 50 hit called "Ain't Gonna Tell Anybody" in 1964, the Fireballs all but disappeared from radio playlists and took a self-imposed hiatus. Jimmy, who said he could read music only well enough to just get by, enrolled in Eastern New Mexico University to increase his understanding of music and explore the possibility of entering law school. But his return to school lasted less than a year. The Fireballs went back into the studio in 1967 and cut some hot new material, including "Bottle of Wine." Misinterpreting the intent of the song's lyrics, which condemned the deleterious effects of alcohol abuse, label owner Randy Wood labeled the song offensive and refused to allow its release on Dot, a label of primarily traditional artists including Pat Boone, Debbie Reynolds, and bandleaders Billy Vaughn and Lawrence Welk. Likewise, ABC-owned radio stations in key markets, including New York, Detroit, and Chicago, unthinkingly banned the record.

Jimmy Gilmer in May 1996. Courtesy of Jimmy Gilmer.

"It was absurd," said Gilmer. "When Dot passed on the record we let Randy know we felt very strongly about it because it had tested really well on our previous tour. Randy told us that if we felt that strongly about it, he wasn't going to hold us back, and he gave us a release from our contract. So we shopped the record, ATCO picked it up, released it and Bam! The dang thing started up the charts. I remember I was in school and here come the booking agents from William Morris and I had to drop out of school again. I never went back after that time."

The Fireballs rode the momentum generated by "Bottle of Wine" into 1969, but were unable to duplicate that level of success again. Incompatibly packaged in tours with other Atlantic-ATCO artists of the time, including Vanilla Fudge, Sonny and Cher, the Bee Gees, Iron Butterfly, Buffalo Springfield, the Allman Brothers Band, and the Rascals, the Fireballs seemed out of place. The band members decided to dissolve after fulfilling a dance club date in Colorado Springs on New Year's Eve 1970. "I was so burned out, I was ready. I hated the last six months," Gilmer confessed. "I was tired of the road and although I loved the music business, I needed a change. My original idea was to go to California and put a new band together, get a new manager and start over."

But instead of going west to LA, he went east, to Nashville, at the invitation of an old school pal, Eddie Reeves. For a time Reeves had run a New York office for the Fireballs and was involved with Norman Petty's publishing interests. Reeves, who would in the 1990s become senior vice president and general manager of Warner Brothers in Nashville, was working for United Artists Music when he called Gilmer in early 1971. Reeves knew that Gilmer had been dabbling in production and management and had signed an act to Atlantic. Eddie asked Jimmy if he'd like to be involved in establishment of a United Artists publishing operation in Nashville. Gilmer replied, "Nashville? That's country music. What do I know about country music?" But with encouragement from Reeves and other United Artists executives, Gilmer joined United Artists Music that February.

"It was me and a secretary, and my job was to find some writers and build this company. I knew nothing about publishing. I remember my boss at that time said, 'As a performer, you knew good songs when you heard them. Just find good songs and go get them cut.' That was my mandate," said Gilmer. He remained with that publishing operation for 26 years. At the time Gilmer joined the firm it was called United Artists Music, a division of United Artists films. The United Artists stable of artists brought Gilmer into contact with numerous old friends, including Bobby Goldsboro, with whom he and the Fireballs had toured. In his new position Gilmer published Goldsboro's songs.

Over the years United Artists underwent several mergers and acquisitions, and was known at various times as CBS Songs, SBK Songs, and EMI Music Publishing. In differing capacities, Gilmer worked with songwriter Alex Harvey and country singer-songwriters Billy Edd Wheeler, Billie Jo Spears, and Del Reeves. He was particularly proud of signing country artist Mary Chapin Carpenter to a publishing contract. At times, Gilmer supervised up to 40 songwriters.

When the company was known as SBK, Gilmer was vice president of the southern region, supervising pop and country music product. The acquisition by EMI in 1989 led to establishment of SBK Records, for which Gilmer was placed in charge of discovering and signing composer-artists to the label. Although the pop market was doing well for the label, the company grew impatient and decided to collapse its country music

The Fireballs in 2022 at the Surf Ballroom in Clear Lake, Iowa: from left, lead guitarist and leader George Tomsco; singer and guitarist Jimmy Gilmer; guitarist and drummer Jerry MacNeish (who also is a nationally certified classic car appraiser and authenticator); keyboard player Michael Jackson of Amarillo, Texas; and bassist Paul Goad of Ruidoso, New Mexico. Photo by Dawn Lark.

component in Nashville. Gilmer returned to publishing for the company until his departure in April 1997 to launch his own artist management firm, called JAG Management. Although he pronounced the company name "Jag," it was derived from the initials of his name — James Axley Gilmer. Within his first few months of operation, he had already signed three country music acts — Cactus Choir, Brad Paisley, and Melodie Crittenden — and had secured major recording agreements for each. At his side was Susan Sherrill, his assistant since 1980. She was married to Billy Sherrill, one of the leading producers and recording engineers in Nashville. In the corporate environment, Gilmer worked with artists only during certain phases of their careers. He started JAG management to enable him to more fully guide the careers of artists.

Jimmy's father worked all his life, and even after retirement from the petroleum business dabbled in commercial real estate until his death in 1990. Jimmy's mother remained in Amarillo until her passing.

Jimmy, who originally married in 1966 but divorced eight years later, raised his son Drew, who was born in 1970. In 1976 Jimmy married Carolyn Downey, and together they raised her two children, Carla and Bobby Baker, from a previous marriage. Jimmy was proud of the achievements of all three kids. "I had a good spiritual foundation built by my parents. I was singing in church choirs from a very early age. During my wandering years I was about as far away from the church as you can get, and I think there were some times in my career that I really could have taken a wrong turn, but somehow I was given divine direction and I pulled myself through that," said Jimmy, who recalled his own youth experiences when raising the three kids. "Those years between 18 and 28 are risky times, but somehow I made it through that tunnel and now they've all made it through. Today you see so many families with kids who are just kind of lost. I've tried to maintain good honest principles in this business," he added.

Carolyn's death at age 60 due to cancer in 2002 depleted Jimmy's motivation. He retired from JAG Management, returned to Amarillo, and gradually resumed performing with the Fireballs for a pleasant diversion. He appeared on stage for the last time in Clear Lake, Iowa, in February 2022 as his own health began to decline. Jimmy died September 7, 2024, in Amarillo, only eight days short of what would have been his 84th birthday. He had been diagnosed with Alzheimer's disease two years earlier.

Quarter to Three

Gary "U.S." Bonds

In the early '60s era of high school sock hops and college fraternity beer bashes, no artist did more to define the genre of party music than Gary "U.S." Bonds. In a soulful rasp overdubbed multiple times and layered over a raucously throbbing beat, Bonds perfected a penetrating vocal style that drove him into the national top 10 with his very first release, produced a No. 1 hit on the *Billboard* Hot 100, and eventually brought him nine top 40 hits spanning three decades.

But seven years before he became known to the world as Gary "U.S." Bonds, he was a 14-year-old boy named Gary Anderson who was looking for something to do with his friends. It was 1953, and while the Korean War raged in its final months and the Soviet Union detonated its first hydrogen bomb, life droned on in Norfolk, Virginia, where young Gary lived. The emergence of early rhythm and blues artists inspired Gary and his friends to try a cappella singing and they chose a street corner for their stage.

"There was not that much to do in Norfolk so my friends and I just said, 'well let's sing.' None of us knew how, but we'd practice songs on the radio by the Flamingos, the Drifters, and the Mills Brothers until we actually started sounding pretty good," recalled Gary. "We'd just stand on the street corner, what we'd call *our* street corner, at night, in front of Mr. Boone's Market. We'd get out there and just keep all the neighbors awake, into the wee hours of the night, until they'd run us away, and then we'd go home and go to bed."

Night after night they gathered to sing, and as the months stretched into years, they improved their harmonizing by sheer determination. It was there in the Brambleton section of Norfolk that transplanted New Yorker Frank Guida, owner of a record store named Frankie's Birdland at 817 Church Street, stopped to listen to the boys one evening in 1957. He said, "You guys sound pretty good. I'm getting my money together and in a couple of years I think I want to open up a studio and a record

Gary "U.S." Bonds jumping for joy at a "Quarter to Three" in 1961 (Photofest Archives).

company. Would you guys be interested in recording?" In 1959 Guida achieved his ambition by purchasing the struggling Norfolk Recording Studio on W. Princess Anne Road near Colonial Avenue, but by that time the other members of the street corner singers had joined the service and Anderson was the only one left.

Guida had achieved initial success in 1959 with "High School U.S.A." That novelty record became a national hit through the aggregate sales of 28 different versions, on each of which singer Tommy Facenda revised lyrics to mention local high schools.

"Guida came by and he said, 'OK, I'll take you.' And we went down to his studio and he gave me a song called 'New Orleans,' which was a country and western song written by Joe Royster, a guy who worked in the shoe department in one of the major department stores in Norfolk. Joe eventually became the staff engineer and songwriter, and I guess everything else around the studio. It really wasn't hard to be an engineer back then; the recording equipment was only two track. All you had to do was find some tape and turn it on and, bingo, you were an engineer," chuckled Gary. Legrand had a studio band of talented musicians: along with saxophonist Gene "Daddy G" Barge, a core group that became known in their own right as the Church Street Five: pianist Willie Burnell, trombone player Leonard Barks, saxophonist Earl Swanson, bassist and tuba player Ron "Junior" Fairley, and drummer Emmett "Nabs" Shields. Barge, who was a high school music instructor, subsequently became a producer for Chess Records, for which he worked with Muddy Waters, Fontella Bass, Little Milton, Billy Stewart, and the Dells.

With the Church Street Five backing him, Bonds' spirited recording of "New Orleans," issued on the Legrand label, hit the pop charts in the fall of 1960, driving to No. 6 on the *Billboard* Hot 100, on which it impressively remained for 14 weeks. Seeking a gimmick to attract the attention of disc jockeys, Guida credited the vocal to Gary "U.S." Bonds and inscribed the message "Buy U.S. Bonds" on the sleeves of promotional copies that were sent to the radio stations. So at the age of 19, Gary Anderson became Gary "U.S." Bonds.

After "New Orleans" concluded its run on the charts, Anderson wrote and recorded a song called "Not Me," which radio stations refused to play because of lyrics they regarded as lewd. "I never did find out what the supposedly dirty lyrics were," said Anderson. In 1963, the female vocal group the Orlons recorded "Not Me," which garnered significant air play and became a top 20 hit.

Bonds worked magic for his second hit, turning a prosaic instrumental into one of the most rollicking party records of the rock 'n' roll era. In 1961, Guida employed a studio band called Daddy G and the Church Street Five, which previously recorded an instrumental called "A Night With Daddy G." Guida asked Gary to come up with some lyrics for it. "I went into his little office, sat down for about 15 or 20 minutes, came back and said, 'I've got something.' And Guida said, 'well, let's record it.' And we recorded 'Quarter to Three' based on 'A Night With Daddy G.'" The song became Gary's strongest record. Five weeks after its premiere on the *Billboard* Hot 100 on May 22, 1961, "Quarter to Three" diverted Pat Boone's "Moody River" from the top of the chart, held onto the No. 1 spot for two weeks until "Tossin' and Turnin'" by Bobby Lewis tossed it aside, but remained on the charts for 15 weeks, throughout the summer of '61. Songwriting was credited to Frank Guida, Gary Anderson, Gene Barge, and Joseph Royster. Gary's successes on the singles charts prompted Legrand to record more tracks for that year's release of Gary's first album, *Dance 'til Quarter to Three with U.S. Bonds.* Dick Clark wrote the liner notes for the 12-track album, which in addition to the title song included "New Orleans," "School Is Out," and Gary's rendition of "Not Me." The album, distributed by Rust Records, a subsidiary of Laurie Records, peaked at No. 6 on the U.S. album charts.

Following the success of "New Orleans" and "Quarter to Three," Gary joined the premier summer stage show, the Dick Clark Caravan of Stars. That traveling entourage toured much of the nation, beginning in Atlantic City, New Jersey, on July 29, 1961, and ending in Detroit, Michigan, that September 4. He toured the country by bus, appearing with Chubby Checker, Freddy Cannon, the Shirelles, Bobby Rydell, Fabian, and other top artists of the time. While he was on tour, Gary scored a well-timed hit with "School Is Out," his third chart single, which hit the *Billboard* Hot 100 on July 24, 1961, when school was indeed out for the summer. Songwriting credits went to Gary Anderson and Gene "Daddy G" Barge. Bonds sported a curled forelock on the single's picture cover sleeve. "School Is Out" rose to No. 5 and remained on the chart for 11 weeks. Shortly after that record dropped off the chart, his follow-up "School Is In" hit the Hot 100 on October 23, 1961, when school was back in session. Bonds shared writing credits as Gary Anderson with Gene "Daddy G" Barge. The single reached the No. 28 spot and remained on the chart for five weeks.

While many of the 1960s dance crazes were short lived, the popularity of the twist spanned more than two years. From late 1960 through 1962 the twist inspired numerous song titles including Chubby Checker's "The Twist," "Let's Twist Again," "Slow Twistin'" and "Twist it Up"; Joey Dee and the Starliters' "Peppermint Twist"; Sam Cooke's "Twistin' the Night Away"; and King Curtis' "Soul Twist." In early 1962, Gary "U.S." Bonds managed to keep the craze going with a twist style of his own with his fifth hit, "Dear Lady Twist," which premiered on the *Billboard* Hot 100 on December 11, 1961. Frank Guida wrote the infectious saxophone-driven party song. Other performers who recorded "cover" versions of the song included guitar-twanging Duane Eddy, twist king Chubby Checker and — seriously — poet and composer Rod McKuen. "Dear Lady Twist" rose to No. 9 and remained on the chart for 16 weeks. On March 18, 1962, Gary appeared on *The Ed Sullivan Show* to perform his newest hit, "Twist, Twist Señora," which made its chart debut on March 31, 1962. The song was written by Frank Guida, Gene Barge, and Joseph Royster. "Twist, Twist, Señora" rose to No. 9 (just as its predecessor, "Dear Lady Twist" had three months earlier), and it remained on the chart for 10 weeks. "Dear Lady Twist" and "Twist, Twist Señora" were featured on Gary's second Legrand Records album, *Twist Up Calypso*.

Gary proposed an idea that gained popularity during the summer vacation of 1962 with his fifth hit, "Seven Day Weekend," which premiered on the Hot 100 that June 23. The song was written by singer-songwriter "Doc" Pomus (Jerome Felder) and pianist Mort Schuman, whose prolific songwriting output also included "You've Got the Magic Touch," "Marie's the Name of His Latest Flame," "Viva Las Vegas," "Hushabye," "Save the Last Dance for Me," "A Teenager in Love" and "Sweets for My Sweet." Bonds' "Seven Day Weekend" was featured in the British film *It's Trad, Dad* (released in the United States under the name *Ring-A-Ding Rhythm*), directed by Richard Lester — who directed the Beatles' films *A Hard Day's Night* and *Help,* as well as *How I Won the War,* starring John Lennon. "Seven Day Weekend" peaked at No. 27 and remained on the chart for seven weeks. Unfortunately, not every U.S. Bonds release was a hit. "Copy Cat," his eighth chart single, made its debut on the Hot 100 on August 25, 1962, but went no higher than No. 92 and remained on the chart for only three weeks.

Gary enjoyed telling the story about firing his backup band, which had been known as the Silver Beatles. "During my first trip to Europe, I was on the bill with Gene McDaniels, who had the 1961 hits 'A Hundred Pounds of Clay' and 'Tower of Strength.' Our backup band, which people would later know as the Beatles, was just not cutting it. At that time they really didn't know the feel of rock and roll," said Gary with a grin. "So we hired another band when we got back to home base in London. That band was worse than the Beatles! So we had to rehire them."

Some of Gary's fondest memories include meeting idols Sam Cooke, Jackie Wilson, and B.B. King for the first time on a bus tour in 1960. He recalled, "They really wanted to turn me around because I was very rigid on stage, since I had no training. I was from Norfolk, Virginia. What the hell did I know? I had a hit record, I went out on stage and I sang. I didn't move, I didn't talk, I didn't dance. So one afternoon, after we left one of the venues, Sam Cooke said to me, 'B.B. and I have a limousine, and we want you to ride with us in the limousine to the next gig. We want to talk to you.' So I said, 'Oh, OK.' And I got in there and they started telling me, 'You talk to us backstage and you're mouth almighty but when you get on stage you don't say nuthin', you don't move. We've gotta loosen you up a little bit.' And they started showing me a few things and telling me some things to say. They said, 'So the next gig you go out and you do that, OK?' And I said, 'Oh, yessir, OK.' And the next gig I didn't do it. And they put me back in the limousine again and they talked to me, and they said, 'At the next gig you do it,' and I didn't do it. The third gig, when I was coming off the stage, after I didn't do it again, Sam Cooke slapped the shit out of me. As soon as I hit the side of the stage, BAM! And he says, 'the next time you go out there, dammit, do it, or I'm gonna punch you.' I've been a dancing fool ever since," he laughed.

On another early '60s bus tour through the South and into Texas that included Dick and Dee Dee, Anderson was the only Black performer. "I remember they used to smuggle me into the hotels because, you know, Blacks weren't allowed. But they got me through it. Dick and all the guys. They'd say, just hang here for a minute, we'll make sure you're in. I'd go to the side door and run."

Anderson toured as well with other legendary rhythm and blues performers, including the Shirelles, the Cadillacs, the Flamingos, Bobby Lewis, and Bo Diddley. "I remember Bo Diddley cooking chicken in the back of the bus. Being young I didn't mind sitting in that bus for 20 hours. Everybody was playing cards and gambling. Oh, God, and no mothers and fathers. We were drinking and smoking cigarettes. Man, I thought it was great," Anderson laughed. "A lot of times we wouldn't get to a hotel, and it got pretty funky in there for a couple of days. We'd just do our gig, get back on the bus, stop at a truck stop or whatever and kinda wash up a little bit, get to the next gig and perform. Then maybe we got to a hotel room, took a shower and cleaned our clothes up a little bit. I think the bus tours were the most memorable things I can remember doing. I got to see the world, make money, and chase the girls."

In addition to bus tours, Anderson occasionally played theaters during the '60s, including the Apollo, the Regal, and the Royal. "I also went down South and got into the chitlin' circuit, they called it, the chicken shacks. We all did those with James Brown and whoever else. They were fun. A little rough, but fun. We were young so we could run real fast," he laughed.

In 1962 Gary introduced the late Jimmy Soul to Guida, who produced Soul's recording "If You Wanna Be Happy," a No. 1 hit in 1963. "Jimmy and I used to sing together in Suffolk. This was before either of us had a hit record. Jimmy was 'wonder boy' and I was 'nature boy.' We didn't wear many clothes back then. The place we were working was really strange so we tried to find a gimmick. It was like a long corridor with the bandstand in the middle, so we'd come swinging in on ropes from both ends wearing little loincloths. Thank God I don't have to wear that damn loincloth anymore," he said, erupting into laughter.

Bonds returned to the *Billboard* Hot 100 chart on April 25, 1981, after a 19-year absence, as the result of a collaboration with Bruce Springsteen. E Street Band member Steve Van Zandt and Springsteen produced Bonds' recording of "This Little Girl," a Springsteen composition that EMI America released. "This Little Girl," Bonds' ninth chart single, rose to No. 11 and remained on the chart for 18 weeks, which was the longest duration of any of his 11 hit singles. "Jolé Blon," Gary's 10th chart single, made its debut on the Hot 100 chart on July 18, 1981. The infectiously lively Cajun-flavored love tune included vocal accompaniment by Bruce Springsteen. Rockabilly pianist and composer Aubrey "Moon" Mullican wrote the new interpretation of the traditional Cajun song, which Gary recorded for his album *Dedication*. Bruce Springsteen and Steve Van Zandt produced the EMI America release, which peaked at No. 65 and remained on the chart for six weeks.

"Out of Work," the 11th chart single for Gary "U.S" Bonds, premiered on the *Billboard* Hot 100 on June 12, 1982. Springsteen wrote the song, which became the last Bonds single to make the charts. Springsteen and Van Zandt produced the EMI America release, which peaked at No. 21 and remained on the chart for 16 weeks.

Long afterward, Gary "U.S." Bonds continued performing, appearing on stage in concert appearances for welcoming audiences, well into the mid 2020s.

GARY "U.S." BONDS

U.S. HIT SINGLES ON THE NATIONAL CHARTS

Debut	Peak	Title	Label
10/17/60	6	New Orleans	Legrand
5/22/61	1	Quarter to Three	Legrand
7/24/61	5	School Is Out	Legrand
10/23/61	28	School Is In	Legrand
12/11/61	9	Dear Lady Twist	Legrand
3/31/62	9	Twist, Twist Señora	Legrand
6/23/62	27	Seven Day Weekend	Legrand
8/25/62	92	Copy Cat	Legrand
4/25/81	11	This Little Girl	EMI America
7/18/81	65	Jole Blon	EMI America
6/12/82	21	Out of Work	EMI America

Billboard's pop singles chart data is courtesy of Joel Whitburn's Record Research Inc., Menomonee Falls, Wisconsin.

Epilogue: Gary Anderson

Singer

Gary "U.S." Bonds was always as fun loving and full of life as his music. His light-hearted humor and infectious laughter revealed his enjoyment of life. With nine top 40 hits under his belt, Gary didn't let any grass grow under his feet. He continued electrifying audiences for decades with lively performances while pursuing a newfound career in a food products company and serving as a goodwill ambassador to Third World countries.

Born to Gary and Irene Anderson in Jacksonville, Florida, on June 6, 1939, Gary "U.S." Bonds carved out a career for himself beginning in high school and spanning

Gary Anderson in the 1990s flanked by his wife, Laurie (at left) and his daughter, Laurie. Courtesy of Gary "U.S." Bonds.

more than four decades. His father was a university professor and his mother, a piano teacher. In the early '40s, Anderson's family moved to Norfolk, Virginia, where Gary was first introduced to theater when he was 8 years old. He recalls his mother taking him to the Booker T. Washington Theater in Norfolk, which featured musical performers such as Bull Moose Jackson, Pigmeat Markham, and Ivory Joe Hunter. "The first time I saw Bull Moose Jackson with all the lights, stage, and sound, I thought 'this is what I want to do,'" Anderson said.

Gary Levone Anderson attended Booker T. Washington High School but dropped out of school before graduating when he landed his first record deal with Frank Guida. "I had to make a choice of either going to school or going out and making money," he said. "My mom was all for me going out and making money, but my dad didn't like it because he was a university professor."

Gary's father had taught math and science at Florida State University for many years before taking a job at Hampton University in Virginia, where he taught science and woodwork. "He always loved to do woodwork and when he was getting ready to retire, he said 'I want to teach woodwork,' so he did," said Anderson. "There's a man who went to school all of his life. He had every degree there was, and he didn't take too kindly to me quitting school."

Gary recalled one time his father agreed to attend one of his performances. "He sat in the back and watched the show, and on the way home I didn't say anything. He didn't either. He just shook his head. Finally, he said, 'I don't understand it. I don't know how you make money doing that.' He didn't understand it till the day he died."

In 1962 Gary met his wife-to-be, Laurie Davis, in Atlantic City, New Jersey. She had been a member of a doo-wop vocal group called the Love Notes, who recorded the R&B hit single "United" for the New York-based Holiday label in 1957, and she also recorded as a soloist under the name Lucy Rivera. When Gary met her she was singing at a nightclub on the Boardwalk near the club in which Gary was performing.

"I stopped by to have a drink. I saw her and said to myself, 'Wow. She looks pretty good.' After the show, she came around to see me and we went out to breakfast. We've been seeing each other ever since," he chuckled. Married since 1963, Gary and Laurie performed in the 1990s with their daughter, also named Laurie, traveling throughout the country with a five-piece band. They set up a recording studio in their Long Island home, where daughter Laurie wrote and produced music with her father. Gary was still performing in 2026 — 66 years after he first took to the stage. "Our show is based around good times. We go out and create a party," said Gary. "We try to create a 'Come on! Let's dance, let's sing' atmosphere. So I guess I'm perceived as some old good-time, happy guy." Since the late 1980s, Gary and his wife, Laurie, have been managing their own musical engagements. "Now when the money's missing, I know who's got it. It's either me or my wife," he laughs.

Gary was regarded in the music industry as an accomplished songwriter as well as a singer. "She's All I've Got," a song that Gary wrote and country music singer Johnny Paycheck recorded in 1971, was nominated for a Grammy award and earned Gary a nomination for the

Country Music Association's "Songwriter of the Year." In 1971 Freddie North's recording of the same song reached the top 10 on the R&B charts, and in 1997 the song became a top 10 hit for country artist Tracy Byrd.

Anderson regarded his association with Frank Guida and Bruce Springsteen as his two biggest breaks. He met Springsteen in 1979 while working at a club in New Jersey. At the time Springsteen was involved in a lawsuit and wasn't recording. "He saw me and said, 'Maybe I'll just work with you until this court thing is over with.' And that's what he did." With a sterling roster of backup singers and musicians, including Ben E. King and Chuck Jackson, Springsteen produced the 1981 Gary "U.S." Bonds album *Dedication* released on EMI. That was followed a year later by another successful album, *On the Line*. "And then we had two kids and Bruce left. And I'm still upset over that," Anderson joked. Springsteen-produced "This Little Girl" and "Out of Work" rose to 11th and 21st positions on the charts in 1981 and 1982 respectively.

Springsteen and Miami Steve Van Zandt presented Anderson with the Pioneer Award for achievement in the music industry at the 1997 Rhythm & Blues Foundation awards ceremony at the New York Hilton. The award included a plaque and a $15,000 cash award.

Gary "U.S." Bonds played a role with Bo Diddley cast as a member of the Louisiana Gator Boys in the 1998 movie *Blues Brothers 2000*. "I performed 'New Orleans' and I also sang backup for B.B. King in the movie."

In 1973 and again in 1983, Anderson met Yank Barry, former lead singer of the traveling Kingsmen, who had the hit single "Louie, Louie," at a benefit golf tournament that Barry was sponsoring. "I love golf, man, I'll fly anywhere," said Anderson. "We met each other in Myrtle Beach, South Carolina, and struck up a friendship. One day Yank came back from South Africa where he had been doing some recording with a philharmonic orchestra. At that time he was producing Engelbert Humperdinck and Tom Jones. He had met a scientist over there, who had an idea for a high-protein, soy bean-based food product, and he asked me if I would be interested in joining him in it, and investing some money. I said, 'This sounds like a good idea. I don't know anything about food, and I don't know anything about investing, but I trust you. Let's go with it.' And thank God, it's been a great thing for me."

The products, under the VitaPro name, are low in fat and calories, and high in protein. VitaPro is a line of meat substitutes created from soy isolate with the taste and texture of meat. Because it's dehydrated and requires no refrigeration, the food is ideal for famine relief. Barry, who was involved with the "We Are the World" relief project, believed strongly in donating a percentage of the company's revenue to hunger relief in the United States and throughout the world. In August 1997, Anderson joined Barry, former world heavyweight boxing champion Muhammad Ali, singer Celine Dion, and other celebrities and supporters in a relief mission to Côte d'Ivoire in western Africa. The project supplied food, medicine, wheelchairs, toys, and writing materials to a rehabilitation center there that housed and cared for 480 disabled, orphaned, and abandoned children who fled civil strife in Liberia.

"We took *Entertainment Tonight, Life* magazine and our own camera crew. In all there were 67 people, including a number of African reporters that we picked up in Abidjan. The president of the Ivory Coast gave us his plane to fly around in, and that was cool." Following the trip, Anderson appeared on *Entertainment Tonight* with Muhammad Ali and Yank Barry. "When you've got Muhammad there, you become background. So I became background, and I was glad to be there."

The trip was deeply revealing for Anderson. He said, "Some of the children had malaria, cholera, polio, one leg, one eye. It was really, really cruel. When I think about it, I feel really bad, but it was the greatest thing that ever happened to me in life. And I didn't get paid for it. People can't understand that I would do that. It was fantastic. It really was."

Anderson told us that he was happy with his career and life. Driven by his love of golf, Gary became involved in several PGA celebrity golf tournaments. He also enjoyed recording, performing, and throwing parties for his neighbors. "I would have moved out of this neighborhood years ago, but our neighbors are fantastic. We all look out for each other and there's no problems within a half-mile radius of here," Gary told us in 1997. "I never work New Year's eve so I can throw a party at my house. Since about 1985 we've invited all of our neighbors to walk to our house for a party so that no one has to drive, and we have about 60 people here on New Year's Eve. It's a lot of fun."

Communicating with people was one of Gary's greatest strengths, but he surprisingly said that singing was not. "I'm not that great a singer. Even though I've learned a lot over the past 40 years, I haven't quite reached the stature of singer that I would like to be, like a Sam Cooke or Jackie Wilson. But I can hold my own. With Sam Cooke slapping me and Jackie Wilson showing me things, I can do it," he laughed. Anderson's greatest

Gary "U.S." Bonds in 1996.

pleasure remained spending time with his family. "We have the greatest time together. That's why we're always here alone. Me and my wife and daughter. We sing and dance and watch movies. I also like working around the house. I'm one of those fixit guys. Even though I can't fix it that good, I like doing it."

Anderson told us that he wants to be remembered not only for his music but also for the societal contributions he made. "It's very important. I like to feel that I made some impact on somebody's life. That's why it gives me such a thrill that I'm doing something with the Champions for Children with Muhammad Ali and Yank. Not only for self-gratification, but also for people to know that the family I'm involved with, my family, is part of something that may change something for somebody in this world. When I'm gone, I don't want people to say 'this guy was here, and he didn't do shit.' Especially for my daughter, I want them to say, 'her father made a meaningful contribution to society.'

3

The Lion Sleeps Tonight

The Tokens

In the summer of 1961 four guys from Brooklyn walked into the RCA Victor recording studio for what might have been the last time. The oldest among them was not quite 23. The youngest was 14. Known initially as Those Guys, they had changed their name to the Tokens. They'd previously scored one national hit, "Tonight I Fell in Love," on another label, Warwick. But when the boss at Warwick told them they wouldn't be paid because their record hadn't cleared a profit, they took their songs and brought them to RCA, which offered them a three-record contract.

Their first two sessions for the RCA label in the spring of 1961 yielded two releases, "When I Go to Sleep at Night/Dry Your Eyes" and "Sincerely," neither of which registered on the *Billboard* Hot 100. At the next recording session, which was likely to be their last, the producers huddled with the quartet members to review the songs they'd brought. The RCA execs weren't impressed by what they heard. They asked the Tokens if they had any other songs.

Well, yes, there was one other song. An African-style folk melody they'd been singing at music gigs and adapted to their own style. It was called "Mbube," and it was also known as "Wimoweh." The producers at RCA loved it. With English lyrics added by a team consisting of George Weiss and session producers Hugo Peretti and Luigi Creatore, the Tokens recorded the song and released it under a new name: "The Lion Sleeps Tonight."

The public loved it as well. At the close of 1961, it became the first African song to top the American pop charts. And while other African melodies, including Miriam Makeba's pulsating "Pata Pata," have found success, none has so endeared itself to pop fans as "The Lion Sleeps Tonight," performed by Jay Siegel, Hank Medress, and Phil and Mitch Margo: the Tokens. But the Tokens ultimately proved to be more prolific behind the controls than they were in front of the microphone. Making

The Tokens in 1961. From left: Hank Medress, Mitch Margo, Phil Margo, and Jay Siegel.

an overwhelmingly successful transition to production work, the Tokens became the first group to produce a No. 1 record by another group: "He's So Fine" by the Chiffons.

Hank Medress first began harmonizing with drummer Phil Margo and his piano-playing brother Mitch in December 1959. Realizing their need of a lead singer, they recruited Jay Siegel, who sang with Hank in two other neighborhood vocal groups. The four began writing songs, then bought some time in Allegro Recording Studios on Broadway in Manhattan. They recorded a demo of a song called "Please Write," and with that master tape, the Tokens were able to start shopping their song to record labels. They headed for the "Tin Pan Alley" sector of midtown Manhattan, populated by music publishers and record labels. Hank took the elevator to the top floor of the fabled Brill Building at 1619 Broadway at the northwest corner of W. 49th Street and started knocking on doors, floor by floor. "In those days you'd find about 10 independent labels on every floor," Hank told us in July 1997. While "Please Write" didn't convince anyone to sign on the bottom line, the owner of Warwick Records liked the Tokens' composition "Tonight I Fell in Love." The label signed the group, and recorded and released the song in February 1961, just after John F. Kennedy took office as president. Phil and Mitch Margo and Hank Medress wrote the song, and the Fields-Madera Orchestra backed the singing group in the session. The single made its debut on the *Billboard* Hot 100 on March 6, 1961.

In less than two months "Tonight I Fell in Love" brought the group into the national top 20 and onto *American Bandstand.* "At that time, to us, you didn't get any bigger than that," mused Hank. A robust doo-wop tune, "Tonight I Fell in Love" reached No. 15 and remained on the chart for 14 weeks. The Tokens took to the road. Pittsburgh. Cleveland. Detroit. "In those days groups promoted records by lip-synching at record hops. Back then, we didn't perform live. We'd do seven record hops in one night."

None of the group members anticipated the success they would achieve. After his graduation from high school in 1956, Medress had entered Brooklyn College with thoughts of becoming a teacher. He began studying elementary education, but found difficulty visualizing himself teaching school for a lifetime. His career choice became solidified after "Tonight I Fell in Love" became a hit. He left college during his junior year. "I had a better perspective then of where I was going," Hank said.

Phil Margo likewise enrolled in Brooklyn College following his graduation from high school in 1959, and began working in a stock brokerage firm. His brother, Mitch, five years his junior, was still in junior high school.

Although Jay Siegel enjoyed singing tremendously, he hadn't given serious thought to a career in the entertainment business. Upon graduation from high school in 1958, Jay also enrolled in Brooklyn College, then transferred to New York City Community College, where he obtained a degree in retail market research. He entered the trade as a merchandise buyer for Rainbow Shops, a retail chain. "I never thought that music would be my career, because people I knew who had jobs didn't really enjoy what they did. So it never occurred to me that I could have a career and make money doing something that's so much fun," said Jay.

In the fall of 1961, he was newly married and had a back-office job doing cost analysis for Lerner Shops, a chain of women's apparel stores. When "The Lion Sleeps Tonight" began its five-week climb to the top of the charts in mid-November 1961, the attorney handling financial affairs for the Tokens advised Jay to quit his job. Jay's parents, wife, and in-laws greeted that suggestion with an identical reaction: "Quit your job? What are you, crazy?" Jay pondered their pleas. On December 18, 1961, "The Lion Sleeps Tonight" displaced the Marvelettes' hit "Please Mr. Postman" from the No. 1 position on the *Billboard* Hot 100. And Jay quit his job.

The Tokens returned to *American Bandstand* when "The Lion Sleeps Tonight" returned them to the charts. "That was difficult for us to lip-synch because 'The Lion Sleeps Tonight' doesn't have an instrumental introduction. It begins with my falsetto," said Jay. "So I held my head down so my lips couldn't be seen, until I heard the first note come through the speakers, and then I looked up and lip-synched with the song." On January 9, 1962, the Recording Industry Association of America awarded gold record certification for "The Lion Sleeps Tonight," which remained on the chart for 15 weeks. The soaring Tokens hit remained No. 1 for three consecutive weeks, until January 13, when "The Twist" by Chubby Checker topped the chart for the second time.

"B'wa Nina (Pretty Girl)," the Tokens' follow-up to "The Lion Sleeps Tonight," made its debut on the *Billboard* Hot 100 on February 10, 1962. The production team of Hugo Peretti and Luigi Creatore wrote the song with George David Weiss. Peretti and Creatore, who were cousins, produced Elvis Presley's early RCA Victor recordings, the Isley Brothers' "Shout," and Sam Cooke's "Twistin' the Night Away" and "Chain Gang," among many other pop standouts. The numerous hits that Weiss co-wrote included Kay Starr's "Wheel of Fortune," Presley's "Can't Help

Falling in Love," Nat King Cole's "That Sunday, That Summer," and Louis Armstrong's "What a Wonderful World." Sammy Lowe conducted the orchestral backing for the "B'wa Nina (Pretty Girl)" session. The recording, on the RCA Victor label, reached No. 55 and remained on the chart for five weeks. The Tokens followed that with "La Bomba," their tribute to Ritchie Valens' "La Bamba." Hugo Peretti and Luigi Creatore infused the Tokens' joyful rendition with a rich orchestral arrangement and more lavish production than Valens' original. However, after making its debut on the *Billboard* Hot 100 on June 30, 1962, "La Bomba" reached no higher than No. 85 during a five-week stay on the chart.

"Hear the Bells," the Tokens' final chart record for the RCA label, made its debut on the *Billboard* Hot 100 on August 24, 1963. All four Tokens — Hank Medress, Jay Siegel, and brothers Phil and Mitch Margo — shared writing credits for the song with Sammy Lowe, who was the orchestral conductor for the session. Hugo and Luigi produced the recording. The single, on the RCA label, remained on the chart for five weeks but went no higher than No. 94.

As stunning a success as "The Lion Sleeps Tonight" had been, it proved enigmatic for booking engagements. "We just didn't fit in anywhere. We weren't folk, we weren't rock. We had this wonderful record, but nobody knew what it was," said Phil. "After doing some college gigs we found that we needed to accompany ourselves. That's what inspired us to learn how to play our own instruments. Hank played bass, I played the drums, Mitch played the guitar, and Jay sang lead and occasionally played guitar."

On the record hop circuit, the Tokens became friends with the Angels, the Marcels, Dion and the Belmonts, Del Shannon, and with Tony Orlando, who as a solo artist was out on the road promoting his records "Halfway to Paradise" and "Bless You." A decade later, the Tokens would produce Orlando's hits with Dawn and resurrect his flagging career.

Although they continued recording and releasing songs that generated some chart action, the Tokens were unable to crack the national top 40 for four more years. While the public may have thought that the group was suffering from a creative drought, quite the opposite was true. The four Tokens, who had always played a large role in the production of their own records, were still writing songs and producing sessions for other artists. "It was a natural progression," observed Hank. "I didn't think we were that great as a performance group. I didn't see

The Tokens in 1962. Clockwise from left: Mitch Margo, Hank Medress, Phil Margo, and Jay Siegel.

any real longevity, but we made really terrific records." Top executives agreed at Capitol Records, which signed the Tokens as producers. Their association with Capitol was brief but fruitful.

There, the Tokens produced a record by a then-unknown vocal group that had come their way. Capitol, which had first right of refusal, didn't think much of the track that the Tokens had produced. After shopping the recording without success at other labels all over the city, Hank and Phil emerged with a deal at Laurie Records. The song that the Tokens had produced was "He's So Fine" by the Chiffons. The deal with Laurie was for an advance and royalty, and the Tokens used the advance to buy out of the contract with Capitol. The gamble on "He's So Fine" paid handsomely, as it rose to No. 1. "With 'He's So Fine,' we became the first group to produce a No. 1 record by another group," declared Jay. On the strength of that musical masterwork and their business acumen, the Tokens leaped from the ranks of doo-wop vocal group to top producers under the name Bright Tunes Productions.

Their record production credits mounted with "Denise" by Randy and the Rainbows and all of the Chiffons hit singles to their credit. Working both sides of the glass, the Tokens threw themselves fully into every phase of music production work: song writing, instrumentation, background singing, arranging, producing, and mixing. "We were having more success as producers than we were having as artists," said Phil with characteristic candor. "Right from the beginning, we produced our own demos. You see, a career in entertainment at that time for rock and roll groups was very short. Who knew that 35 years later we'd still be working? I never could have imagined that, because 10 weeks after 'The Lion Sleeps Tonight' was no longer No. 1 we were forgotten. So if we wanted to remain in the business, we had to do something else. We seemed to have a natural ability for producing — we all had good ears, we all had solid music backgrounds, we all knew what a good song was," Phil told us in July 1997.

Hank Medress concurred. "I remember one period during the 1960s when we had five or six records on the charts at the same time," said Medress. "And we continued to perform even after we had begun producing records and had formed corporations with our lawyer and business manager, Seymour Barash." The corporations the Tokens formed included Bright Tunes Music — their publishing firm named in honor of their Brighton Beach home — and B.T. Puppy Records, their own label established in 1964. The "Puppy" portion of the name was a satirical reference to Nipper, the dog that appears on the RCA logo. The group's first release on B.T. Puppy, "He's In Town," became the Tokens' sixth chart record, which made its debut on the *Billboard* Hot 100 on August 8, 1964. Gerry Goffin and Carole King wrote the emotional tune, a version of which the Rockin' Berries recorded in the U.K. "He's in Town" described a boy's anxiety after the return of his girlfriend's former flame following an absence. The recording, distinguished by beautiful harmonies, reached No. 43 and remained on the chart for 8 weeks.

After a two-year gap, the Tokens returned to the charts with "I Hear Trumpets Blow," a top 30 hit released on B.T. Puppy in the spring of 1966. The song was written collaboratively by all four Tokens, and they produced the recording (as Big Time Productions), with musical arrangement by Trade Martin and engineering by Bill McMeekin. Trade Martin also produced or arranged recordings by Lesley Gore, Solomon Burke, Rick Nelson, and Ian & Sylvia. Bill McMeekin's credits include work on sessions for the Four Seasons, Del Shannon, and Phil Spector. "I Hear Trumpets Blow" took the Tokens' to No. 30 and remained on the chart for eight weeks.

They followed that with "Portrait of My Love," which Steve Lawrence had recorded in 1961. The Tokens' rendition premiered on the *Billboard* Hot 100 on April 15, 1967. Matt Monro and the Lettermen also recorded versions of the song, which was written in 1960 by musical theater conductor, arranger, and composer Cyril Ornadel and lyricist David West. The Tokens produced their "Portrait of My Love" session through their company, Bright Tunes Productions, with musical arrangement by Jimmy Wisner. The recording marked the Tokens' debut on the Warner Bros. label, reached No. 36 and remained on the chart for eight weeks. In their version of "Portrait of My Love," the harmonies of the Tokens were somewhat reminiscent of the Lettermen.

That turned out to be the Tokens' last appearance in the national top 40 for six years, during which time their releases for Warner Bros. and their next label, Buddah, languished. Those included "It's a Happening World," which first appeared on the *Billboard* Hot 100 on July 22, 1967. Prolific songwriters Barry Mann and Cynthia Weil wrote the tune. The dozens of hit tunes that Mann and Weil wrote include "Uptown" and "He's Sure the Boy I Love" for the Crystals; "Blame it on the Bossa Nova" for Eydie Gormé; "It's Getting Better" and "Make Your Own Kind of Music" for Mama Cass Elliot; "(You're My) Soul and Inspiration" for the Righteous Brothers; "Hungry" and "Kicks" for Paul Revere and the Raiders; and "Here You Come Again" for Dolly Parton. Jimmy Wisner performed musical arrangement for "It's a Happening World," and the Tokens

The Tokens in 1967. Top: Jay Siegel and Hank Medress; bottom: Phil Margo and Mitch Margo.

produced the session. The recording, on the Warner Bros. label, reached No. 69 and remained on the chart for four weeks.

"She Lets Her Hair Down (Early in the Morning)," the 10th chart single by the Tokens, premiered on the Hot 100 on December 13, 1969. Paul Vance and Leon Carr wrote the song, versions of which Gene Pitney, Ben E. King, and Bobby Sherman also recorded. Vance and Carr, both of whom were prolific composers with dozens of hits to their credit individually, also collaboratively wrote Johnny Mathis' 1962 hit "Gina." Norm Bergen arranged and produced the gently swinging music for the Tokens' take on "She Lets Her Hair Down (Early in the Morning)," and the Tokens produced the session. The song reached No. 61 and remained on the chart for seven weeks.

The Tokens' remake of the Beach Boys' 1964 hit "Don't Worry, Baby," which premiered on the Hot 100 on March 7, 1970, went no higher than No. 95 and was on the chart for only two weeks. The Tokens produced the session, with orchestration arranged and conducted by Norm Bergen. That Buddah release turned out to be the 11th and final Hot 100 chart single by the Tokens.

In 1973 Jay Siegel and Phil and Mitch Margo formed a country-rock trio they called Cross Country and signed with the ATCO label, for which they recorded an album and several additional tracks for single releases. One single, a ballad interpretation of the Wilson Pickett song "In the Midnight Hour," cracked the national top 30, but neither their self-titled album nor other Cross Country single releases did well, so they disbanded the project in 1974.

Meanwhile, the Tokens also became deeply involved in producing music for television and radio commercials, including spots for airlines, cigarettes, beer, and other products. "We spent a good four or five years writing and producing jingles. It was a very lucrative business," said Siegel.

Even so, lion tracks would follow them throughout the remainder of their career. "The Lion Sleeps Tonight," heard on the soundtrack of 11 motion pictures, emerged once again with the June 1994 release of the Disney animated feature *The Lion King.* That family favorite introduced the captivating song to an appreciative new generation.

In 1996 on their B.T. Puppy label, the Tokens released *Tonight the Lion Dances,* an album of beautifully performed Latin-flavored tunes. The 17 songs on the album included "La Bamba," their tribute to Ritchie

Valens. It was their way of settling a 34-year-old score over an earlier version that they found disappointing. They had first recorded the song in 1962 for RCA Victor, which the label released under the title "La Bomba." That recording, with a rich orchestral arrangement, made its debut on the *Billboard* Hot 100 on June 30, 1962. Phil Margo attributed the variant spelling to "a typo or bad research by the RCA staff." On June 11, 2012, Phil told us, "by the time we saw it, the labels and jackets were already printed. By the way, 'La Bomba' means 'the bomb' — an okay expression for today but back then it had a different meaning [a referral to failure]. It also was nowhere near the record I wanted to make. The version in *Tonight the Lion Dances* was the way I wanted to go. As a matter of fact, I remember having a big snit at the RCA Studios on 24th Street when the orchestra was running the tune down. It induced [producer] Luigi Creatore to call me 'insufferable.' I probably was."

Oldies music radio channels typically obtain their music in packages from broadcast production firms. Even though "I Hear Trumpets Blow," "Portrait of My Love" and "Tonight I Fell in Love" all cracked the national top 40, they're often excluded from the packages that satellite radio and streaming channels acquire. But no oldies channel worthy of its title would be without a copy of "The Lion Sleeps Tonight." Their listeners still love that record — a token of their esteem for Hank Medress, Phil Margo, Mitch Margo, and Jay Siegel: the four guys from Brooklyn whose passion for music then transcended an ocean and now transcends time.

The Tokens — saxophonist Jay Leslie, singer-percussionist Phil Margo, guitarist-keyboard player Mitch Margo, and guitarist Mike Johnson — performing in the Solano Community College Theater on Suisun Valley Road in Fairfield, California, on Thursday, January 21, 1999. Photo by Jeff March.

The Tokens continued performing into 2026 with Phil's son Noah Margo (drummer and singer); Phil's grandsons Solomon "Solly" Margo (guitarist and singer) and Ethan Ginsberg-Margo (keyboardist); horn player Jay Leslie; bassist and singer Nico Wicklin; and singer Rebecca Curci.

THE TOKENS
U.S. HIT SINGLES ON THE NATIONAL CHARTS

Debut	Peak	Gold	Title	Label
3/6/61	15		Tonight I Fell in Love	Warwick
11/13/61	1	▲	The Lion Sleeps Tonight	RCA
2/10/62	55		B'wa Nina (Pretty Girl)	RCA
6/30/62	85		La Bomba	RCA
8/24/63	94		Hear The Bells	RCA
8/8/64	43		He's in Town	BT Puppy
3/19/66	30		I Hear Trumpets Blow	BT Puppy
4/15/67	36		Portrait of My Love	Warner Bros
7/22/67	69		It's a Happening World	Warner Bros
12/13/69	61		She Lets Her Hair Down (Early in the Morning)	Buddah
03/07/70	95		Don't Worry Baby	Buddah
08/18/73	30		In the Midnight Hour*	ATCO
08/20/94	51		The Lion Sleeps Tonight	RCA

▲ symbol: RIAA certified gold record (Recording Industry Association of America)

*released under the group name Cross Country

Billboard's pop singles chart data is courtesy of Joel Whitburn's Record Research Inc., Menomonee Falls, Wisconsin.

Epilogue: Hank Medress

Singer

November 19, 1938 – June 18, 2007

From its northern terminal in The Bronx, the subway B train burrows its way down the Upper West Side of Manhattan under Central Park West and clatters beneath Broadway at 53rd Street before traversing the Manhattan Bridge and drilling underground once again in Brooklyn. The train finally emerges from the darkness and roars past the backyards of houses in the neighborhoods of Flatbush, Millwood, and Sheepshead Bay. After crossing over Neptune Avenue, the train veers in a wide sweep to the right and squeals to a stop on the elevated steel platform atop the intersection of Coney Island Avenue and Brighton Beach Avenue.

In the 1950s, the grimy streets below were lined with luncheonettes, laundries, shoe repair shops, small appliance stores, newsstands, sawdust-floored butcher shops, pizzerias, Chinese restaurants, Jewish delicatessens, and open-front produce markets. Seven-story brownstone apartment buildings shadow the narrow side streets leading to the boardwalk and beach a block away. Farther from the beach, the apartments yield to brick duplexes and modest clapboard cottages built around courtyard enclaves that turn their backs on the streets.

Hank Medress in the 1990s. Photo by Jane Medress, Artextures Design.

Back in 1955, Brighton 5th Place, Brighton 8th Place, and other courtyards were tight-knit communities. Hank Medress, who was only 2 years of age when his father died, lived in a Brighton Beach apartment building with his mother, who worked as a bookkeeper. As teenagers, Hank and Neil Sedaka were neighbors on the same block. From his bedroom, Hank could hear Neil practicing classical music on his piano each day after school until 5 p.m. That's when Hank would dash across the courtyard, Neil would start pounding forbidden boogie-woogie on his keyboard, and the two would harmonize doo-wop tunes.

Hank — an only child who enjoyed shooting hoops with other kids in the courtyard — played basketball and ran track at Lincoln High School, which Neil also attended. With his consistent athletic performance, Hank had the potential to capture a sports scholarship from a small college. But he loved music too much. He and Neil decided to form a musical group with three other Lincoln High School friends, Eddie Rabkin, Cynthia Zolitin, and Jay Siegel. They called themselves the Linc-Tones before adopting a new name: the Tokens. They performed during their junior and senior years, recorded a few tunes including a Sedaka-penned song called "I Love My Baby" for the small Melba label, and then disbanded in 1956 after two years together.

Hank Medress, born November 19, 1938, was first drawn to music when he began listening in the early '50s to pioneering disc jockey Martin Block's "Make-Believe Ballroom" on New York radio station WNEW. In an era of live big-band broadcasts, Block played phonograph records and counted down the most popular songs of the day by Patti Page, Don Cornell, Eddie Fisher, and Perry Como.

Then came Alan Freed in the fall of 1954, broadcasting a steady diet of doo-wop and rock and roll on WINS. Freed played "Earth Angel" by the Penguins, "Goodnight, Sweetheart, Goodnight" by the Spaniels, "Tweedlee Dee" by LaVern Baker, and "Sh-Boom" by the Chords. "Now that was music," said Medress, who began going to the Brooklyn Fox and the Brooklyn Paramount to see the Moonglows, the Harptones, the Flamingos, and other groups.

As that first Tokens combo dissolved, Hank joined a group called Darrell and the Oxfords. He remained with them only long enough to record one tune for the Roulette label called "Picture in My Wallet," which became a local hit in New York. He wasn't distressed about the group's lack of momentum because he was distracted by the notion of forming a new group. He thought first of the Margo brothers, and with them and Jay Siegel formed a new Tokens group, an association that would last more than a decade.

The Tokens remained intact until the early '70s, but Hank began drifting away to pursue his own production interests. "We ran the Tokens as a partnership. If I wrote a song, all four of us were credited with writing it. If another one of the guys wrote a song, we all divided the credit equally. If I produced a record, all of our names went on it. And I left the group partly because I felt there was an inequity to that arrangement," Medress confessed. Pivotal in his decision was the association that the group began with producer Dave Appell, who operated the Tokens' publishing firm.

Appell had worked at Cameo Parkway Records, where he had considerable success as a songwriter and producer working with Chubby Checker, Dee Dee Sharp, and Bobby Rydell. "He found the song 'Candida,' played it for me, and I knew it was a hit," declared Hank. In the original session in 1970, Phil Margo and Jay Siegel played instruments and Frankie Paris, a blues singer in the B.T. Puppy fold, performed the lead vocal. After the mix, it seemed the vocals needed a different treatment. Hank thought of Tony Orlando, who'd enjoyed a solo singing career in the early '60s but who by then had gone on to work for April-Blackwood Music as a music publisher. So at lunch Medress met with Orlando and asked him to try to think of a singer who could record the track. Orlando had no suggestions, but Medress had one. "Tony, you do it," Medress finally said. "Hank, I can't do it," sputtered Orlando. "I've got a job." Medress replied, "Look, I'll tell you what. We'll use a group name and nobody will ever know that it's you." Orlando finally relented and he cut the lead vocal track, with backgrounds provided by Jay and two female singers, Toni Wine of the Archies and jingle singer Leslie Miller. "Only Dave Appell and the engineer and I knew that Tony's voice was on 'Candida' by Dawn. We kept it a secret. And after 'Knock Three Times,' same thing. And, finally, I said, 'Tony, this is insane. You're losing all kinds of money you could be making.' Eventually he agreed to change the group name to Tony Orlando and Dawn."

In early 1972 Medress and the other Tokens produced a re-make of "The Lion Sleeps Tonight" by Robert John, a version for Atlantic Records that returned the song to the charts and captured another gold record. Medress and Dave Appell continued collaborating in record production through the 1970s.

Together they worked with Frankie Valli, Melissa Manchester, Mac Davis, and other popular artists. Medress also began producing on his own in the early '80s, at first inauspiciously. "I started feeling like maybe life was passing me by a bit," Medress acknowledged. "I wasn't a kid anymore and the phone wasn't ringing. I didn't think that I had lost anything but when I was approached to become a staff producer I went to work in my first corporate job." Medress was hired in 1986 by a firm called the Entertainment Music Company, which was later to become SBK Record Productions, ultimately subsumed by the preeminent EMI enterprise. AT SBK, Medress worked with Olivia Newton-John and produced albums for Buster Poindexter, the Nylons, the Weather Girls, and Dan Hill, including "Never Thought (That I Could Love)" and the top-10 hit "Can't We Try" in collaboration with John Capek.

Medress was content — for a while. "In 1990 I woke up one day and decided I needed to do something else. Recalling how much he'd enjoyed Toronto while recording the tracks for Canadian Dan Hill's album, he wrote a memo to EMI executives observing that the company's lack of an EMI music publishing office in Canada was detrimental because Canada's treaty with China was better than that of the United States. EMI liked the idea and asked Medress to open a Canadian office, of which he was named president. "I spent the next two and a half years in Toronto, started the company and within two years we were voted publisher of the year. But the business was totally insane," said Medress.

He likened his role to that of the character played by Peter Sellers in the 1979 motion picture *Being There*. With the mentality of a child, Sellers works as a gardener named Chance but through happenstance and misunderstanding is elevated to executive status when his childlike observations are accorded deep insight. "I was equally out of position with EMI in Canada," Medress conceded. "I was wearing Armani suits, attending board meetings, preparing economic forecasts, and doing other functions that had no relationship with what I had done my whole life until then. I was a creative music person, yet there I was doing that rhetoric bullshit. I hated it." Medress endured that job for more than two years before resigning in 1992. "I was 54 years old, still feeling good, I ran marathons, I was still playing basketball, didn't look my age, had tons of energy and I didn't know what I was going to do. And the phone didn't ring," said Medress.

He concentrated on life with his family — his wife Jane, an interior designer, and youngest son, Zach, born in 1986, along with children from two previous marriages: Danny, born in 1976; Sarah, born in 1972; and Julie, born in 1964.

Time passed. Then Hank happened to see Allan Pepper, a friend of his who owned a nightclub on West 4th Street in lower Manhattan called the Bottom Line. Knowing that the club habitually recorded the performances of the legendary artists who appeared on its stage Hank said, "Allan, it's the 20th anniversary of the club. It would be great to document these past two decades of performances, maybe in a PBS special or something." Allan said, "I don't have the time to do it, but if you want to, you have my blessings."

Applying some of what he'd learned at EMI, Medress developed a business plan and started making phone calls. Among the people he contacted was former Sony Music executive Walter Yetnikoff, subject of the book *The Hit Man.* Together, Hank, Walter, Allan, and Bottom Line associate Stanley Snadowski decided to launch an independent record company on which to sign new artists as well as draw from archival recordings made during performances at the Bottom Line. With the assistance of other investors, they opened Bottom Line Records in October 1996. "It's a dream come true," said Medress, a partner in the venture. "I get to nurture artists and do what I came here to do 35 years ago."

On its first anniversary the label issued the first release in the Bottom Line Encore Collection: a double CD of a performance by Harry Chapin recorded live at the Bottom Line. The club's vault of archival recordings included an eclectic selection of artists encompassing Jerry Garcia, Merl Saunders, Bruce Springsteen, Gary "U.S." Bonds, Karla Bonoff, Canned Heat, Eric Carmen, Jim Carroll, the Chambers Brothers, John Cougar, the Chieftains, John Hammond, Kiki Dee, Rick Derringer, Dion, Flo and Eddie, the Turtles, the Four Tops, Hall and Oates, John Hartford, Richie Havens, and Hiroshima.

"When I wake up in the morning I can't wait to get to work. I think I'm where I belong at last," said Medress. "This is a business in which people ask, 'What have you done lately?' and windows of opportunity close quickly. I wasn't blessed with great musical ability or great tools," Medress said with honest humility, "and consequently I'm very proud of what I've been able to accomplish." Yet he acknowledged that he remained a work in progress. "I think even at my age, I'm very judgmental and because I expect too much from people I become disappointed. I'm beginning to think that the disappointment I feel when someone fails to live up to my expectations may often result from my own misjudgment."

As he worked on that personality trait, Hank told us that he intended to grow old gracefully. "At this point my priorities have really changed. I don't have to impress anybody anymore. As a result, I was able to show up for my daughter's wedding in San Francisco and was with her again when my granddaughter was a few months old. I missed those kinds of special times in the earlier part of my life when I was too wrapped up in my career. So now," Medress said in a 1997 conversation, "I'm 58 years old and I'm going to go out and run tomorrow. I'm going to wake up in the morning and kiss my son hello. I've gone from riding in limousines and cabs to riding in subways, and I like the subways now."

Henry "Hank" Medress lived 10 more years after that. He died of lung cancer at 68 years of age at his home in Manhattan, New York City, on June 18, 2007. Divorced at the time of his death, Hank left behind two sons, two daughters, and two grandchildren.

Epilogue: Jay Siegel

Lead singer

To audiences and business associates, Jay Siegel always looked calm and in control. His confident countenance concealed worries. Jay always was a worrier. On the road he worried about getting to the next musical gig on time. As manager of a recording studio he worried about attracting new clients. As a marketing executive for a music publishing firm he succeeded in persuading Perry Como to record John Lennon's "Imagine" but worried that the Beatles songs for which his firm held copyright intimidated most artists. He declined an invitation to join the Lettermen because he worried that their road concert schedule might harm his family relationship. At production sessions during the peak popularity of the Tokens, Siegel quietly worried about what songs to record next and how to arrange them.

Jay Siegel in the 1990s. Photo by Chuck Goehrig.

Lead singer of the Tokens throughout their hit recording era of the 1960s, Jay Siegel gave the group its characteristic falsetto sound epitomized by the soaring a cappella introduction of "The Lion Sleeps Tonight." Although the group bisected when members Phil and Mitch Margo took root in Los Angeles, Siegel remained the emblematic persona of the East Coast branch of the Tokens. Siegel's involvement with the Tokens dates to 1955, when he joined fellow Lincoln High School students Hank Medress, Neil Sedaka, Cynthia Zolitin, and Eddie Rabkin as a member of the Linc-Tones vocal group.

Jay sang for the fun of it. His musical talent became apparent by age 10, when he began singing in his neighborhood community choir for the holidays. "I soon gained an appreciation for harmony," said Siegel. "I was a boy alto, and my voice was really high. I sang in a 12-person choir in which I was one of only two kids, yet the choir master gave me a lot of solos." In high school, Jay joined the chorus, where he was taught how to regulate his breathing for singing but was given only minimal individual voice training. Choir music was OK, but the rock and roll music the Linc-Tones performed was much more fun for Jay. Although he studied guitar for a year when he was about 15, singing remained his primary interest.

Jay and his brother, Jerry, were the sons of hardworking parents. Their father, Louis, came to the United States from Austria when he was 16 years old. "He found work as a furrier in a sweat shop in New York City. It was a terrible, terrible job, and my heart breaks every time I think about it," said Siegel. "He rode the subway and when it was 95 degrees he sat in a factory that was not air conditioned and worked on furs on his lap, sewing fur coats together. My mother, Yetta, who died in 1989, stayed home and made dinner and cleaned the house and took care of the kids."

As a young man, Jay was most pleased by the success of the Tokens in recording and production because it enabled him to buy things for his parents: a color television, a stereo system, a new couch, a washing machine. "My ability to help them out gave me the biggest joy in my life. My mother was one who thought the sun rose and set on whatever my brother or I did. When I would bring them to see me perform, it was the same thing as handing them $10 million. It was just as important for them to see the people applaud me — their son. My father was always worried. He'd urge me, 'Get a real job.' My mother was just as worried as he was, but she always encouraged me to stick with the music. They were always very supportive."

Siegel, who was born October 20, 1939, treasures the years of his youth. "I had the greatest childhood growing up in Brighton Beach. There was a singing group on every corner and a lot of talent in Brooklyn," said Siegel, noting that Lincoln High School students included flutist Herbie Mann, actors Harvey Keitel and Lou Gossett Jr., and playwright Arthur Miller. "It was great growing up in the summer by the beach. We used to hang out on the beach and we were singing all of the time. That's how we attracted girls."

Siegel said his neighborhood encompassed a mosaic of cultures. "But we were similar in financial status, which ranged from medium to poor. All of our mothers stayed home and took care of the kids. I have only happy memories. We used to climb over the rooftops to get from one street to the next. When I tell my kids these things they just don't understand. We used to walk from Brighton Beach to Coney Island, but we didn't hang out at Coney Island because of the tough kids, who used to ride their motorcycles to the Cyclone roller coaster. We went to Coney Island only to go to Nathan's to eat the best frankfurters. For 25 cents you'd get a frankfurter, a drink, and french fries. The aromas from Nathan's — there was nothing like it in the world. We used to love to go on all of the rides, have a frozen custard at Nathan's, and then leave to avoid the tough kids."

Another favorite haunt of Jay's was Mrs. Stahl's Knishes, a tiny stand of Jewish delicacies tucked in under the elevated train on Brighton Beach Avenue. "In the summertime it was probably 120 degrees in there but that didn't matter because no place else had potato knishes like Mrs. Stahl's. We'd hang out on the Boardwalk in Brighton, or we'd go down to Manhattan Beach. There was a delineation. Manhattan Beach kids had money and cars, Coney Island had the tough guys, and Brighton Beach was in the middle. I remember playing football on the beach in the fall, and I remember the clean ocean breezes. Every Tuesday night during the summer, fireworks would shoot from a barge off Brighton Beach. We used to meet every Tuesday night on the Boardwalk and that's where we'd get together and sing."

Jay and the other neighborhood kids also played games like "kick the can" and "stoopball." In New York, the term "stoop" refers to the steps leading to the front door of a house. Stoopball was a game of points played by throwing a rubber ball at a stoop with the hope of hitting the nose of a step to achieve maximum bounce. They also played "stick ball," a game derived from baseball in which an old broom handle typically served as a bat and sewer covers were used as points of demarcation. "There were storm sewers down the street and if you stood on one sewer and you hit the ball down the block past three more sewers, it was a home run," Siegel recalled. "One sewer was a single. Our kids have no idea what we're talking about."

Inspired by his culturally vibrant surroundings, Siegel developed an interest in folk music as a high school student. "I would listen to music that most other people never heard of," said Siegel. He became a fan of the pioneering folk music group the Weavers, whose repertoire included an intriguing African melody. He discovered that the same song had been captured on tape by a folklorist named Alan Lomax who, beginning in the 1930s, spent six decades recording indigenous music throughout the world. His documentary collection includes songs of Appalachia, of the rural South, and of Africa, Australia, the Caribbean, and South America. A label called Rounder Records catalogued and distributed the recordings Lomax made of work songs, blues, spirituals, ballads, and nursery rhymes. One of those tracks, a rhythmic chant called "Wimoweh," fascinated Siegel. He rearranged the Weavers' adaptation of the chant to emphasize the falsetto line and sang it to the other members of the Linc-Tones, and later to his fellow members of the Tokens.

"We rehearsed it and every time we'd sing it for our friends or to an audience, they loved it," said Jay. So did producers at RCA Victor, who thought the song needed lyrics to achieve commercial potential. "Hank, Phil, Mitch, and I were very much opposed to that idea initially," said Siegel. But he determined that if lyrics had to be written, they must be appropriate. He visited the South African consulate in New York, where he learned that "Wimoweh" was a traditional African hunting song. "The chant 'Wimoweh' had meaning about a lion hunt, and said that if everybody remained quiet, the lion would sleep and they would be able to make their kill. 'The Lion Sleeps Tonight' derived from that traditional meaning."

Although they functioned as a team, each of the four Tokens assumed specific roles in the production process. Mitch and Phil worked on instrumentation. Hank oversaw mixing and other technical functions in the booth. And Jay worked on vocal arrangements. "The result was a kind of magic that we worked together."

But then the magic wore off. "When the Tokens disbanded, it wasn't the result of dislike or disharmony," said Jay. "Nobody ever had a fight. We're all very good friends. We just weren't having any success after awhile, and it was getting stale." Hank began collaborating in music production with Dave Appell. Phil and Mitch moved to California. And in 1974 Don Kirshner Productions hired Jay as music coordinator for all the firm's television productions, including the syndicated *Rock Concert* television series, beginning an 11-year association. Jay also served as a backup singer and in-house producer for Kirshner's music production firm, for which he co-produced sessions by Kansas and other groups.

After Kirshner left the business, Siegel joined a British company called ATV Music, which owned copyrights to the Beatles music catalog. As manager of the company's American operation, Jay was responsible for persuading record producers to choose songs that ATV owned. That proved more difficult than it seemed. "I encountered a lot of resistance to recording Beatles songs because performers believed their rendition would be measured against what the Beatles had done," said Jay. Consequently, he attributed his only success in that effort to Perry Como, who had the courage to record John Lennon's "Imagine."

Siegel remained in that position for about a year until Michael Jackson purchased the company in September 1985. Jackson released all ATV executives and staff members because he already had his own organizational structure in place.

From there, Jay became even more embroiled in marketing when he was hired in 1986 to manage Mayfair Recording Studio on 47th Street in midtown Manhattan. About 80 percent of the studio's business came from advertising agencies that used Mayfair to produce commercials for Coca Cola, Miller Brewing, and other national accounts. The studio also produced music for the Bill Cosby Show for about a year, as well as some session work, notably for Blondie and Ian Hunter. Jay sang on numerous commercials he produced for Häagen Dazs Ice Cream, Quaker Crunchy Granola, and Wendy's Hamburgers, for which he sang "Only Wendy's…" based on "Only You" by the Platters. But running the business monopolized his time. "I had to wine and dine advertising executives to try to get them to use our studio instead of the hundreds of other studios around New York," said Siegel. "It was a tremendously competitive business and I didn't enjoy it at all. In fact, I hated it." Siegel remained in that high-pressure business for about five years until the studio's landlord gave notice that the monthly rent would triple to $12,000. Mayfair shut its doors.

At that point Siegel declined another tempting offer. In their version of Steve Lawrence's "Portrait of My Love," the Tokens blended their voices in a style somewhat reminiscent of the Lettermen, who also recorded the song. Perhaps that's what led Hank Medress to produce the Lettermen in the 1980s and prompted Lettermen member Tony Butala to invite Jay Siegel to join the group. "I had to decline because the Lettermen stay on the road so much and I didn't think I was ready to do that, considering my family and kids," explained Siegel.

He instead decided to resurrect the Tokens in New York, as Phil and Mitch Margo had done in California. He put together an East Coast version of the group that began performing, at first on a modest scale. "Demand increased until it became a full-time job," said Siegel. The group's audiences often included families with children who wanted to hear what they called the "jungle song." For them, "The Lion Sleeps Tonight" was fresh and new, and Jay said that knowledge energized his performances.

Jay said no feeling rivals the exhilaration that a standing ovation gave him. Yet, after all the shows in which he performed over seven decades, he still agonized over the rigors of the road. "Traveling to concert dates is very stressful because we want to make sure things are the way they're supposed to be when we get there. And like other performers, I worry about when the next job is going to come. I guess I'm the group worrier. That's my job. Even if this year looks good, I find myself hoping next year is going to be as good."

Siegel, who continued entertaining audiences into 2026, said that he preserved his voice by living a normal life. "I get up at 9 a.m. and I go to sleep at midnight. I have a family. I have three kids. When I'm on tour and I've finished working at night I go back to my hotel room. I don't hang out and I don't smoke. I live the same type of life that an accountant would live."

Jay's only marriage has endured since 1961. He and his wife, Judy, who met while students at New York City Community College, have a son, Jared (born in 1975), and two daughters: Stacy Dawn (who was born in 1963 and whose middle name inspired the name for the group Dawn), and Jamie (born in 1965).

"One day I'll retire and watch my grandchildren grow," Jay mused, "but in the meantime I'll keep on performing as long as it makes people happy."

Epilogue: Mitch Margo

Singer and pianist

May 25, 1947 – November 24, 2017

Mitch Margo tried to treat May 25, 1997, like an ordinary day. But it was a difficult day for Hank Medress, Jay Siegel, and Mitch's brother, Phil. On that day Mitch turned 50. He handled it gracefully, but his fellow Tokens were suffering disbelief. Mitch, after all, had always been the "baby" of the group. Born Mitchell Stuart Margules on May 25, 1947, he was 13 years old when the Tokens recorded "Tonight I Fell in Love." The group achieved international stardom when he was 14. By his mid-teens he was a partner in the group's own label, B.T. Puppy. And he was but 24 years old when the Tokens dissolved.

Mitch Margo of the Tokens vocal group following a January 1999 performance in the Solano Community College Theatre on Suisun Valley Road in Fairfield, California. Photo by Jeff March.

"When Phil, Hank, and Jay showed up for my 50th birthday party in New York, they kept looking at me and saying, 'This is not right. It's just not right.' The baby was not supposed to be 50."

Being the kid of the group had its advantages and its disadvantages. "I got treated special by the kids in my regular high school to a certain degree," said Mitch. "I tried to remain a regular guy as much as I could. But after a couple of years in regular high school my parents enrolled me in Quintano's High School for Young Professionals in Manhattan, where I attended class for a few hours each morning before going to the office the rest of the day." Young actors and actresses populated the student body at Quintano's, which enabled students to juggle school and work schedules. Patty Duke is an alumna of the school, and Mitch's classmates included Bernadette Peters. "Luke Halpin, the kid from Flipper, also went to that school," added Mitch. The office where Mitch spent his afternoons was Bright Tunes Productions, at 1697 Broadway in the heart of legendary "Tin Pan Alley." At Bright Tunes, Mitch was still in school in a sense because he had no specific role with the company at that time. "I was a kid. I didn't know nothin'. I composed songs and wrote lyrics and contributed in that way."

Mitch was self-effacing as well about his role in the Tokens' best-known production work of the mid-'60s. "For 'One Fine Day' by the Chiffons we used the piano from the original demo track recorded by Carole King, who wrote the song. In the studio the guys added a bass and a saxophone, and my brother came up with the idea for the 'shoo-bee-doo-bee-doo-wah-wah' thing. The Tokens sang background in the bridge, but actually, my job on that record was when I got home from school one day, they called me up and played it for me on the phone. I said, 'Yeah, that sounds good.' That was my job on that record." Mitch always loved that recording. "It's just a wonderful piece. Carole was a big inspiration to me, and she and Gerry Goffin greatly influenced my writing."

Carole King's piano artistry particularly captivated Mitch, who had been playing piano since age 5. When his parents, Leon and Ruth Margules, realized his uncanny ability to play songs by ear, they enrolled him in lessons under the tutelage of their rabbi's wife, a piano teacher. The piano teacher observed Mitch's music notation ability and encouraged him to compose. And he began to sing. "I knew I had an ear for singing, though I wasn't too crazy about my voice. I didn't have much warmth or trill in my voice, but I developed a very good ear for harmony by singing along with Everly Brothers records on the radio, and I could blend well with background parts," Mitch told us in September 1997. "The first song that my brother Phil and I ever sang together in person was 'All I Have To Do Is Dream.' And we still perform that in person sometimes."

Phil and Mitch continued to pride themselves on their rich harmonies. After perfecting their richly harmonized rendition of the National Anthem at sporting events throughout Southern California, including Anaheim Ducks hockey and Los Angeles Dodgers baseball games, they took their show on the road in 1998. Out of their love of baseball, their country, and performing, they paid their own way in an "Anthem Tour" in which they sang the national anthem before games at all 30 major league baseball parks — setting a record for a singing group the same year in which Mark McGwire set his 70-home-run record. "We do a nice chime-off at the end: …'the land of the free-free-free-free-freeee.' It's a good moment," said Mitch.

He had come a long way since the spring of 1964 after he had tumbled to the bottom of a cruel slide from ovation to dejection. At 17, an age when most teenagers are contemplating career paths to follow, Mitch thought he'd reached the end of his, the victim of changing musical tastes. Mop-tops, Merseybeat, and Britain were in. Preppies, doo-wop, and Brooklyn were out. "I had written 'I Hear Trumpets Blow,' which gave our recording careers a boost, but by the time I was 17, I was the most depressed I've ever been in my life," said Mitch. He had become aware that the music business that had once been so much fun was not as it appeared. "I was confronted by the realization that people you trust are not always honest. That's why I wrote the songs for the *Intercourse* album," said Mitch, referring to a 1968 recording that remained in the vaults for three decades.

After the Tokens finally slipped off the charts in 1971 and Hank headed out on his own, Mitch, Phil, and Jay signed a production deal with Don Kirshner for a few years, but ultimately the Margo brothers split off from that arrangement, leaving Jay behind. Phil and Mitch signed a production contract with RCA and moved to the West Coast, where their projects included production of an album by Kristy and Jimmy McNichol. In 1981, Hank, Jay, Phil, and Mitch took to the stage at Radio City Music Hall in New York for a reunion concert. That was the last time they performed together. Mitch quietly walked away from the spotlight. "There were a few years in the early 1980s when I didn't know what I was doing. A few bad years," said Mitch. "I became a house-husband while my wife was supporting the family. I say it with pride, even though society doesn't really accept it. I was delighted to be home with my little boy Ari. I remember dancing around the living room with him in my arms to the *Thriller* album by Michael Jackson. He was a little baby. It was great."

As a result of the alienation that set in when he was 17, Mitch remained cautious, like a pup abused by the master who feeds him. "I basically spent most of my adult life avoiding the music business. I've been staying on the outskirts. I don't jump in. I don't make a lot of calls. It's really almost a crime," Mitch sighed. "I'm sure there are some nice people out there, but I've been that frightened off by it. Although I have scored the music for several TV movies, I was never one to peddle my wares, and I never got good at that, to this day. So I write songs that I seldom play for people."

Still, if you were to ask Mitch what he filled in on the blank line next to "profession," he would have told you "entertainer and composer."

With the Tokens group based in Los Angeles, he continued performing at casinos, fairs, corporate parties, conventions, clubs, concerts, and stage shows. The group closed out 1997 playing a New Year's Eve bill at the Riviera Hotel and Casino in Las Vegas with Frankie Avalon and Bobby Vee. "Our live show has become very good. We've learned what audiences enjoy, and it's a lot of fun to do. Even when we don't perform it as well as we can, it still works really well. It's better than we are," Mitch laughed. In addition to Mitch, who played guitar, bass, drums, and keyboards, and drummer Phil, the group included Phil's son Noah on drums as well, and Mike Johnson on keyboards, along with saxophonist Jay Leslie, a former member of the Sha Na Na retro doo-wop vocal group of the '70s. Mitch could sub for Mike on keyboards, Phil and Noah alternated on drums, and all the members of the group sang. All the members of the audience sang, as well. After four decades in show business, Phil and Mitch perfected an infectious blend of music and comedy. Tokens performances were joyous celebrations that encouraged laughter and invited enthusiastic audience participation.

Although they often reserved "The Lion Sleeps Tonight" or a dance medley for their show closer, they began performing "Only in My Dreams," a song that Mitch composed in 1996. He wrote the song, reminiscent of the music of another era, when he heard that production had begun for the 1996 Tom Hanks motion picture *That Thing You Do,* about a fictional one-hit 1960s rock band. "Only in My Dreams" just missed the cut for inclusion in the movie soundtrack, but the Tokens liked it so much they included it on an album they released in 1997 on their resurrected B.T. Puppy label. Several cuts from that album were used on the daytime television drama *The Young and The Restless.* The album was titled *Tonight the Lion Dances (Esta Noche el León Baila).* "It's an album of Latin doo-wop — Latin and oldies," grinned Mitch. "When Phil was a kid, he used to go to dances at the community center on weekends, where they would play a mix of styles — some Latin, some old rock and roll, some Sinatra, this and that. Phil and his friends would hang out and listen to records like that, and I guess that had an effect on me as well. We wanted to recall those feelings and re-create them in this album. And it's a delightful album. It might be our best production to date."

Mitch said the album reflected his musical preferences as well. "I have eclectic tastes. I like all kinds of music," said Mitch. His music collection at home encompassed Bartók, Bach, Zappa, the Beatles, the Beach Boys, Ladysmith Black Mambazo and the King's Singers. By then divorced from his wife, Sherry, Mitch was living alone. Their elder son, Damien, who was born in 1973, became an independent computer animation artist in the San Francisco Bay area. Damien also enjoyed drumming, and sat in with the Tokens when Phil's son Noah was unavailable. Mitch refrained from trying to influence Ari's decision about a career path. "I want him to follow his bliss," said Mitch, borrowing a sentiment from author Joseph Campbell. "I take that to mean find whatever your heart is telling you and follow it."

Mitch counted his children and the creation of "The Lion Sleeps Tonight" among his proudest achievements. "It seems to be loved by the world as a whole, and it's likely that it's being played on the radio somewhere right now. And that amazes me," Mitch said with sincere humility. "I feel very fortunate to be a part of it."

Although he said that he still loved performing and considered entertainment a joy, he also had talent in another medium of artistic expression: painting, which he enjoyed since the age of 16. He created the cover art for two Tokens albums, *Oldies Are Now* from 1994 and *Tonight the Lion Dances.* "The second cover I designed so that it would look good on a cassette as well as on a CD. For the first one I did just a square painting, and it didn't fit a cassette box very nicely," explained Mitch, who worked in watercolors, acrylics, and oils. "You live, you learn." Mitch had a couple of showings in galleries, and sold some of his paintings. He also dabbled in animation, using images he created in watercolor. His first effort was an eight-minute short called *It's Okay to Laugh,* which was broadcast on the USA Network. He used a technique called cutout animation, photographed the images with friend Ray Templin, and transferred them to video. "It was an interesting project and a fun way to do animation. Something tells me I should have been doing more of that in my life."

The B.T. Puppy catalog also included *Intercourse,* an album recorded in 1968 during Mitch's era of deep depression. "Writing the songs for the *Intercourse* album was my therapy," Mitch said in liner notes for the album. *Intercourse* had been gathering dust for nearly three decades because Warner Brothers, for which they were recording in the late '60s, declined to release it. Mitch considered the album, on which the Tokens played all their own instrumental accompaniment, an artistic triumph. "I was crushed when Warner Brothers didn't release it," he said. Mitch also lamented the disappointing response to *Cross Country,* an early '70s album with a country music flavor that Atlantic-ATCO released without the benefit of enthusiastic promotion. The album, in which he, Phil, and Jay displayed their singing virtuosity as well as their ability to cast familiar songs in a new light, was distinguished by a ballad treatment of Wilson Pickett's raucous 1965 hit "In the Midnight Hour."

Although Mitch's artistic and musical talents both emerged in his youth, he didn't ascribe much of his adult persona to his family environment. "Although I see I have certain traits from my parents, I don't think my lifestyle has turned out to be much like theirs at all," he said. His parents, Leon and Ruth, operated Ruthie's Clothes Closet, a clothing store in Brighton Beach for a time. Leon also held various jobs over the years, including work as a presser for a dress manufacturer. "My dad passed away a while back. He was good man, a humble man, and I was close with him. My mom, thank God, is still around, and she's great." Leon Margo died at age 67 in 1983, and Ruth died at age 101 in 2020.

Mitch's mother often cautioned him, "Love many, trust few, always paddle your own canoe," words that Mitch took to heart. Those were among the words that Mitch was able to understand. "My parents used Yiddish as a code language, so they could say things we wouldn't understand as kids, which I kinda wish they hadn't. I would liked to have been able to speak Yiddish." Still, he said he managed to learn "a bissel" — a little of the language. "I love Yiddish. It's a very expressive language, and plenty of Yiddish sayings are rich in wisdom. And a lot of people don't realize how much Yiddish has become common usage. If you say you saw a schmaltzy performance, you're talking Yiddish."

As he turned 50, Mitch reflected on his life. He regarded himself as a good person, a principal ingredient of which is respect, he said. "It's essential to have respect for life — respect for your own life, and respect for the lives of others, in that order. I think that by and large people are inclined to take life for granted, to forget that they're alive. And that's why I often remind myself that every second is a miracle. Every second is a miracle. I say that because I happened to notice that is true," said Mitch. "I truly go through life astonished that I exist."

Curly-haired Mitch, with a warm, endearing smile, continued to perform with his older brother, Phil, in the West Coast contingent of the Tokens into the autumn of 2017. He unexpectedly died in his sleep at age 70 on November 24, 2017.

Epilogue: Phil Margo

Singer, guitarist, pianist, and drummer

April 1, 1942 – November 13, 2021

In 1967, with a new recording contract from Warner Brothers and a Tokens single, "Portrait of My Love," climbing the charts, Phil Margo bought a new Oldsmobile convertible. Thirty years later, long after the record faded from the airwaves, Phil was still driving that Oldsmobile. That's not to suggest that Phil didn't do well for himself in the ensuing years. Quite the contrary. He was living in Beverly Hills and established himself in the tightly knit television production circle in Hollywood. But Phil was governed by a sense of reserve that appeared to be the product of an oddly disparate set of guiding influences: frugality, humility, savvy, artistic creativity, adventurousness, and a strong undercurrent of Brighton Beach brashness.

Phil Margo of the Tokens singing group following a performance on January 1999 in the Solano Community College Theater on Suisun Valley Road in Fairfield, California. Photo by Jeff March.

Phil Margo was a self-sufficient man. Not only could he sing for his supper, he also could drum, play guitar and piano, compose songs, write screenplays, pilot his own plane to concert dates and, in a pinch, manage the careers of other performers. That's a pretty diverse set of skills for a guy who once sought to become an aeronautical engineer.

Phil's entrée to music was circumstantial. "My dad played the violin a bit, and my grandfather played the clarinet, but I had no reason to expect that I had any talent," Phil claimed.

"I was just a kid growing up. The whole thing was an accident. It was just a set of circumstances that led me from one thing to another. I guess life is like that. Some people know what they want to be when they're 3 years old and pursue that course right until they get there. I never knew what I wanted to be. I still don't," Phil told us in July 1997. "That's why I got into producing movies, I got into writing for television, all kinds of things because they interest me and I don't feel that you have to be locked into one thing for your whole life."

At age 6 or 7, Phil happened to like the 78 rpm records by Frankie Laine, Xavier Cugat, and Dinah Shore that his parents had in their collection. He'd sit in the living room and listen to those songs on the record player. Born Philip Frederick Margules on April 1, 1942, he went all the way through his elementary school years without showing an indication of possessing any musical talents of his own. But entering his sophomore year at Abraham Lincoln High School in the fall of 1956, he participated in the mandatory tryouts for chorus. "We had to go up on the stage and as the music teacher played notes on the piano we would have to sing along," Phil recalled. "I was able to sing all of the notes. I really had no clue that I would be able to do that. The piano teacher said to me, 'Very good. You're in the chorus.' Who wanted to be in the chorus? Yuck! But that was it. I had no choice." Phil had designs on becoming an aeronautical engineer. "But in high school I confronted math and decided I didn't really want to do that."

Meanwhile, his musical interest and abilities had begun to develop. By his junior year in the spring of 1958 he decided he wanted to be a musician in the Catskill Mountains, a resort area in southeastern New York state about 75 miles from Manhattan. "It was cool to be a musician in the Catskills. Only problem was I didn't play anything. So I decided to learn how to play the piano. I tried lessons for about two weeks and I asked when I would start playing songs." The piano teacher replied, "That's not for six months yet." Phil said, "Six months is too late. I could already have a job by then." So at age 16 he taught himself to play piano using a "fake" book that had the chords of the song and notations for the right hand. "The book didn't have both staffs of the sheet music — bass and treble. It just had the notes of the song, with the chords written on top of the bar line. So I learned how to play chords. Now they teach that way, but back then they didn't," said Phil. "That summer I learned how to play and by fall I had a little band with a trumpet player, a drummer, a guy who played saxophone and clarinet, and me on piano. We got gigs like sweet sixteens and stuff like that, where we made about $10 each per night, which was pretty good for a kid in 1958."

Phil made it to the Catskills in the summer of '59 following his graduation from high school, then settled back in New York City where his uncle Mal helped him land a job with Steiner, Rouse and Company, a stock brokerage firm. Meanwhile he enrolled in Brooklyn College as his band continued to play gigs around town. Phil's drummer, Lenny Budnick, heard that Lincoln High alumnus Hank Medress was seeking to produce an instrumental for Roulette Records. Hank was a member of Darrell and the Oxfords, a singing group that had begun recording for Roulette. Phil, then 17, brought his 12-year-old brother, Mitch, along to record a demo. They played a boogie-woogie version of "Chopsticks." The demo session itself was disappointing, but it led to development of a relationship with Hank. "Hank just saw something in us and we started writing together," said Phil. "In December of 1959 we sang the background part of 'A Teenager in Love' together for the first time, and we recognized that we sounded good. I knew I could sing harmony because I had sung it in chorus." They were particularly pleased with their three-part harmony that complemented the lead vocals of Jay Siegel. Two years later, Phil, Mitch, Jay, and Hank would have two hit records to their credit, with more to follow. Seven years later, they would be partners in a recording and production enterprise beyond their wildest dreams.

Following the formation of B.T. Puppy Records, Phil set about fulfilling another dream: attainment of a college degree. In the late '60s he began attending night classes at Kingsborough Community College in Brooklyn and Rockland Community College in Suffern, N.Y., about 25 miles northwest of Manhattan. He earned his bachelor's degree from Empire State College, an alternative liberal arts adult education program of the State University of New York, in 1977.

Around that time he'd begun participating in production of an album for Kristy McNichol, who was then starring in the ABC television dramatic series *Family.* At one point Phil met with Kristy at the Osmond Brothers' studio in Orem, Utah, where she was filming a special for ABC. In an adjacent studio, production was under way on an episode of the *Donna Fargo Show* in which actor Robert Guillaume was making a guest appearance. Margo and Guillaume met and started talking. Guillaume was between managers. He and Margo found they got along well, and that began a 10-year business relationship during which Phil served as Robert's personal manager. "Robert didn't have any reason in the world to think that I'd be any good as a manager, but yet he had a certain degree of faith in me."

Phil quickly learned what it took to be successful in management. "Balls. You need a set of balls, you need to be able to ask people for ridiculous things, you need to be able to say, 'Robert doesn't like this, Robert should be in first class' and you need to be able to take advantage of opportunities. And you need to have a brain to figure out how soon to stop negotiations. You need to know when you've pushed them as far as they can go. You also learn to never take the first offer." That axiom is true, he said, when managing a star. "It's different when you're first starting out. Then the rule is 'tread marks on your back.' We didn't get paid for our first hit record. They never paid us a cent in royalties. We don't know to this day how many copies of 'Tonight I Fell in Love' sold. And even RCA tried to screw us out of the money for usages in movies. They used 'The Lion Sleeps Tonight' in five or six movies and when I told them they never accounted for that, they told us it's not in our contract. I said, 'What do you mean it's not in my contract? If it's not in my contract, you're allowed to use it?' Finally after two years, we settled it, but it was a nightmare."

Margo continued managing Guillaume until 1988. "It was time for both of us to move on. We just went our separate ways. It was amicable," said Phil. "Afterward he appeared on 'The Lion Sleeps Tonight' video that was broadcast on the Learning Channel. He's a good guy, he's a good friend and I love him very much. He gave me some of the most joyous times of my life. We were at the White House twice. We did some wonderful things together."

Exposure to Guillaume's projects persuaded Phil to begin writing and producing movies for television. He conceived the idea for *The Kid From Left Field,* a 1979 movie starring Guillaume and Gary Coleman. After that Phil wrote and produced two other movies starring Coleman: *The Kid With the 200 IQ* and *The Fantastic World of D.C. Collins,* another movie for ABC in 1985 called *This Wife for Hire* starring Pam Dawber, and *Goddess of Love* as well as 1997's sensational *Asteroid* for NBC. All the while he was writing scripts and producing films, Phil continued performing with the Tokens. He also became a novelist. We edited the manuscript of his intriguing 2010 science fiction adventure novel *The Null Quotient,* which was published in hardcover and e-book formats.

"I was off shooting *Asteroid* in Denver, and I get a call saying I had to be in LA the next day because we're doing *The Tonight Show.* So I'm on the plane, doing *The Tonight Show* the next day with the Tokens. We did a Jay Leno version of 'The Lion Sleeps Tonight.' We had written it because a guy who sometimes does publicity for us said, 'Look, if you want to do the Jay Leno show, do a parody.' So I wrote a parody of 'The

Lion Sleeps Tonight' and I sent it to them and that was all forgotten. Then seven months later, *The Tonight Show* people said, 'We have a parody of 'The Lion Sleeps Tonight.' I said, 'Good, I'm glad you thought of it.' I didn't care. As long as it got on the show. It was a very nice spot for us."

On the road, the Tokens' drummer was Phil's son Noah, who was born in 1969. Noah's twin brother, Joshua, who completed doctoral studies at UCLA in East Asian languages and cultures, became a successful account executive for a fulfillment company handling major accounts. Phil and his wife, Abbie — who married in 1966 — also had a daughter, Neely, born in 1974. Phil and his brother, Mitch, were partners in B.T. Puppy Records with their sister, Maxine Margo, and Paula "Rusti" Wolintz. The label, resurrected in 1993, operated out of an office in the small town of Millwood, N.Y., about 20 miles north of Manhattan.

Phil shunned flamboyance and lived modestly. "While I've never had a full cup, I've never had an empty cup either. I don't go on vacations often, I don't go to the track, I don't spend big bucks, I don't have expensive clothes," he said. "I do have some nice old cars: a 1967 Oldsmobile convertible, which I've had since it was new, and a 1966 Mustang convertible. And I teach kung fu with my son Noah. I started taking the course with my sons when I was 44 years old. It was something I could do with them and it was a good outlet for exercise. Now we're high-degree black belts, which has given me a great deal of confidence."

Phil sometimes flew his Varga Kachina, which looks like a little fighter plane, to gigs, and he periodically covered air shows for *In Flight* magazine. "If I wasn't doing what I'm doing, I would be working in the aircraft industry — flying, preferably," said Phil, who had been a pilot since 1963. He takes to heart the old song "Fly Me to the Moon" — and beyond. "If somebody said to me, 'Phil, we're going to Mars tomorrow, you want to come?' I'm gone, man. I try to make my life an adventure. But I can also be very reclusive. I can disappear in my room for days at a time and watch television and smoke cigars. I'm as shy or as bold as anybody else. You just have to pull on a particular trait when you need it. You take a circumstance and turn it into something."

Mitch Margo enjoyed telling a story about his multi-talented brother. "Phil was originally a drummer," said Mitch. "He plays percussion now with us when we perform. He also played drums on hit records. He was the drummer on 'He's So Fine,' 'Denise,' and 'Candida.' As a matter of fact, Max Weinberg, the drummer on *NBC's Late Night With Conan O'Brien,* once said that one of his favorite drum parts was the drumming on 'Denise,' but said that he didn't know who the drummer was. And I'm not sure if he knows to this day that it was my brother, Phil."

Phil died November 13, 2021, at age 79 at a hospital in Los Angeles of complications from a stroke. The singer's death came 60 years to the day after the group's smash hit "The Lion Sleeps Tonight" premiered on the *Billboard* Hot 100 chart. Phil and his wife, Abbie, had three children — twin sons Noah and Joshua and daughter Neely — and eight grandchildren.

My Boyfriend's Back

The Angels

While most teenage girls of the late '50s were giddily coiling themselves on the sofa beside the telephone, hair in curlers, painting their nails bright red in anticipation of a boy calling to ask them out to the weekend sock hop, three determined and multi-talented New Jersey teens were writing songs and planning their weekend musical performances. Friendly rivals Peggy Santiglia of the Delicates and Barbara and Jiggs Allbut of the Starlets had been performing for years at dances and local events, and singing professionally as session group artists before joining forces as the Angels and unleashing their wildly popular denouncement of male boorishness, the million-selling "My Boyfriend's Back."

The Angels first hit the charts with the ballad "'Til," popularized in 1960 by Tony Bennett. Pianist Roger Williams, the vocal group the Vogues, and Tom Jones also recorded the song. The girls' version was released by Caprice Records and made its debut on the *Billboard* Hot 100 on October 16, 1961. Carl Sigman and Charles Danvers wrote the tender ballad, which the Angels gave a dramatic reading., accompanied by the Hutch Davie Orchestra. Angels member Barbara Allbut wrote "A Moment Ago," the tune on the flip side. "'Til" rose to No. 14 and remained on the chart for 14 weeks. At that time the group consisted of Barbara, Jiggs, and Linda Jankowski (whose stage name was Linda Jansen). By early 1962, the trio scored again with "Cry Baby Cry," which made its debut on the *Billboard* Hot 100 on February 17, 1962. The song, written by Morris Bailey Jr., reached No. 38 and remained on the chart for 11 weeks, but performed even better on the R&B charts. The success of those two singles led Caprice to send the Angels into Regent Sound Studios at 24 W. 57th Street in New York City. There they recorded the remaining tracks for an album cleverly titled *And the Angels Sing,* which Caprice released in 1962. The 12 songs on the LP included the title track as well as their two pop hits, with a variant spelling of "Till." But then the Angels found themselves in a slump with chart presence eluding their next three successive singles — "Everybody Loves a

The Angels in 1963: Barbara Allbut, Peggy Santiglia, and Jiggs Allbut (Photofest Archives).

Lover" (released in May 1962), "You Should Have Told Me" (September 1962), and "A Moment Ago" (March 1963). The tame, safe ballads by which Caprice had defined the Angels were no longer resonating with radio programmers or audiences. During that period, they began earning money by recording demo tracks for three songwriters and producers who were shopping their tracks to various labels. The songwriters were Bob Feldman, Richard Gottehrer, and Gerald Goldstein, and they operated as FGG Productions. After lead singer Linda Jankowski left the Angels to pursue other interests, Peggy Santiglia stepped in and provided the tough girl attitude that the FGG crew needed for one of their newly composed songs: "My Boyfriend's Back." The three songwriters quickly realized that the Angels' electrifying version of the song was more than merely a demo track. It was just what they'd been searching for.

Feldman, Gottehrer, and Goldstein helped the Angels terminate their contract with Caprice and negotiated a contract for them with Mercury Records, which assigned them to the subsidiary Smash label and immediately pressed "My Boyfriend's Back" as a vinyl single. The chart-topping Smash Records single that served as a warning for all unwanted suitors made its debut on the *Billboard* Hot 100 on August 3, 1963. The song began with Peggy's searing monologue. "He went away and you hung around — and *bothered* me, every night," she scolded. "And when I wouldn't go out with you — you said things that weren't very nice." That triggered all three to sound off, "My boyfriend's back, and you're gonna be in trouble…." Four weeks later, on August 31, "My Boyfriend's Back" unseated Stevie Wonder's "Fingertips" from the No. 1 position and held onto that slot for three consecutive weeks, until Bobby Vinton's "Blue Velvet" slid into the top spot. "My Boyfriend's Back" remained on the chart for 14 weeks. Songwriters Feldman, Gottehrer, and Goldstein later became the behind-the-scenes performers of the studio group they named the Strangeloves (known for the 1965 hits "I Want Candy" and "Cara-Lin").

Barbara and Jiggs had known Peggy for a few years before she joined them. "We had met Peggy when our group, the Starlets, and Peggy's group, the Delicates, played local record hops. In fact, we all did a New York TV show together." During that show, the producer instructed the girls to assume an unanimated pose while their record was being played. "We didn't know what was going on, so we just kind of stood there," said Jiggs. "As the record was playing we saw this guy off-camera wildly gesturing and saying, 'Come on, do something, sing, move, do!' So we started lip-synching, doing our little routine, swinging and playing to our beautiful ballad. When we finished, the program producers were furious with us and told us, 'Well, now we have to pay you because you performed.' They didn't want to pay us, but there happened to be someone from AFTRA [American Federation of Television and Radio Artists] there at the time, and he was the one who had been gesturing to us. When someone from the show called and asked us to give back the check, we called Peggy and asked her what the Delicates were going to do. We all agreed to keep the money."

Naive, maybe, but the Angels were insightful enough to know how to manage their own career and money. They signed with managers from time to time, but didn't allow them to monopolize their livelihoods. "In getting out of our Caprice records contract, we did get involved a little bit with people some might characterize as unsavory. However, I think that brought us some of our very best, most prestigious jobs. There was never any problem connected with it in any way," said Jiggs. "We did a lot of really cool stuff with them. We always got our money, things were done for us. As far as how I think a manager is supposed to perform, that possibly was the best of them. And there were many bad ones out there."

Peggy, Barbara, and Jiggs were dulcet harmonizers, but they were looking to transform their image from a trio crooning innocuous, albeit beautiful ballads, to a group with a more fun, aggressive style. "We were looking for a song that was really different — something you could dance to," Peggy explained. "And we found it in 'My Boyfriend's Back.'"

"I Adore Him," the fourth single by the Angels to hit the *Billboard* Hot 100, made its debut on the chart on October 26, 1963. Jan Berry (of the singing duo Jan and Dean) wrote "I Adore Him" with songwriter and producer Artie Kornfeld, who also co-wrote the Jan and Dean hit "Dead Man's Curve" with Brian Wilson and Roger Christian. Kornfeld was a co-creator of the Woodstock Music and Art Fair of 1969. Feldman, Gottehrer, and Goldstein produced the session, and prolific arranger, producer, and composer Alan Lorber arranged and conducted the accompanying music for "I Adore Him," which reached No. 25 and remained on the chart for seven weeks. The flip side song, "Thank You and Goodnight," charted on its own, premiering on the Hot 100 on December 7. Feldman, Gottehrer, Goldstein, and Marty Sanders (of Jay and the Americans) wrote the song. For two weeks, both of the Angels songs were on the chart, but "Thank You and Goodnight" stalled and went no higher than No. 85.

The album version of "My Boyfriend's Back," published by Blackwood Music, had an extra chorus that was cut from the single version to comply with the preference of radio programmers for records of about two-and-a-half minutes. "One time we did a TV show lip-synching 'My Boyfriend's Back' and they had the wrong version of the song. We didn't know what to do because we didn't really remember the extra chorus at all. We had been doing it the short way for so many years, it was a shock," chuckled Jiggs.

"Wow Wow Wee (He's the Boy for Me)," the final chart single by the Angels, hit the *Billboard* Hot 100 on January 18, 1964, just as the "British Invasion" began. A quintet of songwriters —Feldman, Goldstein, and Gottehrer, along with Robert Spencer and Peggy Farina — were credited for writing the song, describing how a girl was able to attract the attention of a boy she liked. Feldman, Goldstein, and Gottehrer produced the recording session. The single, on the Smash label, topped at No. 41 and remained on the chart for seven weeks.

Although they had been performing professionally for years, Peggy, Jiggs, and Barbara were still kids when "Boyfriend" went national on the Smash label. "At the time, it was a bit more difficult for females in rock and roll groups, I think, because it was sort of unheard-of, and it was a bit frowned upon, that nice girls would want to be traveling with rock and roll bands," recalled Peggy. "It was a little scary at times. I can remember in some situations people trying to pull us off the stage, and security on the stage grabbing one leg and somebody in the audience pulling the other."

One of the highlights of Peggy's career was her first visit to Europe. The group was part of a musical entourage assigned to entertain the American troops at various Army and Air Force bases there. "We were shocked and thrilled with all of the attention we were getting," admitted Peggy. "But don't forget, here's all these young American guys, without their wives or girlfriends. They just wanted to see women. It really spoiled us. We got back to the United States after one of the extended tours and wondered, "gee, why aren't people falling at our feet any more?"

In addition to military shows, the group performed in a few nightclubs in Europe, becoming wildly popular with the Germans. Philips Records, the Dutch parent company of Mercury and Smash at the time, recorded an album featuring the Angels singing their songs phonetically in German. In the 1970s Peggy recorded a Brazilian Latin-charged album called *Sweet, Sweet City Rhythm* with a group called Fantasia.

A good part of the trio's career involved singing background for other artists — either individually or collectively. Between Angels appearances Barbara, Jiggs, and Peggy began recording together as background singers for other musical entertainers, arrangers, conductors, and record producers, including Neil Diamond, Anthony Newley, Bob Gaudio and Frankie Valli of the Four Seasons, Quincy Jones, Don Costa, Alan Lorber, Lee Holdridge, Steve Lawrence and Eydie Gormé, Patty Duke, David Geddes, and Frank Sinatra.

"We had breaks all the way along. Our first break was finding our first record deal, because that led to the second record deal. After ''Til' and 'Cry Baby Cry,' we spent a lot of time in New York singing backgrounds and doing demos for various artists and that led to our meeting the producers and writers who wrote 'My Boyfriend's Back' for us. We had done some demos for them and they wrote the song specifically for us," said Barbara. "So I think we had good luck all the way through. One thing led to another and to another."

When "My Boyfriend's Back" was released, Peggy had been vacationing with her parents, and Barbara and Jiggs telephoned her saying, "Come back now! It's a giant hit!" The record remained No. 1 on the charts for four weeks and in the top 40 for three months. This national recognition earned them spots on *The Ed Sullivan Show,* Bill Dana's Las Vegas Show, *American Bandstand* with Dick Clark, *The Merv Griffin Show, The Tonight Show With Johnny Carson, Shindig,* and numerous local TV shows. "We played at Madison Square Garden, the Apollo Theater, the Copacabana, Nassau Coliseum in New York, at Army and Air Force bases in the United States, Germany, and France, and many, many other places," said Barbara. "We went from rock and roll to the nightclub act to, in later years, the oldies shows."

Contributing to their long-lasting friendship and success was the mutual agreement that each member could accept other assignments throughout the trio's career. That creative freedom allowed Jiggs to pursue acting, and singing in numerous commercials, including spots for Caravelle watches, Thom McAn Shoes and a Money Store advertisement with former New York Yankees shortstop Phil Rizzuto. Barbara sang jingles in New York for Wendy's, Peter Paul Candy, and for many other well-known commercial spots. During the late '60s Jiggs and Barbara continued performing as the Angels with another lead singer while Peggy toured and recorded with the Serendipity Singers. Peggy recorded one album called *Love Is a State of Mind* with the "Dips," as the Serendipity Singers jokingly referred to themselves. She then went on to record as a member of Dusk, the female counterpart to Dawn, for former Tokens member Hank Medress, producer for Tony Orlando and Dawn. With Dusk, Peggy had two chart records, "Angel Baby" and "I Hear Those Church Bells Ringing," which neared the top 40 nationally and reached top 10 in some secondary markets. She later rejoined the Angels and began playing the oldies circuit.

Barbara, who was responsible for taking care of the business end of the trio, left the group in 1978. It was an amicable departure and the three singers remained very close. Jiggs recalled, "After we were all older and we married, being away that much became tough on us. Barbara was the one who started the whole thing. And she was just so much more entwined in the business end than I ever was. She finally came to a point where she just couldn't do it anymore. She said, 'I can't just half-heartedly continue and if I pursue the music career the way I really need to do it, then I'm not going to have anything else.' I shouldn't speak for her, but this is how I saw it."

Jiggs and Peggy tried to replace Barbara twice but it wasn't meant to be. "Both replacements were great singers, but it just wasn't us. We were bending toward their style, rather than having them bend toward ours, because they couldn't. They just didn't have the background that we had, they didn't begin their careers during the time we did," observed Jiggs. One of Barbara's replacements had a Broadway singing style. Jiggs and Peggy agreed she was an excellent singer and had a compatible personality, but she didn't fit their musical style. "We performed with her in an HBO special with Robert Klein, and I think maybe that was the point at which we said, 'Oh, my goodness, listen to us.' We had never really realized we were having to sing more in her style because she couldn't bend to ours. So we said, 'This is not going to work at all,'" recalled Jiggs. The duo then signed Jiggs' husband, Stan Sirico, a multi-talented conductor and guitar player, to complete the ensemble.

But with only two Angels on the bill, Jiggs said she and Peggy got a lot of flack from agents. "They said to us, 'Oh, no one's going to book you, they want three girls, blah, blah, blah.' But the first job Peggy and I did without Barbara was a New Year's Eve party in Brooklyn," said Jiggs. The worst part was that our guitar player, Stan Sirico, who now sings our third part, had already taken another gig that evening. But the band that we worked with was fabulous. They rehearsed with us a couple of times and did some background singing with us. Once we got that under our belt we were OK and we didn't have much trouble getting booked." One of Jiggs' daughters, Karalyn Hugo, filled in as the third Angel on some of the group's appearances.

The number of Angels' performances varied from year to year because Jiggs and Peggy could afford to be selective about their gigs. "One year we toured for a month on the West Coast, including a week in Alaska," said Jiggs. They also welcomed weekend jobs and one-nighters near home.

And while audiences appreciated their musical versatility displayed with varying styles, arrangements, and tempos on familiar as well as new material, fans invariably broke out in wild applause at the smoldering spoken recitation that introduced "My Boyfriend's Back."

The Angels continued performing intermittently through the first two decades of the 2000s. Peggy, Barbara, and Jiggs got together again, along with Jiggs' husband, Stan, and her daughter, Karalyn, in 2008 to record a new album called *Love, the Angels.* The 15-song package, released on their own Angel Sound label, opened with a new version of "My Boyfriend's Back" and closed with a refreshed take of "'Til."

Linda Jankowski Russo, who for a while had her own group called Linda Jansen's Angels, died unexpectedly at age 74 on February 19, 2019. The Angels continued concert touring until the death of member Barbara Allbut Brown in July 2021.

While superficially "My Boyfriend's Back" was a bouncy ode to teenage indignation, it presaged a new, assertive attitude for females in rock music that ultimately gave rise to numerous other dynamic female performers.

Pretty good for a group of high school kids who decided they had more to do than just wait for the phone to ring.

THE ANGELS
U.S. HIT SINGLES ON THE NATIONAL CHARTS

Debut	Peak	Title	Label
10/16/61	14	'Til	Caprice
2/17/62	38	Cry Baby Cry	Caprice
8/03/63	1	My Boyfriend's Back	Smash
10/26/63	25	I Adore Him	Smash
12/7/63	84	Thank You and Goodnight	Smash
1/18/64	41	Wow Wow Wee (He's the Boy for Me)	Smash

Billboard's pop singles chart data is courtesy of Joel Whitburn's Record Research Inc., Menomonee Falls, Wisconsin.

Epilogue: Peggy Santiglia

Singer

A performer since the age of 11, Peggy Santiglia spent almost every weekend of her early teen years singing at record hops and at the Brooklyn Fox and the Brooklyn Paramount. Although she loved school and had a great curiosity for learning, landing a hit record immediately out of high school set her on a fulfilling musical career path for the next three decades. It wasn't until the '80s that Peggy's yearning to learn sent her back to school. In 1990 she graduated Phi Beta Kappa (the highest scholastic distinction given by an American college or university) from the prestigious Goucher College, originally affiliated with Johns Hopkins University, in Baltimore, Maryland, when women were not permitted to attend Johns Hopkins.

Extremely bright as well as talented, Peggy went on to earn a master's degree in clinical psychology from Loyola College in Baltimore in 1995.

As a psychotherapist, Peggy established a clinical practice in Baltimore called Positive Approach to serve a dual clientele — people in need of comfort for life-threatening illnesses, and performers who required psychological coaching to help them face an audience. Peggy's

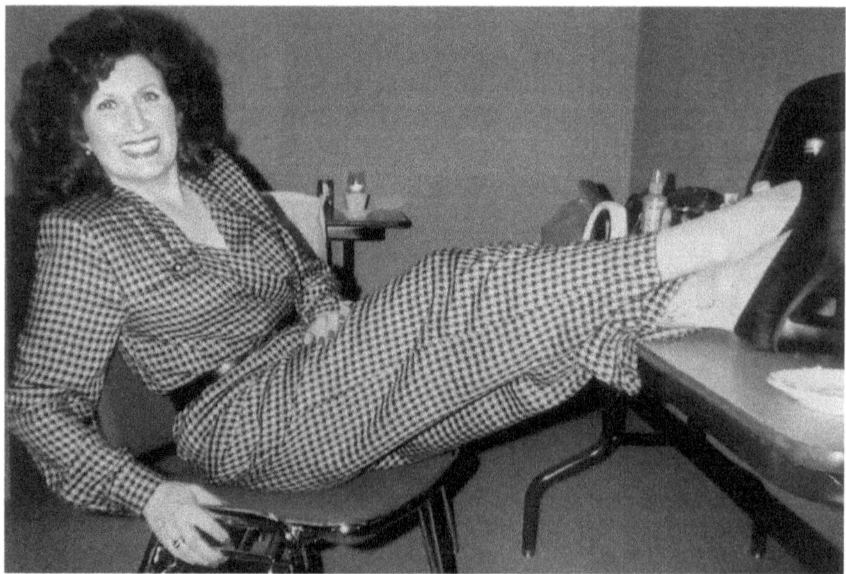

Peggy Santiglia (Davison) Ricker in the 1990s.

passion became helping her critically ill patients gain the strength to overcome their fears and embrace the future. Although professionally trained to detach herself from her clients, Peggy admitted to going home with her stomach in knots at times. Using a lot of the same techniques she learned to combat her own stage fright in show business, Peggy worked with a variety of people, from the business executive who must speak to a corporate board of directors, to a mother who wanted to talk in front of her local PTA. "I mostly work with 'worried wells,' not people who have serious psychological problems," explained Peggy. "And I do get a lot of gratification working with people who are undergoing treatment for a life-threatening illness. I've grown a lot from helping people and learning about and living life's most important moments."

Born Margaret Santiglia on May 4, 1944, and raised in Belleville, New Jersey, Peggy grew up in a musical household. As far back as she could remember, Peggy's father, Pietro (Peter) Santiglia, played woodwind instruments, guitar, and mandolin, and everyone in the family sang well. During holidays and family get-togethers, aunts, uncles, and cousins would all sing and play together. Her mother, Michelina (Margaret), wrote an early singing commercial that a department store in New York used for its promotion, and her sister, Ann, attended Juilliard School of music and sang opera. "I guess I recorded professionally the first time in seventh grade," recalled Peggy. The year before, she and two school chums, Arleen Lanzotti and Denise Ferri, had formed her first trio, the Delicates. "We would write songs just about our friends and not being able to date. We kept all these songs in our heads. We made up the tune and the words, and we also harmonized. One of our songs was called 'Too Young to Date,' which we later recorded, and it became a regional hit on the United Artists label." The Delicates sang at many public events in Belleville, and Peggy wrote a song about the mayor that the Delicates performed at his victory party.

In the seventh grade Peggy took the initiative to meet influential disc jockey Murray "the K" Kaufman, who was later described as the "fifth Beatle" for his involvement in bringing the Beatles to America. Murray the K had a radio show on WINS in New York City. "I decided in my naiveté that Murray the K needed me to write a theme song for him. So I got together with my friend and we wrote something called "Meusurray," because he used to talk sort of a pig-Latin, based on his name Murray. He also used to joke about watching the submarine races, which really meant making out on the beach or something, because that's what you'd tell your parents: you were watching the submarine races. So we wrote

'The Submarine Race Watcher's Theme.'" One day in the middle of winter, Peggy and her friend played hooky from school and took the bus to Manhattan to deliver their songs to Murray the K. "We probably had more nerves than brains," laughed Peggy. "But we found the studio in this huge building and pretended we had an appointment with Murray the K. They knew just by looking at us that we were just kids, but they humored us. They introduced us to Murray and we sang our little songs. Not only did they like it, they instantly recorded it right there in the studio. Imagine, I had no idea that people got paid for writing songs, which is something I loved to do." Murray the K recorded the song and by the time Peggy got back home, she heard her songs on the air.

The Delicates were invited to appear on the show many times after that. During one of the radio sessions, Billy Mure, a well-known studio guitar player for the Unart subsidiary of United Artists, heard about the Delicates and brought them into a studio to record a demo of their song "Black and White Thunderbird." He brought the demo to Don Costa, then head of A&R for United Artists, who recorded many well known performers such as Steve Lawrence and Eydie Gormé and went on to produce Frank Sinatra sessions. "We went to meet him and we brought our little songs written on school notebooks and paper bags. He was so encouraging and very nice, and booked a recording session. I remember being so innocent thinking the 40-piece orchestra was all for us. In actuality, he had tagged us onto the end of somebody else's session and, since they were still paying for the musicians, the orchestra backed us. Our songs titled "Too Young to Date" and "The Kiss" turned out wonderful, and we got quite a lot of regional airplay in three or four states," recalled Peggy.

Following the Delicates' regional success with "Black and White Thunderbird," Peggy met Barbara and Jiggs Allbut. Barbara and Jiggs were in a group called the Starlets, which also included Peggy's distant cousin Linda Malzone. They, too, had a hit, "P.S. I Love You." Since the Delicates and the Starlets were too young to play in nightclubs, they frequently met at record hops, becoming friendly rivals. When they realized their voices and styles blended well together, they became friends and together started singing backgrounds for notable artists, such as Neil Diamond, Anthony Newley, Bob Gaudio and Frankie Valli of the Four Seasons, and others.

"The first time I appeared on the Dick Clark show, I was with the Delicates, which was even before the Angels. Maybe I was in ninth grade at the time. The vice principal of my high school didn't want to announce that I was going to be on Dick Clark, because, you know, rock and roll in those days. It's laughable now what people thought was shocking," Peggy said with a chuckle.

Peggy said that she was never content doing just one thing at a time. Often while she was attending college as a non-traditional age student, Peggy would fly home from a concert and go directly to school. "It was hard work, but I graduated Phi Beta Kappa," she said proudly. Although Peggy's parents weren't able to share the excitement of seeing her receive her bachelor's and master's degrees in psychology and her induction into a brand-new career, they were always very proud of her achievements.

"Both of my parents died in the early '90s — in fact, my father died the day of my mother's funeral," said Peggy. "While my parents were thrilled about me going back to school because they knew that's what I wanted to do, they wouldn't be any less proud if I didn't. My family was just so down to earth, not your typical stage mother or stage father. And I'm happy they were the way they were because I never took myself too seriously. I knew at a very young age that we weren't any better than anyone else just because we had some good fortune. There are a lot of very talented people out there who have never performed professionally, and there are also a lot of non-talented individuals who happen to be very famous."

Peggy was the youngest of three children. Her sister, Ann, who attended The Juilliard School for performing arts, sang opera and performed in many prestigious places throughout the country at a very young age. "Because my sister was a little bit older, I was very influenced by seeing her sing, but I knew I couldn't sing opera. I can remember being 11 years old, sitting on my front porch — we had this wonderful big, old wooden house, my grandparents' house that I lived in. My grandparents grew everything. We had peach trees, pear trees, and a big garden. Anyway, I remember sitting on the steps and just thinking, 'Well this is want I want to do. I'm going to be a singer' and planning how I was going to do this. My sister still has a beautiful voice, but she didn't like performing in front of an audience," Peggy told us in June 1997.

Peggy also enjoyed listening to '50s R&B in her pre-adolescent years. She recalled a high school teacher, Dr. Peck, who was very encouraging. "I guess he knew I had some natural musical abilities, and he was very encouraging along those lines. I was already singing in the school glee club, and by that time I had already been recording in grade school. But he gave me confidence in myself that I was very musically gifted. He gave me the encouragement that my singing and song writing was legitimate. Most adults at the time didn't put rock and roll in the same category as 'real' music."

Connie Francis attended the same high school Peggy did in Belleville, although she graduated about six years ahead of Peggy. "A cousin of mine was very good friends with Connie, who influenced some of the very early things that I wrote after the Delicates." We were in the Columbus Day Parade together because I was singing with my little local school group and she had come back to make special appearances. I thought, 'Well, here's another person who not only came from the same cultural background, but also went to the same high school and had hit records. I didn't have a big hit record yet but I was already recording, and it made success more plausible."

After the loss of her parents, Peggy's clinical psychotherapy pursuit took on even greater meaning. "Although I do have the education to be able to professionally detach myself, part of the ability to help others stems from genuine caring," asserted Peggy. "But I can't say that it's not stressful if I know my clients are in dire straits and their doctors have sent them to me to cheer them up and, hopefully, give them enough support so that they can face their chemotherapy or other medical challenges. It's something that I can do and should do, and my life certainly has been enriched by it."

Although Peggy said she has had many happy endings, each individual case presented its own complexities. "Very strong people cry and very strong people say 'Why me?' There's no expert, especially with things for which we don't know all the answers. So we just try to encourage each other to face the future as bravely as we can and to enjoy and live life to the fullest for whatever time we have left. None of us really knows whether it's a day, or a year, or 10 years. And the singing has helped me in a lot of ways not to sweat the small stuff. I used to envy friends who envied me. They'd say, 'Ooh, traveling all over the country. Ooh, you never know where you're going to be and what you're going to do.' Right. But they had the security of knowing what they were doing. When I'm dealing with people in very serious situations, it has helped me because I've been somebody who has been all over the country and all over the world, and I've been exposed to so many different types of people and cultures. And show business has definitely made me a very nonjudgmental person."

But show business was not all rosy for Peggy. "I've seen people die from drugs, people who I cared about very much. I haven't been sheltered from life. Nothing anybody can tell me is going to shock me. I just feel very fortunate not only to be alive, but to have these diverse sides to my life and that I've been able to use my brain because my singing came absolutely naturally to me."

Peggy met her second husband, Jim Davison, on a blind date. "I had been married many years ago, but I had been single for a long time when I met Jim. I owned a very small cosmetics company called Face Concepts, and earlier was in regional management for a division of Revlon and involved in some projects in Baltimore." A couple of business friends thought Peggy should meet Jim. "I didn't want to meet anybody, and he didn't want to meet me — this crazy rock and roll person. So we just appeased our friends and went on a blind date." The couple married in 1981.

Peggy had no tolerance for promoters making money from "bogus" oldies rock groups. "Unfortunately, I don't think a whole lot of people know the names of individual members of '60s rock groups. There's no other form of show business in which impersonators are not called impersonators, except oldies rock and roll. And that is a little disturbing to those of us who really were the people who sang the songs and grew up in that time period. I'm not blaming the performers; it's the promoters and producers who are being deceitful to people in the audience. Oldies fans, very much like country fans, are very sincere, wonderful people. I can't tell you how lucky we are. People come to see us from all around the country. I love to talk and reminisce with fans. We're usually associated with happy times, so they feel like they know us."

Peggy was proud of her achievements but a bit humble. "I knew that I could do well in school, but I was also worried about it at the same time. Going back to school many years later and never really having been in college, I did feel really proud to be a Phi Beta Kappa graduate. That is not easy to do. And I didn't do it with a plan. I mean, I wasn't even thinking about Phi Beta Kappa when I went into school. And I was also very proud of my thesis. I worked really long and hard on it, and I'm gratified that I was able to mix real life and my experiences and my educational background and actually see it come to fruition by helping people. That does make me feel very proud," Peggy told us. "And as far as my show business career, at risk of sounding corny, I guess I'm most proud that I'm able to have gotten through this whole long career without any serious regrets about what could have been. I feel what happened to us and what we achieved was wonderful, especially that we were kids, and I feel very proud that we're still very good friends. We got through all the ups and downs of show business, good and bad. Because for every wonderful thing that happened — all the first big network television appearances, all the singing at famous places all over the world — there were also lots of background problems inherent in that."

Peggy's upbeat attitude enabled her to withstand more hardship in her life. Her sister, Ann Santiglia Daniels, died at age 91 on September 1, 2018. After her second marriage came to an end, Peggy married Dwight Ricker, a U.S. Department of Agriculture food program specialist, but he succumbed to illness at age 71 on September 5, 2020.

Peggy found purpose volunteering as a big sister in the Big Brothers and Big Sisters program and resumed writing songs, which she said she intended to continue for the rest of her life.

"I didn't ever really feel like I changed careers, because the singing has just been such an important part of my life. I can reach people emotionally with my voice. And in turn, I get a lot of wonderful feeling back."

Epilogue: Phyllis "Jiggs" Allbut

Singer

Through the decades, rock music performers have had a penchant for nicknames. Fats Domino, Ringo Starr, and Count Basie all adopted monikers reflective of their adult personas. But Jiggs Allbut has carried her nickname since infancy. Born Phyllis Allbut, Jiggs was given her nickname by her mother, who thought she resembled the monocled character in the comic strip known as "Jiggs and Maggie" in some cities and "Bringing Up Father" in others. "There was this little fat Irish guy who always used to get beat up by his wife, but he did bad things and he deserved it," Jiggs recalled with a grin. "My mother thought I looked like him when I was a baby. I had a big, fat face with a clump of hair sticking up, so she called me Jiggs." She's always been known as Jiggs, except of course by the IRS, banks, insurance companies, and the like.

The youngest of two girls, Jiggs grew up in a musical family. Her sister, Barbara, took piano lessons at a very early age, and both girls sang, Jiggs providing harmony. Their desire to become professional musicians came in their early teen years. Both born on

Jiggs Allbut Sirico backstage before a performance in Baltimore in the 1990s. Courtesy of Jiggs Sirico.

September 24, two years apart — Barbara in 1940, and Jiggs in 1942 — the girls each received cash for their birthdays one year. They didn't use it to buy clothes or jewelry like most teen girls, but instead pooled it to finance their first recording. "We found a little recording studio near our home in Orange, New Jersey. Barbara played the piano, and we harmonized some of the songs that she had written," said Jiggs. "We met some little guy there named Bob Minete, who wrote songs, too. With his guitar accompaniment, we moved on to a larger studio and sang some of his songs for a demo."

That sparked the beginning of a long and accomplished recording career. Barbara and Jiggs continued singing backgrounds for other artists, moving up to a larger studio in New Jersey where they met the two girls who joined them in becoming the Starlets. The foursome recorded "P.S. I Love You" on the Astro Records label in Hillside and it became a regional hit. Peter Tripp, a New York deejay, began regularly playing the Starlets' version of "P.S. I Love You" on his WMGM radio show. "We were getting a lot of airplay and then all of a sudden, we tuned in one day and no more Peter Tripp. He'd been charged with payola," said Jiggs. The small New Jersey recording company attempted to make a distribution deal with Canadian American Records in New York once the song began getting some additional airplay, but the deal went sour.

Disappointed, but not defeated, Jiggs and Barbara were constantly working on new songs. Shortly after the "P.S." deal fell through, Barbara, Jiggs, and lead singer Linda Jankowski adopted the name Blue Angels, later dropping Blue from the name.

For Jiggs, entering into showbiz at such a young age made the adjustment to stardom second nature. "We were young, we were all single at the time and we were having fun. Although, in those days, the thing that got so many people into trouble was thinking, 'this is fun, this is great, this is what I want to do.' And there were not that many people there to take care of you. Our parents were not showbiz parents by any means. They were normal, middle-class people, and all of a sudden this new kind of rock and roll music was here, and they didn't know what was going on. So we were a little naive, I guess."

In 1976, Jiggs met her husband, Stan Sirico, in Connecticut when the band auditioned for a drummer. "Stan came with his friend to the audition to make him feel more comfortable," recalled Jiggs. "We liked Stan's guitar playing so much that we asked him if he wanted a job, too, and he said, 'Yes.'" Stan and Jiggs were married in 1986.

After living most of their lives on the East Coast, Jiggs and Stan moved to California in 1991 when his employer, AKG Acoustics in Connecticut, offered him a transfer and promotion. AKG Acoustics is a Viennese company that produces microphones and headphones for stage, studio, and the sound reinforcement industry. About a year after the transfer, the company moved to Nashville, Tennessee, and Stan and Jiggs opened their own electronic business in the San Francisco Bay Area city of San Leandro called Sirico Instruments. Their company supplied AKG and other companies with electronic components including power supplies for microphones.

With a long and successful musical career and a track record as business owner as part of her impressive resumé, Jiggs still asked herself, "Gee, what am I going to do when I grow up?" She decided, among other things, to finish her undergraduate degree and obtain a teaching credential from Thomas Edison State College (later renamed Thomas Edison State University) in Trenton, New Jersey. "Teaching was something I never thought was right for me. But then I got involved with Project Literacy at the library, teaching reading as a volunteer, and it was so fabulous. I would come home and say, 'Gee, that was really good.' I'm remembering different teachers in school, and how they taught things, what I thought of them and what I got out of their teaching.

Jiggs said she never loved performing more than she did by the 1990s. She enjoyed escaping from the routine responsibilities of being home and running a business. "We met some wonderful people on our tours. We took our CDs and we sold pictures and T-shirts at the shows, we signed autographs, and it's wonderful. Here you are and people are asking you to sign an autograph for them, they're buying your things, and it's just fabulous. Then you have to come home and walk the dog and scoop poop and, you know," laughed Jiggs. "Sometimes when we're out for a while, we get inspired and we start writing. Not me so much, but Stan and Peggy do, and I try to contribute what I can. In fact, they wrote a country-oriented song a while back that's really good. Things like that happen to us when we're out for a long time and totally into music."

When the Angels were on the road, a lot of prep work had to be done to make sure each of their other businesses continued running smoothly. For example, although Stan and Jiggs didn't have permanent employees, they often hired help to get them through some of the busy times of year. "We had certain things that had to be done at certain times. And when we were going away, we either worked real hard before or worked real hard after to make sure that tasks would be completed by their deadline," explained Jiggs.

Jiggs raised two daughters: Karalyn, born in 1969, and Samantha "Sam," born in 1987. "Karalyn is a very good singer and plays piano. In fact, she played piano with us years ago. She was in high school and, to tell you the truth, I never knew how well she could sing because she was shy about singing. But when we realized how well she really sang, we were amazed." Sam, the more outgoing of the two daughters, also played piano and loved art.

Jiggs described herself as "adaptable" and not particularly talkative, especially about her feelings. She considered her ability to get along with just about everyone among her greatest strengths. But on stage she could ham it up with the best of them. "I remember over the years being willing to do just anything on stage. I used to put on a stupid hat and do a drunk act."

A former aerobics and yoga instructor, Jiggs enjoyed weight training, exercise walking and yoga. She told us, "I also like to watch tennis and baseball. We're big New York Yankees fans. We play a lot of ping pong, and a lot of pool and it's fun, and I'm getting a little bit better, although I don't think I'll ever be a pool shark."

With her enjoyment of all types of music, including jazz, classical, and oldies, Jiggs claimed to be able to sing 99.9 percent of the songs that play on the oldies radio channels. "My husband's always amazed," she said. "He wants to put me on *Name That Tune*. I do like to sing along." Growing up, Jiggs listened to the early Alan Freed rock and roll and R&B hits by Black artists "before they were made hits by the white artists." She also loved to listen to the great harmony groups, including the Four Aces and the McGuire Sisters. "I used to love to go to the movies, too. I did study acting for a while. I never really pursued it because our singing career usually got in the way, but I did voice-overs and things like that. And that's something that someday I'm going to do again."

Epilogue: Barbara Allbut

Singer

September 24, 1940 – July 10, 2021

A multi-talented singer, music writer, pianist, and businesswoman, Barbara Allbut was instrumental in forming the Angels and overseeing the early business dealings of the group. Her keen business sense also contributed to the success of Peter Brown Associates, a commercial construction management company she owned with her architect husband Peter Brown. Although she no longer performed professionally after the late '70s, Barbara always had music in her blood and continued to satisfy her musical cravings by playing her 1917 Bösendorfer piano in her Santa Barbara home on the flanks of the Santa Ynez Mountains, overlooking the city and the Pacific Ocean.

She said that her interest in music began when she was toddling around at the age of 3. "My mother told me I'd walk around the house humming notes from operas that I'd heard on the radio," recalled Barbara. "Whenever we would go to a department store — I remember this — I would head for the piano department. They had a whole floor full of pianos and I'd go and sit there and play. I was just crazy about pianos."

When she was 5 years old, Barbara began taking piano lessons, playing mainly classical music. "I studied for 11 years until I was 16, and I just didn't like to practice. A couple of years before that I became interested in rock and roll. So I quit piano lessons, and I started writing songs, singing, and making up harmonies."

That was the beginning of her early performing career and the catalyst for her lifelong close relationship with her sister, Jiggs, with whom she shared the same birthday: September 24. Two years to the day older than Jiggs, Barbara — born in 1940 — formed musical groups with her friends in their Orange, New Jersey, junior high and high schools, performing for classmates and teachers. Barbara played the piano and everyone sang.

Reminiscing about her childhood idols, Barbara recalled, "At age 15 I saw Jo Ann Campbell at the Brooklyn Fox. She was a sexy little rock 'n' roll singer who electrified audiences in the Alan Freed rock 'n' roll concerts in the '50s. She recorded a song called 'Wait A Minute.' When I saw her up there, I was possessed by a powerful feeling that I was going to be a performer."

In about 1959 Barbara and Jiggs were singing duets in a little studio in New Jersey when they met a couple of other girls who had also been recording there. The foursome decided to form a quartet and they called it the Starlets. At the studio, they met a disc jockey who became the Starlets' manager and proceeded to make them a record deal with the small Astro Records label in Hillside, New Jersey. "We recorded a song called "P.S. I Love You" that started to climb the charts in New York," said Barbara. "At that time Peter Tripp was a popular deejay on WMGM in New York, and he just loved our record and was pushing it. But very shortly thereafter he was thrown off the air on payola charges. So that wiped everything out at the time."

Barbara's mother thought that show business was full of dishonest and underhanded people preying on the success of talented performers. "She was right, it really wasn't too nice. People got cheated left and right and we were kids and there were a lot of not very nice people who would take advantage of you." On the other hand, my father was wary but he was secretly proud. He would play our record on the jukebox whenever he went to the diner and he'd tell people, 'Those are my daughters,'" said Barbara with a smile. "When we were on *The Ed Sullivan Show* my mother apparently wouldn't sit in the room to watch it. My father said he was watching the television, and she kind of peeked around the corner and then made her way into the room slowly after she saw that we weren't going to fall on our faces." The girls' father loved to sing bass and his sister was a concert pianist. Their mother also played the piano. Barbara and Jiggs' mother died in 1977 and their father in 1979.

After 21 years on the road with the Angels, Barbara was tired of traveling and decided it was time to do something else. "In 1978 I began singing jingles in New York. I did a commercial for Wendy's, Peter Paul candy, some milk commercials, and stuff like that," said Barbara. She then met Peter Brown, who was an architect at Skidmore, Owings and Merrill, a large architectural firm with offices in Chicago, New York, Washington, San Francisco, and London. Peter and Barbara were married in 1986 in Santa Barbara, California, after Peter was transferred to the firm's Los Angeles office. In 1988 he decided to leave the firm to start his own business, Peter Brown Associates in LA.

"He's an architect, but this is not an architectural firm," explained Barbara. "We do construction project management for building developers. We do budgeting, scheduling, and assist in hiring project architects as well as advising and making sure everything is done right, on time, and on budget." The company's projects were mainly large commercial buildings, hospitals, and hotels.

"We've done numerous projects for Kaiser Permanente and the Equitable Insurance Company. We're doing Western Digital's new headquarters, projects at Loma Linda University Medical Center, Children's Hospital in Los Angeles, Century Plaza Hotel, Nikken North America world headquarters, the Aventine complex in La Jolla, and a lot of large law firms," she said. "We worked on a 25,000-square-foot house in Beverly Hills, and we just finished another one that's just over 30,000 square feet. Those are like commercial buildings."

The successful company had six employees. Most everyone in the firm was an architect by training, but they all functioned as project managers. Barbara was the business manager, responsible for payroll, billing, financial reports, and supervision of clerical personnel. Although she enjoyed running the office, it consumed most of her time. In 1998 she resumed writing music, studying arranging and composing. "I'm working on five songs that I'm very excited about," said Barbara. She spent three-and-a-half to four days a week in her Santa Barbara home, which looked out over the Pacific Ocean, 90 miles northwest of Los Angeles. The couple also maintained an apartment in the Bunker Hill area of downtown LA, within walking distance of their office.

Barbara attended two semesters at The Juilliard School of performing arts in her early 20s. "I took those night courses, and I studied theory, sight singing, and choral music. It was wonderful," she said. But her mother insisted she have something other than music to fall back on and encouraged her to go to secretarial school. "I've done some legal secretarial work here and there in the past. But that's it. I didn't have time to go to college with all of the performing we were doing." Although her company's project managers take care of several multi-million dollar projects, Barbara said her job was not particularly stressful. "There's a lot of work, but we have somebody wonderful working for us — our project assistant, Jackie. We get along really great. We love to go to out to lunch together, to try all the restaurants around here. Everybody in this firm gets along well with everybody else"

Barbara loved to travel, but being on the road and having to perform every night is not the type of traveling she liked to do in her mature years. "I love traveling on vacation," she said. "Although I do miss performing in a way, especially the interaction with the audience. When it was great it was so great. We became high from those performances. The thing I miss most, actually, is the vocal arranging, listening to what it sounds like with the group and hearing the harmonies. I love being in a recording studio, and I'm looking forward to getting back into studio work. I did a lot of work on my own when I was singing jingles. I would practice and tape myself and sing all the parts. And I really loved hearing how it would come out."

Barbara considered herself a quiet person who loves her freedom. "However," she said, "that would change when I'd hit the stage. I felt like I was two different people. When I got up on stage I was a big ham. People would say, 'Wow, you're not at all like you usually are.' I don't mean that I was dull; I think I'm quite interesting. But I did change when I got on stage. I don't like complications, although I have to field some of that in my job. I think I'm a kind person, I'm very fair, fun, hardworking, and smart." Although she had no children of her own, Barbara adored Jiggs' two daughters and visited with them as much as she could. She also was very close to her sister. "Jiggs and I talk all the time. She's the greatest sister ever. Everyone should have a sister like my sister," Barbara told us in August 1997.

In addition to her musical talent, Barbara found that she had a knack for being extremely organized at running her business and managing people and projects. "I really never thought I would necessarily have any talent in managing financial affairs. It was not something that I ever liked at all. I've sort of had to do it. But because I take care of the administrative end of the business, we don't have to have anybody from the outside doing our bookkeeping. If you'd have told me a few years ago I'd be doing this, I would never have believed you." Barbara also organized various projects in her Santa Barbara neighborhood. "I live on a private road and we've done a lot of improvements together principally because I got the ball rolling. So I seem to be able to get people to respond."

In her spare time, Barbara loved tennis and followed the pro tennis tour. "I go to as many matches as possible. I read every result every day. This started about 1985 when I first saw Boris Becker win Wimbledon, and I've just been a total fan ever since. I still play a little bit, but I have a very bad arm and I can't play very much. But I love it, and I love being at home with Peter and puttering around our home."

Barbara remained extremely proud of both her music career and her administrative career. Recalling her days with the Angels, she said, "Even though things hadn't necessarily been easy for us, we made it happen. And I think besides luck we also had great drive. I'm very proud that we had our hit records and we stuck with performing for so long, and I'm also proud of myself for what I'm doing now." She admitted that if she could go back in time, she'd satisfy her great longing: continuation of her studies at Juilliard. "I would have probably become a composer-arranger, perhaps for movies. I would have expanded my musical career through personal learning. I would have gone to school and really done something with it. I think of myself first as a musical person. But it's never too late, and I intend to continue with my music."

When Barbara first became interested in performing, she enjoyed listening to the early rhythm and blues music of groups such as the Moonglows, the Harptones, and the Paragons. "I love every kind of music now. I listen to pop music and Alanis Morissette, I'll listen to Mozart, I'll listen to Chick Corea, Manhattan Transfer. And at Christmas, I love Fauré's Requiem, and I love Pavarotti. I guess I like all music, except rap."

When asked how important it is for people to remember her, Barbara grew pensive. "I didn't think it was that important for me to be remembered until a few years ago," she slowly replied. "At one of the Angels shows, Jiggs and Peggy were singing, and I was in the audience. It just struck me that we had really pioneered for the girl groups, and we really made a contribution to the history of music. I was very 'up' that night, and it just dawned on me what we had really done. So I, too, want to be remembered."

Throughout her later life Barbara continued writing songs and early in 2021 recorded and released an extended-play collection of music called "Love Songs" in collaboration with her niece Karalyn Bord (the daughter of her sister, Phyllis "Jiggs" Allbut Sirico). Among the recordings on the EP is a composition titled "My Song For You," which Barbara wrote for her husband, Peter, who died of Parkinson's disease at age 69 in August 2012. Barbara died in Scottsdale, Arizona, at 80 years of age on July 10, 2021, as the result of a procedure to remove a pulmonary embolism.

A World Without Love

Peter and Gordon

When the Beatles catapulted to the top of the American music charts in early 1964, they did so in sovereign style, scoring four No. 1 singles in rapid succession. So overpowering was their influence that British artists reigned supreme all but 10 weeks during the first half of the year. While scores of British recording artists followed in the months to come, the Beatles shared the top position during the first half of '64 with only one other British musical act: Peter and Gordon.

The musical success of Peter and Gordon was preordained in a sense. At a time when anything bearing the Beatles imprint turned to gold, Peter Asher and Gordon Waller had the distinction of recording a new song by Beatles composers John Lennon and Paul McCartney. The song "A World Without Love" helped validate the music composition credentials of the Lennon-McCartney team while giving Peter and Gordon a career-launching, million-selling record.

Peter Asher and Gordon Waller met as teenagers at Westminster School in London, where they were students. Westminster, a residential public school founded in the 12th century by the Benedictine monks of the Abbey of St. Peter in Westminster, counts philosopher John Locke, actors Peter Ustinov and John Gielgud, and musical composer Andrew Lloyd Webber among its alumni. After Waller and Asher discovered that they shared an appreciation for the guitar and the silken harmonies of the Everly Brothers, they realized they had more in common. Both had fathers who were physicians. Neither dreamed of becoming pop music stars. Waller's father wanted Gordon to be a doctor. Gordon wanted to become a cowboy.

Evidently Gordon had his mind more on riding the range than on his schoolwork in his early school years. His recollection of what he was studying? "Nothing!" Although he was enrolled in physics, chemistry, and biology, he passed only physics with an unremarkable grade. "I wasn't academic and I'm still not," he insisted as a mature adult. Yet on

Peter Asher and Gordon Waller at a south London railway station in early 1965.
Photo by Chris Walter, Photofeatures.

the urging of his mother, who had been a nurse, and his father, Waller pressed on, transferring from his "junior school" in Pinner, Middlesex, to Westminster in London.

"I couldn't get into any other school," Waller candidly admitted. The "common entrance exam" required of British schoolchildren tested knowledge in numerous subjects, including chemistry and physics. The test revealed young Gordon's weakness in the sciences. "I was hopeless," he said. But although Westminster was considered a difficult "scholarship-level" school, its entrance exam consisted only of an English paper and a math test. "Those just happened to be subjects that I found pretty easy. I was a big hero in my junior school when it was announced that I passed into Westminster with flying colors because I got a couple of sports scholarships. I played everything that the school played."

And more. As schoolmates, Peter and Gordon developed a repertoire of gentle ballads and folk music, relying heavily upon songs by the Everly Brothers and Joan Baez. Accompanying themselves with acoustic guitars, they played local nightspots including the Pickwick Club, an exclusive dinner club frequented by show business personalities. Actors Harry Secombe, Michael Caine, and Trevor Howard were among the regulars. At the time, Asher had no particular career ambitions.

Following graduation from Westminster School, Peter studied philosophy in his first year at King's College, University of London. "I think I chose philosophy because it was the vaguest subject you could choose," he reflected. Asher thought of music more as a diversion than a potential career. As their audiences grew more appreciative, however, Peter and Gordon began to treat their music more seriously. After Peter made the decision to leave school, Gordon followed suit in July 1963. Then 18 years of age, Gordon told his father of his entertainment ambitions.

"I'll give you six months," said Gordon's displeased father. "If you can't make it as a music professional within six months, you'll go back to school."

Gordon protested, saying, "Dad, it's not that easy."

His father left him no choice. "Well, those are your options," he declared.

The clock began ticking.

Up on stage, Peter and Gordon continued singing their ballads and weaving harmonies. Gordon performed to the rhythm of a six-month metronome unheard by anyone but him. Before long, people began to express interest in recording them. Despite the urgency, they exercised remarkable discretion.

"We weren't really interested because they weren't the type of people we wanted to work with. I hadn't heard of the record companies they mentioned," said Waller. "I suspect the reason we became successful is that we waited for a decent company."

That company was EMI and its North American subsidiary, Capitol Records. After the duo finished a set at a London nightclub one evening, a man named Norman Newell approached them. He was an A&R specialist with EMI Records, a well-respected British label with good recording facilities and resources for strong promotional backing. Newell invited Asher and Waller to audition. They went to the label's studios and performed a few of the folk songs that constituted their on-stage repertoire. Newell offered them a recording contract. Peter and Gordon put their signatures to the contract just as Gordon's six-month time limit drew to a close.

As they considered material to record, their thoughts turned to a composition by an acquaintance: Paul McCartney. In early 1964, Paul took a fancy to a girl named Jane Asher — Peter's sister. Jane, who became Paul's girlfriend through the mid-'60s, introduced Paul to Peter and Gordon. "As we began thinking about material to record in our first session, I remembered a song that Paul said he had been working on but which wasn't finished because John [Lennon] decided he didn't like it," said Asher. "So I asked him if we could have it, and he said we could." The song, "A World Without Love," became Peter and Gordon's first record and cemented their success. After premiering on the *Billboard* Hot 100 on May 9, 1964, it soared to No. 1 on the British and American charts. Released by Columbia in the U.K. and by the Capitol Records label in the United States, "A World Without Love" remained on the *Billboard* chart for 12 weeks.

On June 27, the same day on which "A World Without Love" completed its seven-week climb up the chart by knocking the Dixie Cups' "Chapel of Love" out of the No. 1 spot, Peter and Gordon's second single, "Nobody I Know," premiered on the *Billboard* Hot 100. That song also was written by John Lennon and Paul McCartney. Released

Gordon Waller (left) and Peter Asher in 1965.

by Columbia in the U.K. and by the Capitol Records label in the United States, the record rose to No. 12 and remained on the *Billboard* chart for nine weeks. They still had more to offer in '64, courtesy of yet another Lennon-McCartney composition. "I Don't Want to See You Again," the duo's third single, premiered on the Hot 100 that October 3. Although the record did not reach the charts in England, it rose to No. 16 in the States and remained on the *Billboard* chart for nine weeks.

Instant fame was anything but traumatic to Asher.

"I really enjoyed it. I can't pretend there were any huge stresses attached to it. It was all fun at the time," he admitted. When fame came, Asher's studies ceased. "I went to my 'tutor' at the university — that's like a counselor in the States — and told him that we had a No. 1 hit record and that we'd been invited to travel to America to tour and appear on *The Ed Sullivan Show*. I asked if he or the university would consider giving me a year's leave of absence to go off, and then I'd come back and finish my studies. And to his credit, he consented. Unfortunately," Asher added, "he's still waiting for me to come back. I never did, and I'm still a dropout."

Even if he entertained any thoughts of returning to school, those must have vanished when Asher stepped off the plane on his arrival in America on Monday, June 15, 1964, exactly one week before his 20th birthday. He and Gordon, who had just turned 19, were booked to perform in their first U.S. concert tour beginning with three dates later that week at the New York World's Fair. "Screaming girls at the airport were carrying big signs that said 'We love you, Peter and Gordon" and tearing at our clothes. That was thoroughly enjoyable."

The live performances turned out to be less so.

"The business was very badly organized back then," recalled Asher. "The gigs were horrible. They were in some awful gym or roller rink. It was a good thing our shows lasted only a half hour because there were no stage monitors and we couldn't hear ourselves. The production aspects of the shows were very amateurish then. It was a complete nightmare," Asher asserted. Well, not a complete nightmare.

"The good side was I enjoyed singing with Gordon," Asher added. "He was a terrific singer. We sang very good harmony together. I greatly enjoyed being in America, being in LA. Here I was, with a No. 1 record, driving down Sunset Boulevard for the first time in my life in a convertible Mustang while girls recognized me and asked if they could jump in the car. Life doesn't get much better than that."

Although Peter and Gordon's first three hits had been written by John Lennon and Paul McCartney, Asher and Waller turned to a song composed by Del Shannon for their fourth hit single, "I Go To Pieces," which premiered on the *Billboard* Hot 100 on January 9, 1965. Released by Columbia in the U.K. and by the Capitol Records label in the United States, the record rose to No. 9 and remained on the *Billboard* chart for 11 weeks.

On April 17, 1965, Peter and Gordon sent their fifth hit song, the Buddy Holly tune "True Love Ways," onto the charts. Although Holly's version of "True Love Ways" had not been a hit in the United States, it was popular in the U.K. Peter and Gordon's version of "True Love Ways," released by Columbia Records in the U.K. and by Capitol Records in the United States, rose to No. 14 and remained on the *Billboard* chart for 11 weeks. Without missing a beat, Peter and Gordon slightly changed the Teddy Bears' 1958 song "To Know Him Is to Love Him" (written by Phil Spector) and made it "To Know You Is to Love You." They gave the song a far more robust reading than the original, blending their voices powerfully. That gave the duo their sixth chart hit, which made its debut on the *Billboard* Hot 100 on July 10, 1965. The recording, released by Columbia Records in the U.K. and by Capitol Records in the United States, rose to No. 24 in the States and remained on the *Billboard* chart for seven weeks. In the U.K., "To Know You Is to Love You" became the duo's fourth top-10 hit, soaring to No. 5.

Peter and Gordon followed that up with "Don't Pity Me," which they wrote themselves. The recording, with musical arranging and conducting by Geoff Love, made its debut on the Hot 100 on November 6, 1965. The flip side of the Capitol single in the United States was "Crying in the Rain," the Carole King and Howard Greenfield composition that was a top-10 hit for the Everly Brothers in early 1962. In the U.K., however, "Don't Pity Me" was the "B" side of the duo's Columbia Records single "To Show I Love You," a song that Tony Hatch wrote. That single, released in June 1966, did not reach the British charts. The Capitol Records release of "Don't Pity Me" in the United States was on the *Billboard* chart for four weeks, during which time it stalled at No. 83. Peter and Gordon would follow with one of their biggest hits a couple of months later.

Throughout their recording careers, Peter and Gordon retained an association with the Beatles and collaborated with Paul McCartney in a celebrated bit of musical subterfuge. When unwavering fan loyalty planted seeds of doubt in Paul's mind about the depth of his songwriting talent,

Peter and Gordon (Gordon Waller at left, Peter Asher at right) promotional photo
for the 1965 American International Pictures film *Go Go Mania.*

he asked Peter and Gordon to consider recording a song he wrote under the assumed name of Bernard Webb as his means to see if the public would appreciate music he composed without the magnetic draw of the McCartney name. The song, "Woman," premiered on the *Billboard* Hot 100 on February 12, 1966, and quickly became the eighth hit for Peter and Gordon. McCartney's alias was quickly uncloaked because the publishing company's paper trail wasn't well concealed, but the appeal of "Woman" proved his intended point and reassured him of his lyrical talents. Released by Columbia in the U.K. and by the Capitol Records label in the United States, the dramatically orchestrated recording of "Woman" rose to No. 14 and remained on the *Billboard* chart for 12 weeks. It peaked at No. 17 on the *Cash Box* chart, and at No. 28 in the United Kingdom.

"There's No Living Without Your Loving," the ninth chart single for Peter and Gordon, premiered on the *Billboard* Hot 100 on May 7, 1966. Gene Pitney and Manfred Mann previously recorded and released the song (written by Jerry Harris and Paul Kaufman) but only Peter and Gordon managed to send it onto the charts. Released by Columbia in the U.K. and by the Capitol Records label in the United States, "There's No Living Without Your Loving" peaked at No. 50 and remained on the *Billboard* chart for seven weeks. The duo's 10th chart hit, "To Show I Love You," made its debut on the Hot 100 on July 30, 1966. The song was written by Tony Hatch, who wrote or co-wrote most of Petula Clark's hits. John Burgess produced the recording, for which Bob Leaper did musical arrangement and conducting. Released by Columbia in the U.K. and by the Capitol Records label in the United States, "To Show I Love You" was on the *Billboard* chart for only two weeks, and went no higher than No. 98. The duo's follow-up release, however, proved to be their second-biggest hit: "Lady Godiva."

That slightly naughty novelty tune, which captivated the imagination of the duo's fans, made its debut on the *Billboard* Hot 100 on October 8, 1966. The song was written by Mike Leander and Charles Mills. Leander had been musical arranger for most of Marianne Faithfull's single releases, and Mills worked primarily as a lyricist. John Burgess produced "Lady Godiva," the Capitol Records release of which in the United States rose to No. 6 and remained on the chart for 14 weeks. Columbia released the single in the U.K., where it peaked at No. 16. It was a No. 1 hit on the Columbia label in Australia. With much the same musical feeling, "Knight in Rusty Armour" made its debut on the Hot 100 on December 24, 1966. Like its predecessor, the whimsical song was written by Mike Leander and Charles Mills. The U.K. release on Columbia (as

"The Knight in Rusty Armour") did not reach the British charts, but the American release on the Capitol Records label rose to No. 15 and remained on the *Billboard* chart for nine weeks.

"Sunday For Tea," Peter and Gordon's 13th chart recording, made its debut on the *Billboard* Hot 100 on March 25, 1967. The song was written by John Carter and Ken Lewis, members of the band called the Ivy League. John Burgess produced the recording session, with musical accompaniment under the direction of Mike Vickers, who played saxophone, flute, and guitar with Manfred Mann. Burgess was a prolific recording producer who also worked with Freddie and the Dreamers, Matt Monro, Adam Faith, the English Congregation, and Toto. Released by Columbia in the U.K. and by the Capitol Records label in the United States, "Sunday For Tea" rose to No. 31 and remained on the *Billboard* chart for six weeks.

"The Jokers," Peter and Gordon's 14th and final U.S. chart recording, made a one-week appearance on the *Billboard* Hot 100 the week beginning June 24, 1967. It was from the motion picture of the same name, starring Oliver Reed and Michael Crawford. The song was written by Mike Leander and Charles Mills, who also wrote two of the duo's preceding hits, "Lady Godiva" and "Knight In Rusty Armour." Mike Leander arranged and conducted the musical accompaniment, and John Burgess produced the recording session.

In all, Peter and Gordon produced 11 top 50 American hit singles for Capitol Records during a three-year period. The duo amicably went their separate ways in 1967 but remained friends. Nearly four decades later, they reunited in August 2005, beginning with a performance to benefit Dave Clark 5 keyboard player and lead singer Mike Smith, who had sustained paralyzing spinal cord damage in a fall from a fence at his home in Spain. Peter and Gordon continued making appearances together for four more years after that.

PETER AND GORDON

U.S. HIT SINGLES ON THE NATIONAL CHARTS

Debut	Peak	Title	Label
5/9/64	1	A World Without Love	Capitol
6/27/64	12	Nobody I Know	Capitol
10/3/64	16	I Don't Want to See You Again	Capitol
1/9/65	9	I Go to Pieces	Capitol
4/17/65	14	True Love Ways	Capitol
7/10/65	24	To Know You Is to Love You	Capitol
11/6/65	83	Don't Pity Me	Capitol
2/12/66	14	Woman	Capitol
5/7/66	50	There's No Living Without Your Loving	Capitol
7/30/66	98	To Show You I Love You	Capitol
10/8/66	6	Lady Godiva	Capitol
12/24/66	15	Knight in Rusty Armour	Capitol
3/25/67	31	Sunday for Tea	Capitol
6/24/67	97	The Jokers	Capitol

Billboard's pop singles chart data is courtesy of Joel Whitburn's
Record Research Inc., Menomonee Falls, Wisconsin.

Epilogue: Peter Asher

Singer

Peter Asher, CBE, always was a model of modesty. One of the most artistically prolific and powerful figures in the recording industry, he confessed to being a man without career plans. His career path, he said, was anything but mapped out. To hear him tell it, he simply had a knack for wandering down the right pathway at the right time.

Peter Asher in the 1990s. Courtesy of Peter Asher.

"I don't really have any ambitions. All of the career changes that I've made have been unplanned. They were not the result of ambitions," Asher confessed. "When I was a university student I had no ambition to be a pop star, when I was a pop star I had no ambition to be a record producer, when I was a record producer I had no ambition to be a manager, and when I was a manager I had no ambition to become a senior record company executive. So it seems almost pointless for me to think of any ambitions at this point," he told us in June 1997. "I think I have done a lot by succeeding at whatever I was doing by doing my best at it, but ambition has been more a function of the opportunity that presents itself. When there's an opportunity to jump, I jump."

Asher apparently jumped with impeccable timing. He gracefully leaped from the role of pop star to pop star-maker, emerging in the 1970s as a highly sought producer of scores of musical performers including James Taylor, Linda Ronstadt, Neil Diamond, Cher, Randy Newman, Olivia Newton-John, Bonnie Raitt, 10,000 Maniacs, John Stewart, Kenny Loggins, Dan Fogelberg, Billy Joel, Diana Ross, and Ringo Starr. The latter association served as a reminder of the ways in which Asher's career was interwoven with the Beatles, who provided Peter and Gordon with their stunning debut song, "A World Without Love," and for whose Apple label Asher was hired in 1968 as head of A&R (artists and repertoire).

His success as a music producer was validated by the Record Industry Association of America (RIAA), which presented him with awards for 37 gold albums and 22 platinum albums. In addition, he earned many accolades internationally. Eight of the recordings he's produced won Grammy Awards, and he received additional Grammy recognition as producer of the year in both 1977 and 1989.

Born in London on June 22, 1944, Asher grew up in a musical household in a flat at 57 Wimpole Street in the Westminster sector of London. His mother, Margaret, was a professional oboe player and professor of music at the Guildhall School of Music and Drama. Her students, long before Peter met any of the Beatles, included a young George Martin, who later became the Beatles' producer. Young Peter spent the first few years of his life on the road with her as she toured with English orchestras entertaining military troops. Peter's father, Richard, was a physician.

"During the last couple of years of the blitz, he spent most of his time sewing up people who had been in the bombings," Asher wryly observed. For relaxation, when he found time, Peter's father played piano. Music filled the household. Even so, Peter's initial musical experience wasn't encouraging. "I was very bad at my piano lessons, and I can't read music properly to this day," he acknowledged. Just as his sisters Jane (two years younger) and Clare (four years younger) took an interest in theatrics and became child actors, so did Peter, who appeared in several motion pictures and TV show episodes between 1952 and 1957. Peter's affinity for music blossomed when he discovered rock and roll. In school he developed an interest in the guitar. "But it didn't become serious until I started singing in school with a friend of mine, Gordon."

Three years after Peter and Gordon arrived in America on the first wave of the British Invasion, the ride came to an end. The breakup of the act in 1967 was gradual rather than cataclysmic. "We just became a bit less successful, and began to enjoy each other's company a bit less," Asher explained. By then he had already given thought to developing a career in music production.

Fascinated by the process of record production, Asher mentioned his interest to Paul Jones, lead singer of the Manfred Mann combo. Jones, who had observed Asher in the studio during Peter and Gordon sessions, asked Asher to produce some tracks for him.

"That was quite brave of him," Asher said. A music producer is somewhat analogous to the head chef of a fine restaurant. Producers typically help artists choose songs to record, select the musicians, consult on the musical arrangement, oversee technical direction of the mix, direct the pacing and phrasing of vocals and instrumental passages, and more. All the while Asher was testing his wings in the booth with Paul Jones, he received encouragement from his friend Paul McCartney. The two frequently hung out together, and McCartney spoke to Asher at length about a conceptual project he and the other Beatles were in the process of developing. The project was the formation of the Beatles' own label, Apple Records, and on its launch Asher was hired as head of A&R. Just four years after he'd been signed to his first recording contract, Asher was given a major role in determining which artists the new Apple label should sign, what kinds of recordings they'd make, and who would produce their sessions. Within the Apple culture, such decisions were a shared responsibility.

"I would have weekly A&R meetings with as many Beatles as wanted to attend, and usually some sort of a 'Beatle quorum' would be present when we made decisions," Asher recalled. One of his first developmental assignments was the signing of Welsh singer Mary Hopkin, whom Paul McCartney had spotted on a local talent show on television. Asher sought her out and promptly signed her to a contract with the intention of recording a particular song.

"Paul already had in mind the song he wanted her to do," said Asher. "It was a song he had heard at a folk night club. Although the couple singing it had written English lyrics, it was really a Russian folk song." Asher assisted with arrangements for the hauntingly melancholic "Those Were the Days," which sold a million copies in the fall of 1968.

Shortly after joining Apple, Asher entered into an enduring creative relationship with another artist who would grow to legendary stature. The association began through a mutual friend, Danny Kortchmar, who'd been a member of a band called the King Bees that backed a few Peter and Gordon gigs during an American concert tour. Asher and Kortchmar developed a close friendship and stayed in contact through the years.

After Asher arrived at Apple he received a phone call from a young American visiting in London. He'd been in a band called the Flying Machine, in which Kortchmar played after the breakup of the King Bees. The young visitor's name was James Taylor. Asher agreed to listen to Taylor's audition tape.

"I'd like to sign you to a recording contract and produce your records," Asher told Taylor.

"Fine," Taylor calmly replied.

Taylor's relaxed demeanor couldn't mask his awe when, barely two weeks after arriving in London, he was in the studio meeting the Beatles. During his tenure with Apple, Peter met and began dating American-born rock music publicist Elizabeth "Betsy" Doster , whom he married in October 1970. The marriage did not endure long, however, and ended in divorce.

The debut James Taylor album was the first — and only — record that Asher produced for Apple. After American business executive Allen Klein was hired as the Beatles' business manager in 1969 to restore order to the band's imbalanced finances, he restructured Apple by terminating numerous employees and releasing several performers, including Taylor, from their contracts. Asher followed Taylor back to the states in 1971 and assumed management of Taylor's career. Although Asher knew nothing of talent management, he received coaching from a friend named Nat Weiss, the Beatles' American business representative and attorney. For several decades, Weiss remained Asher's friend and Taylor's attorney.

Under the tutelage of Weiss, Asher learned the ropes quickly and competently.

"Management, as I always thought it was, turned out to be based upon common sense," observed Asher. In short order Asher inked a

Peter Asher with Gordon Waller (moments before his wedding to Georgiana Steele) on August 15, 1998, in the home of Terry Holland and Kathy Holland, the duo's business manager, in Simi Valley, California. Photo by Jeff March.

record deal for Taylor with Warner Brothers, for which he produced Taylor's stunning second album, *Sweet Baby James.* From that success in early 1970 Asher's fortunes spiraled. As slowly and carefully as he built Peter Asher Management into a talent powerhouse, Asher's production career took on brilliance as well. He orchestrated a succession of critically acclaimed works not only for James Taylor, but also for Linda Ronstadt, whose chart debut with the Stone Poneys came at about the time the recording career of Peter and Gordon was fading.

Asher began managing Ronstadt in 1973 and produced the albums that propelled her to superstardom, beginning with 1974's country-flavored *Heart Like a Wheel* and encompassing Ronstadt's chameleonic musical progression through *Prisoner in Disguise, Hasten Down the Wind, Simple Dreams, Living in the U.S.A., Mad Love, Get Closer, Canciones de Me Padre,* and *Cry Like a Rainstorm, Howl Like the Wind,* running the gamut from reggae to rock to ballads to punk. When Ronstadt collaborated with orchestra leader Nelson Riddle in creating three albums of lush sentimental ballads in the mid-'80s, Asher was at the creative helm. By then Peter had met art curator and collector Wendy Worth, whom he married in May 1983.

Beverly Hills-based Peter Asher Management prospered and grew, shepherding the careers of Randy Newman, Warren Zevon, and other artists. Asher was perfectly content overseeing his enterprise until the phone rang one day in early 1995 with an offer too tempting to refuse. Asher accepted, and became senior vice president at Sony Music Entertainment, the New York conglomerate encompassing Columbia Records, Epic Records, and other labels. Although involved in corporate planning and decision-making, Asher remained within the realm of talent development, scouting, and nurturing new acts. He also continued to produce recordings for Sony Music artists.

Asher's role in corporate management was in keeping with his candid view of his performing talents. "I always saw myself as a harmony singer, not a lead singer, so I never wanted to be the guy in front of the band," Asher confessed. "But I enjoy singing harmony and I still do from time to time, whenever there's a part to which I think I can usefully contribute."

Asher's position with Sony required a lot of travel, so he kept a tiny apartment in Manhattan not far from his office, as well as a flat in London. He spent much of his time in Los Angeles, where he preferred to schedule recording sessions. His primary residence was in Malibu, where he and his family owned a home. Asher and his wife, Wendy, welcomed a daughter, Victoria, in 1984. Asher remained with Sony until 2002, when he resumed his career in personal artist management — first with Sanctuary Artist Management until 2007, when he joined Strategic Artist Management. He also reunited with Gordon Waller for occasional concert appearances from 2005 until Waller's death in 2009. He subsequently toured regularly as a soloist, as well as pairing with Jeremy Clyde (of the Chad and Jeremy duo) and with celebrated guitarist Albert Lee, known for his associations with Emmylou Harris, Eric Clapton, and the Everly Brothers.

For a man who in school studied the complex philosophies of ancient scholars, Asher adopted a disarmingly simple philosophical approach.

"I think my philosophy has always been the same," he mused. "I find myself very uncomfortable with any kind of deceit. I've never been any good at it. My management company developed a reputation of being very straight ahead and honest. But that shouldn't be the exception upon which to grow a reputation. In my estimation it doesn't do any good to weave a web of confusion and deceit because it makes life too damned complicated. I can't say that I've always told the truth, but one tells as much of the truth as possible without causing anyone tremendous upset or huge social disruption."

Indeed, Asher agreed that he has not been without his faults.

"I admit to impatience and unwillingness to put up with foolishness," he said without hesitation. But he also saw himself as intelligent and level-headed.

"I don't get daunted by problems," said Asher. "I'm convinced that if you think hard enough, everything can be sorted out."

On February 24, 2015, Queen Elizabeth II appointed Asher a Commander of the Order of the British Empire (CBE) for his services to the British music industry.

Epilogue: Gordon Waller

Singer

June 4, 1945 – July 17, 2009

By the time he was 15 years old, Gordon Waller had made an important discovery. "The guitar was a very good vehicle for social attraction by the male species," he observed. "If you played the guitar you got invited to parties." And so young Gordon set about learning to play the guitar. He'd already become enamored of the rock and roll music of Buddy Holly, Eddie Cochran, Elvis Presley, and the Everly Brothers.

Gordon Trueman Riviere Waller, born June 4, 1945, in the Scottish Highlands town of Braemar, took his guitar with him when he went off to school in London. He learned he was one of very few guitar players at Westminster School, where classical music was emphasized and the guitar was frowned upon. Fellow student Peter Asher, a year older than Gordon, shared his interest in the guitar.

"Peter's tastes were more jazz and folk-oriented than mine," said Gordon. "But when we got together we realized that our voices suited each other, so we started doing a bit of work in local clubs — probably the happiest days of my life." From that comfortable association, they found themselves at the avant-garde of the British Invasion, scoring a string of hits from 1964 until 1967. Waller wasn't prepared, however, when the warm glow of fame chilled and he and Peter went their separate ways.

Gordon Waller (right foreground) performing in 1996. Courtesy of Gordon Waller.

"When it stopped, I carried on trying to live the same way — that was my first mistake," Waller said candidly. "I ran out of money, and that's when it hits you bad. But I survived. I tried different things."

He made an unsuccessful attempt to continue performing on his own.

"The guy we had as a manager thought that I had a very good chance of making it solo, but he had his fingers in too many pies. He was managing too many people. He had a couple of people very similar to me so he didn't concentrate enough. It might have worked if there had been a bit more time and effort put into it, and if someone controlled me a bit more. I was fairly uncontrollable then. Eventually I decided to go off somewhere no one would know where I was, including me."

Gordon found the anonymity he sought in the countryside of Northampton, where he moved into a 17th-century farmhouse and started a landscaping business in which he did the physical labor himself. "It's good work, it keeps you fit," he explained. He dug in the dirt by day and played music in clubs by night. That, he said, kept him out of the pubs. He shared the quiet life in his cottage with his five dogs, a few dozen ducks and geese, a horse, and a parrot named Proby. In the ancient stables he kept his tractor along with his car, an elegant 1936 Austin Seven saloon — the British term for sedan — which he restored himself.

His interest in acting, an ambition Gordon held in his youth, was stirred when he received a call from his friend Tim Rice, lyricist of *Jesus Christ Superstar, Evita,* and other musicals. Rice had collaborated in a new theatrical production with composer Andrew Lloyd Webber, who had been a classmate of Gordon's at Westminster School. On Rice's invitation, Gordon tried out and won the role of "Pharaoh, the King" in the Webber-Rice musical *Joseph and the Amazing Technicolour Dreamcoat.* Gordon appeared in performances at the 1972 Edinburgh Festival, the Roundhouse, and the Young Vic Theatre in London and in 1973 at the Albery Theatre (since renamed the Noël Coward Theatre) in the West End of London.

Despite laudatory reviews in which critics praised his performances as "superlative," Waller grew disenchanted after appearing in a couple of other stage musicals and three or four plays. "I didn't like acting much because you have to be there all the way through and you don't get any individual applause afterward, which is something the ego side of me used to love about music — the adoring fans." After concluding a performance run of Joseph at the Seymour Centre in Sydney, Gordon returned to England and bought a house in Everdon, West Northamptonshire.

There, through a mutual friend, he was reacquainted with a young woman named Gay Robbins whom he had met in Australia in 1964. They married in 1975, and Gordon set out in search of "proper employment." At the age of 32 he took a bottom-rung sales position with Rank Xerox, a British office equipment firm. He remained there three years, until 1980, when he became angry at his boss one decisive day.

"I slung about a year's paperwork out of the 13th floor window and they didn't want me back again," he said.

He spent the next four years with a big Canon office equipment distributor, where he rose to the position of sales manager.

"I got sacked from that. I got sacked from most places because I find that I lose respect for people," said Waller. "Some of these guys think they know the ins and outs of everything but they're not quite as cute as they really would like to think they are."

Recognizing the potential of emerging cellular telephone technology, Waller started a cell phone dealership in 1984, then sold out within two years as prices and profits plummeted.

Waller counted his ascension in office equipment sales among his proudest achievements. "When I was selling office equipment, I worked myself up to a pretty powerful position. Nobody thought I would do it because I was an ex-pop star, but I said, 'Just watch.' And I think that was an achievement, because I really had to work at it," said Waller. "I had to work at being a little bit more polite to people, and I had to learn to control my impatient attitude. I do get very impatient. I hate being late for anything and I hate people being late for me. I do tend to lose my temper about it. Like when I'm with someone and it's quarter to seven and we've got half an hour drive and we're supposed to be there at seven, and they say, 'Oh, don't worry, everyone in California turns up late.' And I say, 'I don't give a shit about people in California being late. If I say I'm going to be somewhere at 7, and it's possible, I'm going to be there at 7.' That's just part of the stubborn Scotsman in me."

Through his wandering years, it took Gordon quite some time to find himself. But he eventually did. "Thinking back on all of the things I should have done and didn't, I should have taken myself a little more seriously instead of being the happy-go-lucky kind of guy I was. I probably would have been bored stiff, working my brains out day in and day out, but making a lot of money. I don't miss a lot of money, but I don't like being absolutely without any. I've never been without any," Gordon added quickly.

Waller's greatest test of survival did not involve finances, but rather his battle with the bottle. He regarded excess drinking as the worst mistake he made. "I'm just about over that. I do love Guinness, but I used to drink too much bloody whiskey and it made me violent," he admitted. "It doesn't make me violent now; it just makes me silly and I go to sleep. I know Peter used to hate my drinking. It would make him pretty irate. Peter is a very moderate, very clever, easygoing, thoughtful person. He thinks out every move, even from the bad dream in the middle of the night. And, God bless him, we get along far better now than we did when we parted company. We get along great now. He sent me a great big bunch of balloons for my birthday, which arrived in a truck. The message just said, "from Peter, with love."

The balloons arrived at the Los Angeles-area office of Steel Wallet Publishing, a small music publishing firm Waller launched in the early '90s with a business partner, longtime friend Georgiana "Georgie" Steele. Gordon first met Georgiana in April 1966, when she was working with the Gazzari Dancers, who appeared regularly on Dick Clark's television program *Where the Action Is*. The Steel Wallet name was inspired by a friend of Waller's, who long referred to Gordon as "Mr. Wallet" because he always seemed to have 20 pounds in currency with him, no matter what his financial state. "Mr. Wallet, this is your round," he'd tell Waller. Most of the songs that Steel Wallet published were written by acquaintances of Waller's.

Although all of the hits that Peter and Gordon went on to record from 1964 to 1967 were written by other composers, the duo did write several of their B-sides and album tracks. Gordon, who had no formal musical training, composed music on the piano, which he taught himself to play. Gordon continued to write songs into his 50s, even though he never learned to read or write music. "I don't actually write the notes, but I write down the chord changes," Waller told us in June 1997. "I find that with song writing, if you can't remember the bloody thing, it probably wasn't worth doing."

In 1997, Gordon composed music for *James Dean: Race With Destiny,* a motion picture about the later years of James Dean's life. The film starred Casper Van Dien as James Dean, with Robert Mitchum's granddaughter Carrie Mitchum (Van Dien's wife at the time) in a leading role. Robert Mitchum also appeared, along with Mike Connors and Connie Stevens. "There's quite a collection in the cast," said Waller. "A whole lot of old rags," he added smiling, "like me." To maintain authenticity, music for the film was recorded using techniques common in the 1950s. Waller packaged the motion picture music on a CD that the Swil Records label released.

Even though the publishing enterprise remained modest, Waller said that he never was at a loss for finding something to do. He had a knack for turning dabblings into dollars. He shaped model railroad construction, a pursuit he began as a hobby, into a marketable enterprise. He kept a workshop in the spare bedroom of a Southern California house. He converted the shower stall in an adjoining bathroom, equipped with an air compressor, into a paint spray booth. Soldering irons, drills, and the bits and pieces associated with metal fabrication clutter the sink area. He built an elaborate train layout, with impressively detailed structures, terrain, and scenery, in his two-car garage. Serious O-gauge train hobbyists, lacking the patience and mechanical skills that Waller developed, commissioned him to hand-build rolling stock for them. Although the locomotives and freight cars he built were derived from kits, he fashioned extensive modifications with exacting precision and historical accuracy.

"Wherever possible I use brass instead of plastic," said Waller. "It's a lot more solid and a lot easier to correct errors. If you make a mistake while you're soldering, you can just re-solder it back to shape. But if you make a mistake with plastic it melts away and so you have to make a new piece. It's time-consuming, but it's also very relaxing. And it requires an analytical approach in finding solutions to problems. I do like a challenge of that sort. I can sit here working for literally a whole day except for slipping out to get a cup of tea or going to the loo [toilet]. In England, I've got a huge rail layout."

Waller's love of model railroading was laden with sentimental value. "It was just a childhood thing that was re-kindled when my first daughter was 1 year old," said Gordon, speaking of Natalie, who was born in December 1976. "My father and mother asked, 'What are you going to give Natalie?' And I said, 'I'll give her an electric train set.' They thought that was very funny, but lo and behold, that is what Natalie got from my mother and father. She loved it. As she became older, she said, 'Let's go to the shops, Dad, and buy more.'"

Gordon's second daughter, Phillippa, was born in January 1980. Waller said he was grateful that his show business career had little effect upon the childhood experiences of his daughters. While he always was supportive of Natalie and Phillippa, he did not try to influence their ambitions the way his own father urged him to pursue a career in medicine. "I have no premeditated ambitions for them. I just hope that whatever they do, they're happy at it. If they're happy with life, that's half the battle. I haven't encouraged them to go into show business because I don't know enough about it to help them. I don't think anybody really does. Phillippa is the model type. So that's about as close to show business as she gets. She also has a great voice but she won't use it. She's embarrassed. I've said, 'Come on Phillippa, I was making my bloody living when I was your age singing.' She said, 'Yeah, but that was you, Dad, and I'm a girl.' Natalie [was] into hotel management. A nice steady job. One thing for sure, there will always be hotels. I did tell her, 'Make sure that whatever you do, it's something people will need. Get involved with cars, food, hotels, office equipment.' That's where the money is and always will be."

Waller's father died in 1981. His mother remained near London and the spark of vitality that she shared with Gordon still burned within her. For her 80th birthday party in September 1997, she declared that she wanted a swimming party. "She wanted to have all of her grandchildren splashing around," Gordon explained. "She was still a very good swimmer. If we went anywhere there's a pool, she would definitely get in. I had to stop her from jumping off my boat once."

Gordon Waller at his California home, working on his model train layout on August 23, 2001. Photo by Jeff March.

Waller, who was at once disarmingly honest, brutally self-critical, hopeful, and pragmatic, developed somewhat of an aversion to fame after the breakup of Peter and Gordon. "I like all the very basic things in life, which is probably why I didn't pursue the music career too damn seriously after Peter and I split up," he reasoned. "I really wanted to do what I never had a chance as a teenager to do. For example, I couldn't go down to a local pub and have a couple of pints, because I'd just get lynched. People would say, 'Are you looking at my girlfriend?' And I'd say, 'No, I'm not, I wouldn't bother.' And then they'd hit me because I didn't like their girlfriend."

As the turn of the millennium approached, Waller still had ambitions. "To survive. Just to have enough to be going along with. It would be nice if the James Dean soundtrack CD is picked up by a recording company and perhaps if someone wants to invest in my recording another album before it's too late. But if it doesn't happen, it doesn't happen," he said. And he meant just that. "I've got a friend who just finished recording a CD for which I've published all of the songs, and he's worried sick that he's not going to make it. I told him that's the wrong attitude. He shouldn't even think about making it or being successful. He should just think about making good records and enjoying it. If he should get a hit record and become successful, that would be a bonus. You can make a good living if you've got a good band even without any chart successes."

Although Waller tended to shun the spotlight in his latter years, he did occasionally perform when asked. "Whenever I sit in with a band, they say, 'You still have a fantastic voice and it's great that you're here.' I appreciate hearing that because in England, nobody gives a shit about Peter and Gordon, especially Gordon. There's no nostalgia like that. Over here [in America], it's quite embarrassing to me because I'm just a normal person and always have been, apart from the days when I obviously had to act a little bit differently. I'm just a bloke who can play guitar and sing. Having come over here [to America] in 1996 for the first time in 25 years, I find that I'm getting recognized." Stopping at a bar with a friend in San Diego shortly after his return to America, Gordon was invited to sit in in with the band. "We had a really good evening," he said. "That was good fun for me. I'm quite happy to keep it that way."

Gordon turned in one of his most stirring performances on August 15, 1998, when he sang at his own wedding. After the dissolution of his 22-year marriage to Gay, Gordon exchanged vows with his longtime friend and business partner, Georgiana Steele. As best man, Peter Asher once again stood by Gordon Waller's side during the casual backyard ceremony. Wedding guests included former Monkees member Micky Dolenz; Spencer Davis and his keyboardist, Jim Blazer; Billy Hinsche of Dino, Desi, and Billy; singer Chris Montez; former Byrds member John York; Tom MacLear, who played with the Faces and Rod Stewart; and singer-guitarist Terry Reid. Many of them, along with bassist and guitarist Don Adey, lead guitarist Dave Pearlman, and drummer Jovan Popovic, played long into the night.

The evening turned magical when Gordon coaxed the reserved Peter to the microphone. Together, hesitatingly at first, and then bolder, they began singing "A World Without Love." It was the first time they'd sung together in 29 years. Encouraged by the cheers of their guests, they resurrected their characteristic sweet harmonizing with a tender rendition of their 1965 hit "I Go to Pieces," and then mesmerized their guests and musical colleagues with an emotionally powerful performance of "Woman," during which Gordon gazed adoringly at his bride, Georgiana.

"Woman" is the song that for Waller epitomized Peter and Gordon. It's also the Peter and Gordon song of which Waller remained fondest.

Georgiana Steele and Gordon Waller moments before their wedding on August 15, 1998, at the home of Terry Holland and Kathy Holland (business manager of Peter and Gordon) in Simi Valley, California. Photo by Jeff March.

"You can sing it without any music, you can sing it with just one guitar, you can sing it with a band, or you can sing it with a bloody orchestra. I think it envelops a lot of our other songs from that period, which were basically all love songs."

Following the dissolution of his marriage to Georgie Steele, Gordon moved to Las Vegas, Nevada, then met Josenia (Jen) Couldrey, whom he married in March 2008. The couple moved to Connecticut but the duration of their marriage was tragically short. Gordon died of cardiac arrest at age 64 on July 17, 2009, at a hospital in Norwich, Connecticut, near his home in Ledyard. Gordon, who signed his email messages with the slogan "There is no world without love," left behind not only his wife, Jen, but also his two daughters, Natalie and Phillippa, and by his two sisters, Diana and Annie.

The Beau Brummels

Among American bands of the mid-'60s, the Beau Brummels stood apart not only for their melodic hit singles and critically acclaimed albums, but also for the musical trends they pioneered. No city made a more indelible impression on the music of the 1960s than San Francisco. While Jefferson Airplane, the Grateful Dead, We Five, Moby Grape, Quicksilver Messenger Service, Country Joe and the Fish, and other bands solidified the San Francisco sound, the Beau Brummels were responsible for first bringing national attention to the Bay Area music scene of that era.

Contrasting dramatically with many of the chirpy pop tunes of the day, the early releases by the Beau Brummels were rich in texture, with elaborate harmonies and complex arrangements. The Brummels, whose music contributed to the emergence of folk-rock and presaged the psychedelic music era, also were at the forefront at the close of the decade in plowing the country-rock field in which the Byrds, Bob Dylan, Linda Ronstadt, and the Eagles followed.

Consisting of vocalist Sal Valentino, composer-guitarist Ron Elliott, Irish-born singer-guitarist Declan Mulligan, bassist Ron Meagher, and drummer John Petersen, the Beau Brummels were a product of San Francisco's eclectic North Beach district. While playing in a bar called the Morocco Room at 2010 S. El Camino Real in San Mateo, on the peninsula 15 miles south of San Francisco, the Beau Brummels were discovered in 1964 by legendary KYA radio disc jockeys Tom Donahue and Bob Mitchell, partners in the fledgling Autumn Records label. Looking much like Orson Welles, the bearded Donahue had a voice like rolling thunder — booming, yet soothing. He had a finely tuned sense for musical talent, and he liked what he heard the first time he saw the Beau Brummels play.

Composer Ron Elliott was the architect of the musical repertoire of the Beau Brummels. Ron's love of light opera and show tunes undoubtedly contributed to the admiration he felt the first time he heard Sal Valentino sing. Like Ron, Sal lived with his family in an apartment

The Beau Brummels in 1965 — clockwise from left: Declan Mulligan, John Petersen, Ron Meagher, Sal Valentino, and Ron Elliott (in front). Photo by Dick Gilfether.

building in San Francisco's North Beach sector. Although Sal's junior
by two years, Ron attended the same parochial grade school and knew
that Sal would go to the basement of his building every day after school
to sing. "I remember the first time I heard him sing 'Summertime,' I
almost fell off my chair because he had a beautiful voice. He didn't have
control of it yet, so he would hit a note by sliding up to it. He would sing
'summertiiiiiiiiime' and he'd finally get up there," Elliott fondly recalled.
Ron and Sal, who had been singing with other groups, began singing
together. And Ron shared with Sal his theories about music. "When
Sal listened to advice from other people, he started sounding like Bob
Dylan," Elliott asserted. "But when he listened to me, he sang very well
because he has a wonderful voice."

Sal shared an affinity for country music with Ron, whom Sal met
when he was about 15. "Ron was the best guitar player I'd ever heard,
and even though he liked country music, too, he was already writing light
opera and musicals." The two began performing together at benefits for
the local boys' club and for the grammar school they had attended. With
Ron strumming and Sal singing, they began to perform at weddings,
dances, and other social events. "I just enjoyed singing. But Ron was
serious, probably the most serious of all of us. He wanted to do music,
and he was a gifted writer. And still is."

Although Ron attended St. Ignatius High School while Sal went
to Sacred Heart, they continued to hang out and perform together
periodically. During that time Ron remained consumed by his interest in
composing, and during his teenage years he wrote several unpublished
musical theater and light opera scores. He developed his compositions
on the guitar, and as he did he became increasingly proficient on the
instrument even though that was not his intention. "Everyone considered
me a guitar player, but I was a songwriter who happened to play guitar.
That's how I saw myself," said Elliott flatly. "I would have learned piano
if we had room for a piano, but you do with what you've got."

Ron was a student at San Francisco State College in the fall of
1963 when he, Sal, and drummer John Petersen had begun playing gigs
together informally. It was at one such performance that they met another
singer, Declan Mulligan, at an Irish Cultural Center dance. Sal, John, and
Ron had begun rehearsing with Dec Mulligan and a bass guitarist named
Ron Meeker. Although Meeker didn't fit well with the band, his ultimate
replacement was a guy with a nearly identical name: Ron Meagher.
Through the girl he was dating, Elliott was introduced to Meagher, who
had been a high school classmate of hers. "And that's how we put the
Brummels together," said Elliott.

Sal was uncertain which member of the quintet suggested the name. But it's likely the inspiration derived from the Beau Brummell Barber Shop in North Beach rather than from early 19th-century British gentleman George Bryan "Beau" Brummell, known for his dapper style of dress. "I didn't know who Beau Brummell was at that time, and I don't think the other guys did, either," Sal grinned.

The Brummels' first booking was at a North Beach joint called El Cid, where Sal had previously sung as a soloist. They played there until the club owner learned that Ron Elliott was underage. But word about the band had reached Rich Romanello, owner of the Morocco Room in suburban San Mateo, where the regulatory environment was more relaxed. Billed as the house band at the Morocco Room in the spring of 1964, the Brummels were booked to play each Thursday, Friday, and Saturday night, at $40 per night apiece. Acting as the band's self-appointed manager, Romanello persuaded a rep from Warner Brothers Records to audition the Brummels. They recorded four demo tracks, but the label declined to offer a contract.

Meanwhile, local KYA disc jockeys Tom Donahue (real name Thomas Francis Coman) and Bob Mitchell (Michael Guerra Jr.) had already become expert in scouting rock music talent. After getting their feet wet conducting record hops, they began staging larger shows in San Francisco's Cow Palace auditorium. They parlayed their profits from those shows into establishment of their own record label, Autumn, for which they enlisted Sylvester Stewart as producer. Born in Denton, Texas, Stewart grew up with his four siblings in the San Francisco Bay Area community of Vallejo, where his family formed a gospel group through their Pentecostal church. As a high school student he was in a couple of R&B bands, and then after attending Vallejo Junior College and the Chris Borden School of Modern Radio Technique in San Francisco he gained popularity as a disc jockey on two Bay Area soul music radio stations — first at KSOL San Francisco before moving to KDIA Oakland. With Stewart as producer, Autumn Records scored a hit with its second release, "C'mon and Swim" by Bobby Freeman, which climbed to No. 5 on the *Billboard* chart in the summer of 1964.

Then Donahue and Mitchell dropped into the Morocco Room. They'd been invited by Romanello and his girlfriend, a nude model named Judy who called herself Judette the Nudette. "She's now a preacher," grinned John Petersen. When Donahue and Mitchell appeared at the Morocco Room, they were far more serious than were the band members. "Those guys were players. But we were only 18 years old

The Beau Brummels in 1965. From left: Ron Meagher, Sal Valentino, Declan Mulligan, John Petersen, and Ron Elliott. Photo by Dick Gilfether.

and we didn't care. We were just having fun. It was the funniest scene I've ever seen in my life," said Petersen. "We're jamming away, playing good stuff and in walks this big guy wearing a trench coat. It was Tom Donahue, and with him were Bobby Mitchell, much smaller than Tom, and Carl Scott, who was about the same size as Donahue and later became an executive vice president at Warner Brothers. With them was Sly Stewart, who produced our first couple of albums. He also was working for Autumn Records for $80 per week."

Sandwiched between the imposing Donahue and Scott, Bobby Mitchell blurted out, "Look at these guys — Tweedledum and Tweedledee," referring to two corpulent characters from Lewis Carroll's book *Through the Looking-Glass, and What Alice Found There*. Petersen and Mitchell immediately got along well after they discovered a mutual interest in cars. "It was 1964 and the Mustang had just come out. So we signed a contract and never made one penny of royalties. Not one cent." He was referring to record sales percentages for the songs they had recorded with producer Sylvester Stone, primarily at Coast Recorders, 960 Bush Street in San Francisco.

Touring, however, was profitable for Petersen and the other band members. "After a concert tour, we would come home with our preapproved money as well as with gate receipts," Petersen explained. "In those days it probably cost $6 or $7 to get into a concert. We'd each get paid a briefcase full of $1 bills, because that's what the gate took in." Other funds were channeled to pay for the band's per diem expenses, including travel costs, overnight accommodations, and meals. "A lot of that money I never saw. But it sure was fun to get a load of $1 bills, and I bought my parents new furniture and a color TV. I bought myself a 1965 Pontiac Grand Prix. Two-door, hardtop, black leather, navy blue. Everyone bought a car but Sal. He didn't drive. He sort of just hitched a ride. That's Sal. He wasn't into possessions. He's very unpretentious."

Once the Brummels signed with Autumn, their transformation from house band obscurity to national pop stardom occurred with blurring speed. "Laugh, Laugh," their first recording released on Autumn Records, hit the *Billboard* Hot 100 on January 2, 1965 and peaked at No. 15. Ron Elliott wrote the song, which remained on the chart for 12 weeks and established the Beau Brummels at the vanguard of the emerging San Francisco rock music scene. Their follow-up release, "Just a Little," did even better. Ron Elliott and his frequent collaborator Robert Durand wrote the song, which made its debut on the *Billboard* chart on April 17, 1965, reached No. 8, and remained on the chart for 12 weeks.

Even before they had a chance to define themselves, they were propelled into the high-profile role of pop style-setters, viewed as one of the first legitimate American challenges to the British pop music Invasion. And if composer Ron Elliott was the musical architect of the project, Autumn recording session producer Sly Stone was the general contractor. "None of us had really wanted to grow up to be rock stars. I wasn't that kind of guy, and neither were the others. We were kind of quiet, and in the recording studio we tried to play and sing as perfectly as we could. Sly was a great help to us because he was loose. He was like a cheerleader who helped loosen us up and get our energy going."

Among the individuals contributing to the success of "Laugh, Laugh" was the late Sonny Bono, who as an independent record promotion man helped generate radio airplay for the record. The Brummels appeared on stage with Bono as he and Cher launched their own meteoric recording careers. "They appeared with us at the Cow Palace, dressed like prehistoric people. Sonny was a funny guy," Sal fondly recalled.

Donahue and Mitchell deliberately withheld putting the Brummels on tour until "Laugh, Laugh" was a solid national hit. And then they hit the road. "The first place we performed in concert was the Sacramento Memorial Auditorium. We were on the bill with Gary Lewis and the Playboys, who were on the charts with 'This Diamond Ring,' and we closed the show," recalled Sal. That was on Friday, January 22, 1965. The Memorial Auditorium became a favorite stop for the Brummels, who played there several more times with other groups, including the Beach Boys.

In May 1965 the Brummels made a triumphant return to the Bay Area, appearing in a KYA-sponsored concert with the Rolling Stones, the Byrds, Paul Revere and the Raiders, and the Vejtables at San Francisco Civic Auditorium. They played the Cow Palace in the San Francisco suburb of Daly City, the Whisky à Go-Go in Hollywood, and on a Murray the K bill at the Brooklyn Fox. Sal recalled, "We did a show at the Fox with the Lovin' Spoonful, Marvin Gaye, Martha and the Vandellas, Brenda Holloway, the Temptations, the Four Tops, Stevie Wonder, and Patti LaBelle, who opened the show. Patti LaBelle took the house down every day. Just killed 'em. And the girls went crazy for Marvin. We did all right, too." The Brummels made television appearances on *Where the Action Is* and *American Bandstand.* "Dick Clark was special. He either really remembered our names, or he always did his homework," said Sal. "He knew what we were doing, and it was always nice to appear on his show." The Brummels also appeared on *Hullabaloo, The Mike Douglas Show,* and *Shindig.*

Their third release, the Ron Elliott composition "You Tell Me Why," landed on the *Billboard* Hot 100 on July 24, 1965. The gently rocking ballad epitomized the San Francisco folk-rock style of the mid-'60s. Produced by Sylvester Stewart, the single reached No. 38 and remained on the chart for seven weeks. The popularity of the Brummels persuaded many radio stations to play the "B" sides of their records, including the rousing "Still in Love With You Baby." Other tracks that added to the band's popularity included "Ain't That Lovin' You Baby," "Sad Little Girl," and "Don't Talk to Strangers," the latter of which became the Brummels' fourth chart single. Ron Elliott wrote the song with Durand, who had been a high school buddy of his. The session, produced by Sylvester Stewart, was distinguished by rich harmonies and brilliant 12-string guitar runs. The single, which made its debut on October 9, 1965, rose to No. 52 and remained on the chart for eight weeks.

But touring also aggravated tensions within the band, leading to the departure of Dec Mulligan by the fall of 1965. With Ron Elliott unable to withstand the rigors of the road, guitarist Don Irving substituted, leaving only three original members on tour. The Brummels turned to a John Sebastian composition, "Good Time Music," for their fifth chart single. The pulsating track had a raucous, garage-band attitude that contrasted strongly with the band's signature folk-rock sound. Autumn Records co-owner Bob Mitchell produced the recording, which appeared on the *Billboard* Hot 100 for only one week, at No. 97, beginning December 25, 1965.

The Brummels excelled in the studio, releasing two fine albums on Autumn — *Introducing the Beau Brummels* in April 1965 and *The Beau Brummels Volume 2* in August '65. They recorded a third, but before its release the financially struggling Autumn Records label shuttered its doors and sold the band's contract to Warner Brothers Records in 1966 along with the Mojo Men, the Vejtables, and the Tikis, who subsequently found success under the name Harpers Bizarre. At about that time, Irving was drafted into the U.S. Army. The Brummels' first Warner Bros. single release was their interpretation of Bob Dylan's "One Too Many Mornings." After making its debut on the *Billboard* Hot 100 on June 4, 1966, it turned out to be the final chart single for the band. The track was credited to Autumn Productions; Lenny Waronker produced the song, which remained on the chart for three weeks but rose no higher than No. 95.

Since the Warner deal did not include master tapes, the Los Angeles-based label immediately sent the band into the studio — to record *Beau Brummels 66,* a largely unappreciated album of "cover" songs with which other bands had previously scored hits. Label executives came to their senses in 1967, when the remaining three members of the band — Ron Elliott, Sal Valentino, and Ron Meagher — recorded *Triangle,* a new album of original material. The Brummels' last album for Warner Brothers, *Bradley's Barn,* fused modern country and rock, which had grown far apart since the "rockabilly" style at the roots of pop music. Over the ensuing six years Warner Bros. tried to perpetuate the band's success, releasing six more singles: "Here We Are Again," "Two Days 'Til Tomorrow," "Lower Level," "Lift Me," "Long Walking Down to Misery," and "Cherokee Girl," but none of those made the charts. After its subsequent breakup in 1968, the band reassembled to record *The Beau Brummels,* a reunion album in 1975. But the original chemistry that ignited the Brummels in 1964 had become inert. And the band's final Warner Bros. single, a re-recorded version of their 1965 tune "You Tell Me Why," did not reach the charts.

As they went their separate ways to pursue new careers, Ron Elliott, Sal Valentino, John Petersen, Ron Meagher, and Declan Mulligan left behind a timeless body of work profuse in lyrical substance, technical virtuosity, and artistic depth.

Autumn Records co-owner Michael Guerra Jr. (aka Bobby Mitchell and Bobby Tripp) died of Hodgkin lymphoma at 48 years of age on July 19, 1968. His business partner Thomas Coman (aka Tom Donahue) died of a heart attack at age 46 on April 28, 1975. Sylvester Stewart, better known as Sly Stone and leader of the prolific R&B funk group Sly and the Family Stone, died at age 82 on June 9, 2025, in his home in the Los Angeles neighborhood of Granada Hills. His death was attributed to long-term chronic obstructive pulmonary disease (COPD) and other underlying health problems.

In 2000 the DIG Music label issued the band's only on-stage recording, *Beau Brummels Live!* The 19-track album, produced by Dennis Newhall, captured the original five-piece band in a performance at the Shire Road Pub, an intimate venue in the Sacramento suburb of Fair Oaks. Ron Elliott contributed to the album's graphic design work. Bay Sound Records released an 18-track Brummels album titled *Continuum* in 2013. Music archivist Alec Palao compiled and mastered a collector's dream: an eight-CD, Beau Brummels box set titled *Turn Around: The Complete Recordings 1964–1970,* which the Now Sounds label released in November 2021. The 228 tracks in the set encompass the entire Autumn and Warner Bros. catalogs of the Beau Brummels.

THE BEAU BRUMMELS

U.S. HIT SINGLES ON THE NATIONAL CHARTS

Debut	Peak	Title	Label
1/2/65	15	Laugh, Laugh / Still in Love With You Baby	Autumn
4/17/65	8	Just a Little	Autumn
7/24/65	38	You Tell Me Why	Autumn
10/9/65	52	Don't Talk to Strangers	Autumn
12/25/65	97	Good Time Music	Autumn
6/4/66	95	One Too Many Mornings	Warner Brothers

Billboard's pop singles chart data is courtesy of Joel Whitburn's Record Research Inc., Menomonee Falls, Wisconsin.

Epilogue: Ron Elliott

Singer, guitarist, and composer

Ron Elliott became an artist because he had to be. He created not with the intention of selling his work, but because the art was inside him and he was the instrument to release it. If someone happened to like what he did, he found that rewarding. But Ron Elliott would have created his art even if it meant nothing to anyone else, for it meant everything to him.

Ron Elliott in the 1990s. Photo by Expressly Portraits.

The onetime composer, guitarist, and architect of the Beau Brummels evolved into a graphic artist working in acrylics, photography, and computer imaging, Elliott considered himself an artist ever since a vision came to him at age 10. "That's when the music just started coming out of me. I had to write it, and I learned how to play guitar just so I could get my melodies out. Right then I knew I was an artist and would remain an artist for the rest of my life, no matter what. And that's what I've done," Elliott said.

"I've gone from music to a few years of painting to graphic arts. I haven't thrived but I haven't starved either. I'm one of the wealthiest people I know because I've done only what I was supposed to do, and I'm really happy. I don't regret being unable to write music anymore. When the music was in me, that's what I did. Strangely enough, when I was 10 years old, I saw a vision of what my life was going to be like. I knew I'd have a taste of success at a young age. And I knew that in the long run, in the end, if I pursued this self-premonition, I'd be recognized maybe even after my death."

Wearing a tan canvas photographer's vest and trademark wide-brimmed fedora, a likeness of which graced his business card, Ron Elliott spoke softly, deliberately, carefully composing each thought before the words left his lips. At his side was a thick travel case that contained the two greatest compelling forces in his life: his portfolio of magnificent florals and landscape art, and the equipment and medications necessary to monitor and control his diabetes. Seated in one of his favorite restaurants on Clement Street in San Francisco on a mild September day in 1997, he savored the anonymity that he was denied during his years as a reluctant pop star.

The only child of Charles and Lola Elliott, Ron was born October 21, 1944, and spent the first five years of his life on his family's ranch 70 miles north of San Francisco, in the rural Sonoma County town of Healdsburg, California. But two years of devastating drought in the Russian River country crumbled Charles and Lola's finances, and they moved to San Francisco in search of employment to pay off their debts. Charles learned steam engineering in the merchant marine, found employment with the PG&E (Pacific Gas and Electric) utility company, and ultimately erased all his debts.

Charles, who played drums, and Lola, who played accordion, contributed in large degree to Ron's interest in music. For their own enjoyment, they'd play popular songs of the day with a saxophonist or clarinetist. Ron's earliest musical awareness dates to his early childhood, when his parents listened to records by Lefty Frizzell and other popular country music performers of that era.

Ron's premonition about his life of artistry preceded by two years the diagnosis of his diabetic condition. During a protracted bout with the flu at age 12, he began losing weight. "I went from 120 pounds to 90 pounds within two weeks," he said. Realizing that Ron had been in bed for two weeks without taking a bath, Charles went into Ron's room. "When he took my pajama top off, he gasped at how much weight I had lost, even though I had been scarfing up food. The morning I went to the hospital, I ate six eggs, six pieces of bacon and six pieces of toast. My parents were thinking, 'He's going to be a monster.' And there I was, shrinking away. The fact that I had the premonition before I got diabetes was the only thing that kept me focused."

Ron had become an instrument for the creative forces he felt within himself. "Diabetes attacks the nervous system, attacks sensitivity, and although I did not know it then, musical time was running out and creativity would eventually fade. At the start, however, the music was just pouring out. I had to write," said Ron, who shunned pop music in favor of the theatrical stylings of Jerome Kern, Irving Berlin, Rodgers and Hammerstein, Rodgers and Hart, and Cole Porter. "I probably would have had more success had I gone to New York and gone into theater, because I was more of a composer than a song writer."

Elliott was characteristically blunt in his description of the music he wrote for the Beau Brummels. "It was simple, unsophisticated music, lots of steps backward from the music I had been composing. 'Laugh, Laugh' has a very complex chord structure, but instead of using the major seventh chords and the passing chords that I prefer, I wrote the song in flat major and minor keys using a simplified tonal structure. But you have to remember, I was coming from a theatrical rather than from a rock and roll perspective. That was all new to me and I never really did figure it all out."

For Elliott, the role of pop music raconteur was an arduous task. "I felt under pressure from beginning to end to produce and keep it together. I worked three hours before we got together for a rehearsal or recording session, I was working the whole time we were together, and I worked three hours afterward organizing, writing chord charts, and figuring out lyrics." Elliott, who said lyrics were his curse, often collaborated with Bob Durand, a high school buddy of his who had a way with words.

Performance was an even greater source of unease for Elliott, a self-professed introvert who felt uncomfortable in the presence of more than two people. He required several hours of mental preparation before each stage performance, after which he was emotionally drained for the remainder of the day. "I was never good at performing because I had no relationship with the crowd. I was always testing myself, wondering, 'Am I OK? What's the next song?' When things went wrong, I always had a prepared solution, so I was inner-directed the whole time. I approached music like a playwright. I didn't have to learn the lines. I knew the lines. I knew the harmonies. I had no real communication abilities, but not because I resented the audience," Elliott explained. "It was a matter of self-preservation, the result of the combination of my personality and my health condition. And that's what I had to do to survive those ordeals."

The rigors of the road proved too great for Ron. He was unable to continue touring, which compromised his health and strength, as he tried without success to maintain his strict medication and dietary regimen. "In those days people with diabetes had no glucometers to test blood sugar. It was all guesswork. That was the biggest obstacle that I ever had to face," Elliott said.

Even so, the dissolution of the band in 1968 proved nearly as challenging. "When Tom Donahue sold the band to Warner Brothers, he sold our tapes to someone else, and he sold the publishing elsewhere. So he figuratively cut off our heads," Elliott asserted. "When Warner Brothers discovered what they didn't have, that marked the demise of the Beau Brummels. We became a tax write-off for them."

At that point, in 1968, Elliott called upon a skill that he had regarded only as incidental: guitar playing. He became a studio musician in Los Angeles, where he was in high demand through the '70s and well into the '80s. He was a rehearsal guitarist for Barbra Streisand, worked recording sessions for Dolly Parton, Little Feat, the Everly Brothers, Van Dyke Parks, and Van Morrison, and performed on seven Randy Newman albums. He produced the melodious *Living in the Country* album by Dan Levitt and Marc McClure in 1969 for Warner Brothers, and an album by a group called Joyous Noise in 1971 for Capitol Records. Elliott also recorded a 1969 solo album of his own called *The Candlestickmaker* for Warner Brothers. "It wasn't 'get your girlfriend in bed' music. It was a suite, a picture of a person in crisis." Despite Elliott's high aspirations for the album, it received little promotion and consequently was accorded little notice.

Disillusioned, he returned to the Bay Area, where he resumed playing weekend gigs with Dec Mulligan. Something was different, but he couldn't quite put his finger on it. He knew what it was by the time he turned 50. The music had faded away. "It just wasn't there anymore," said Ron, who set his guitar on its stand in 1994 and let it remain there. "I walk past it 10 times a day, and I don't even look at it. It never even occurs to me." Elliott hardly even listened to music anymore. "I listen to sports and have very little desire to hear music. When I do listen to music, it's short bits of opera, American theater or movies from the '30s produced by MGM. I love that stuff. I wish that we could again make entertainment programs that give people hope and laughter instead of despair."

When the music died Ron's art was born. He began working in acrylics in 1994, painting interpretations of floral and landscape photographs, such as those he took in nearby Golden Gate Park. By scanning his paintings and manipulating them with image-editing software on his Macintosh computer, he created hauntingly beautiful impressionistic artworks, composed in delicately hued pointillistic patterns.

Ron Elliott in the summer of 2024.
Photo by Ron Meagher.

Elliott learned to paint the same way he learned to compose music and play guitar: by teaching himself. A voracious reader, Ron learned what he needed to know about artistic techniques from books. "The main lesson you learn in school is how to learn," he observed. He studied the techniques of other artists and adapted them to the moods he wanted to convey. "Those paintings are my songs," he said. They also were his progeny. Married briefly to the young woman who introduced him to Ron Meagher, then married to another woman in the 1970s, the twice-divorced Elliott has no children. Following the passing of his parents, he moved to San Mateo, near the home of his former bandmate Ron Meagher.

Even after completing well over 100 paintings and illustrations, Elliott has not exhibited his artwork. "I'm an extreme introvert, and consequently I don't talk to many people. I need to make some contacts," he admits. "But in the art world, I know no one."

Unlike the other band members, Elliott continued to derive some income from the Beau Brummels as composer of their songs. "The Brummels didn't make squat. But I wrote the material and that's what makes money. I'll make a penny here and a penny there and by the end of the year, I have a few pennies," he allowed.

Elliott believed his life would have taken a dramatically different course if not for his diabetes. "But having it isn't that bad. As long as you watch your stuff — watch the clock, watch your diet, watch the dosages and live a relatively boring life, you're fine." The greatest limitation it imposes, he said, is time. "I have to watch my insulin doses and my blood sugar. That's much easier now than it used to be, when it was all guesswork. Still, when you're young and your blood sugar drops, you can sense it. Now, at my age, I don't have a clue. I don't know if it's low or high. That's because of the damage that diabetes does to the nervous system. That's why I have to rely on a glucometer to measure my blood sugar level."

Elliott's characteristic pragmatism was induced to large degree by management of his diabetes. "I've sold a few paintings but not because I was trying to sell them. I just try to create artwork that is very harmonious. Like a good scheduled diabetic lives his life. That's the kind of artwork I want to do," he explained.

After spending the first three decades of his life manipulated by the sounds in his head, Ron Elliott enjoyed the silence. At last he had the opportunity to fulfill what he regarded as his destiny, saying, "I continually explore the art I was born to create."

Epilogue: Sal Valentino

Lead singer

Sal Valentino in 1998. Photo by Amanda Domingues.

Having Sal Valentino escort you around San Francisco in the mid-1960s would have been like touring Boston with James Taylor. Or comparable to strolling the streets of Liverpool with Ringo Starr. Like Beau Brummels composer-guitarist Ron Elliott, Sal Valentino grew up in San Francisco — along with his two younger sisters — in the colorful Italian-flavored North Beach neighborhood. Born Salvatore Spampinato on September 8, 1942, he enjoyed singing from the time he was a young child, although he never thought of it as a career. Sal — whose father had been a Golden Gloves amateur boxer and worked professionally as a boxing trainer, ringside "cutman" treating injuries, and *Daily Racing Form* agent for Northern California horse racing tracks — tried his hand at a variety of laborious jobs. Sal worked in drayage, he unloaded boxcars, he drove trucks, he was a warehouse laborer, he took bets as a racetrack cashier. But his parents always supported his interest in music. Sal's father, in fact, suggested Sal's adoption of the name Valentino, in honor of heavyweight boxer Pat Valentino.

As Sal entered his teenage years, his parents paid for lessons from a voice teacher. Sal learned to sing standards — "Don't Blame Me" (which premiered in 1932) and "It Had to Be You" (from 1924). Sal received a lot of support from his mother, who worked for most of her life at a San Francisco credit union, as well as from his father, whose own youthful musical ambitions had been discouraged. "My father played saxophone when he was young, but he didn't play long," said Sal. "His father, who was a fisherman, used to complain. He'd say, 'I go out, I hear the foghorns out there. Then I come home, I hear the foghorns here, too.' So I guess my father got discouraged. He didn't tell me about that until I was almost 20."

Like his father, Sal took up baseball. A lefty, Sal played first base until high school, when he made the school's football team as a receiver. His play earned him a spot on the All-City team and scholarship offers from the University of Utah, Oregon State, and the College of the Pacific, but Sal decided he didn't want to play football. He wanted to sing. Working solo and pairing with other musicians, Sal started working gigs in the neighborhood — weddings, dances, and clubs with names like Bimbo's, La Rocca's Corner and El Cid. He first called himself Sal Valentino in 1961 at age 19, when he cut a record called "I Wanna Twist" for a couple of local guys. Released on the Falco label, the record earned Valentino several appearances on *KPIX Dance Party* with host Dick Stewart, which aired on TV channel 5 in San Francisco.

His success with the Beau Brummels, then, was no surprise to those who had followed his rising star in the San Francisco Bay area. But the sale of the Beau Brummels' contract to Los Angeles-based Warner Brothers in 1966 took Sal as well as his Bay Area fans by surprise. Working with Warner Brothers producer Lenny Waronker, the band recorded two albums, *Triangle* and *Bradley's Barn,* which were artistic achievements but received little supportive airplay. "They were the most highly acclaimed records we ever did, but *Triangle* came out just before the Beatles' *Sgt. Pepper* was released, and once that hit the air, nobody heard anything else." The Brummels went to Nashville to record *Bradley's Barn,* an acoustic album in which Valentino and Elliott reached back to their country roots. Despite the artistic integrity of *Triangle* and *Bradley's Barn,* the Brummels were lacking something they had when they recorded their debut album. "We had timing the first time. We didn't have that again." By 1968, the band ceased to exist.

After Warner Bros. brought Valentino into the studio to record some tracks produced by Waronker and Van Dyke Parks, he turned to background singing on an album for Screamin' Jay Hawkins. Sal also worked on Ron Elliott's *The Candlestickmaker* album and he discovered Rickie Lee Jones for Warner Brothers. "I took her to Lenny, and he loved her demo tape," said Sal. "I wanted to get an A&R [artists and repertoire] job out of it, but I didn't," he told us in June 1997.

Meanwhile, Tom Donahue had returned to radio after the sale of Autumn Records, of which he was co-owner. He devised a format that was the antithesis of frenetic, jingle-punctuated, singles-dominated Top 40 radio. His freeform approach transformed little-known San Francisco FM station KMPX into the nation's first "underground radio" outlet, emphasizing long album cuts and a low-key delivery. Duplicated in Southern California at Pasadena's KPPC, as well as stations in New York, Chicago, Detroit, Boston, and other markets, the format metamorphosed into "progressive rock," the precursor of the "album rock" format.

By 1971, Donahue turned his attention to another project. By then, Warner Bros. had cut Sal loose. "Tom Donahue came to rescue me. In fact, with only one exception, Tom got me all the record deals I've ever had," said Sal. Donahue had become involved with production of a rock music motion picture called *Medicine Ball Caravan,* the acts in which included a power trio called Stoneground. Promotion plans called for a five-week national concert tour to launch the motion picture. Donahue added Sal and three female backup singers to strengthen Stoneground's stage presentation. "We did three concerts — in Taos, New Mexico, Boulder, Colorado, and Winnebago, Nebraska, along the way to a final performance at the Lincoln Memorial in Washington, D.C. By the time we got to D.C., Warner Brothers signed us, and that's how we became a recording act."

Donahue produced Stoneground's first album, with Sal assisting on some tracks. Released on GRT Records, the album included several compositions by Ron Elliott, who became increasingly involved in writing for the band. In 1971 Stoneground headlined at Sacramento Memorial Auditorium, locale of numerous Beau Brummels triumphs. Sal sang, played guitar and produced cuts not only on Stoneground's self-titled debut album in 1971, but also on the follow-up *Family Album* the following year, and on *Stoneground Three* in 1973. Upon completion of the Stoneground Three album Valentino left the band, resurfacing two years later in Southern California with Elliott, Mulligan, Meagher and Petersen in a Beau Brummels reunion. The band recorded an album titled simply *The Beau Brummels*, but it lacked the spark of their previous efforts. Within a year, the band members parted for the last time. In San Francisco, Tom Donahue died of a heart attack on April 28, 1975, at the age of 46.

The reunion was a sad counterpoint to the glory days of 1965. Valentino thought the band was misunderstood — in 1975 as well as in 1965. "'Laugh, Laugh' is listed as one of the 500 most influential songs in the Rock and Roll Hall of Fame, but I never thought we were a rock and roll band. You know, 'Laugh, Laugh' is not like a Chuck Berry or Fats Domino or Little Richard tune. Its chord structures are based in the musicals that Elliott was writing. In '75 he wrote some real nice songs for us. We just didn't have a market anymore."

The Brummels reunion soured Sal. "I found out too much about the music business then. It broke my desire to make any more records for anybody," he said. "And then my father was diagnosed with cancer." Sal returned to Northern California, to be closer to his family. And to find work. As a teenager, he'd worked as a laborer. He could always do that again. "I've had other jobs outside of music. I didn't know what I was going to do, but I knew I didn't want to wind up singing in bars," he said. He worked a succession of jobs, unloading freight, driving forklifts, stocking warehouse shelves. Ultimately, Sal heeded the call of his father, who by then had regained his health and was working as the agent for the *Racing Form* at Northern California horseracing tracks. "I never was much interested in that, but I didn't have anything else to do at the time. So he put me to work as a parimutuel clerk at racetracks."

For the next decade, Sal's stage was a teller window, where he took bets and cashed winning tickets. Sal was working at a betting window in the Southern California coastal town of Ventura in 1993 when he bent down to pick up a $20 bill. A paralyzing pain seized his

Marti Smiley Childs, Sal Valentino, and Jeff March during a book signing event for *Where Have All the Pop Stars Gone? Volume 3* at the now-defunct Sacramento Rock and Radio Museum on Saturday, October 8, 2016, when it was at 911 20th Street in Sacramento, California. Photo by Ken Shuper.

back, and he was unable to move. Sal was forced to go out on disability with a herniated disc in his lower spine. Sal once again was the victim of circumstances beyond his control. For the first time in 15 years, he thought about resurrecting his singing career. He considered singing jingles for commercials. "I was getting tired of the voices I was hearing on commercials, with the exception of Bob Seger," he said. Still living in Los Angeles, he began practicing, using his tape recorder at home, but was unsuccessful in landing any assignments.

While the advertising agencies didn't call him, a member of a band in Reno did in early 1994. The caller had named his band the Beau Brummels, and he hoped to include at least one member of the original Brummels. Sal agreed, but didn't move to Reno, instead relocating 120 miles away in Sacramento because of friends and fond memories there.

The first time Sal Valentino appeared in Sacramento, in early 1965, he and the Beau Brummels were welcomed by thousands of screaming, adoring fans. When he returned to the Northern California city in 1994, he came quietly and unnoticed. After years of living in Southern California, the San Francisco native rented a small apartment in Sacramento, 11 blocks from the auditorium in which the Brummels had played their first concert. The apartment, at 27th and J, was owned by a friend of his who also owned Harlow's restaurant and nightclub, on the ground floor of the building. In that nightclub, a friend introduced him to Catherine Kopinski, a school teacher who had moved recently from Michigan. Sal and Catherine developed a friendship, began dating, and in March 1995 began a marriage that lasted until their divorce nearly two decades later.

Valentino performed in the mid 1990s with the Reno Brummels for about a year, until concert producer Donnie Brooks called. Brooks, a singer who hit the top 10 with "Mission Bell" and "Doll House" in 1960, packaged oldies shows on which he also performed. Sal did shows for Donnie in 1995 and 1996, resurrecting "Laugh, Laugh" and "Just a Little" for appreciative fans and starring for three months in "Juke Box Giants," a Brooks-produced review at the Flamingo Hotel in Laughlin, Nevada's newest gaming and entertainment town.

Gradually, Sal became interested in performing new material. He readily credited Ron Elliott as a pivotal musical influence in his life. "I'm fortunate I had Ron writing songs for me. That made a big difference. I didn't fully realize that until after I worked with others," he said. With that realization, he began gaining new confidence in himself, sufficient to resume songwriting and record three solo albums. The first was *Dreamin' Man*, for which fellow Stoneground band member John Blakeley collaborated with him in songwriting and recording for release by Global Recording Artists in 2005. That was followed by the bluesy folk-rock album *Come Out Tonight*, recorded in Austin, Texas, and released by Fat Pete Records in 2006. The third was *Every Now and Then*, his seasoned take on six decades of living (including a reprise of the Brummels' "Laugh, Laugh") on the Dig Music label in 2007.

In his personal life, however, he didn't remain solo. After meeting Roberta Landis in 2017, he married her and the couple settled in Folsom, in eastern Sacramento County.

Sal said regardless of any additional recording or performing he may do, he'll always remain proud that he was able to carve a place in musical history. "I could have done a lot worse if I weren't lucky."

Epilogue: Declan Mulligan

Singer and guitarist

April 8, 1938 – November 2, 2021

When turntable tone arms lowered onto the first Beau Brummels record in 1965, the first sound that emerged from the vinyl was Declan Mulligan's melancholy harmonica. Wailing like a lonesome train whistle across the prairie, Dec's playing set the somber tone for "Laugh, Laugh," the song that sent the San Francisco quintet to the top of the charts.

Declan Mulligan in the 1990s. Photo by Tanya G. Mulligan.

Pop music stardom was an unanticipated dalliance in the life of Dec Mulligan, who had come to San Francisco three years before to learn the insurance trade in expectation of an eventual return to his native Ireland. But for most of his life he remained in San Francisco, where he continued to perform music for decades after the breakup of the Brummels.

Contradicting record label biographies and liner notes that made him appear two years younger, Dec freely admitted that he was born April 8, 1938, as John Declan Mulligan. As a teenager in the town of Clonmel, County Tipperary, Ireland, in the 1950s, Dec was exposed to a lot of music. Although television wasn't available in the hilly, wooded Fethard region where he lived and BBC radio was out of range, he was able to receive Radio Luxembourg, which on Sunday nights relayed the U.S. Armed Forces Network's broadcast of the top 20 tunes. "It was a thrill to hear American accents. That's where I heard a lot of the early rock and roll, songs by the Everly Brothers, Fats Domino, and Elvis Presley," said Mulligan.

"My uncle, Dick Gough, lived in the United States and he would come to visit every now and then. One visit coincided with the release of Elvis' first movie, *Love Me Tender,* and my uncle brought two Elvis records — *That's All Right,* and *Mystery Train.* He brought me a guitar, but nobody in the town played guitar, and I didn't even know how to tune it. I saw somewhere that you tune it E-B-G-D-A-E, but our piano at home was out of tune and didn't sound right, so I went into the convent where the nuns teach music and I tuned it there." Painstakingly, Dec taught himself to play guitar.

Because Dec's father, William, made a comfortable living as a divisional manager for a large insurance company, he was able to send Dec to boarding schools for the last three years of his high school education. "Although my father didn't attend college, he was a very refined man and articulated like someone with a college degree. My mother, whose name was Mary, was well educated," Dec said lovingly.

As a student, Dec began to play with local skiffle bands and learned to play many of the American songs that were popular at the time. "Every hit that was a hit in America was copied by a British artist," recalled Dec. "For example, Tommy Steele copied Guy Mitchell's 'Singing the Blues.' Frankie Vaughan looked a bit like a young Tony Franciosa and he sang Jim Lowe's 'Green Door.' Cliff Richard was an English version of Elvis Presley." When Dec enrolled at University College Dublin, to study business administration, he began playing in "show bands," which typically had acoustic bass, drums, guitar, piano, trumpet, trombone, and saxophone players.

"I was on guitar, and I was feeble because I was playing rhythm and also trying to play some of the leads. Ireland had a lot of natural talent but musical education was very much according to the nuns. Wind instruments and piano dominated the musical scene, not the guitars. You learned to play an E flat, an F, C sharp, B flat, and if you went into a band and someone asked, 'What key do you play this in?' and you say, 'I do it in A,' you could feel the vibes in the horn section — like get out of town right now. They didn't want to play in E or A or G — which are good-sounding keys for guitar. So most of the time I ended up in conflict with these guys. I'd sing a song in F or I'd play a song in B-flat and kill myself trying to play these bar chords on the guitar — with bad action, also, I recall. My fingers would be throbbing by the end of the night."

At that time, Mulligan didn't regard music as a potential career. His ambition was simply to travel to the United States. After completing college in 1960, Dec made it across the Atlantic and stopped in Toronto, Canada — where he stayed for two years after landing an underwriter's job with the Fireman's Fund Insurance Co. Several years from retirement, his father planned to open an insurance office of his own in Clonmel, and Dec intended to learn the general insurance business to supplement his father's concentration on life insurance. In the summer of 1962 Dec transferred to the San Francisco office of Fireman's Fund, fulfilling his dream to journey to the United States. The following year, at an Irish dance at Richmond Hall, an auditorium at 309 Fourth Avenue at Clement Street in San Francisco, he met three other young men who would change the course of his life: Ron Elliott, Sal Valentino, and John Petersen.

Tanya and Dec Mulligan in 2005. Photo by Scott Shea.

Dec was faced with a decision: choose between music and his insurance job. "Thinking about living a life as a musician was scary, even though I loved music. Coming from a strict Catholic background, as I did in Ireland, the guilt trip began working on me," Dec told us in September 1997. But the lure of music was too strong and the pull of the stage lights was mesmerizing. And, after all, the Beau Brummels did work steadily during their extended stay as the house band in the Morocco Room in San Mateo. Dec remembered one unforgettable Wednesday night at the Morocco Room.

"Rich Romanello, who owned the Morocco Room, had an attractive girlfriend named Judy. She did some modeling under the name 'Judette the Nudette.' She had told us that she wanted to help us. On this particular night," Dec recalled, "she walked in, accompanied by a big imposing figure and a black man. Heads turned. The big man was Tom Donahue of Autumn Records and with him was Sly Stone, his producer. Tom Donahue was a very handsome man, bearded, probably about 6 foot 2, weighed about 275, and when he spoke he had a commanding presence. He asked us to come to Coast Recorders on Bush Street that Friday. And that was the start of it. Tom liked the sound of Sal's voice and Sal looked good. Then he and Bob Mitchell began to talk about us on the radio. When Ron picked me up to drive to the Morocco Room, he said, 'Muggins' — that's what he called me — he said, 'Look at all of the people!' They were lined up around the block to see us, because of the power of radio. That's how the Beau Brummels were created, by Tom Donahue and Bob Mitchell."

During his time with the Brummels, Dec met another person who would later become very important in his life. Her name was Tanya Goodhill. Only 16 at the time, she was a reporter for her high school newspaper and she wrote stories about celebrities. After interviewing Sean Connery at the Fairmont hotel in San Francisco, she was assigned to do a story on the Beau Brummels while they were performing at a nightclub in the bohemian, avant-garde North Beach neighborhood. Her parents wouldn't let her go there alone, so her British-born mother and her brother accompanied her. "When Declan heard my mother's English accent, he began talking to her, and my mother wound up inviting him to enjoy a home-cooked meal at our home," Tanya recalled. Dec took a fancy to Tanya, and began taking her out on dates. "My parents weren't happy with that because of the age difference. Dec was almost 11 years older than I was," she explained.

"I dated her for a little while but then I went away to Los Angeles, she went away to school and we thought that was the end of it," said Dec. That seemed all the more so after Tanya met and wound up marrying another man, with whom she had four children.

Life on the road with the Brummels didn't sit well with Dec. Tensions that arose contributed to abbreviation of his tenure with the band. "I was unhappy on the road. But my departure was partly my fault," Mulligan admitted. "I thought things would come easier than they did. I thought if I had talent, I didn't have to work at it. I realized later that even though you may have talent, you've got to work at it." That realization came too late for the Brummels. "When we came back off the road in the summer of '65, Donahue called me and said, 'Hey, the boys don't want to play with you anymore.' In every band some personalities don't fit," Mulligan philosophized. "I've since learned that no matter how good you think you are, there's always someone out there better than you."

Dec took little time to form his own band called Mulligan Stew, which for three years was the house band at the Carousel Ballroom, a dance hall above the Les Vogel Chevrolet dealership at 10 S. Van Ness Avenue at Market Street— which was later to become Bill Graham's Fillmore West. Looking for something new, Dec began assembling another group called the Black Velvet Band, just as the Beau Brummels were in the process of dissolving. Ron Meager reunited with Dec in the Black Velvet Band, along with lead guitarist Fuzzy Dean and drummer Don Abbott. "The Black Velvet Band was one of the hottest club bands in San Francisco in that era," declared Mulligan. He and Meagher remained with the Black Velvet Band until the ill-fated Beau Brummels reunion in 1975.

The reunion of the Brummels seemed like a good idea at the time because each of the original members had enriched their musical experiences during their time apart. But the band's resurrection germinated the seeds of dormant animosity, which resurfaced during the earliest rehearsals. Dec envisioned a larger role for himself in singing and songwriting. His suggestion to include a couple of original songs from the Black Velvet repertoire was rebuffed and Mulligan became agitated. "Muggins, calm down, calm down," urged Ron Meagher. "Let's just go along with it. Don't worry about it. Let's just do the other songs. You blew it before when you left the band and everything went haywire. We might make some money this time." Four months after the band members signed their new contract, Mulligan recalled, Ron Meager was dismissed. The others managed to remain together for another year before parting for the last time.

Dec Mulligan at home in April 2009 with his golden retriever, Bailey. Photo by Tanya Mulligan.

"It became boring for me to play with the Beau Brummels in 1975 and revert to the old songs," said Dec. "By comparison, the Black Velvet Band had matured so much as a band. We were playing anything and everything." Unfortunately, they played too few self-penned compositions. "We probably could have signed with a label if we had more original material. The door opens only once and if you're not ready to walk in, it slams in your face. Then I got to be a smart ass on top of that. This was a period when bands were receiving large advances to sign. When a guy from Capitol told us, 'I really like you guys. You should be signed up,' I asked him, 'Where's the brown case?' He looked at me with a puzzled expression on his face and asked, 'What case?' I said, 'The case with all of the money in it that all the other bands are getting. Where is it? I don't see it.' As he turned and walked away, the Capitol rep hissed, 'Who's that smart-ass Irish guy?' I've kicked myself many times after that for not doing a little brown-nosing."

Although not as volatile as he once was, Dec was still driven by restless energy into his 50s and beyond. In the years since the second breakup of the Brummels, he worked in the San Francisco Department of Public Works and held a managerial position with the golf course at the Presidio. He also devoted much of his time to his son, Sean, who was born in 1980. Sean lived with Dec between the ages of 3 and 14 after Dec's relationship with Sean's mother disintegrated. Sean went to spend the remainder of his teenage years with his mother in Oroville, a Sacramento Valley town about 150 miles northeast of San Francisco.

But Dec was not destined to live alone. In 1989, he heard from an old friend. Tanya, whom he had dated when he was with the Brummels, got in touch with Dec after an absence of more than 20 years. She and her husband had divorced, and she was calling to say hello. Dec and Tanya resumed their relationship, married in 1991 and moved into a comfortable home clinging to a San Francisco hillside. Tanya, who had stepped away from her medical-surgical nursing career to concentrate on raising her children, resumed nursing in pediatric care after she and Dec married.

Tanya's career in nursing inspired Dec in 1997 to join the staff of a Marin County residential care facility for physically and developmentally disabled people. In his position, as he transported residents to medical appointments and relayed critical information about their care, he discovered the power of music to bring joy and elicit responses from people who were largely noncommunicative. "He developed and maintained a music therapy program for the residents," Tanya said.

Energetic and trim, Dec still ran on nervous energy. Music remained an important part of his life. "I play a little. I write a little," he said with a shrug. Awaiting the arrival of a fellow musician before a wedding gig late one afternoon, he paced, craning his neck to see the street down below. Clearly a man who wore out shoe leather faster than he did seat cushions, Dec remained in a state of flux. "I'm kind of retired right now," he told us in 1997. "My dad died in 1973 and my mom died in 1988, and they left me some money that keeps me going. I have to be frugal to exist."

Dec turned his thoughts abruptly to the Brummels. "Autumn Records neglected the Beau Brummels. [Beatles manager] Brian Epstein focused all of his attention on the Beatles. Why didn't Autumn do that with the Beau Brummels?" Dec gazed out the window. "We were like five guys pushing a Cadillac up a hill who were within 10 yards of the top but got tired and rolled back. And if they'd gotten us to the top of the hill, we could have been cruising down the other side for a long time."

But Dec wasn't dwelling on the past. Far from it. He had plans: "To stay healthy," he said. And to continue performing. "I'd love to record some of my songs. Because I think I sing better now than I did 30 years ago."

The doorbell rang. Dec bolted down the hall, grabbed his guitar case and gave Tanya a tight hug as he headed out the door and down the stairs to sing once more.

After the couple relocated 40 miles north to Petaluma, Dec continued performing at weddings and other musical gigs, as well as working at the residential care facility through his 70s, even while working through his own physical setbacks. "Over a period of time Declan had three heart attacks, and one day while walking he tripped over our golden retriever, took a really bad fall, and shattered his left shoulder. As a result he lost complete use of his left arm, which meant that he no longer could play the guitar or play golf — and he had been a scratch golfer. Because of his age and other complications, he didn't qualify for shoulder replacement surgery, so his only treatment was physical therapy. But after his third heart attack, something was changed. In 2017 I noticed he was showing some symptoms associated with Parkinson's — rigidity and staring," Tanya told us in January 2026. Physicians in fact confirmed a diagnosis of Parkinson's disease. Stumbling and falling occurred with increasing frequency. "Then he had a stroke. He was gone within a week."

Declan died November 2, 2021, at age 83 of causes related to advanced Parkinson's disease. At the time, Brummels bass guitarist Ron Meagher wrote to tell us, "Dec passed away peacefully in his sleep and in the arms of his loving wife, Tanya. He will be missed."

Epilogue: John Petersen

Drummer

January 8, 1945 – November 11, 2007

Most people go through life wondering when their day of reckoning will come and what it will bring. John Petersen already knew beforehand. It was January 11, 1985. Unemployed after ownership squabbles crippled the Mother Lode restaurant in which he had worked as a chef, Petersen and his wife, Roberta, had driven 150 miles to San Francisco, where his mother had taken ill. They intended to care for her and cook some food to put up in her freezer. As his mother began to improve, John heard that his former Beau Brummels mates Sal Valentino and Dec Mulligan were performing at a bar across town.

"I'm sitting at an intersection in my blue Ford pickup, on my way to go hear them play, and my light turns green," Petersen recounted. "I go and some guy running the red light hits me going about 70 miles per hour. The crash broke my neck in five places." John was in the hospital when he regained consciousness, heavily braced and dazed. He spent the following three months in San Francisco in a "halo" brace that immobilized his neck and head. "I stayed at my Mom's with my wife in the room that I grew up in." Fortunately, the residual effects of the injury were limited to partial paralysis of his right thumb and forefinger.

Roberta and John Petersen celebrating their 25th anniversary in 1994.
Courtesy of John Petersen.

Just as John had recovered sufficiently to permit him to travel, Roberta received a call from her former employer: Warner Brothers Records, where she had been on the A&R (artists and repertoire) staff. The label wanted her back, this time as a vice president. She accepted. John, who had during the previous two decades played with a half-dozen bands, managed two ice cream parlors, sold men's clothing, operated a bed-and-breakfast inn, and rolled burritos, took stock of where he'd been and where he wanted to go. Still suffering from headaches related to the collision, he wasn't yet strong enough to work, but he was up to reading. And so he began studying for his real estate license. After passing his real estate test in April 1986, he began selling homes in Southern California. During the ensuing years, John avoided dwelling on the past, but every now and then he would pour himself a drink, put a Beau Brummels recording on the stereo, and listen with pride.

Born January 8, 1945, and raised in the Outer Mission District of San Francisco, John Louis Petersen began his childhood musical instruction with trumpet and accordion lessons. But he was more interested in banging on the kitchen pots and pans. That was a particularly prophetic fusion of two interests that would dominate much of his life: music and cooking. To quell his abuse of kitchen utensils, his parents, Louis and Marie, bought him a drum set when he was about 12. John's father was somewhat musical. "My dad, who was a cabinet maker, played spoons and he played harmonica just for fun." His older sister, one of his four siblings, was an accomplished piano player. But John pursued music more zealously than anyone else in the house.

Petersen played in the band in junior high and at Balboa High School in San Francisco, but he also became involved with a musical group called the Sparklers, so named because the band members wore sparkle shirts and white bucks shoes. The Sparklers played luncheon meetings for Lions Clubs, the Veterans of Foreign Wars and other fraternal and civic organizations. They recorded two sides, "Sparklers Theme" and "Freight Train Boogie," at Sound Recorders, later renamed Coast Recorders, the eventual site of the Beau Brummels recording sessions for Autumn. At age 12, John sometimes made as much as $50 or $60 per week playing with the Sparklers. "I realized that if I just kept playing drums and making music I wouldn't have to shop at JC Penney anymore. Even then, I thought I would either play music the rest of my life or be in the restaurant business."

John continued playing with the Sparklers as well as with other San Francisco musicians, and by the fall of 1963, he was earning $21.40

union scale each Friday night while playing with Sal Valentino and Ron Elliott at the Irish dances in San Francisco, where they met Declan Mulligan. So began the Beau Brummels, as well as a relationship that was often stormy. John still felt pangs of distress decades later about the friction that developed between him and Dec Mulligan in the months before the fiery Mulligan and the Beau Brummels parted. "Declan and I came very close to fist fights. But you know what? It was probably a big mistake for that band to break up at that point," Petersen declared. "Although we thought Declan was behaving like a jerk, it was a mistake for us to say, 'Leave,' instead of trying to work it out. We were all just too immature."

The disintegration of the band was foreshadowed even before Autumn sold the Brummels' contract to Warner Brothers in 1966. "Elliott was married and Meagher was married, and they and their wives were all living together in Laurel Canyon. Sal, Meagher, and I had actually started another offshoot of the band because Elliott wasn't healthy and they had drafted Don Irving to play lead guitar," explained Petersen. "Irving was really cool. He played all of Elliott's licks perfectly. By then we had three albums and we were still a good draw but the vibes in the band weren't healthy. It was really strained. I would go out to Laurel Canyon and people weren't talking to each other. By the time we got sold to Warner Brothers, we weren't the same band anymore."

He was musing over that realization while staying at the Hollywood Sunset Hotel at 8300 Sunset Boulevard in late 1966 when he received a call from Carl Scott, who had been the Brummels' manager. The Tikis, who had been on the Autumn roster and were dealt to Warner Brothers along with the Brummels, needed a drummer. At Carl's request, John met with Ted Templeman and Dick Scoppettone of the Tikis. John agreed to join the Tikis, who soon became known as Harpers Bizarre. "And that's how I met my wife," John told us in October 1997.

Roberta Templeman, Ted's sister, joined Warner Brothers in 1967 as a "listener," screening audition tapes and demo tracks by aspiring recording artists. Demonstrating a natural sense for detecting musical talent and hit-making potential, she rose quickly through the ranks and held A&R executive positions with increasing responsibility at Warners for 25 years, before joining Geffen Records in 1993.

The Tikis, as Harpers Bizarre, had recorded "59th Street Bridge Song (Feelin' Groovy)" before the arrival of Petersen. But Petersen was a part of the band when the song hit the charts in March 1967, and played at the session that produced Harpers Bizarre's follow-up hit, "Come to the Sunshine" three months later. "I found a second life," said Petersen, who toured with Harpers Bizarre for three years. "I had a lot of fun with Harpers, but I would have to say the Brummels were much closer to my heart."

John and Roberta married in Santa Cruz, California, in 1969, a year before Harpers Bizarre disbanded. Petersen subsequently took a job at a local Taco Bell fast-food outlet. "I did cooking jobs, I did whatever it took. I'm not ashamed of that," he said. "You've got to take care of yourself and your family. I had three cars and I couldn't put gas in them all." Petersen called Ron Elliott one day and asked if he'd like to form another band. "Cool," Elliott replied. They recruited Butch Engle to sing lead, Pappy Smith on bass, and named the band Crap. After playing some gigs in San Francisco, they relocated to Southern California, moving into a big house in Malibu together. "We were just this funky little band doing covers and acting goofy on stage," said Petersen. Unable to tolerate the communal environment in the Malibu house, Roberta moved in with Ted, and his wife, Kathy, who lived in Pasadena. When Crap dissolved a couple of weeks later, John moved in with Roberta, Ted, and Kathy. A few days passed before Roberta told John, "You probably should go get a job."

After landing a job as a cook at a Pasadena coffee shop, John moved into management at the Pasadena and Beverly Hills locations of Wil Wright's, an upscale ice cream parlor chain. After some time Petersen responded to a "help wanted" ad placed by Bruno's for Men, a locally owned clothing store. Hired as a salesman at age 26, Petersen advanced to become a buyer and eventually general sales manager of Bruno's, which expanded from its single location to four stores during the time he was there.

Roberta and John were both doing very well in 1975, when Ron Elliott called to say he wanted to resurrect the Brummels. "That sounds cool to me," John replied. He and Roberta rented out their house, Roberta moved back in with her parents in Santa Cruz, and John returned to San Francisco to rehearse with Elliott, Valentino, Mulligan, and Meagher. "We got a contract with Warner's, recorded the Beau Brummels album, went on the road, and it was a disaster." Ron Meagher quickly departed, John's drumming was criticized, and simmering tensions between Dec and John reached the boiling point. After appearing with Fleetwood Mac in Phoenix and Tucson, the band arrived in Portland, Oregon, the next tour stop. In John's room, he and Dec began a fierce argument. "I just about took off his head. I didn't know if I could beat him up or if he could beat me up. It didn't matter. I was mad," said Petersen. "So I took a walk, bought a raincoat and tried to figure out what I wanted to do with my life." At 5 the following morning, John boarded a plane. He and Roberta returned to their home in Southern California, where John rejoined Bruno's.

"I'll probably always regret leaving the Brummels, because it was what I always wanted to do, ever since I was 10 years old. This is probably the first time I've ever vocalized that," Petersen confided to us. "But I guess my ego was too big. I couldn't take the criticism. I'm not Ginger Baker, I'm not Russ Kunkel, I'm not like some of the great drummers out there, but I was always good for the band. We were always about simple licks and simple lyrics. At the recording sessions for the 1975 album nobody ever got loose and it was all too technical. And on stage in 1975 we didn't play anything that we used to, other than 'Laugh, Laugh' and 'Just a Little.' The rest was new stuff. We should have been playing 'Still in Love With You Baby' and other fun old stuff. That's what people came to hear." After Petersen's departure the Brummels played only a few more gigs with a different drummer before disbanding for good.

At Bruno's, John was promoted to buyer, then manager. In 1981 John and Roberta became restless, sold their home in urban Pasadena and moved 40 miles away to Thousand Oaks, beyond the western suburbs of Los Angeles. John quit his job and occupied his time by stripping furniture. Six months later they moved 400 miles north to Placerville, a Gold Rush town with a narrow, twisting main street lined by 19th-century buildings. John and Roberta bought and remodeled an old Victorian home at Coloma Street and converted it to a bed-and-breakfast inn. Working with a local handyman, they fashioned bathrooms out of closets, stripped generations of paint from fine old wood, repaired leaks, and replaced poor plumbing and outdated electrical fixtures. When completed, the Petersen Inn accommodated eight guests.

In 1983 John and Roberta sold the inn and bought a house in Twain Harte, another historic California town along State Highway 108, a mountain pass route that is routinely closed in winter by Sierra snowfalls. John took a job as a night clerk in a liquor store for $4.25 per hour until the real estate agent who sold the Petersens their home decided to open a restaurant with a business partner. Since neither of the new proprietors knew anything about the restaurant business, they persuaded John to quit the liquor store and become the chef and manager of the eatery they named Moby Dick's seafood restaurant, where he remained for the next two years. "I had some great recipes. I was doing San Francisco-style dishes like swordfish with avocado butter and great scampi dishes." But business declined and John was laid off after squabbles erupted between the two owners. It was then that Roberta and John drove to San Francisco to help John's mother during her illness.

During John's recuperation from his devastating automobile collision that occurred during that visit, Roberta sold the house in Twain Harte. And as John progressed, Warner Brothers Records offered Roberta an executive position that she accepted. Once John was able to travel, they moved to Pasadena, where John studied for his real estate license. He sold homes in the Pasadena area for 12 years, until leaving real estate in August 1998 to pursue a longtime dream: owning and operating his own record label. With two partners he formed Lawless Records, based in Pasadena, quickly signing alternative rock singer Caron and her band as the label's first act.

Petersen was modest about his time in the spotlight. When his real estate clients asked what he did before he entered real estate sales, he answered, "I was in the entertainment business and I was in retail." That's often as much as he revealed to new acquaintances. He mentioned the Brummels only if questioners persisted. "I never tell people that I meet for the first time. When they find out later, they're thrilled but, still, that has little bearing on what I do today," said Petersen.

Although he and Roberta had no children of their own, he spoke lovingly of his niece Sissy and nephew Peter, the children of his older sister, Susan, and her husband, Jack. John's younger brother Bobby worked in the printing trade all his life. John playfully described his older brother Ernie as a "goofy entrepreneur." John's younger sister Judy died of leukemia in 1976 at the age of 28. John's father died in 1975 following a short illness. John learned something important about his father shortly thereafter.

"Some of the fathers of the '50s didn't express themselves. They didn't hug you and tell you they love you, like fathers do now," observed John. He was never certain how much his father loved him until after he died. "When we were going through my Dad's stuff, I went out into the car and I happened to pull down the visor on the driver's side. Clipped to the visor," John said slowly, "was a picture of the Beau Brummels. He was not unwilling, he was simply unable to say, 'I'm proud of you.' I never knew he was proud until that moment."

John Petersen in August 1998 on the front porch of his home in Pasadena, California. Photo by Jeff March.

Although John in later life continued playing drums for personal enjoyment, he developed new interests. Like fellow Beau Brummels member Ron Meagher, he became interested in photography and enrolled in a class. I've been thinking about my passions," he declared. "I'm comfortable, I drive a nice car, I wear nice suits, I have a great history behind me, but I'm looking to find another passion." Even before launching Lawless Records, Petersen mused, "One thing I'd like to do is open a night club. I'd like to do some acting. And I'd like to have a restaurant with maybe 15 or 18 tables and cook for people." John Petersen was not a person who wanted his life defined by what he did when he was 22 years of age. "I think my future is probably a lot more important than my history."

He lived only 10 more years after that. While residing in Pasadena, California, John died of a heart attack on November 11, 2007. He was 62 years of age.

Epilogue: Ron Meagher

Bassist

There was a time, before the Beatles and other British acts caught the fancy of teenagers around the world, that American teenage boys all wore their hair short and neatly trimmed. A time when their standard attire was straight-leg blue or white Levi's jeans, red or green plaid Pendleton shirts, white tennis shoes, and white socks. A time when the only leather apparel item they wore was a belt. Such was the time when teenagers Ron Elliott, Sal Valentino, John Petersen, and Dec Mulligan formed the Beau Brummels. It was the late autumn of 1963, and the four boys with the Ivy league looks had begun practicing in the downstairs room of Ron Elliott's family home while awaiting the arrival of a bass guitarist who had been invited to audition for the band. The staircase leading to the downstairs room revealed visitors' feet first, step by step.

The four boys had never met the bassist, who was an acquaintance of a girl Elliott knew. His arrival brought the room to silence.

Late 1980s self-portrait of Ron Meagher with his wife, Cheri, and their son, Aaron, and Canaan, Ron's son from a previous marriage.
Courtesy of Ron Meagher.

First they saw black Beatle boots. Then black pants. A black guitar case. A black leather jacket. Black sunglasses. And a face framed by long, dark hair. That was their introduction to Ron Meagher. He plugged in his amplifier. They asked if he had heard of the Beatles, who were little-known in America at that time. To their surprise, he had. They asked if he knew how to play "I Want to Hold Your Hand." Meagher told them he did. With Mulligan singing lead, the band began playing the song.

Barely 15 seconds into it, Mulligan laid down his guitar and, with an astonished expression, motioned with outstretched palms to stop playing. "Whoa, whoa, whoa! That's it, that's it! He's doing it!" Mulligan was indicating to the others that Meagher was playing the intricate bass line the way that Paul McCartney did. Replicating McCartney's playing required a difficult hand stretch, and other bass guitarists that the group had interviewed failed because they took a lazy approach. That night, Meagher became a Beau Brummel. No big deal to him, because he was already playing with 12 other bands.

Ron's early musical interest was a product of the public school system in Oakland, California, an industrial and commercial center across the bay from San Francisco. Ronald Carl Meagher, born October 2, 1945, displayed natural musical aptitude that an elementary school teacher easily identified. Ron learned to play every stringed instrument he could wrap his hands around, but was disappointed to learn that the school would provide training only on orchestral instruments. Unable to learn to play the guitar in school, he decided to try the upright bass. "I remember carrying that upright bass home every afternoon so I could rehearse. It was unusual to see a 13-year-old kid walking around with a bass fiddle on his hip," Ron laughed.

But the ability to play that upright placed him in high demand at an early age. He played with jazz combos, folk groups, Latin ensembles, and orchestral dance bands by the time he entered high school. And he carved his own path into rock music when he heard a trio called the Off-Beats performing music of the Ventures during lunch at high school at the beginning of the fall 1961 semester. Meagher approached the group, which comprised drummer Richard MacDonald, lead guitarist Graig Cahill and rhythm guitarist Jimmy Eala, and asked, "Would you like to have a bass player?" They agreed. With that opportunity and his 16th birthday approaching, he chose an electric Fender Jazz bass guitar and an amplifier rather than the '57 Chevy that his parents had offered to give him.

Every evening after completing his homework, Ron assiduously practiced with his new instrument. After his parents went to sleep, he'd plug headphones into his amplifier, muting the speakers, and he'd perform bass lines into the early hours of the morning. Ron polished his skills, and during his junior and senior years of high school rotated among 12 musical groups, including the Off-Beats, which by then were known as the Blue Echoes. At a time when few Americans had heard of the Beatles or Cliff Richard and the Shadows, Ron and the other Blue Echoes were buying British albums in a local record store that had a small selection of imports. "I Saw Her Standing There," the leadoff cut on the *Please Please Me* album, had an unusual bass line by Paul McCartney. Ron Meagher was intrigued. He studied McCartney's playing style until he was able to replicate it himself.

In his junior year at Oakland High School, Ron understudied the lead role in the musical *Oklahoma*. During the staging of that play, he struck up a friendship with a girl named Kay Dane, a senior who was also in the cast. Kay would play a more important role in Ron's life a couple of years later. After enrolling at San Francisco State College, Kay developed a close friendship with fellow student Ron Elliott, whom she would later marry. Upon Kay's suggestion, Elliott and his buddies invited Ron Meagher to that basement audition with the band that became the Beau Brummels.

At 18, Ron Meagher was the youngest member of the band, a year younger than Ron Elliott and John Petersen. Meagher celebrated his 19th birthday on October 2, 1964, on stage at the Cow Palace, where the Brummels were appearing with a slate of 10 acts that included Sonny and Cher, Sam Cooke, the Temptations, and Glen Campbell. "Laugh, Laugh" had just been released, and Meagher was as yet the only member of the Brummels with long hair. Master of ceremonies Tom Donahue, KYA disc jockey and Autumn Records co-owner, went to the mike to introduce the individual members of the Beau Brummels.

"That was our first performance before a large audience. I remember we were wearing yellow bolero jackets with no collar," Meagher laughed. He was the last band member in Donahue's introduction. "When Tom called my name, I bowed, my long hair came down and the place went nuts. The girls were screaming like crazy. All the other band members looked over at me and thought, 'Oh. Isn't this interesting?' That was the end of the ivy league look of the Beau Brummels and shortly after that, one at a time, they started growing their hair longer." After the introductions were complete and the screams subsided, Donahue carted across the stage a huge layered birthday cake topped with a candle. After being presented with the cake, Meagher carried it offstage. There, Glen Campbell approached him, affectionately said "Isn't this great?" and promptly smashed his hand into the cake. "We ate the cake anyway," said Meagher.

Ron remained with the band through its relocation to Los Angeles, through the sale of the band's contract to Warner Brothers in 1966, until he was called up for military service. "I remember being right in the middle of a recording session for the *Bradley's Barn* album for Warner Brothers and I had to leave with about only three-quarters of the tracks laid down. I had to serve Uncle Sam." After his military discharge in 1970, Meagher returned to San Francisco. At the time Dec Mulligan was performing in an Irish bar in San Francisco with his own group called the Black Velvet Band. "Declan recognized me sitting in the audience. He was kind enough to ask me to come up and join his band, and I just happened to have a guitar sitting in the back of my car," Meagher smiled. The band became regulars at Paoli's Old Library, a San Francisco restaurant and night club stocked with old library books. After joining the Black Velvet Band, Ron married San Francisco State College Student Linda Lasdon in May 1970. The couple had a son, Canaan, but the marriage did not endure.

Meagher and Mulligan continued to perform with the Black Velvet Band until the 1975 reunion of the Beau Brummels. With Dec playing bass for the Brummels, Meagher moved into the lead guitar slot, but he was uncomfortable with the change. When the Brummels went on tour performing their new tunes, Meagher stayed behind, replaced by Danny Levitt. Meagher reactivated the Black Velvet Band in the East Bay, and recruited drummer Will Riddick and bassist Tony Del Favero, later adding female singer-keyboardist Britani Bartelme. "She not only had a wonderful voice, she also had one of the first keyboard synthesizers in the area," said Ron. The trio began a gig in the Emeryville location of Tia Maria, a Northern California restaurant-cocktail lounge chain. Adjoining Berkeley and Oakland, Emeryville is a commercial center and transit hub for East Bay commuters. The band continued playing there for more than four years. "During that time, I met a beautiful blue-eyed blond named Cheri, and we became engaged," Ron smiled. Unfortunately, the Tia Maria chain was sold by the owner to bankroll other investments in San Francisco. "If the chain had remained open, we'd probably still be there," chuckled Ron.

With the closure of Tia Maria, the Black Velvet Band increased its availability for dates at social events, including business parties and weddings. During one wedding gig at the prestigious Olympic Club in San Francisco, Ron's mind began wandering as he pondered his future. His gaze fell upon the bride and groom dancing as the wedding photographer snapped pictures of them. Leaping around the reception hall to capture memorable images, the energetic photographer riveted Ron's attention. Ron introduced himself to the photographer, Tony Machado, and told him he'd like to learn how to become a wedding photographer. "No kidding," Tony replied. "I always wanted to learn how to play the guitar." The two agreed to teach each other. Tony invited Ron to accompany him on several assignments. As Ron lugged the photographer's bag of equipment, his determination was cemented.

Ron began his quest for a new career by securing a sales job in Berkeley at Brooks Cameras, a chain of retail photographic equipment stores. As he learned more about the stock, he was promoted to assistant manager. Meanwhile, Tony introduced Ron to Jim London, another photographer who had just bought some new lighting equipment and was considering selling his old gear. Ron not only bought the equipment then and there, but he bought Jim's house and studio as well years later, after Jim's retirement from the business.

"I'm just starting wedding photography," Ron announced to Jim. "Would you like someone to come out and carry your equipment for you?" Ron had no idea that Jim London was among the most prominent wedding and portrait photographers in Northern California at the time. Ron went to four wedding photo sessions with Jim, and noticed that Jim didn't run around as Tony did. He was relaxed as he stood in front of the church waiting for the bride and groom. Jim simply exercised control over the shoot and knew what was going to happen next. That impressed Ron. After his informal apprenticeship, Ron got his first paid wedding job, and he applied all he had learned. When the 200 proofs were returned from the color lab, Ron showed them to Jim before the bride and groom saw them. Impressed, Jim said, "You and I have to talk." Eventually Jim and his wife nicknamed Ron "the sponge" because of how much information he absorbed and applied so quickly. "It was just what I did with music — I heard it and duplicated it," explained Ron. "I simply observed photographic styles and applied them."

In 1978 Ron launched his new career, working weekends as a wedding photographer for the next seven years while working weekdays in sales management at Brooks Cameras. It wasn't long before Ron's talent as a professional photographer was recognized, as he won several local, regional, and national awards for his work in portrait and wedding photography. Although photography was both artistically satisfying and lucrative, Ron felt drawn in yet another direction that would provide more long-term stability. And so after he finished counting receipts and shut down the Brooks offices at night, he would walk up the hill to the University of California, Berkeley, where he began taking Extension courses in computer science.

Ron's interest in the computer industry was first aroused back when the Black Velvet Band was playing at Tia Maria. There he struck up a friendship with a company financial executive, Marvin Katich, who balanced Tia Maria's books using IBM mainframe computers and software. After leaving Tia Maria, Katich went to work selling peripherals for California Computer Products, a Silicon Valley firm that devised pen plotter technology used for engineering drawings. Katich persuaded the branch manager of his office to interview Meagher, who was hired as a salesman in 1981.

Ron Meagher had made the transition to the corporate world. He excelled at Cal Comp, where he earned numerous awards of recognition and remained for nearly three years until his manager's prophecy materialized. Marvin had long maintained that the brass ring would go to the first company to develop a color plotter.

A Xerox subsidiary called Versatec was first to introduce a color electrostatic plotter, which printed images composed of tiny dots at high speed. In only one minute, an electrostatic plotter could generate a drawing that a pen device required a half hour to complete. As Ron considered approaching Versatec, the company's sales manager recruited him in 1984 after observing his effectiveness selling in their territory. Versatec's high-end equipment was not an easy sale, considering the cost: plotters and their controllers carried price tags of as much as $150,000. Nevertheless, Ron excelled at Versatec, earning a succession of promotions from senior sales engineer to regional manager of local OEM (original equipment manufacturing) accounts — then ultimately western regional OEM sales manager for Xerox, covering 11 western states. During an 11-year period, during which time the company became known as XES — Xerox Engineering Systems — Meagher opened several new markets in the reprographics and graphic arts industries.

"I'm proud of those accomplishments. Before my arrival at Versatec, architects would take their files on diskette to a service bureau, where a pen plotter would create the drawing, copies of which they would produce on a blueprint machine. So I was instrumental in introducing black-and-white electrostatic plotters to that industry," Meagher explained.

Ron Meagher self-portrait photographed in the summer of 2024. Courtesy of Ron Meagher.

Meagher, whose territory covered only the industrial areas of the East Bay cities, had customers who needed only black-and-white output. Color plotters were primarily marketed to the high-tech semiconductor firms of Silicon Valley across the bay, out of Ron's territory. "I could sell only black-and-white plotters, but I still made my quota," said Meagher, whose sales colleagues dubbed him "Monochrome Meagher." After one of Ron's customers told him, "I will never buy a color machine," Ron took that as a personal challenge. Meagher's breakthrough into a new color market came by means of a prospect in Berkeley named Harry Bowers, who was interested in the potential of color plotters to produce wallpaper or other large photographic images.

Versatec and Xerox Engineering Systems had concentrated on the semiconductor, petroleum, architectural, engineering, and construction industries, but disregarded the emerging desktop publishing segment. But after a new company called Bowers Imaging Technologies emerged from Harry's experimentation in electronic digital imaging technology, XES was persuaded to enter the graphic arts environment. Ron was credited for enabling the Xerox entry into the new graphic arts industry segment, in which plotters were viewed as tools to create photographic imagery rather than just engineering drawings. "Suddenly we were selling new color plotters to people we never imagined would be interested," Ron said proudly. XES plotters were being used to create advertising displays, billboards, and other applications requiring large color images. He racked up lots of sales awards, and also acquired a new nickname: the "Color Guy." Xerox eventually created a new business unit called Xerox ColorgrafX Systems, dedicated to this single vertical market. "To think that a former rock musician could make a difference in one of America's premier corporations," Meagher mused.

But Ron's success in creating the close affiliation with the graphic arts industry ultimately contributed to relocation of the entire division to Rochester, New York, where many Xerox corporate functions were concentrated. Ron's parents were elderly and Cheri did not want to uproot their family, so he left Xerox in the summer of 1995 and took a sales position with another computer firm in the San Francisco Bay Area.

There in the home they purchased from photographer Jim London, Ron and Cheri raised their son Aaron, who was born in 1984 — the year they moved into the house — and Ron's older son Canaan, who was born in 1974 during his first marriage.

A display case in the home contains a singular collection of symbolic Beau Brummels mementos. Mint-condition copies of the two original Autumn albums. Playbills and tickets from Beau Brummels concerts. Newspaper clippings. Wonderful old photographs. Less than two miles away, a parking garage has replaced the Morocco Room. Nothing remains of the building in which five young guys in yellow bolero jackets made music that the world would recall with fondness decades later.

Wooly Bully

Sam the Sham and the Pharaohs

By early 1965, much of the mania that characterized the mop-top British Invasion had settled somewhat. Even while the Vietnam war raged and racial unrest in cities seethed to a low boil, the pop charts showed that America turned a blissfully deaf ear. Roger Miller tickled his fans' fancy with "Do-Wacka-Do," Freddie and the Dreamers flapped along with "I'm Telling You Now," and Herman's Hermits honed their huggable image with their serenade to puppy love lost, "Mrs. Brown, You've Got a Lovely Daughter."

Sam the Sham and the Pharaohs in 1965. Left to right: guitarist Ray Stinnett, saxophonist Paul "Butch" Gibson, drummer Jerry Patterson, bassist David Martin, and organist-singer Domingo "Sam" Samudio in a promotional photo for the MGM motion picture "When the Boys Meet the Girls." From Photofest Archives, New York.

Through that squeaky-clean panorama a flamboyantly attired group from America's South burst onto the charts with a raucously improbable blend of Tex-Mex salsa and Memphis rhythm and blues. While parents settled in for a quiet evening watching Lawrence Welk set the bouncy rhythm of his televised "champagne music-makers" with his trademark "uh-one and a two-and-uh," their kids cruised the boulevard with radios blaring a far different beat that Sam the Sham launched with his inimitable Tex-Mex countoff: "Uno, dos, one-two, tres, cuatro." So began the boisterous "Wooly Bully," which remained on the charts longer than any other record in 1965, and so began the outrageous hit recording career of Sam the Sham and the Pharaohs.

Dressed in robes and brightly colored headdresses inspired by the attire of King Ramses in the motion picture *The Ten Commandments,* Sam and the Pharaohs arrived at gigs in a 1952 Packard hearse. Sam had polished his act over a two-year period, beginning in clubs around Dallas, at isolated roadhouses in steamy southwest Louisiana, and finally in the thumping nightspots of the legendary home of the blues, Memphis.

Bearded Texan Domingo "Sam" Samudio, singing lead vocals and playing rhythm on organ, fronted the four Pharaohs: bassist David Martin, guitarist Ray Stinnett, saxophonist Paul "Butch" Gibson, and drummer Jerry Patterson. In their hometown of Dallas, Samudio and Martin had been high school classmates, performing together in a local band with drummer Vincent Lopez before going their separate ways.

As an aspiring singer in the early '60s, Sam worked any kind of gig that would pay a few bucks and put him in the spotlight. When the house band at a Dallas bar called the Blue Room needed an organist who could sing, he auditioned and was hired even though he'd never played the organ. Sam traded a bass guitar and a flute for a Wurlitzer 4040 organ to practice at home, and three days later his phone rang.

David Martin was on the line from Louisiana. He and Vincent Lopez had joined Andy and the Nightriders, a band led by guitarist Andy Anderson. They were playing at a club in Louisiana when their organist quit, and they heard that Sam had picked up the organ. Sam agreed to join them, but after he arrived in Louisiana, his rudimentary keyboard skills earned him a new nickname.

"Andy and the Nightriders started introducing me as Sam the Sham because they knew I couldn't play the organ well," said Samudio. "Shamming also refers to cutting up, and I did a lot of that." It was the spring of 1963. As Leroy Gordon Cooper orbited the earth 22 times in the last Mercury space mission, Andy and the Nightriders were kicking in the afterburners down in New Llano, Louisiana. "Every night was like Saturday night on Highway 171 in Vernon Parish. We were a hot band," Sam proudly recalled.

The lights were bright and the music was loud, but home was a motel room that Samudio shared with David Martin. There, the two forged their dreams. Lying on his bed one muggy sleepless night, Martin said, "You know, while we're sitting here in this rathole, there's bands out there not half as good as we are making thousands of dollars a night."

"So I asked him what he thought it would take to get there," said Sam. "David answered, 'one gold record.' I told him, 'Let's go get one.' David got closer to my face and he said, 'I'm not joking.'"

"Neither am I," Sam affirmed. They shook on it.

By the summer the band members felt ready. "We packed everything up in a U-Haul and headed for Memphis, eating onions and sardines," said Sam.

When they pulled into Memphis, they checked into the Crystal Motel at 1750 S. Bellevue Boulevard and took a look around town. The place was pulsating. Jerry Lee Lewis was pounding piano at the Hi-Hat Club on Highway 61, the Mar-Keys were struttin' in a club across the way, Willie Mitchell was bumping out blues just up the road, and Ace Cannon and Bill Black's Combo were gigging in town. Undaunted by the competition, Andy and the Nightriders started making the rounds. Within four days they landed a gig at a place called the Diplomat Club. They hit the stage in full stride.

"Oh, we were hot," confirmed Sam. "We were playing six hours a night and we never came out in the daytime. But about sundown that hearse would roll out of the driveway. We were on our way to rock. On stage, Andy would hit a couple of notes on lead guitar and we were on. He was way ahead of his time."

Time was running out for Andy and the Nightriders, however. After a couple of months in Memphis, Andy's homesickness for Louisiana became overpowering. He announced his intention to quit the band and return home. Vincent Lopez was losing confidence as well. Figuring that meant the breakup of the band, Sam was tempted to return home as well. But David Martin, whose musical talents Sam deeply respected, persuaded him to stay and form a new unit. Sam was concerned how the band would survive the loss of its lead guitarist and drummer. "We'll find others," David assured him.

Sam the Sham and the Pharaohs outside Sun Studio in 1964, after signing their first recording contract with XL Records. Left to right: David Martin, Sam "the Sham" Samudio, Jerry Patterson, Paul "Butch" Gibson, and Ray Stinnett. Courtesy of Sam Samudio.

Guitarist Ray Stinnett and drummer Jerry Patterson had been close friends for two years before Sam and David had even arrived in Memphis. Ray recalled that he was standing at a Memphis bus stop in 1961 when he first met Jerry, who ran stock cars at the time. "Jerry had a big ole pink Oldsmobile that he called the pink elephant," said Ray. The initial conversation focused on engine rebuilding before the two discovered their mutual interest in blues music. "We instantly became buddies," said Ray. "I helped him build his car back up, and the two of us started playing music together at roadhouses, honky-tonks, clubs, bars, anywhere we could play."

After a while they started doing gigs with Sonny Wilson, an early Sun recording artist, and Memphis singer-pianist Eddie Carroll. That led to some backup work on demo sessions at Fernwood Recording Studio at 297 North Main Street. Ray and Jerry began moving easily through Memphis music circles. They hung out at Satellite Record Shop at 926 East McLemore Avenue just as it was metamorphosing into Satellite Studios — the precursor to Stax Records. Satellite Record Shop was run by Estelle Axton, the mother of Charles "Packy" Axton, who played tenor sax with the Mar-Keys.

Ray, who with Jerry also began doing some session work at Sonic Studios on Madison Avenue, remembers a particular recording date one morning late in the summer of '63. "While I was waiting for Sonic to open, I looked across the street and noticed this tall dark-haired guy with a big beard. He looked kind of like Fidel Castro," said Ray. "He was with a guy who looked like Cochise or something. I said to myself, 'these are some weird-looking dudes.' I walked across the street to them and said, 'You've gotta be musicians,' and they said, 'We're from Dallas.' So we sat down on the stone wall and started talking." The guy with the beard was Sam Samudio. With him was David Martin.

"They said they had a band called the Nightriders and that the other two guys were off having breakfast," said Ray. "They told me they had been in Memphis a few weeks and they had a gig playing at Eddie Bond's place, the Diplomat Club." Then Andy and Vince, the two other Nightriders, showed up. "They said they thought they were wasting their time in Memphis and wanted to go back to Texas or Louisiana. Sam and David said they wanted to stay but they needed a guitar player and drummer." Ray asked them what kind of music they play. "Blues, rock, soul, gut-bucket kind of blues," Sam responded.

"That sounds like something I'm familiar with," said Ray with a sly smile. "This might be your lucky day."

As they talked, the studio opened its doors for a scheduled demo session with Dick and Dee Dee. Ray invited the Nightriders in. "On that session, Sam contributed a little organ and I played a little rhythm guitar, and when the demos were done, the Nightriders hooked up and played a couple of tunes. But the whole time Andy was mumbling and complaining that they were wasting their time in Memphis," recalled Ray.

Sam spoke next. Pointing to Ray, he said, "Hey, look, let this red-headed guy sit in and see what he can do." As Ray began to play, Andy packed his guitar and left. Sam said, "We're staying. We found a guitar player already. You want a job, Booger Red?" he asked Ray.

"He started calling me that. He had a talent for coming up with names for people," said Ray, who was hired on the spot. "I told them about this drummer friend of mine. Sam said, 'If he can play as well as you can, bring him on in to the Diplomat Club.' Jerry joined us, and that was the beginning of the Pharaohs."

The quartet had good chemistry and quickly evolved into a tight unit. Their repertoire consisted principally of funky rhythm and blues tunes like "Long Tall Sally" and "Every Woman I Know (Crazy 'Bout an Auto)." The Diplomat was a big club and Sam the Sham and the Pharaohs quickly drew crowds. "We were the only predominantly white band in Memphis that played hardcore blues. The club was packed every night," said Ray. In addition to their own shows, the band also backed two nightly performances by singer Jumpin' Gene Simmons, who owned an independent label called Tupelo Records. On Tupelo, with their own money, Sam the Sham and the Pharaohs recorded their first single, the 1958 Chuck Willis hit "Betty and Dupree," backed with "Man Child," a tune penned by Sam. Disappointed by their inability to penetrate the soul music market with that release, the band members decided they needed the added dimension that a saxophone player could provide.

As a pre-medical student at Southwestern at Memphis (later renamed Rhodes College) in 1962, saxophonist Butch Gibson began moonlighting with a band named Joe Davis and the All-Stars that was fronted by a trio of black vocalists. The band, which played dates at colleges throughout the South, had a brush with stardom in 1963 when they recorded as the Avantis. They cut a tune on the Argo label called "Keep On Dancing" that became a top-10 hit two years later for the Gentrys. In January 1964, when Butch was halfway through his second year of college, Joe Davis called him aside. "Hey, man," Joe told Butch, "there's a group in town that you need to hear. They play your kind of music, but they don't have a sax player. They call themselves Sam the Sham and the Pharaohs."

Butch headed to the Little Black Book, the club where Sam the Sham and the Pharaohs were playing at the time. He introduced himself and they invited him to audition on stage with them. The Pharaohs liked what they heard. And that evening as Butch became a Pharaoh, he decided to quit college.

"That was a real smart thing to do," said Butch sarcastically, "but I wouldn't change that now because it afforded me a lot of opportunities and exposure to the world that I wouldn't have had otherwise." Butch had begun a two-year adventure that would take him to the heights of bliss and the depths of depression.

After the arrival of Butch, the band members recorded their second single, Johnny Fuller's "Haunted House," and tried their best to promote the record, which was released on the independent Dingo label. "We went on George Klein's TV show, *Dance Party,* and I sat on Butch's shoulders and we were made up like some kind of 10-foot-tall spooky 'haint' from the haunted house," chuckled Ray. "Sam and the other guys acted out the story line of the song and then Butch and I chased them all over the studio in this ridiculous getup. We worked really hard at promoting 'Haunted House.' We went out on the road knocking on radio station doors, asking them to play the record," said Ray.

After the band had shopped the record from Memphis to Birmingham and everywhere in between, Gene Simmons said that a larger label, Hi Records, was interested in releasing "Haunted House," but wanted Sam and the Pharaohs to re-record it with a somewhat different arrangement. The deal didn't feel right to Sam. Simmons appealed to Sam to reconsider, but Sam was resolute in sticking with Dingo. "So Gene went over to Hi Records and recorded "Haunted House" himself," said Stinnett. The Simmons version eclipsed the Pharaohs' disc and charted nationally in August 1964.

As chart success eluded them, Sam the Sham and the Pharaohs continued enjoying a strong following in the nightspots of Memphis. After the closure of the Diplomat Club for curfew violation, the band quickly found other gigs, first at Quentin's Club and then at a place called Smoochie's Show Bar. Owner Jerry Lee "Smoochy" Smith was the original piano player with the Mar-Keys and a member of the famed Sun Rhythm Section. As a solo act, Smoochy had a local hit called "Hot Nuts," with eye-winking lyrics. Sam the Sham and the Pharaohs, too, went back into the studio and recorded a novelty song called "The Signafyin' Monkey," released on XL Records. To promote that record Sam bought a small spider monkey that sat on his shoulder and occasionally bit him on stage. Although the song failed to live up to their expectations, the next recording session for XL was more productive.

"Do you have anything else to record?" producer Stan Kesler asked. "Yeah, we got something," replied Sam.

What he had was little more than a rhythm pattern without any words. "I told the band, 'kick it off, and we'll make up some words.'" There, in the same recording studio in which Elvis Presley, Roy Orbison, Jerry Lee Lewis, Johnny Cash, and Carl Perkins had laid down tracks for Sun Records, Sam the Sham and the Pharaohs improvised, jotted down some lyrics, and recorded another novelty tune: "Wooly Bully."

Pivotal to the tune's eventual success was its riveting downbeat, the staccato "Uno, dos, one-two tres cuatro" spark plug that ignited the band. The famous countdown was no big deal to Sam. "It was just a Tex-Mex count-off," he shrugged. Sam used it as a timing device to pace the musicians, but hadn't intended it to be part of the recording. Kesler liked it, however, and argued in favor of retaining it on the pressing. Sam finally agreed. "Put a label on it, that's a hit," Sam said. It was, but not right away.

During the smoldering days of "Wooly Bully," before it became a wildfire hit, the band continued playing at Smoochie's. Wishing to increase business at the club, the band members decided they needed a gimmick. "At the time we wore brocade jackets and we looked kind of like the Blues Brothers. We bought our clothes at Lansky Bros. and we were mod, dapper dudes," said Ray.

"Then we got the idea that the Pharaohs should dress up like pharaohs, so we went to a drapery shop and bought some pieces of fabric and decorative cording. We made some head coverings out of them and dyed some bed sheets, and made them into robes. We didn't wear the pharaoh outfits all of the time, just for special occasions. They were a pain," Ray acknowledged. "We couldn't hear very well, they were hot, and we tripped over the sheets. But we used them to attract attention. We started riding around town in Sam's hearse dressed like the pharaohs. We got ourselves boots with real high heels and we looked like we'd just ridden in on camels. We'd run into clubs and yell, 'Smoochie's Show Bar' and leave, and Smoochie's started filling up."

Even while playing at Smoochie's, the band made short runs on the road, promoting their record and doing one-nighters in other Southern cities. Duke Rumore, a Birmingham disc jockey who liked the band's music, packaged rock shows at the local National Guard Armory and at a beach stage in Panama City, Florida. "He would rent out those places and we would pack them," said Ray. Opening for Sam the Sham and the Pharaohs one night was a band called the Sundowners, whose guitarist was a very young Tom Petty. With help from Duke, "Wooly Bully" hit number one in Birmingham. That's when MGM Records took notice. "A couple of MGM reps came out to Smoochie's Show Bar, took one look at us in our pharaoh outfits and said, 'That's it, deal's closed. You guys are on MGM Records.' It was just that fast," said Stinnett.

Released nationally in March 1965 on MGM Records — the label of Herman's Hermits — the thumping "Wooly Bully" premiered on the *Billboard* Hot 100 on April 3. By June 5, it had shot to No. 2, a position it held for two consecutive weeks on the *Billboard* Hot 100 at the height of the British Invasion. "Wooly Bully," with Sam credited as writer, remained on the chart for 18 weeks. *Billboard* declared it the top song of 1965, the Recording Industry Association of America awarded it gold record certification on August 5, 1965, and it went on to sell 3.5 million copies. The solemn pact that Samudio and Martin had made in that dim motel room in Louisiana had been fulfilled; they had their gold record.

In short order, the band that had existed by living in flophouse motels and eating bologna and onion sandwiches was on tour in Europe and introduced to a national television audience by Ed Sullivan. Making the leap to the drive-in screen, the fully garbed Sam and the Pharaohs appeared with Herman's Hermits in the MGM motion picture *When the Boys Meet the Girls,* starring Connie Francis, Harve Presnell, and Sue Ane Langdon, with cameo appearances by Louis Armstrong and Liberace.

Dick Clark booked the band even before "Wooly Bully" had made it to the top of the charts. "He was a visionary," Ray said with admiration. "He knew a good thing when he saw one coming. We were booked on the Dick Clark Caravan of Stars tour for a small amount of money. We lived on a bus for about 30 days and slept in the luggage racks, on the floor, whatever."

Butch also recalled with fondness his days touring with the Caravan of Stars. "We toured on the West Coast with Ike and Tina Turner, James Brown, the Beach Boys, the Righteous Brothers, and others," Butch said wistfully. "Dick Clark was without a doubt, the greatest guy in the music business in the whole world and always will be. If Dick Clark told you that tomorrow is Easter, you have to color your eggs tonight. Whatever he said is real. We went up the West Coast into Portland and then down to Reno. I'll never forget the night that we played in Oakland, with James Brown the marquee leader on the show. We had a blues song called 'I Found a Love' that was done originally by the Isley Brothers. We held it for the last song of our set, and I mean we really played it. James Brown came out of his dressing room with his silk robe on, and stood in the wings with his hands on his hips and watched us sing that song. He wanted to know who was singing because the crowd was going crazy. He didn't smile, applaud, nothing. When we were done he just turned around and walked off. And that was kind of like his approval."

Capitalizing on the success of "Wooly Bully," MGM rushed the group into the studio to record a couple of cookie-cutter follow-up hits, "Ju Ju Hand" and "Ring Dang Doo." The Pharaohs headed for the swamps and invoked a voodoo theme for "Ju Ju Hand," which Sam Samudio wrote. Stan Kesler produced the session for MGM Records. After the single premiered on the Hot 100 on July 31, 1965, it climbed to No. 26 and remained on the chart for seven weeks. "Ring Dang Doo," the band's third chart single, premiered on October 9. Joy Byers and Bob Tubert wrote the song in the "Wooly Bully" vein, and Stan Kesler produced the session for MGM Records. The recording peaked at No. 33 and remained on the chart for nine weeks.

"Red Hot," the fourth chart record by Sam the Sham and the Pharaohs, premiered on the *Billboard* Hot 100 on February 5, 1966. Billy "the Kid" Emerson wrote the song, and Stan Kesler produced the session for MGM Records. The pulsating recording was an attempt to capture the energy of "Wooly Bully," but it gained only a lukewarm response. The recording with Sam Samudio's snarling lead vocal stalled at No. 82 and remained on the chart for five weeks. For 10 months the band toured relentlessly throughout the United States and Europe, pausing only to record three albums. The pace took its toll by the spring of 1966.

"Our management unmercifully worked us on the road," said Ray. "We were all young, married, and had young children except for Sam, even though we lied and told all of the fan magazines that we were single. As soon as we'd get home and see our wives, the phone would ring, and we'd be told, 'You gotta come to the studio' or some such thing." Despite the grueling schedule, it seemed to have its rewards — at first. The band members managed their own funds initially, counting their earnings after each show and keeping their mounting cash reserves in shoe boxes. Then financial management was assigned to a team of New York accountants. The band members were given expense accounts, and small allowances were sent to their homes. That arrangement seemed satisfactory until the day Butch called the accountants' office and asked for $1,000 to buy a motorcycle. "The accountant laughed and told Butch, 'You don't have $1,000' and we all freaked out because we'd figured we should have had about $100,000 in the account by then," said Ray. "So we went to meet with them and they showed us stacks of statements showing where all of our money had been spent. We had 70 people working for us who we didn't know, in offices we'd never seen, and bills we were unaware of. It was horrible."

Sam remembers the day the band broke up while staying at a Ramada Inn on the road. "It was a Wednesday," by Sam's recollection. "They asked when we would be going home. And I told them, 'This is home.' They were weary. They wanted to go out and try it on their own. I said, 'OK,' but I turned to David and asked, 'Where are you going Dave?' He said, 'I think I'll go with them.' And that's how we parted. The following day I flew to New York."

Owwwooooooooo. Who's that I see walkin' in these woods? In New York, Sam assembled a new group of Pharaohs from a band called Tony Gee and the Gypsies. The recruits included keyboard and saxophone player Frank Carabetta, singer and bass guitarist Tony Gerace, drummer Billy Bennett, and guitarist Andrew Kuha.

Searching for a new hit formula for the reconstituted group, MGM concocted a nursery rhyme scheme. Surprisingly, the initial effort of that new direction, "Lil' Red Riding Hood," clicked and gave Sam and company their second top-10, million-selling single. The 45 rpm release "Lil' Red Riding Hood" (shown on the corresponding album label as Li'l Red Riding Hood") premiered on the *Billboard* Hot 100 on June 11, 1966. The song was written by Ronald Blackwell, who composed several other tunes for Sam the Sham and the Pharaohs, as well as songs that the Everly Brothers and Roy Orbison recorded. Stan Kesler produced the session for MGM Records. The record peaked at No. 2, a position it held for two weeks, and remained on the chart for 14 weeks. On August 11, RIAA awarded it with a gold record. The Pharaohs followed that with another Blackwell novelty tune, "The Hair on My Chinny Chin Chin," which hit the chart on October 1, 1966. It performed well, peaking at No. 22, and remaining on the chart for eight weeks. But personnel turmoil continued. Billy Bennett exited and was replaced by Louis Vilardo. Ronnie (Spiderman) Jacobsen became bassist. The band was given a new dimension with the addition of the Shamettes, a female vocal backup trio consisting of Fran Curcio, Loraine Genero, and Jane Anderson.

The Pharaohs' last top 30 hit was yet another Ronald Blackwell tune, "How Do You Catch a Girl," which premiered December 24, 1966, peaked at No. 27 and remained on the chart for eight weeks. Sam and the new Pharaohs tried again with "Oh, That's Good, No, That's Bad," written by Ron Blackwell's brother Dewayne Blackwell and produced by Stan Kesler. A female trio called the Sham-Ettes (at times also spelled Sham-ettes or Shamettes) joined the five Pharaohs on the recording. Although it became the eighth chart record by Sam the Sham and the Pharaohs after premiering on the Hot 100 on March 18, 1967, and it remained on the chart for six weeks, it peaked no higher than No. 54. In their prime, Sam and the group had surmounted heavy odds and taken their barroom beat to the top of the charts. "Wooly Bully" was named record of the year for 1965 by *Billboard* magazine. Ronald Blackwell, who had been born in Woodland, California, in October 1938, tragically died in a car crash at the age of 27 on April 24, 1966.

By the time "Black Sheep" was released in June 1967, the novelty of Sam the Sham and the Pharaohs had lost appeal. "Black Sheep," the group's ninth and final chart record, had the ingredients for success. The song, which premiered on the Hot 100 on June 17, 1967, was produced by Stan Kesler and written by prolific country music songwriter Bob

Jerry Patterson, Paul "Butch" Gibson and Sam Samudio were guests at a book signing on Sunday, August 20, 2000, for *Echoes of the Sixties* by Marti Smiley Childs and Jeff March at Borders Books and Music, 6685 Poplar Avenue in Germantown (Memphis area), Tennessee.

McDill, who went on to write "Amanda," which Waylon Jennings recorded; "Gone Country," a hit for Alan Jackson; "Good Old Boys Like Me," "It Must Be Love" and "Say It Again," recorded by Don Williams; "Nobody Likes Sad Songs," recorded by Ronnie Milsap; and "Song of the South," recorded by Alabama. During its six-week run on the charts, "Black Sheep" peaked at No. 68. The group's next single, "Banned in Boston" appeared to be banned everywhere else as well; it didn't even crack the top 100. But that was probably more a measure of the times than an indictment of Sam the Sham and the Pharaohs.

The summer of 1967 was the summer of love, of Monterey Pop, of Haight-Ashbury, when the Beatles' landmark *Sgt. Pepper's Lonely Hearts Club Band* helped to usher in the era of psychedelia. America left Tex-Mex and Memphis behind as it tripped off to San Francisco.

SAM THE SHAM AND THE PHARAOHS
U.S. HIT SINGLES ON THE NATIONAL CHARTS

Debut	Peak	Gold	Title	Label
4/3/65	2	▲	Wooly Bully	XL, MGM
7/31/65	26		Ju Ju Hand	MGM
10/9/65	33		Ring Dang Doo	MGM
2/5/66	82		Red Hot	MGM
6/11/66	2	▲	Lil' Red Riding Hood	MGM
10/1/66	22		The Hair on My Chinny Chin Chin	MGM
12/24/66	27		How Do You Catch a Girl	MGM
3/18/67	54		Oh That's Good, No That's Bad	MGM
6/17/67	68		Black Sheep	MGM

▲ symbol: RIAA certified gold record (Recording Industry Association of America)

Billboard's pop singles chart data is courtesy of Joel Whitburn's Record Research Inc., Menomonee Falls, Wisconsin.

Epilogue: Sam Samudio

Lead singer and keyboardist

Sam Samudio in 1966.

Fort Polk, Louisiana. 1963. A car rolled to a stop at the entrance gate of the U.S. Army base. A young soldier stepped out of the guard shack, approached the vehicle, and addressed the driver.

"Sir, please state your business," declared the soldier.

"My passengers and I are expected at the Officers' Club," said the driver, Andy Anderson.

When the soldier said, "I'll need to see identification," a voice from the back seat of the vehicle asked, in Spanish, "¿Qué dijo?" — meaning "What did he say?"

"Hold it right there," said the soldier as he peered into the vehicle to see who had spoken. There, seated in the rear, was a dark-haired, bearded man wearing military fatigues and a garrison cap. He was clenching a large cigar in his teeth. In those tense times, the persistent armaments threat posed by revolutionary bearded Cuban Premier Fidel Castro kept American military forces in an uneasy state of alert. Placing his hand on his holstered .45 service weapon, the young guard said," Sir, you'll need to report to the provost marshal's office."

The man in the fatigues was Domingo "Sam" Samudio, and he and the other musicians went on to play their set in the Officers' Club without incident. The band was called Andy and the Nightriders, the precursor to Sam the Sham and the Pharaohs. Although the Fidel Castro impersonation was typical of the stunts the band members occasionally did for their own mischievous enjoyment, it reflected the proclivity for costumes that would help propel Sam to international stardom in a robe and turban.

Sam had put in some military time of his own, a four-year stint in the U.S. Navy. After his discharge in December 1959, the lanky 6-foot-1 Samudio became a construction laborer — as his father, Santiago "Jim" Samudio, was — in order to save enough money for the entrance fee to the

206

University of Texas at Arlington. While studying English and music there, he worked beer joints, singing and playing harmonica for $6 a night. Sam grew restless in college, however, as he pondered his ambitions. He wanted to be a movie star. He wanted to be a bull fighter. He wanted to be a singer. More than anything else, he wanted to be a singer.

Born February 28, 1937, Sam made his performing debut as a first-grader singing "I'm Always Chasing Rainbows" in a contest broadcast on a radio station in his hometown of Dallas. As a high school student at Crozier Tech (later renamed Dallas High School), Sam took voice lessons and began performing lunch-hour concerts in a band with two fellow students: bassist David Martin and singer Trini Lopez. After quitting college, Sam united with Martin, drummer Vincent Lopez and two other friends in forming a band that pounded out Tex-Mex music and blues. They called themselves the Pharaohs. Mirroring the interest in ancient Egypt stirred by the motion pictures *The Ten Commandments* and *Cleopatra,* an image of King Ramses adorned the Pharaohs' bass drum. The Pharaohs played funky clubs that paid each musician as little as $5 per night. After the group disbanded, Sam did what he could to survive, including selling french fries and hot dogs on the midway at the Texas State Fair, and cutting truckloads of fir trees in the forests of New Mexico for the Christmas season.

Not everyone in Sam's family was pleased that he had begun to pursue an entertainment career. His sister, Esterina Samudio, who received a master's degree in education and special education, encouraged Sam to continue with his studies. Sam's older half-brother, Onesimo Hernandez, who was a physician, offered to pay Sam's way through law school if he'd promise to relinquish entertaining. But the siren call of the stage was too loud, and it drew him to Louisiana and then to Memphis, where Sam the Sham and the Pharaohs began their rise to fame.

Although distressed by the breakup of Sam the Sham and the Pharaohs in the spring of '66, he took pride in the success achieved after he re-formed the band, casting aside doubts about his durability.

"People were saying I'd never do it again. They said I was a one-trick pony," said Sam. "That was before we recorded 'Li'l Red Riding Hood.' It sold over a million and a half." That was in the summer of '66. Sam and the reconfigured Pharaohs went on to drive two more novelty tunes into the top 30, but the group's popularity sagged after the release of their January 1967 single, "How Do You Catch a Girl?"

Sensing the inevitable demise of the group, Sam recorded and released a solo album titled *Ten of Pentacles* in 1968. With a title taken from the occult, the album revealed Sam's interest in the mystical arts, including tarot card reading and astrology. Four years passed before his next recording endeavor. Long after the expiration of the MGM contract, Sam was in a club in London hanging out with blues guitarist and singer Freddie King. A man walked up to him and tersely introduced himself. "Sam. Sam the Sham," he said. "Ahmet. Ahmet Ertegun. Atlantic. Do you have a contract with anybody?"

Sam "the Sham" Samudio in the 1990s. Photo by Mickey O'Keefe, Majestic Entertainment Co.

"No, I'm not signed," Sam replied.

"Would you like to do an album for us?" Ertegun asked.

"Yeah."

"When you get back to New York, call me," Ertegun said as he walked off.

Freddie King turned to Sam and said, "Man, that was Ahmet Ertegun from Atlantic Records."

Sam returned to New York, took up Ertegun's offer, and Atlantic sent him to Criteria Recording Studios in North Miami, Florida, to record with a cadre of top-notch musicians. The Dixie Flyers formed the rhythm section and the Sweet Inspirations sang backup. The result was a heavily blues-flavored album of which Sam was proud but which received little airplay or public attention. Still, his work on the album, called *Sam Hard and Heavy,* gleaned some redemption when he was presented with a Grammy Award for best liner notes. Written as a personal acknowledgment of those who had helped and inspired him, the liner notes also revealed Sam's pain and exposed those who inadvertently strengthened his character by mistreating him. His list of those to thank began with "The people who mistreated me as a child, 'cause they made me strong." He thanked "the people who refused me service, for they made me save my money." He thanked "the people who rejected me because of the color of my skin and the texture of my hair, for they made me realize that I was different." He thanked "the towns I was run out of, for they ran me to better places." He thanked the women who loved him, and acknowledged that loving the wind would have been easier. He thanked his children "for having chosen me as their father in this life; for they alone gave me the will and strength to continue when all other sources of energy were depleted." Finally: "And most of all, God for letting me be a musician, for in doing so he's given me a taste of Paradise."

Sam packed and went west to fulfill the acting ambitions he'd harbored since his college days. But when he was unable to navigate his way into the inner circles in Hollywood, Sam took up a pen and began writing music and recorded some tracks with a number of top session musicians in LA. He was surviving financially, he said, on a guaranteed 10-year salary from MGM. Just about the time he began to experience some artistic freedom, the Internal Revenue Service came to call. Sam and the Pharaohs had long questioned royalty payments they said they never received and expenditures by their agents they said they never authorized. "I was doing OK until the IRS came after me for money I had never seen," said Sam. He let himself slip into a boozy, hallucinogenic mire. He'd previously been hospitalized for collapse of the lower lobe of his left lung, which he almost lost. "It was caused by smoking, cocaine, and the dusty dumps I'd played in for so many years," he said. Now he reached bottom, figuratively and literally, when he found himself on the floor of his Hollywood Hills apartment, staring up at the sky. Sam heard a voice — the voice, he said, of God.

"Lord, give me a break, because I know this is going to take me out," Sam pleaded, referring to drug abuse. "If you would just remove the desire, I'll go wherever you want me to go and do whatever you want me to do. I just want to ask you to take care of my kids." Sam, saying he "felt a peace," experienced a transformation. "That night I felt the power of God come into the room. He spoke to my heart and said, 'I gave you a talent and look what it's come to. I'm going to put it back together for you and the way I'll put it back together no man will be able to take it apart." And I said, 'God, I love to stay high.' And the Lord spoke to my heart and said, 'I'll keep ya high. But it won't be on anything cheap. The high that I'll keep you on is so expensive, it cost my son his life.' And I said, 'You know Lord, I love to run that highway.' And the Lord said, 'You can run that highway, but you'll run it for me.' And when I made that deal with the Lord I walked away from rock and roll."

Sam concluded that he really was a sham. Uncertain about what to do with his life, he lingered in LA until 1976. "Then I returned to

Memphis and went through some more changes," said Sam, ticking off a succession of events. "Got married. To the wrong woman. By that time it was the third marriage."

When that marriage went awry, Sam headed back to Texas — not to Dallas, but down along the Louisiana border through Sabine Pass to the shipyards on the Gulf Coast. There he signed on as a deckhand, doing labor on the ships that shuttled workers and supplies to the offshore oil rigs in the Gulf of Mexico. Sam shaved his trademark beard and quietly, anonymously toiled, working his way up through the ranks and reading his Bible in his room. No more hearses, no more turbans, no more "Wooly Bully." Just Sam, the sea, and his God. Sam rose to the rank of engineer, then mate, then captain, piloting vessels. He commanded a 100-ton crew vessel and though he battled 23-foot swells in stormy seas, his spirit was becalmed.

Sam "the Sham" Samudio in August 2000 at Sam Phillips Recording Service, 639 Madison Avenue in Memphis, Tennessee, where "Wooly Bully" and other hits were recorded. Sam Phillips was founder of Sun Record Company.
Photo by Jeff March.

Sam did surface briefly from anonymity when slide guitarist and record producer Ry Cooder called in 1982. Cooder, an admirer of Samudio's music, wanted him to record a couple of tracks for the Universal Pictures film *The Border,* starring Jack Nicholson, Harvey Keitel, and Valerie Perrine. Sam's estranged wife, Brenda Patterson, also a singer, helped Cooder track Sam down in the Gulf. The script appealed to Sam and he wrote two songs, "Palomita" and "No Quiero," in Spanish for the soundtrack, which Backstreet Records released. The project brought Sam, Freddy Fender, and Flaco Jimenez into collaboration. Once his work on the project was completed, Sam slipped back to the Gulf oil fields.

Then while out at sea one day in 1985, another conversation with the Lord persuaded him to do more with his life. As easily as he came to the shipyards, he left, and headed once again for Memphis. This time, Sam was on a mission from God. That mission was to spread The Word.

Singer, songwriter and entertainer Rufus Thomas (left) and Sam "the Sham" Samudio chatting on Beale Street in Memphis on Monday, August 21, 2000. Rufus joked that the tail hanging by his side was all that was left of the dog he was walking (a reference to his 1963 top-10 hit "Walking the Dog"). Rufus died 16 months after this photo was taken at age 84 due to congestive heart failure.
Photo by Jeff March.

He did so wherever people would listen. Driving a pickup truck with a small trailer in tow, he'd stop on a street corner, set up shop, and begin preaching and singing gospel songs. For the better part of two decades, he spoke and sang wherever anyone would listen, in nursing facilities, homeless shelters, jailhouses, and maximum-security prisons. He existed on commercial-use royalties from "Wooly Bully" and other songs that he had written. His was accompanied not by Pharaohs, but by a group called Gideon's Few, whose members included reformed drug abusers.

Sam didn't completely forsake his musical roots. In 1994, he went back into the studio and recorded *Won't Be Long,* an album of gospel songs, backed by the Ambassadors for Christ. Released in tape cassette and CD format on his own Samara Productions label — a name that means "protected by God" in Hebrew — the album contained nine songs, including "Prayer Line," "Maranata," and a "Power Medley (What a Friend We Have/There Is Power in the Blood/I'll Fly Away)."

Sam said that his family wasn't religious. Yet one of the few memories he retains of his mother, who died when he was only $3^1/2$ years old, is a prayer she liked to recite. "I'm not into religion," Sam surprisingly told us in July 1997. "It was religious people who nailed Jesus to the cross. I don't really preach. I teach." Sam spoke proudly of the Bible study courses he conducted at several prisons in the Memphis region. He even journeyed to Latin America as an interpreter with a missionary organization called Health Care Ministries. Sam paid his own way. "That was just part of my end of the bargain with the Lord," Sam explained.

Sam, who was married three times before wedding his wife, Ann, expressed humble thanks for her and for the health and happiness of his family, including his two sons, who were born in the 1960s, and his daughter, born in 1980. Referring to Ann, Sam said, "I was resolved to live the rest of my life alone when the Lord blessed me with a fantastic person."

For a long time Sam tried to suppress memories of the old days. While he still performed, he'd sing only gospel, refusing requests for "Wooly Bully." By the mid '90s, however, he began to come to terms with the past, consenting in public appearances to perform a few of the old tunes, along with a gospel number or two. And he held pleasant memories. His fondest thoughts, he said, were of bassist David Martin, who died in Dallas of a heart attack in August 1987. "I loved him. Sometimes you can have a bond with a friend that other people don't understand. Even wives. It was rough in Louisiana, and we went through a lot together down there."

Speaking of his previous wives, Sam said, "Today I have great relationship with the mothers of my children. And I really appreciate that." Looking back, Sam candidly acknowledged, "I imagine any of those situations would have worked if I'd have worked at it." He tempered his tart self-criticism with an apologetic philosophical nougat: "You can't blame a dog for being a dog."

Sam Samudio and his wife, Ann, relaxing in August 2000, on the rear patio of their home in a rural area at the outskirts of Memphis, Tennessee. Photo by Jeff March.

That raised the paradoxical question: who was the real Sam the Sham, and what kind of person was he? "You should ask my enemies," replied Sam in his salt-dried drawl. But quoting Scripture, he found an answer. "Paul the Apostle said, 'In this flesh dwelleth no good thing.' What kind of person am I? I'm not anything but by the grace of God. I guess I'm critical and, at times, I can get full of myself. You know, you must always guard against becoming a legend in your own mind. And, if we're going to serve God, let's really serve God," he urged. "That doesn't mean you have to walk around with a long, drawn face trying to be sanctimonious. Look at me," he offered, grinning that mischievous Sam the Sham grin. "I still keep company with publicans and sinners."

Sam continued making public appearances into the early 2000s, when he went into retirement. He told us in June 2025 that he still was dabbling in writing poetry and composing songs, which he sung only to Ann.

Epilogue: David Martin

Bassist

March 20, 1937 – August 2, 1987

Although the colorfully costumed Sam the Sham and the Pharaohs were most often identified with lively novelty tunes, their roots were in the blues. And while Sam Samudio personified the group's on-stage image, the musical soul of the Pharaohs was embodied in David Martin.

If anyone was truly accountable for the formation of Sam the Sham and the Pharaohs, it was David. It was he who had recruited Sam to join Andy and the Nightriders in Louisiana. It was he who had solemnly declared with Sam the intent to capture a gold record. It was he who had encouraged Sam to persevere as Andy and the Nightriders were preparing to abandon their plans for stardom in Memphis. And it was he who provided musical direction in shaping the repertoire of Sam the Sham and the Pharaohs.

Born March 20, 1937, bass guitarist David Allen Martin had known Sam since high school days. Both grew up in West Dallas, the poor, working-class area that produced notorious '30s gangsters Bonnie and Clyde. Looking for something more than West Dallas could give him, Martin quit school and enlisted in the Army. Assigned to duty in Germany, he promptly joined a country music band called the Redeye Four. He also completed the requirements for his high school diploma. On his discharge in 1959, he returned to Dallas, where he worked in construction for a time before joining a rhythm and blues band called Tommy Brown and the Tom-Toms.

David first showed musical inclinations as a preschooler, when he became separated from his parents at the Texas State Fair. After a frantic search, they found him at the bandstand, where he was mesmerized by the musicians. David's father, Calvin, was a superintendent for an

David Martin in 1965, while on tour with Sam the Sham and the Pharaohs.

electrical contracting firm and his wife, Edna, was a homemaker. They encouraged David's musical development. "His daddy gave him a guitar when he was 11 years old and let him have lessons with a teacher in downtown Dallas. He'd take the bus there every Saturday from the Cement City neighborhood where they lived," according to Jean Martin, who was married to David from February 1964 until his death in August 1987. The first song he learned to play was "Red River Valley," which was popular in the late '40s. Tall and regal in appearance, David Martin had coal-black hair and a rich heritage of Dutch, German, and Native American blood.

Even though he was 6-foot-3, he was so small at birth compared to his four older brothers that his mother started calling him "Tiny." The name stuck. To his brothers and his friends at school, he was always "Tiny." Jean met David on Christmas Eve, when a few friends took her out for a night on the town to celebrate her 19th birthday. They went to the Colonial Club, a nightspot in Arlington, midway between Dallas and Ft. Worth. There, David was playing bass with Tommy Brown and the Tom-Toms. One of Jean's friends was dating a member of the band, and at the break the musicians came over to the table where Jean was sitting. David asked Jean to dance. That began a four-year courtship, during which David told Jean he would marry only when he was sure of his future. Jean herself was cautious.

"He was tall, well-mannered, and good-looking," Jean recalled upon first meeting David. "But I was very leery of dating him because he played in a band and I thought at that time that a man wanted only one thing, and I wasn't about to let him have it. And that's what I told him on our second date. That shocked him, but he was also pleased." Apparently so, because David went home and awakened his mother. "He told her that he'd just met a girl — a good girl. And then he took me to meet her. She told me I was the first girl he'd brought home in five years."

As Martin quit the construction job in 1960 to devote full attention to music, Tommy and the Tom-Toms signed on as the house band at the Guthrie Club — the hottest club in Dallas. While there David met a musician named Andy Anderson, who had his own band called Andy and the Nightriders. David accepted Andy's invitation to join the Nightriders, who had club dates lined up in Louisiana. Before long, David began making a name for himself. Barely in his 20s, he backed and toured with blues greats Jimmy Reed, Elmore James, and Lightnin' Hopkins as well as R&B pioneers Chuck Berry and the Drifters. Jean said his talent was self-evident. "He had a natural ear and perfect pitch, and he could play about anything he set his mind to playing," she observed.

David and Jean continued dating on his frequent returns to Dallas, where she worked in the billing department of Lone Star Steel. In Louisiana, David was joined by his former schoolmate Sam Samudio in the spring of '63. As the band's sound solidified, the bond

David Martin and Sam Samudio in the 1980s.

strengthened between Sam and David as they envisioned a recording career. On the encouragement of David and Sam, Andy and the Nightriders migrated to the music Mecca of Memphis that summer in quest of a gold record. Did David really believe at that time that a gold record was within their grasp? "Oh, yes," reassured Jean. "He believed that with all his heart, and of course he did get that gold record, and he was happy."

Martin's strong conviction weathered the skepticism of Andy and the other Nightriders, who chose to retreat to Louisiana after only a few months in Memphis. He and Samudio formed Sam the Sham and the Pharaohs with the addition of Ray Stinnett, Jerry Patterson, and Butch Gibson. "David was the one who picked all the songs that we played. He was the soul of the band," according to Patterson, the band's drummer. "David knew way more than we did about the blues."

Guitarist Ray Stinnett characterized Martin as a man of creativity, quiet intelligence and unpretentious goodness. Ray was close to David — off stage and on. "He's the guy who I shared a microphone with on more gigs than I can count," said Stinnett. "We used to make lots of jokes about all those onions that Dave ate corroding the mike. I never minded because we loved to sing harmony together. He made the most handsome Pharaoh when we were in our costumes," Ray added. "He had enough charisma to inspire the whole band."

As popular as the band was becoming and as close as he felt to his fellow performers, David couldn't ignore the empty spot in his heart.

At 3 o'clock one morning in January 1964, the phone rang at Jean's house in the South Oak Cliff neighborhood of Dallas. Jean answered.

Dave was on the line. "He'd had a little bit to drink," Jean recalled. "Will you marry me?" he blurted out. She asked him to repeat that. Mustering up a bit more confidence, he repeated, "Will you marry me?" Jean sat silent for a moment before replying, "Yes. Tomorrow will be fine."

The next morning at about 11, Jean phoned David.

"Do you remember calling me last night?" she asked him.

"Yes," he replied.

"And do you remember what you said?"

"Yes," said David.

They were married in a small church wedding on February 17, 1964, the first date David could get off work. They moved into the rented house that all the band members had previously roomed in together, while the other band members rented apartments elsewhere in deference to the newly married couple. And as the Pharaohs began touring, their wives frequently kept each other company, stayed overnight at each others' homes, and looked after each other. So it was when "Wooly Bully" hit. The night the boys headed off on their initial tour, Jean suffered a miscarriage. Saxophonist Butch Gibson's wife, Gwynne, took care of Jean during the difficult weeks that followed.

Even at the height of the group's popularity, David and Jean tried to live normal lives. He treated touring as if it were a day at the office. "To him, that was going to work. That was his job," said Jean.

Their daughter, Denise, was born in 1966, just as the band was breaking up. Leaving Sam behind, David, Butch, Jerry, and Ray remained together for a time and played in a few nightspots around Memphis and other cities in the South. But they were unable to land a steady gig. Money became tight for David and Jean because her accounting job at the home office of Holiday Inn couldn't quite stretch far enough to pay all the bills.

David decided to use his GI Bill benefits and enrolled in an electronics training course through the DeVry Institute. He played gigs by night, and baby-sat Denise during the daytime, studying while Jean worked. "We were kind of passing ships in the night for a while," Jean smiled wistfully as she recalled those times. "David finished his electronics course early and got excellent grades, because he had a high IQ," explained Jean. David landed a job with a big retailer in Memphis that sold home entertainment products and operated an in-store repair service. "He worked for them for about seven months before deciding it wasn't for him because the owners were dishonest," said Jean. "After David would repair a TV that somebody had exchanged because it was defective, the store would turn around and sell it as new again. He didn't care for that. He was a very honest person. He didn't like cheating people."

David Martin in 1986 exploring land on which he had hoped to build a home for his retirement years. Photo by Jean Martin.

So David and Jean opened their own television repair shop in Memphis called Martin Electronics. They built the business with steady clientele but closed in 1975 when Jean's allergies worsened and she developed asthma. They returned to Dallas. "He moved back for my sake," said Jean. There in Dallas, they started a new Martin Electronics store, offering TV and VCR repair. They closed shop nine years later, when their inventory of unclaimed repaired televisions became unmanageable. David remained in television repair, working as a technician for others.

Sale of the business permitted him to spend more time at home with Jean and Denise, which he relished. He had purchased a drum set for Denise when she was 8 years old, and he taught her how to play. Denise had fond memories of those days. "The first song he taught me was 'California Dreamin' by the Mamas and the Papas, and then 'Sloop John B' and 'Tequila.' We liked to clown around and play that. It started out just me and him and then all the kids in the neighborhood wanted to play, too," recalled Denise. "And we'd sing and he'd try to teach me harmony."

Denise said her dad continued playing his guitar, well after he'd gone into TV repair. "That was his relaxation, his comfort zone." Those informal jam sessions rekindled David's interest in music, and he began to consider managing the career of drummer Jeff Hilliard, with whom he had developed a close, paternal relationship. "My daddy loved him as a son," said Denise. But David was unable to fulfill his plan of guiding the careers of Jeff and other musicians.

David was home relaxing one August day in 1987 when he mentioned feeling ill. "He didn't like to go to the doctor, and when he got a feeling of heartburn he didn't think much of it. But when it didn't go away after a few hours and then he said his arm ached, I thought I'd better phone the doctor." David went to the bedroom. As she phoned the doctor's office, Jean heard a thud. She found David collapsed on the closet floor. He was rushed to the hospital, where doctors reported he'd suffered a massive heart attack. They were unable to save him.

Denise, who was 21 when her father died, confessed to having no particular interest in school as a young girl. "My interest was just getting home and being with my dad," she said. "He always gave. He always called me 'Baby,' and he would give me his last dollar for my lunch at school. He was usually home by the time I got home and we'd ride the lawnmower together and play guitar or swim. We had an above-ground pool in the backyard and we'd play water volleyball all the time. You know, he was a mentor, he was a friend. He had an open-door policy with you to find out what was on your mind. And he was that way with all my friends, too."

Married and a mom herself by the late 1990s, Denise bought her son, Dalton, a snare drum for his second birthday. One of Denise's best friends, a young man who studied drumming and talked music with Denise's dad, gave the name David to his first-born son. "What I miss most in my Dad I get to see and enjoy in my son, Dalton," Denise confided. David's brothers Max and Frank remained in the Dallas area, where they operated a freight auditing company. Their sister, Martha Barnes, was a computer operator for a Dallas firm.

Jean said three things mattered most to David: privacy, love for his family, and humankind. "He was a religious person, even though he didn't go to church," said Jean. "He knew his Bible inside out, and he lived life as a Christian daily."

Although David Martin did get his gold record, he never did achieve substantial riches. But that didn't matter much to him. "We both came from struggling families so we thought we were well off," explained Jean. "David always said when he was growing up that he thought the rich kids lived in the projects. We didn't know we were poor. We had love."

Epilogue: Ray Stinnett

Guitarist

Ray Stinnett learned the answer to one of his most puzzling musical questions early in his career. Although he was an apostle of blues music, he was unable to replicate the particular lonesome, melancholy whine that legendary African American blues artists coaxed from their guitars. He found out how one night from one of the masters, when he and drummer Jerry Patterson heard that B.B. King was playing at Club Paradise at 645 E. Georgia Avenue in Memphis. They went there and got a front-row table. Ray sat mesmerized through B.B.'s set, intent on watching his intricate fingering.

"After the set, B.B. stepped off the stage and we went over and talked to him. It was pretty obvious we were musicians because we were the only white guys there," said Ray. "I asked him, 'How do you get that sound with those strings?' And B.B. told me the secret. He said, 'I go down to the drugstore and buy myself a packet of Black Diamond strings and I buy an extra second string and I put that where the third string is supposed to go. All of the white guys use those wound third strings and you just can't pull those strings to get the blues sound, even if you know how to play the blues.' And that's what B.B. told me. The second string is unwound. It's just straight steel and it's thinner. So nowadays," said

Ray Stinnett in his home studio in the 1990s. Courtesy of Ray Stinnett.

Stinnett, "everyone uses an unwound third string. It's more pliable, you can pull it and that's how the blues sound is developed on the guitar. B.B. is the guy who started that sound. I think I was one of the first white guys to use that technique. I started stringing my guitar that way and from that day forward, I was able to play the blues much better than I had before."

Ray attributed his early interest in music to his uncle Mitchell "Mickey" Stinnett, who had played guitar and bass with bluegrass music pioneer Bill Monroe. "When my dad first came home from the war, my uncle broke out his guitar from under the bed, and I was hooked," said Ray.

Born James Ray Stinnett in Memphis on February 18, 1944, the red-haired guitarist went by his middle name as long as he could remember. Ray developed a strong interest in boogie-woogie music by the age of 7, three years before the debut of the earliest rock and roll songs. Inspired by a 12-year-old neighbor who played boogie woogie on the piano, Ray persuaded his parents to buy a piano and enroll him in lessons. Ray's mother was a beautician and his father was a civil service employee who worked for a time in the U.S. space program. Although Ray took lessons for several years, his teacher disliked boogie woogie and taught classical style only. "I'd occasionally get rapped across the knuckles with her ruler for playing boogie woogie," said Ray. "She finally gave up in disgust and advised my parents to sell my piano. She thought I was off on the wrong foot. And my parents listened to her."

Ray continued his musical pursuits at school, where he began playing horns and joined the school band. But "Daddy-O" Dewey Phillips' "Red, Hot, and Blue" radio program on WHBQ caught his ear, and after the station began playing Elvis Presley's recordings, Ray decided he had to have a guitar. "So in 1956 my folks took me down to Nathan Novick's Jewelry and Pawn Shop on Beale Street, the same place Elvis bought his guitar, and they bought me a guitar for $29," recalled Ray. "That same night, as fate would have it, Elvis was cruising Beale Street in his pink Cadillac, and pulled right up beside us at the stop light. I said, 'Hey, Elvis," and he answered, 'Hey, cat.' That provided all the inspiration I needed."

Ray took a few lessons from premier instructor and solid-body guitar maker Lyn Vernon, then began practicing with upright bassist Jimbo Hale, nephew of rock music performer Bill Black. Within a year Ray had hooked up with many other young musicians and eventually formed a band called Johnny and the Electros, which began playing sock hops and other local engagements. "We were highly competitive at Kingsbury High School, where kids who later formed the Gentrys had a rival band.

I started getting paid to play when I was 13 years old." Johnny and the Electros remained together for about four years. "I decided it was time to move on as I became more interested in jazz and black music."

Ray immersed himself in his music, to the exclusion of everything else. Or so he thought. "In January 1963, after telling a close friend I felt so dedicated to my musical pursuits that I was sure I would never get married, I met my true love, Sandra," said Ray. They were married a few weeks later. "She loved me and my music." A few months after Ray and Sandra were married, Sonny Wilson returned briefly from California, where he'd been working, and he invited Ray and Jerry to join him at a gig in San Bernardino, California — about 20 miles from Upland, where Ray and Sandra later moved. They played a few country music places in the area, but that didn't appeal much to Jerry and Ray and before long they returned to Memphis, where in the summer of 1963 they first encountered Sam Samudio and David Martin. That union would make them internationally recognized within 18 months.

Although "Wooly Bully" was a huge hit in major capitals as well as remote outposts, Ray didn't fully realize the vastness of its reach until years later, when he met a man who had done combat duty in Vietnam in 1965. "The guy hung out at a joint in Saigon where the only American tune on the jukebox was 'Wooly Bully' and they literally wore out the record. He said his company used 'Wooly Bully' to march cadence."

After Ray and the three Pharaohs parted with Sam in the spring of 1966, they began calling themselves the Violations and recorded "The Hanging," a song that Butch Gibson and Ray wrote protesting their treatment. Released on Dot Records, the song failed to capture attention and Butch decided to leave the recording business. David Martin, Jerry Patterson, and Ray Stinnett took a new name, the 1st Century, and landed a gig in Naples, Florida. They recorded some songs, including "Dancing Girl" and "Looking Down," which Ray wrote and Capitol Records released in 1968 as a single — but which did not chart. "On 'Dancing Girl,' I played harpsichord and recorder flute, which I had bought just the day before. On 'Looking Down,' I also played an instrument that I had made out of what used to be my dining room door. The door was played like a slide guitar."

The trio hooked up with Sonny Wilson, who invited them to come to California. Once again, Ray found himself playing in San Bernardino. It was the summer of 1967. The Beatles had released *Sgt. Pepper's Lonely Hearts Club Band,* 50,000 people converged on the Monterey

Pop Festival for performances by the Grateful Dead, Jefferson Airplane, Buffalo Springfield, Quicksilver Messenger Service and a dozen other acts, and Scott McKenzie's "San Francisco (Be Sure to Wear Flowers in Your Hair)" was an open invitation to America to come to Haight-Ashbury. Ray responded. In San Francisco, he heard about a place called Morning Star Ranch, a commune in the redwoods of Sonoma County on property owned by Lou Gottlieb, a former member of the Limeliters. Ray called Sandra at home and passionately described what he had found. She promptly sold off most of their furnishings and appliances, shuttered their house, and she and their 4-year-old son, Bobby, joined Ray at Morning Star, where they spent the "summer of love" living in a tent amid the redwoods.

"Before Morning Star, I was heavy into liquor, cigarettes, and the night life. While there, I learned how to have fun again, enjoy nature, and listen to other people play music. It was a sort of spiritual rebirth," Ray told us in August 1997. Morning Star began to attract more widespread attention. The BBC told the story of the commune in a documentary film. "Lou deeded the property to God, and God wouldn't pay the taxes, so that led to the eventual demise of Morning Star," deadpanned Ray.

He and his family returned to Memphis, where Ray reunited with Jerry, who had been playing with other bands. With Jerry, bassist Mike Plunk, organist Bruce Smith, and guest performers, Ray formed the group Sun Tree to perform his original material. In the summer of 1969 he recorded a double album for Buddha Records, produced by R&B stalwart Booker T. Jones. The album was not released, nor was *A Fire Somewhere,* a subsequent Stinnett-Jones collaboration for A&M Records two years later — not because of problems with agents or distribution, but for quite another reason. "I had my second child by that time and A&M wanted to make a superstar out of me, throw me into the bubblegum music market. That sounded like a nightmare to me. I had already gone that route with 'Wooly Bully,'" said Ray. "I didn't want to be a superstar. I just wanted my songs released. That's what I told them at A&M and they weren't too impressed. They said, 'We're going to release you from your contract instead.'" At that point, Ray made a momentous decision — to leave music.

Returning to Memphis, he took an interest in landscape design, inspired by his experience at Morning Star and by a little gardening he'd done while staying at Sam Samudio's apartment in the Hollywood Hills. Ray took a low-paying job with a Memphis landscaping outfit and found out, he said, what hard work was all about. Ray also began taking

Ray Stinnett with his wife, Sandra, in August 1998 in their home in Upland, California. Photo by Jeff March.

Yoga classes, became friends with his Yoga instructor and went into the landscape gardening business with him, working out of an old truck that Ray bought. He and Sandra then tried their hand at operating a health food store, Alfalfa's Good Earth Shop at 610 S. Cox Street in Memphis, for three years.

In 1982 they moved to Florida, where Ray got into construction work and then sold vacation time shares for a company that soon transferred him to Breckenridge, Colorado. When the time-share market weakened, Ray took a job with a construction firm building a Hilton Hotel at the ski resort. For a while the Stinnetts settled down, enrolled the kids in school and enjoyed life. When the construction job ended, though, the money ran out. "In 1987 we moved to Southern California the hard way: broke," said Ray. "We lived in our RV at the beach and went surfing a lot."

Then Ray started getting residential construction work in the communities around LA — first in Castaic, then in Newhall, then in Malibu. There, he found steady work with Sandpiper Construction, which had a heavy roster of celebrity clients. The Stinnetts were able to move from their RV onto a ranch that overlooked the Pacific, around the bend from Dick Clark's home. One morning Ray couldn't resist the urge to visit him. "I knocked on the door, Dick opened it and he asked, 'Are you the carpenter?' I said, 'I am a carpenter but probably not the one you're expecting.' When I told him that I'd worked for him years ago and handed him my card, that blew him away. Dick's a great guy. He showed me around his newly constructed home."

The Stinnetts restored the historic ranch house where they lived for three years while their daughters Christy, born in 1973, and Laurie, born in 1974, attended Malibu Elementary School. Meanwhile, their two older kids Marea, born in 1971, and Aaron, a year younger, were enrolled at Santa Monica High School. Aaron played in the drum line of the school's highly regarded marching band, while Marea played orchestral percussion, including xylophone. Marea became the century-old school's first female drum major and conducted from the podium.

Like other proud dads, Ray enjoyed watching his children perform with the band at Santa Monica High football games. As Ray sat in the bleachers at the football home opener one September evening in 1988, he had an unexpected and emotional reunion with an old friend. There to watch his own son Justyn play football was Carl Wilson of the Beach Boys, with whom Ray and the Pharaohs had appeared in concert at the Seattle Coliseum in 1965. They hadn't seen other in the 23 years since. The two men who had played to thousands of adoring, screaming fans sat side-by-side in the stands.

In 1990 the Stinnetts moved to Upland, in California's San Bernardino County, where Aaron and Christy joined their high school band. They marched in the Rose Parade on New Year's Day 1991, and Aaron performed at the 1991 U.S. Olympic Festival at Dodger Stadium. Although Ray still did construction and creative landscape through his own business, Ray Stinnett Custom Carpentry, he was becoming more interested in the music activities of his other family business, Stinnett Enterprises. Ray and Sandra later relocated to Lake Elsinore, California, where they began composing music and performing together under the name Time Warp and recording for their own label, AxeCut — a nod to Ray's "axeman" musician nickname. Meanwhile, Ray acquired the masters for his 1971 solo A&M Records double album *A Fire Somewhere,* which Light in the Attic Records released in 2012. Ray characterized it as "A perfect melding of Memphis soul and San Francisco psych, folk, and rock."

Dating from their experiences at Morning Star Ranch, Ray and Sandra continued their advocacy for protection and preservation of the

Earth's natural resources, and health through nutrition and exercise. Their lives took a terrible turn on April 28, 2017, however, when an aneurysm ruptured in Sandra's brain, resulting in a debilitating stroke. She died 13 months later, on May 28, 2018. In her memory, and in commemoration of the causes that the couple held dear, he burns sage in the olive memorial garden he created in the yard of his home.

Ray persevered, declaring "Bop 'til you drop." He continued to compose and perform music, driven by his long-held belief in the virtues of patience and hard work. "I intend to continue working hard on my music, which I have never really given up on. I've never hung up my rock and roll shoes. I try to break mine out every now and then and polish them up."

Epilogue: Jerry Patterson

Drummer

November 30, 1941 – August 5, 2020

Jerry Patterson in early 1966.
Courtesy of Jerry Patterson.

Until a momentary catastrophic event deprived drummer Jerry Patterson of the pursuit that had defined more than half his life, he thought he knew who he was. But through tragedy, Jerry learned a lesson in courage that opened an unexpected avenue of achievement.

As a teenager in 1950s Memphis, Jerry wasn't sure what to do with himself. Working the Cotton Exchange or the barges that floated down the Mississippi held no appeal for him. Shelby County kids didn't have many choices back then. Upon graduation from high school, Jerry took a job in a bread bakery. Even while some of his buddies took an interest in auto mechanics, truck driving, or assembly-line work, Jerry was drawn to Beale Street, immortalized by composer-performer W.C. Handy in his 1912 tribute called "Memphis Blues."

Perpetuated by the legendary Johnny Ace, T-Bone Walker, Memphis Slim, Lowell Fulson, Bobby Bland, B.B. King, and other blues artists, the pitch inflections or "bent pitches" that define the blues were infectious. Those "blue notes" hooked Jerry. Particularly captivated by the beat of many of the blues numbers he heard, Jerry bought a set of drums at the age of 19. He bought B.B. King's "Sweet Sixteen," put it on his phonograph, and began playing along. "That was the first record I ever practiced with, and that's how I learned to play," said Patterson.

Jerry was born November 30, 1941, one week before the United States was drawn into World War II. His father worked in a variety of trades in the postwar years. "He had cafes, stores, he worked on the river some," said Jerry. His folks encouraged his musical ambitions. "They were proud of my music career, especially Momma."

Jerry pursued his newfound interest with passion, and began practicing with a couple of local guitarists. "I always had my drums in my car and was ready to play at any time," recalled Patterson. Before long he landed his first paying gig with a rockabilly band at a dance club in Jonesboro, Arkansas. "The place was a concrete block square building along a country road out in the cotton fields. It paid $12 per night, and I had to drive 120 miles from Memphis three nights a week. The bass guitarist in that band, Marcus Van Story, later became part of the Sun Rhythm Section." Jerry had been playing there intermittently for more than a year at the time he met fellow musicians Ray Stinnett and Sonny Wilson, with whom he began playing in Memphis clubs. That led to some session work at a Memphis recording studio called Fernwood, where Jerry and Ray recorded backup tracks for aspiring singers.

Although Patterson wasn't getting rich, he was working steadily, enough so to settle down, he thought. In 1963 he met and married his first wife, Alma Josephine, shortly before he and Ray hooked up with Sam Samudio, David Martin, and Butch Gibson in forming Sam the Sham and the Pharaohs.

"We were young and crazy," remembered Patterson. "I was drinking a lot, doing pills. I was into alcohol and drugs more than anybody else in the band. I liked to have a party every night and sometimes went too far." All the while the British Invasion was spreading across the country, Sam the Sham and the Pharaohs continued pumping out the blues at nightclubs through the spring and summer of '64. That Halloween, the boys decided to have a little extra fun. That's the first time they wore the sheets that eventually led to their costumed stage persona. "During that whole period of time we had standing room only at our gigs, and we just got light-headed about it. Ray and I had never been around any kind of success. We were like stars. We'd drive there to do our show and we'd find a line of people outside waiting to see us. Even a little success can spoil some people," Jerry admitted. "So we got a big head and started getting goofy about it. I'd dye my hair bright orange or blond, and I caught a lot of grief from the rednecks there. But when you're a star, it doesn't matter. We were playing six hours a night and making $80 a week."

Only months after the Pharaohs were working on stage in smoky clubs in Memphis, they were appearing on screen in an MGM motion picture and on tour throughout the United States.

"I guess I knew we were going places when we met at a restaurant one night with a couple of record company guys and a lawyer," said Patterson. "They had mapped out a concert tour, and they had bought us a late-model Ford station wagon to ride in. It looked so exciting. We headed out in the station wagon and the hearse because we had a lot of equipment, including Sam's organ. It was heavy. The first date on the tour was in Holyoke, Massachusetts, and we had to drive there straight from Memphis. The rest of the tour was just as ridiculous, driving long distances like that. Still, we thought it was all right then because we were having so much fun. Later, we started flying to gigs."

But the high-flying days of Sam the Sham and the Pharaohs didn't last long. "Wooly Bully sold a few million copies. By the time that happened, it was all sour," said Jerry. "We figured we'd have a lot of money, about $30,000 apiece, when the first royalty checks came in just before Christmas in 1965. We went to a meeting but instead of money we got a huge statement sheet showing where all our money went for hotels, touring, and managers and stuff, and we walked away with nothing. The stack of statements was about an inch and a half thick. There were expense items in there like Playboy clubs and limousines, and we had never seen a Playboy club. I had a wife and a 2-year-old daughter, Randy Lynn, at home who I'd hardly ever seen. All the fun went out of it because my wife had no car, no money month after month, and for a year I kept telling her that it would get better." Even after he and the other musicians quit and headed home, Jerry somehow thought a solution would materialize because they had planned to retain the name Pharaohs and resume performing on their own. "When we got back, they said we owed them some money. That broke our spirit right there."

Legal action with the record company and talent agents over the use of the name ensued. For a settlement of $1,000 apiece, Patterson, Martin, Stinnett, and Gibson agreed to relinquish use of the name Pharaohs. After MGM told the four they had been in violation of their recording contract, they named themselves the Violations. They landed a recording contract with Dot Records, and with Stan Kesler as producer recorded an R&B-flavored single, "You Sure Have Changed" (which Paul Gibson wrote) backed with "The Hanging" (written by Gibson and Ray Stinnett). After the single failed to appear on any charts, saxophonist Gibson left the group. The three remaining members began playing clubs in Mississippi. Capitol Records offered a contract, but when that fizzled the group disbanded for good.

"We had our shots after Sam," said Patterson, dismissing any notion of bitterness. He and Ray reunited with Sonny Wilson, with whom they'd played before the Sam the Sham days. The trio decided to take their act to California. While playing at a country music bar in Orange County, they were drawn to the "summer of love" movement in San Francisco. "We couldn't stand playing that redneck music anymore and we loved the hippie ideals. So Ray and I drove to San Francisco and we lived in a car on the street for weeks." From there they drifted to the Sonoma County commune called Morning Star, sanctioned by former Limeliters member Lou Gottlieb. "Our wives were in Memphis with no money. After a while Ray brought his wife out. We stayed high a lot, but then I had all I could take of it. My mother sent me some money so I could fly back home. That's when Ray and I finally parted," Patterson said.

Back home in Memphis, Jerry returned to session work, which he did through the 1970s. In 1973 Jerry played with Tony Joe White on the last Creedence Clearwater Revival tour. "It was my last real party. Every night for three months, we had a time," grinned Jerry. "I did a little of everything until age 40." That's when he noticed some lumps on the right side of his neck. A physician told him he suspected the growth was cancerous and ordered a biopsy. During that procedure, the physician nicked a nerve in Jerry's neck. "The whole right side of my body immediately drooped," said Jerry, who is right-handed. "I couldn't raise my right arm for about a year. The biopsy showed that it wasn't cancer, after all; it was cat scratch fever." That's a benign short-term condition characterized by fever and inflammation of the lymph nodes.

Jerry, who knew only to play the drums, was confronted with a stunning reality: his playing career was over. "It was tough, but I think God wanted to get me out of music. I knew it was time to leave music but I couldn't do it on my own." Jerry was undecided what to do until an old friend called him. "Jimmy Day was a musician who I recorded with in the early 1960s. He once had a group called Jimmy Day and the Knights, but he had gone into paint contracting back in the 1970s." Jimmy asked Jerry if he wanted a job. "I don't know anything about painting," Jerry protested. "Well, I'll teach you," came Jimmy's reply. Jerry agreed, and spent the next year and a half working for Jimmy. "After he taught me how to paint, he decided to quit painting. He had a long list of customers and he gave me his list. I started calling people and got jobs."

Divorced from his first wife, Jerry met and married a woman named Joanne. She helped him through his painful recovery, but their marriage didn't survive. By this time his daughter Randy Lynn was married, and his other daughter, Lara Spring, born in 1972, was living with him. He built his paint contracting business, which he named Master's Touch. He began to hire painting crews to handle the growing volume of work. "But they got to be way too much of a hassle," said Jerry, observing an eerie parallel. "Getting a good paint crew together is like trying to get a band together. Many painters are temperamental and drink too much and do drugs. You can't depend on them." Jerry scaled down his operation a bit, hiring only one or two painters at a time as needed. He did home repair work and plastering as well as painting. "Whatever comes up," he said.

Jerry credited his resiliency to a seminal event that occurred in 1978, three years before his life-changing bout with cat scratch fever. "The Bible says no man can come to the Father except through Jesus and you can't come to Jesus unless the Father draws you," said Jerry. "In 1978, I was living with this girl and cutting up and getting drunk every night, but she was patient and she was Christian. One day I came in drunk and she started reading the Bible to me and led me into prayer. The next day I got up and I didn't want any drink or smoke or anything anymore. It's been like that since."

Jerry didn't make a big deal of his past. "I never tell people that I was in that band, but somehow people find out even now," he said. Jerry acknowledged that his music career remained his greatest source of pride. "I think I'm most proud of the fact that I made a living in music for so many years. It's a hard life and most people couldn't do it. Sam and the band went through a lot together, and I'm happy I can call him my good friend today," he told us in August 1997. Jerry continued to regard drumming as his greatest talent. "I can play at church now, but I can't play over 30 minutes at a time because there's a lot of pain."

After Jerry's third marriage, to Lorie, came to an end, he met the love of his life, clinical nurse Jackie Burton, whom he married in September 2009.

Through all the years, Jerry remained true to his musical roots. "The Black music of the 1950s had a profound influence on me. I was really caught up in it all the way. I wasn't a Christian then, but it didn't matter. The rhythms that the Black singers adapted from gospel music and the emotion that they sang with, I still love." Jerry's greatest regret was his abuse of drinking and drugs. "That's what killed my music career," he said candidly. "I would get a really fine job where I could have made steady money and I'd get too drunk some night and couldn't play. Or I'd get in someone's face. You know alcohol is like that. It's the devil. It cost me my first family and a lot of money. But pain is a relative term," he philosophized.

"I've been Christian long enough to realize a lot of fundamental truths; one is that God's in control," Patterson declared. "I believe the Bible, and the Bible says that all things work together for good to those that love the Lord. The bad things that happened to me don't seem so bad because they're working toward my good in the long run. God's not concerned about my comfort here. He's concerned about my spiritual well-being and my eternal life. So not many things cause me pain. I get angry like everybody else. But the pain like I used to feel, I don't feel that anymore." Citing Philippians, Jerry added, "For to me, to live is Christ, and to die is gain."

Jerry Patterson in the 1990s. Photo by Charles Gage.

Jerry Patterson died at 78 years of age on August 5, 2020, of causes related to COVID-19, complicated by the effects of a four-year decline from Alzheimer's disease.

Epilogue: Paul "Butch" Gibson

Saxophonist

Butch Gibson's saxophone has rested for decades in a closet in his home. The horn that helped coax James Brown to his feet has stood in silence since 1966. Dusty and tarnished, the instrument has worn pads that for years have rendered it unplayable. The horn remained a bittersweet reminder of the sadness and happiness of years gone by.

Butch never forgot the first time he heard "Wooly Bully" on the radio. He was listening to WHBQ in Memphis when disc jockey George Klein gave it a spin. Butch should have been excited, but other thoughts were on his mind. "I've got $2 in my pocket, and if we don't get paid at the club tonight, I won't be able to buy enough gas to get home," he thought. A month later, Butch and the other Pharaohs were performing on stage in Atlanta with the Beach Boys.

Paul "Butch" Gibson with his late wife, Gwynne, in the 1990s. Photo by Mary Frances Abernathy Gibson.

The skyscrapers and crowds of Atlanta were leagues away from the small west Tennessee town of Adamsville, where Paul "Butch" Gibson grew up. There, in the country about 100 miles east of Memphis, his folks operated the town's hardware store and a real estate business. Butch took a liking to blues and R&B when he began listening to John R. and Big Hugh Baby Jarrett around 1956 on WLAC, a Nashville radio station that drifted in through the blackness of the nighttime sky. "I listened to them playing Slim Harpo, Lightnin' Hopkins and those guys and I thought, man, that's really good music," recalled Butch, who was born Paul D. Gibson on October 2, 1944, in Corinth, Mississippi.

After taking his first music class in junior high, he began playing sax in his high school band. Following his sophomore year, Butch left Adamsville to attend a military institution, the Webb School in Bell Buckle, Tennessee. It didn't take Butch long to break out his sax and break into a music combo composed of fellow students. After graduation from military school in June 1962 he entered college at Southwestern at Memphis (later renamed Rhodes College). Following the lead of other medical professionals in his family, Butch enrolled in Southwestern's pre-med program, but he moonlighted in music.

His work with Joe Davis and the All-Stars led to his encounter with Sam the Sham and the Pharaohs, which he joined in January 1964. During his two years with the Pharaohs, Butch met and married his wife, Gwynne, who gave birth to Amy, the first of the couple's four children. That event presaged a dramatic change in priorities for Butch. "When Amy was born I realized I really didn't want to be a musician forever," said Butch. His career change came sooner than he had anticipated. "The group broke up over money," said Butch. "It's always about money, the same thing that breaks up homes." So when Sam the Sham and the Pharaohs disbanded in early 1966, Butch was perhaps more prepared than other group members to move on. And while he knew he needed to change directions, he made a lot of wrong turns up dead-end streets before he found his way.

His first post-performing foray was with his uncle's used-car business, but it didn't take long for him to realize he didn't like selling automobiles. From there he spent three years pounding on doors as a collection agent for a Memphis finance company. "That was pretty scary," he admitted. Then he got an inside job, working as a loan officer for a bank. Back outdoors again when he and one of his relatives formed a business installing and operating truck wash equipment at truck stops.

When the truck wash business partnership dissolved, Butch hired on as the manager of a truck stop he had been servicing in West Memphis, Arkansas. Within three years, the company, which operated truck stops throughout the South, appointed Gibson vice president of sales and marketing. In that position he developed a wholesale fuel program called Mid America Petroleum Suppliers. "I bought and sold enough gasoline and diesel fuel in the Memphis area every day to raise or lower the price of gasoline on the street by a penny. We sold a lot of petroleum," Butch reiterated. Butch's high-volume dealings drew news coverage in a national petroleum trade publication, *U.S. Oil Week* in Washington, D.C.

He remained happily in that post for eight years until the early '80s, when his friend and company founder Frank Wagner died and Butch found himself in business with Frank's wife and son. Butch sold his share of the business to them, then with his profits launched his own oil wholesaling business, which he named Phoenix Petroleum. He bought petroleum from refineries and sold it to independent service station operators and regional chains including Total Petroleum, which operated Vickers service stations in Memphis. Oil wholesaling is a tricky high-stakes business requiring impeccable timing. And deep pockets. A wholesaler must have sufficient finances on hand to take delivery as product becomes available at good prices, and try to have the right quantity on hand to match the needs of the service station owners. "Ideally, you want the checks to pass one another in the mail," explained Gibson. "It takes about a million dollars in credit to do it. You don't sleep real well in that business. You just stay in the fast lane, and you either get used to it or get out." Gibson quoted a Chinese proverb: He who rides the tiger has fear to dismount. For Gibson, the fear was well-founded. "The business was doing real well until the summer of 1986, when the price of crude oil dropped from $30 to $10 per barrel. I lost about $600,000 in eight weeks."

Butch decided to try his hand at real estate. Plunging in headfirst, he earned a broker's license to sell commercial real estate and sold properties totaling $1 million within his first three months in the business. "That was easy because I was dealing in commercial properties costing $300,000 to $500,000 or more. I sold $3 million in my first year of real estate business, but I earned only $30,000 due to commission splits. I thought, what's wrong with this picture?"

While in real estate he began taking an interest in the computers he was using. He saw new opportunity, and joined a division of the Ralston Purina Company after taking some courses in computer programming and systems management at Christian Brothers University in Memphis. "I went to work for Ralston as a computer nerd. Another example of being in the right place at the right time." Gibson became the financial systems manager of the company's Protein Technologies International subsidiary in Memphis, where he remained until his retirement in 1999.

By then age 55, Butch was once again prepared to move on. During his years with Ralston Purina, Butch went to Christian Brothers University and earned his bachelor's and master's degrees in business administration. In the spring of 1999, he began pursuing a doctoral degree with plans to inaugurate a new phase of his life, teaching business, computer science, philosophy, and theology at Faulkner State Community College in Bay Minette, Alabama.

Butch's interest in theology is attributable in part to his close call with death in 1992. When complications arose during gall bladder surgery, physicians told Butch's family they didn't expect him to survive the night. "I had an out-of-body experience during which I stood at the junction of two tunnels," said Butch. "One goes there, and the other comes back here. While I was in the tunnel I saw my old friend Frank Wagner, who had already gone on." Butch miraculously survived, but his wife Gwynne didn't. After 32 years of marriage, she died of cancer in 1996, leaving Butch to raise their four kids.

Despite the tragedy, Gibson felt bolstered by what he called the four Cs in his life: character, charisma, credibility, and Christ. "Character is something you get from your own life's experiences — the ups and downs that put the scars on you but give you soul. Charisma is something that you're born with to a degree, but which you enhance as you develop people skills. Credibility is something you earn by going to the well and coming back with water. You can gain credibility from successes, or from awards like college degrees. Then, of course, Christ is available to everybody. You just have to open your heart and say that you want Christ to take over your life and handle it." In that regard, Butch retained much in common with Sam and the other original Pharaohs. "Sam and I talked on the phone periodically. He was in touch with the family when I was so sick, and he was in touch with me when Gwynne died. He did a whole lot of good in his ministry for the homeless and for prisoners," Gibson told us in July 1997.

Butch resumed musical performing for a brief period in the early 1980s, when he sang lead for a Memphis gospel quartet called the Confederates. "We opened up with the Blackwood Brothers for a couple of years in Mississippi, Arkansas, and West Tennessee." Musical performance remained in his past after that, however. "I'm a lot different from the person I was in the '60s when we did the records. And I'm different from the way I was in 1995 before my wife died. I'm settled and comfortable, yet I'm still anxious about what I'm going to see next. I kind of amaze myself sometimes. I'm not afraid to take a risk and to change venues to take advantage of new opportunities. Every move I've made had been with myself and my family in mind. You have to measure the risks."

Although he generally was content with the choices he made, Butch had some regret about one opportunity he let pass him by. "Al Jardine of the Beach Boys was a good friend. We traveled with them. A lot of people have worked for the Beach Boys at various times. When Sam the Sham and the Pharaohs broke up, the Beach Boys came through town. Al called me and said, 'I heard you guys are breaking up.' When I told him we had, he asked, 'Would you like to come to work for us and do some studio work?' I turned him down. There were times later that I'd have changed that decision if I could have."

But Gibson didn't agonize over the past, preferring to focus on the future. "You know, persistence is the key. Just don't give up. It's hard to have an absolute career as a life goal. I think it needs to keep changing, because sometimes the worst thing that can happen to you is for all of your dreams to come true. Because then you ask, 'What now?' A lot of my dreams came true when I was in music, but I really looked forward to teaching college. I came from a small town and had a real strong Christian background. When I went to college, there were a lot of atheist and agnostic professors there who tried to challenge my faith, and that hurt me a lot." Although scholars have an obligation to raise questions and introduce their students to new and sometimes controversial ideas, Butch asserted that a predominant number of academics willfully blur the line between raising questions and forcing their own agendas. "Those professors are out there in increasingly greater numbers. I want to be able to tip the scales in the other direction a little bit."

To that end, he enrolled at Memphis Theological Seminary, where he earned an MAR (master of arts in religion) degree in philosophy and theology in 2005. As he pursued his studies, he met Melissa Michaels. "I have always believed in divine intervention. Meeting Melissa was no exception. By the summer of 1998, I had been a widower for two and a half years," Paul told us in December 2025. "My son was about to travel to San Juan, Puerto Rico, on family business and he needed a place to stay. I am a fan of Hampton Inns but I did not know if a Hampton would be in San Juan. So I called Southern Living Travel Service for advice. Melissa answered the phone. Her voice was so beautiful and calm, she was in no hurry, and when she laughed she sounded exactly like all the women in my family who raised me. I was raised in a home of four women with me and Dad. Each lady had several sisters for a total of 10 and they were all there from time to time for holidays, birthdays, fish fries, and those fun things. They all loved coffee and cold duck, and they all loved to laugh. So when Melissa laughed like my family I thought, 'Oh, man. Who is this?' And it just developed from there. We were married on the beach in 2004. When it's right you really do know it."

Despite earning his theological degree, Paul's academic evolution was not yet done. By 2020 he and Melissa had relocated to Foley, Alabama, and he began work toward another advanced degree, doctor of education (Ed.D.), at the University of West Florida. He conducted

Paul and Melissa Gibson at Gulf Shores Alabama State Park in 2004, celebrating their wedding. Courtesy of Paul Gibson.

original research exploring the experiences and training of teachers at a federally designated Title 1 school with a high percentage of students living in poverty. His research revealed the need for specialized, intensive training to better prepare teachers to nurture low socioeconomic status students.

Upon receiving his doctoral degree in May 2021, he established himself as a consultant, advocate, and researcher for public school systems, students, and teachers working with students living in poverty. He subsequently published studies related to improving training, strategies, and resources for teachers of students living in poverty, and he advocated for teachers who themselves are struggling financially. He also began writing a sermon topics newsletter distributed free of charge to pastors.

Gibson summarized his research findings in his book *Thanking Teachers Working in High-Poverty Schools,* published in August 2025 with the assistance of *For the Record* coauthor Marti Childs and the BookPrep service (www.book-prep.com) that she operates. "Teachers are often the primary caregivers for their students after parents, grandparents, or guardians," Gibson observed. "For the first time in educational research, our study shows that the longer you are a teacher, the deeper your commitment becomes. A new teacher will typically be a caregiver, then with time, a negotiator, then an advocate, and then a crusader. Those who have been teaching for the longest time are typically the crusaders. This discovery is totally new for educational research."

Even as Butch moved on, his time with Sam the Sham and the Pharaohs remained an indelible part of him. "Sam had a great stage presence," he reaffirmed. Butch's memory was etched with the whimsical rap that Sam recited to his audience at the close of each nightclub gig: "That old clock on the wall done caught up with us all, and we're going to roll outta here like a hole in a doughnut. Remember, you've got to be yourself or else you'll wind up by yourself. And like the old gypsy woman told me, life is short and talk is cheap, don't make promises you can't keep. And you know I love you baby, cause if I don't love you baby, grits ain't groceries, eggs ain't poultry and the Mona Lisa was a man."

"We were cool, man," said Butch. "We had it all."

Summer in the City

The Lovin' Spoonful

In pop music, the class of 1965 was resplendent in fresh talent, comprising a striking honor roll of new artists who graduated to the national singles charts for the first time. Performers making their debut on the *Billboard* Hot 100 that year included flamboyantly attired Sonny and Cher, the rock band Them with Van Morrison, rough-hewn, revolutionary folk singer Bob Dylan, Los Angeles-based Dylan disciples the Byrds and the Turtles, the forerunning San Francisco quintet the Beau Brummels, Great Britain's Yardbirds, and an electrified jug band quartet from New York's Greenwich Village called the Lovin' Spoonful.

The Spoonful emanated from the same roots that produced the Mamas and the Papas and Richie Havens, among others. During a prolific three-year run, the Spoonful put 13 memorable singles on the pop charts, the first seven of which all cracked the national top 10. Most were ballads and ditties flavored with the band's lilting "good-time" folk-flavored blend of instruments. But the group is perhaps best remembered for "Summer in the City," a hard-driving full-on dose of rock and roll that jackhammered its way to the top of the charts in July 1966.

The band's bilateral repertoire reflected the divergent backgrounds of its founding members: folk music aficionados John Sebastian and Zalman Yanovsky, who had been entrenched in the Bohemian scene of Greenwich Village, and rockers Joe Butler and Steve Boone from Long Island, New York.

Native New Yorker John Sebastian had honed his musical skills by hanging around the coffee houses of the eclectic Village, where in his late teens he sat in with John Hammond, Fred Neil, and Mississippi John Hurt, formed a backup duo with Felix Pappalardi, did extensive session work playing harmonica for Elektra Records, and performed with the Even Dozen Jug Band. John also worked with a baritone singer named Valentine Pringle, a protégé of Harry Belafonte. At one gig in late 1963 at a club called The Shadows in Washington, D.C., Sebastian and Pringle opened for a group called the Big 3, the members of which included Cass Elliot.

The Lovin' Spoonful in 1967. Left to right in foreground: Joe Butler, Jerry Yester, John Sebastian (wearing glasses), and Steve Boone. Zal Yanovsky, then departing the band, peers out in the rear from behind the barn door. Photo by Henry Diltz.

"Cass was instantly likable and funny, and conversationally astute. I loved her from the minute I met her," said John. The two became friends and kept in touch as the Big 3 grew to include members of a dissolved Canadian group called the Halifax Three, which included Denny Doherty and Zal Yanovsky. The merger of the two groups produced the Mugwumps, which John briefly joined as well.

Sebastian clearly remembered when he met Yanovsky in February 1964. "It was the evening of the Beatles' first appearance on *The Ed Sullivan Show,* which we all watched at Cass' house." A friendship soon developed as Zal and John discovered common musical interests. When the Mugwumps encountered difficulty gaining acceptance and disbanded, Cass and Denny became members of the New Journeymen, which evolved into the Mamas and the Papas. Meanwhile, Zal and John began looking around the Village for a bass guitarist and a drummer.

Since the early '60s, singer-drummer Joe Butler and guitarist Steve Boone had been playing together in a band on Long Island called the Kingsmen. When Steve first joined the Kingsmen as a college freshman in 1962, he was playing rhythm guitar, but was asked to switch to bass when the Air Force transferred the band's bass guitarist to Louisiana. "OK," Steve told the others. "That's two less strings to play."

Joe grew up in a working-class family in largely affluent Great Neck, New York. He led his first band at age 13 and performed music even after enlisting in the Air Force at age 17 in 1959. While stationed at Westhampton, Long Island, he enrolled in college courses through Long Island University, but found himself drawn to Greenwich Village.

Steve, too, slipped into the Village on weekends, taking advantage of the Long Island Railroad's student discount fare. True, the Village was grungy and populated by an assortment of characters. "But the Village was always exciting. That's where all of the action was," declared Steve.

After Joe's discharge from the Air Force in 1963, he continued working toward his college business degree while the Kingsmen changed their base to Greenwich Village, and changed their name to the Sellouts. Joe soon underwent a change as well. "I was introduced to my ex-wife's cousin, Peter Yarrow, one of the first musical celebrities I had met," acknowledged Joe. His reaction to Yarrow: "It struck me that he was just a guy. If he could be a star, I realized that so could I." That revelation provided all the incentive Joe needed to quit school in early 1964, just before completing his degree requirements.

When the Sellouts were playing six 40-minute sets a night at the Playhouse Cafe in the Little Italy section of New York, Joe attracted the attention of Mercury Records, for which he cut a few demo tracks beginning in late 1964. Producer Erik Jacobsen introduced Joe to John Sebastian and Zal Yanovsky, who were seeking a bass guitarist and a drummer. Joe suggested bassist Steve Boone.

Steve had taken a three-month break from college that fall, motorcycling through Europe with a friend. He had just returned from that trip in December when he met Sebastian and Yanovsky, and quickly agreed to join them in forming the band that would become the Lovin' Spoonful. Joe Butler hesitated, reluctant to leave the Sellouts.

Still unnamed, the band rehearsed throughout January at a hotel in Bridgehampton that had been closed for the winter. Steve and John broke camp only to do some session work with Bob Dylan in New York City. The band's eventual name was inspired by Mississippi John Hurt's song "Coffee Blues," in which the legendary scotch-and-coffee-drinking blues singer professed his love for his "baby" by the lovin' spoonful. As the new band took the name Lovin' Spoonful and began playing at the Night

Owl Cafe on West Third Street the following month, the members of the audience included Joe Butler.

"Zally totally hypnotized me and captivated me," said Joe. "He had a tremendous sense of crazy humor. He was loose, relaxed and was having the time of his life. John was a little serious, a little professorial in his presentation. They were doing mostly old jug band things, but a few John Sebastian originals were in the set, and they were good."

Erik Jacobsen finally convinced Joe that joining Sebastian, Yanovsky, and Boone would be a good move. It was late January 1965 when Joe agreed. The quartet began playing at various clubs in the Village — the Night Owl, the Village Music Hall, Café Bizarre — where they worked for peanuts. The four members of the Spoonful, along with Cass Elliot and Denny Doherty, all roomed that icy winter at the rickety Albert Hotel, where they rehearsed in the basement. "We lived on tuna fish and ice cream. Whenever we needed to pay the bill, we'd send Denny down to romance the girl who was keeping the books, and he got us a free ride many times," Joe grinned.

Bob Cavallo, manager of The Shadows nightclub in which Sebastian had previously played, caught the Spoonful's act and inked a deal with them — not for a booking, but as their manager. With front money put up by Erik Jacobsen, the band bought studio time and recorded some original material, including several sides that would go on to become hit records. The major labels were uninterested, but when Kama Sutra Records offered the band a recording contract as well as a publishing deal, the members signed. Though it was small, Kama Sutra had a distribution arrangement with powerful MGM Records.

Issued as Kama Sutra No. 201, John Sebastian's composition "Do You Believe in Magic" was a prophetic debut single for the group. After making its debut on the *Billboard* Hot 100 on August 21, 1965, the record magically took off in the summer of '65 and pushed into the national top 10, and the band appeared on a wondrous succession of television programs. On *Hullabaloo.* On *The Ed Sullivan Show.* On stage with Sammy Davis Jr. and the Supremes. "We went from playing to 200 seats in the Night Owl to playing in front of 60,000 at the Pasadena Rose Bowl," exulted Butler. That summer they recorded their first album, *Do You Believe in Magic,* which Kama Sutra released in October. In addition to the title track, it also contained what would become the band's fourth hit, "Did You Ever Have to Make Up Your Mind?" The amplified Autoharp zither that he played on most of the tracks contributed strongly to the distinctive sound of the Spoonful.

Kama Sutra already had released the Spoonful's second hit single, "You Didn't Have to Be So Nice" by the time the band started recording *Daydream,* the album on which it would appear along with the title track. Spoonful members John Sebastian and Steve Boone wrote "You Didn't Have to Be So Nice," which made its debut on the *Billboard* Hot 100 on November 27, 1965, peaked at No. 10, and remained on the chart for 12 weeks. The Spoonful ushered in 1966 in a "Daydream," the band's third chart single, which premiered on the Hot 100 on February 26, 1966. The John Sebastian composition peaked at No. 2, a position it held for two consecutive weeks, while hitting No. 1 in *Cash Box,* and remained on the chart for 12 weeks. The band's follow-up single, "Did You Ever Have To Make Up Your Mind?" made its debut on the *Billboard* Hot 100 on May 7. Lovin' Spoonful member John Sebastian wrote the song, which was inspired by his adolescent puppy love experience with two sisters at summer camp, and Erik Jacobsen produced the session. The song soared up to No. 2, a position it held for two consecutive weeks, and remained on the chart for 11 weeks. Sebastian also wrote "Didn't Want to Have to Do It," the tune on the flip side.

By 1966 the Spoonful had created such a strong presence that they were enlisted to appeared in and create the score for a wacky Woody Allen film, *What's Up, Tiger Lily?* That year they turned up the heat with "Summer in the City," a sizzling hit that burned up the charts. From the initial throbbing drumbeats to the break with jackhammers and impatient car horns, the track epitomized sweltering summer days and humid summer evenings, teased with the possibilities of nighttime romance. "Summer in the City," the band's fifth chart single, made its debut on the *Billboard* Hot 100 on July 16. John Sebastian and his brother, Mark, wrote the summertime anthem, and Erik Jacobsen produced the record. It knocked the Troggs' "Wild Thing" from the No. 1 spot on August 13, did not relinquish that position for three consecutive weeks, and remained on the chart for 11 weeks, ultimately earning RIAA gold record certification on September 19, 1966. That was one of four hit singles contained in the *Hums of the Lovin' Spoonful* album, which also included "Rain on the Roof," "Nashville Cats," and "Full Measure." John Sebastian wrote "Rain On The Roof," which first appeared on the *Billboard* chart on October 15, 1966. Erik Jacobsen produced the session for the song, which reached No. 10, and remained on the chart for 10 weeks.

Although John Sebastian and Steve Boone wrote most of the Spoonful's material, all the band members played a songwriting role.

They were versatile instrumentalists as well. John played guitar, piano, Autoharp, harmonica, and other instruments. Steve played organ, piano, and bass guitar. Zal played guitar and bass. All four sang and contributed song arrangement ideas.

The guys clearly had fun in the studio, evidenced by their playful use of an old manual adding machine to set a syncopated beat in "Money," and their rollicking performance of Sebastian's "Lovin' You," a good-time tune if ever there was one. The band played credible country music as well, delivering a mischievous poke in the ribs with "Nashville Cats" and "Darlin' Companion." John Sebastian wrote "Nashville Cats" as a playful tribute to the musicianship of country performers. Erik Jacobsen produced the session for the song, which made its debut on the Hot 100 on December 17, 1966. It peaked at No. 8, and remained on the chart for 10 weeks. In the meantime its flip side, "Full Measure," charted on its own beginning on January 7. Spoonful drummer Joe Butler, rather than John Sebastian, sang the lead vocal on that track, which reached No. 87 and remained on the chart for three weeks.

The soundtrack that the Spoonful recorded for Francis Ford Coppola's 1967 motion picture *You're a Big Boy Now* included one of the band's lovelier recordings, a wistful harmonica instrumental called "Lonely (Amy's Theme)," along with Sebastian's "Darling, Be Home Soon," the band's ninth chart single, which made its debut on the *Billboard* Hot 100 on February 11, 1967. The song peaked at No. 15, and remained on the chart for eight weeks.

On the road, audiences adored the Spoonful. Glorious moments included a stellar performance at the Hollywood Bowl in 1967 with Simon and Garfunkel, and an appearance at Fordham University in New York in which the audience coaxed the Spoonful out for nine encores. "Performing was a big party. It was rare to do a concert without continual yelling and screaming. It was wonderful. When they went ape shit, I was in heaven. It was the best response I ever got out of anybody," Joe laughed.

In February 1967 Kama Sutra released a compilation album, *The Best of the Lovin' Spoonful*, containing six of the band's prior hits along with popular album tracks. Fans snatched up that collection sufficiently for the album to earn RIAA certification that July 7.

The band found itself amid controversy in 1967, however, following disclosure of the arrest of Yanovsky and Boone in San Francisco the year before for possession of one ounce of marijuana they had obtained at a party. Under threat of Yanovsky's immediate deportation to Canada, he and Boone reluctantly acknowledged their source of the illegal weed. The story was kept quiet for nearly a year, until the *Berkeley Barb, Los Angeles Free Press,* and *Rolling Stone* learned about the incident.

"It was such a heart-wrenching ordeal that stigmatized me and Zally," said Boone, who with Yanovsky and the other band members paid for an attorney to defend the individual who was charged with selling the pot. Although their cooperation with police was vilified in the "underground press," mainstream kids outside the counterculture enclaves were largely unaware or unconcerned about the incident. Still, the harsh public reaction was a distraction and cause of dissension among the band members, precipitating Yanovsky's departure from the Spoonful in June 1967 and leading to the eventual collapse of the band.

Because he was a close friend of Erik Jacobsen's, guitarist Jerry Yester was aware in May 1967 of Zal's impending departure from the Spoonful. But Jerry said he was surprised when John Sebastian phoned and asked him to join the band. Jerry replaced Zal as lead guitarist in June.

Yester, a member of the highly regarded Modern Folk Quartet who had produced recordings for the Association and Tim Buckley, and performed on recording sessions for the Monkees, had long been friends with the members of the Lovin' Spoonful. He had, in fact, done vocal arrangements for the band and played piano on the recording session for "Do You Believe in Magic."

Erik Jacobsen had produced the Spoonful's first four albums — *Magic, Daydream, Hums* and *You're a Big Boy Now* — encompassing all their hits of 1965 and '66. But a dispute that arose over production of "Darling Be Home Soon" prompted the Spoonful to switch producers. They replaced Jacobsen with Joe Wissert, who produced the Turtles' "Happy Together," "You Know What I Mean," and "She'd Rather Be With Me." The Spoonful had previously recorded at Bell Sound Studios and Columbia Studios in New York City, but Wissert instead booked time for them at Mirasound Recording Studios at 145 W. 47th Street in Manhattan. There, the Spoonful took part in a pioneering technical experiment in 1967, when the group became the first rock band to record an album on an Ampex 16-track AG-1000 tape machine. In December 1967 Kama Sutra released the well-received album, *Everything Playing,* which yielded three hit American pop singles — "Six O'Clock," "She Is

Still a Mystery," and "Money." The driving rocker "Six O'Clock," the Spoonful's 10th chart single, made its debut on the Hot 100 on April 29, 1967. John Sebastian wrote it, and Erik Jacobsen produced the session. The song peaked at No. 18, and remained on the chart for eight weeks. The Spoonful next appeared on the *Billboard* chart on October 28, 1967, with "She Is Still a Mystery." John Sebastian wrote the gentle ballad, and Joe Wissert produced the session for the song, which peaked at No. 27 and remained on the chart for six weeks.

The Spoonful rang in 1968 with "Money," their 12th chart single, which made its debut on the Hot 100 on January 6. John Sebastian wrote the song, and Joe Wissert produced the session. Jerry Yester (who with Sebastian co-wrote the flip side, "Close Your Eyes") was credited for orchestration, with musical conducting by Jim Friedman. "Money" reached No. 48, and remained on the chart for six weeks. The Spoonful came back with "Never Going Back," which made its debut on the Hot 100 on July 27, 1968. That song was written by singer-guitarist John Stewart, whose expansive catalog of compositions includes the Monkees' "Daydream Believer," Rosanne Cash's "Runaway Train," and numerous songs for the Kingston Trio, of which he was a member before becoming a soloist. Chip Douglas produced the session for the song, which reached No. 73, and remained on the chart for five weeks. Following release of the *Everything Playing* album — their fifth — the Spoonful made a triumphant appearance on *The Ed Sullivan Show,* where they performed "She Is Still a Mystery" to a wildly appreciative audience.

Although many pop artists of the era, including the Association, the Animals, the Doors, and Simon and Garfunkel felt compelled to use their music as a forum for political and antiwar statements, the Spoonful purposely avoided doing so. "What set us apart was that we did decide against supporting any political cause," Steve explained. "We felt that if we could be non-political and provide some uplifting moments during some very tense times, that would be a fine mission in itself. But," he added, "by the time 1967 rolled around and a lot of our buddies were coming back in bags or with ugly stories to tell, we could see the handwriting on the wall for the end of good-time music."

After John Sebastian left the band in June 1968 to embark on a solo career, Joe, Steve, and Jerry maintained the Spoonful as a trio. Under Joe's guidance, the band produced two final charted singles, the country-tinged "Never Going Back" in the fall of 1968, and "Me About You," which barely broke into the Hot 100. "Me About You," the 13th and final chart single by the Lovin' Spoonful, made its debut on the Hot 100 on February 8, 1969. The song was written by Gary Bonner and Alan Gordon, who also collaborated in writing the Turtles' "Happy Together," Petula Clark's "The Cat in the Window (The Bird in the Sky)," and Three Dog Night's "Celebrate." Bob Finz produced the session. The song reached no higher than No. 91, and remained on the chart for only two weeks. Although the trio disbanded at the end of 1968, they were able to look back with pride on an association that left behind a catalog of memorable music for millions of lovin' fans.

Lead guitarist Zalman Yanovsky, who was born December 19, 1944, went solo after leaving the Spoonful in 1967, co-produced an album for Tim Buckley, and was lead guitarist on a Kris Kristofferson tour. Zal and his wife Rose subsequently founded and operated the popular restaurant Chez Piggy in Kingston, Ontario, Canada. He died of a heart attack at age 57 on December 13, 2002.

Steve Boone, Jerry Yester, and Joe Butler resurrected the Lovin' Spoonful and resumed touring in 1991. The reconstituted band recorded *Live at the Hotel Seville,* an album recorded in Harrison, Arkansas (where Jerry Yester had moved), and released on the Varèse Sarabande label in 1999. The band was inducted into the Rock and Roll Hall of Fame in 2000 and the Vocal Group Hall of Fame in 2006. Steve Boone, playing keyboards as well as bass, fronted the band that continued performing into the mid-2020s with lead guitarist Rob Bonfiglio, guitarist and singer Jeff Alan Ross, bass guitarist and singer Bill Cinque, and drummer Mike Arturi.

THE LOVIN' SPOONFUL

U.S. HIT SINGLES ON THE NATIONAL CHARTS

Debut	Peak	Gold	Title	Label
8/21/65	9		Do You Believe in Magic	Kama Sutra
11/27/65	10		You Didn't Have to Be So Nice	Kama Sutra
2/26/66	2		Daydream	Kama Sutra
5/7/66	2		Did You Ever Have to Make Up Your Mind?	Kama Sutra
7/16/66	1	▲	Summer in the City	Kama Sutra
10/15/66	10		Rain on the Roof	Kama Sutra
12/17/66	8		Nashville Cats/Full Measure	Kama Sutra
2/11/67	15		Darling Be Home Soon	Kama Sutra
4/29/67	18		Six O'Clock	Kama Sutra
10/28/67	27		She Is Still a Mystery	Kama Sutra
1/6/68	48		Money	Kama Sutra
7/27/68	73		Never Going Back	Kama Sutra
2/8/69	91		Me About You	Kama Sutra

▲ symbol: RIAA certified gold record (Recording Industry Association of America)

Billboard's pop singles chart data is courtesy of Joel Whitburn's Record Research Inc., Menomonee Falls, Wisconsin.

Epilogue: John Sebastian

Lead singer, guitarist, Autoharp player, and composer

Throughout his durable career, John B. Sebastian has performed with some of the most prominent folk and blues artists of the 20th century. Bob Dylan. Judy Collins. Fred Neil. Tim Hardin. Maria Muldaur. John Hammond. The Serendipity Singers. Peter, Paul and Mary. Mississippi John Hurt. Lightnin' Hopkins.

But he derives his greatest sense of professional pride and some of his fondest memories on stage from his association with a blues mandolin player named

John Sebastian in the 1990s. Photo by Catherine Sebastian.

James "Yank" Rachell, whose recording career spanned an astonishing 68 years. Already a celebrated artist in Memphis 15 years before Sebastian was born, Yank Rachell was in his 80s when he recorded some tracks and performed on stage a few times with the jug band in which Sebastian blew diatonic harmonica and played guitar.

Sebastian never forgot the day he was stepping off the stage following a performance with Rachell, who had diabetes and who had undergone dialysis the day before. Turning to Sebastian, Rachell crowed, "Man, if I had a guitar player who could play as strong as you, I might be able to do this for another 40 years." Even though Rachell had grown frail and suffered from painful arthritis, the stage energized him and he continued performing until his death at the age of 87 in April 1997. With an air of reverence, Sebastian said, "To play with Yank and to hear him say the things he told me were every bit as valuable as all the screams for the Spoonful on *The Ed Sullivan Show.*"

While some contemporary pop music stars have professed that they drew their inspiration from rock and roll performers of the 1950s and '60s, John Sebastian cherished the music upon which the rock and roll genre itself is based: blues, country music, traditional folk, ragtime, and jug band music. It was no accident that jug band music was mentioned by name in the very first Lovin' Spoonful hit, "Do You Believe in Magic." Jug band music was a formative interest for John Sebastian as a young man, and the desire to preserve that element of Americana remained a driving force in his life.

With an interest in music stemming from his childhood, Sebastian had learned to play harmonica, guitar, electric bass, and Autoharp before the age of 20. While a member in 1964 of the Even Dozen Jug Band, the members of which made about $25 apiece per gig, Sebastian began getting an increasing amount of work as a session musician, making $51 per three-hour recording session. Sebastian's harmonica was heard on most of the early output of Elektra Records, on recordings by Tom Paxton, Judy Collins, Fred Neil, Tim Hardin, and other folk artists emerging from the Greenwich Village music scene.

Unlike most of his contemporaries, Sebastian didn't migrate to the Village. His family lived there from the time he was born, on March 17, 1944. John B. Sebastian and his only brother, Mark — who co-wrote "Summer in the City" — grew up in a musically rich environment. Their father, John Sebastian Pugliese, was a classical harmonica virtuoso who was born in Philadelphia and later truncated his name, adopting Sebastian as a family name. As a soloist, he played with the New York Philharmonic and the Philadelphia Orchestra, the Tokyo Philharmonic, and orchestras in Rome and Milan. Young John's mother, Jane Bishir, was a script writer in the heyday of radio. Young John, whose middle name is Benson, was known at home and to his friends as J.B.

"My father was the greatest classical harmonica virtuoso who ever lived," proudly declared John B., who began playing harmonica as a 4-year-old. "A diatonic harmonica like the ones I learned to play can produce two or three notes between the regular notes based on chords," Sebastian explained. "If you inhale, you get a seventh chord and that technique came from an African-American tradition. That's the key to playing the blues."

Although he had an idle interest in veterinary medicine and acting during his high school years at Friends Seminary in New York City, he was far more intrigued by what was happening in the neighborhood of his parents' Greenwich Village home on Bank Street. "I was 16 in 1960, a perfect time for my attraction to folk music." The "Sundays at the Park" folk music gatherings in Washington Square were only a few blocks away. His acquaintances there included another young fellow, at that time a portrait artist from Brooklyn who worked with chalk and enjoyed singing doo-wop. The portrait artist was Richie Havens, who in 1969 would appear along with Sebastian on stage at Woodstock.

During the two years of his early adolescence when he had lived with his family in Italy, John B. picked up a bit of the language. So when he was told to go to college, he enrolled at New York University in the fall of 1962 with a major in Italian. "I was a total goofball," he laughed. He spent more time working in a Greenwich Village guitar shop trying to earn a guitar than he did at his studies. He didn't need much of a nudge, and one day he received a phone call from finger picker Stefan Grossman.

John Sebastian in 2021. Photo by Franco Vogt.

"We started a jug band and you're in it and rehearsal is today," Grossman blurted. The model for the new assemblage, called the Even Dozen Jug Band, was the Jim Kweskin Jug Band. The jug band music genre, popular in the South when Yank Rachell was a young man, draws its rich sound from skilled players who can evoke just about any note in any key from ceramic maple syrup jugs. Before the members scattered, the Even Dozen Jug Band quickly achieved renown, playing Town Hall and Carnegie Hall.

The Even Dozen Jug Band, which had as many as 14 members, also brought John B. into contact with Paul A. Rothchild, who would later produce the Doors and most of the artists in the Elektra catalog. It was Rothchild who booked Sebastian for much of that session work. And it was Rothchild who would produce the solo *John B. Sebastian* album for Warner Brothers after Sebastian's departure from the Lovin' Spoonful in 1968.

Sebastian defined the Spoonful's place in the evolution of pop music by saying, "The Lovin' Spoonful was truly the first American band in post-Beatle America that was not seeking to imitate the English sound. We were seeking to combine as many American influences as we could,"

John told us in September 1998. "Now, granted, the Beatles had taken as many American influences as they could to incorporate into their sound. But part of what made them who they were was the fact that they were Englishmen. Rather than to try to imitate Englishness, we decided to follow them only in the sense that we were going to be a self-contained band, without using session musicians and by doing our own writing."

Sebastian left the band in June 1968 because it seemed to him that it had run its course. "As somebody who was there in the beginning, I had a sense of the arc of the success of the group," he said. "By then, not only had I learned a lot about the studio, but I had accumulated friends who were studio musicians. Once three years had gone by people I knew had advanced as members of groups or producers. I also wanted to move forward musically and try to carve out a solo career. I never conceived that the Spoonful would go on. I began to build another body of material and I began to record."

Sebastian's departure from the Spoonful coincided with dramatic change in other aspects of his life. Newly divorced after his 18-month marriage to his wife, Loretta Kaye, Sebastian sold his secluded house in rural North Haven, eastern Long Island. He accepted the invitation of a friend, Modern Folk Quartet member Cyrus Faryar, who owned some outbuildings that were part of an old hunting lodge behind the Warner Brothers television production lot in the hills of Burbank, California. John took up residence on the property in a tent for a Volkswagen Camper van. "It was sufficient because I was mainly on the road at that time," said Sebastian. "I had accumulated a lot of debt, because I had not realized how much I was going to be taxed." Sebastian's financial austerity was exacerbated by a prolonged legal tussle between MGM, distributor of the Kama Sutra label for which the Spoonful had recorded, and Warner Brothers, with whom Sebastian had contracted as a solo artist. Release of his first solo album was delayed a year and a half as a result.

Faryar's property during that time became somewhat of an artistic haven populated by other musicians and actors. While there, Sebastian met a photographer named Catherine Barnett. Over time, they developed a friendship. In 1971 John decided he wanted to take a leisurely drive across the country in a truck and he wanted Catherine to accompany him. She agreed, and during that trip, their friendship grew into a relationship. That trip, on which they were accompanied by another couple, Bart and Carolina Carpinelli, fueled the idea for a Sebastian solo album called *The Four of Us,* which the Warner-affiliated Reprise label released in 1971.

During the following years, John was content to record as a soloist and play small club dates. He and Catherine married in 1972 and settled in the Los Angeles suburb of Tarzana in a home they bought from Iron Butterfly guitarist Erik Braunn. John had just signed with manager David Bendett of Brooklyn in 1975 when a TV producer phoned Bendett. "I'm trying to find a John Sebastian-type guy to write a song for me for a new television show," the producer said. "How about John Sebastian?" replied Bendett.

Sebastian was interested. After reviewing a 10-page show synopsis and a couple of potential scripts, Sebastian wrote "Welcome Back," the theme for the hit television series *Welcome Back, Kotter.* The project came at a time when Sebastian had decided to extract himself from his contract with Warner Brothers Records.

"With Alice Cooper posters on the walls at Warner Brothers, it had become obvious to me that it could be hard to be a John Sebastian-type guy with that label, because I was not going to suddenly show up with studs and leather," Sebastian explained. A few Warner Brothers officials agreed until the label began receiving phone calls from record stores throughout the country inquiring about the Kotter television theme. The label rushed Sebastian into a studio, and he assembled an album incorporating other material he had already written. The single and the album were released in 1975 on the affiliate Reprise label. "It was an odd period when I couldn't get the attention of the record company, yet 'Welcome Back' became the second biggest-selling single of the year," Sebastian said wryly.

"Welcome Back" became a welcome back for Sebastian. "It permitted me another long breath in my solo career. It resulted in some tours that were a lot of fun," said Sebastian. He spent a summer opening stage appearances for Steve Martin, who had just unveiled his "wild and crazy guy" persona. Sebastian also worked with Robin Williams, George Carlin, and Billy Crystal. "I was a very logical opener for a comedian because I didn't need a band, so it made for a very compact traveling unit."

Sebastian quietly continued recording and performing solo through the 1980s, as well as with a group called the Little Big Band, which included drummer James Wormworth and guitarist Jimmy Vivino, who later would join Conan O'Brien's television show. But 1991 brought another professional change into Sebastian's life. A Sony Music executive phoned and said, "You know Sebastian, I'll bet you could put together about the best jug band in the world." Sebastian replied, "You

John Sebastian in 2021. Photo by Franco Vogt.

know, you're absolutely right." Sebastian recruited his friend Fritz Richmond, once the washtub and jug player in the Jim Kweskin Jug Band, along with guitarist Paul Rishell and harmonica player Annie Raines. They formed the core of a musical group called John Sebastian and the J-Band, which began playing summer concerts, rock and roll bars, folk and blues festivals, fairs, and just about any other kind of musical venue.

While touring, Sebastian met Yank Rachell and began the association from which he derived so much pride. "Yank was pleasantly surprised that we were playing in a style he had played 50 years before. He loved the fact that I would stay on this old six-string banjo and that the jug player could play in any key. He knew how unusual that was."

For part of their first jug band album, Sebastian and his group members traveled to a studio in Indianapolis, where Yank lived in his last years. There, Yank recorded two tracks for the first album release by John Sebastian and the J-Band, *I Want My Roots.*

"Yank was 87 years old at the time, and after that we traveled with him to Brownsville, Tennessee, his old home, and did a concert there at a location where he was never allowed to play as a young man." In early 1997 Sebastian's ensemble played a benefit concert in Indianapolis that raised funds to help pay medical costs for the ailing Rachell, who was suffering from kidney failure in the months before his death. Tracks recorded at that concert were included in the J-Band's CD *Chasin' Gus' Ghost,* which was released in early 1999. The album's title honors pioneering jug band musician and composer Gus Cannon, who died in 1979 at the age of 94.

Although Sebastian was enlisted for a lot of session work in the early 2000s, the J-Band remained his principal musical interest. His objective was gaining greater visibility for jug band music.

John, who appeared on stage at the Woodstock Music Festival in 1969 crooning his tender song "Younger Generation" about the joys and trials of parenthood, led a comfortable life three decades later with his family near Woodstock, New York. He and Catherine, a successful anthropological and portrait photographer whose work has graced scores of album covers, raised two children of their own: Benson, born in 1972, and Charlie, who was born in 1986. Sounding remarkably like the parent he had anticipated when he wrote "Younger Generation" three decades before, John was quick to identify the greatest challenge he faced in his life, musical or otherwise: "Parenting. I think that's a real challenge," said John. "Music is easy."

John Sebastian was inducted into the songwriters Hall of Fame in 2008.

Epilogue: Joe Butler

Drummer, guitarist, and singer

Joe Butler relaxing in his hotel room before performing on September 12, 1998, at the Harvest Fair in Placerville, California. Photo by Amanda Domingues.

For more than half of his life, Joe Butler had been a musician, earning income behind his drums and behind a microphone. Then suddenly, when he was 27 years of age, it came to a halt. The breakup of the Lovin' Spoonful in 1968 was devastating to Butler. "It happened very abruptly," he said. "I didn't have any kind of grace time. We received far less money than we had been expecting. I was on the street instantly, and needed to earn money right away." However, he was in anything but the right frame of mind to find other work. "The hardest thing I've ever had to do is keep my spirits up when I was down and out and had given up on myself," he acknowledged. "In the music business, a lot of bodies have washed up on the shore, not because of drugs but because of having their hearts broken."

But Joe, always emotive on stage, took stock of his resources and decided to try his hand at acting. Immersing himself in method acting studies, he achieved remarkable success, doing Shakespeare and Chekhov with the prestigious Circle Theater Company, and landing leading roles in Broadway productions of *Hair, Mahogany,* and *Soon.* Drawn by the cinema, Joe sold his apartment at 105 Bank Street in Greenwich Village to John Lennon and Yoko Ono, and moved to Los Angeles. There, he was cast in a half-dozen motion pictures, including *Born to Win* with George Segal, *The American Game,* and *One-Trick Pony.* Even so, he became disillusioned with Hollywood. "I didn't know the system well enough. I didn't know how to make that crossover from stage to films," he said.

He decided to enter a more welcoming labor market: residential construction. Two years after he was pounding his drums before thousands of fans, Joe was pounding nails into wallboard. One of his first jobs was construction of a home for comic Dan Rowan. Following Joe's marriage to Leslie Vega in 1967 and the birth of his daughter, Yancy, in July 1970, construction work supported his young family. Moving with them back to New York, Joe graduated to more polished finish carpentry and eventually became a foreman, supervising large construction projects. Although he survived the career change, his marriage didn't. By 1978 the relationship was on the rocks, and Joe and his wife divorced.

Living once again in Greenwich Village, Joe answered his phone and heard a voice from the past. It was Kim Ablondi. "She had been a neighborhood kid when I lived on Bank Street in the Village in the early '70s," Joe explained. He had heard that she had moved to San Francisco several years before. She was working as a congressional aide in Washington, she told him. They decided to renew acquaintances. "When I saw her I fell like a ton of bricks," said Joe. They were married in 1982, and took up residence in the Village.

Through the first decade of their marriage, Joe was content to work, anonymously, in construction. After all, he'd been working since he was a kid, unlike many of his more privileged childhood friends. Born September 16, 1941, in Glen Cove on Long Island's largely rural north shore, Joe had a newspaper route during his grammar school years, and at age 12 got a job washing dishes at a soda fountain. "I was under age, and my apron was so long, I had to fold it at the waist so I didn't trip on it," Joe chuckled. "I remember being so proud of having that apron. I didn't want to take it off. It was like I was a grown up because I was earning money. I wanted to contribute to the family."

Joe, whose father was a police officer, credited the formation of his childhood interest in music to his mother, who once sang in a talent contest in which she lost to an adolescent Frank Sinatra. Joe tried his hand at trombone in grade school, but quickly dismissed that instrument when he realized he wanted to sing. He tried guitar but had an unsatisfying experience because of the poor quality of the instrument he was using. Then he paid a kid a couple of bucks for a pair of drumsticks and some brushes, and began pounding out rhythms on newspapers and chair seats. His folks set him up with an old drum set in the basement, where he practiced for hours, singing and playing along with records by Danny and the Juniors and other early rock music performers.

At age 13, Joe started playing in a combo with a guitarist and an accordion player. The group played mostly country music in a local delicatessen, and Joe reveled as Elvis Presley took his rockabilly tunes into the mainstream of pop music. "I shied away from the Irish music," said Joe. "My family was Irish and it was embarrassing when the old timers played their fiddles. Now I love the stuff. Somehow it raises the hackles. If I hear a bagpipe, I'm looking for my sword and a hill to charge down." But Joe grew up in a community in which 93 percent of his high school graduating class was Jewish. He was one of few gentiles, non-Jews. Only later did he learn that his heritage included some German-Jewish blood.

After graduation from Great Neck North High School in 1959, Joe enlisted in the Air Force at the age of 17 to earn money for college. He was assigned for the majority of his time to an installation at Westhampton Beach on eastern Long Island, where he compiled aviation weather forecasts for flight crews. He took courses at Long Island University toward a business degree through much of his four-year stint in the military, but his heart wasn't in it. He felt pressured to get a business degree. "It was the curse of the working class, the fear of the Depression that forced parents in that era to press for something to fall back on," Joe told us in May 1998. Although Joe had enough credits to graduate, he hadn't quite completed the requirements for a business major when he decided to pursue music and moved to the Village in early 1964. "We were in the war, I had grown to dislike the military, President Kennedy had died, and there was a lot of bitterness in the nation." Joe said he viewed the focus of the Greenwich Village music scene on peace and love as a "noble attempt to try to find another solution."

Joe remained proud of his years with the Spoonful, and proud that he survived the dissolution of the band as well. Difficult as that was, it was not nearly as emotionally draining as the breakup of his first marriage. "We went for therapy, which was healing and helping," Joe declared. "A lot of people laugh at therapy until they need it. With the help of therapy, we scrapped the marriage and kept the friendship. We never used our daughter as a weapon, or resorted to other cruel things that some people endure." But the process still brought Joe to his lowest ebb. "I had a feeling of real worthlessness," he confided. His work in construction was the mechanism by which he began pulling himself out of his depression. "Getting some money in my pocket, so I wasn't always out of money and always frightened, helped a lot." But most instrumental was a remark in a speech at his daughter's high school graduation in Brooklyn." When a speaker said, "Remember, it's not the road you take, it's how you take the road that you find yourself on," that struck a chord with Joe. "That thought really gave me solace and comfort. It re-established me. I had joined the human race as a working person and realized that's okay."

Although he came to terms with anonymity, his past shadowed him. Like a scene from the motion picture *Eddie and the Cruisers,* each time Joe heard a Spoonful song, that would be a painful reminder of the money he said the band members were still owed. That unrest ultimately led to the resurrection of the Lovin' Spoonful in 1991. "One of the reasons we got back together was to fight back and claim our money. We had been given a large advance and then cut off and still to this day, we don't have one piece of paper accounting for that money. We fought for and received a settlement. We were granted future royalties, which we collect now," said Joe.

In October 1991, Joe, Steve, and Jerry rented a house near Pittsfield, Massachusetts. After a month of rehearsals, they played a date on Thanksgiving in Kitchener, Ontario, then a New Year's Eve party in Athens, Ohio. The band members lined up a schedule of dates for the following summer, and continued touring after that. In that incarnation of the Spoonful, Butler stepped out from behind the drums as lead singer, performing the classic Spoonful hits, as well as new material.

"One of the reasons we put the band together was to serve as a vehicle for this new music that Jerry, Steve, and I have been writing," Joe told us in May 1998. "Jerry is a virtuoso and could certainly be making records by himself, but I think the most interesting recordings are made by groups of people. I'm a believer that if you have one person, that's just one, but if you have two the square is four, if you have three it's nine, and so forth. So the group concept becomes very powerful. John [Sebastian] had been the only representative in the Spoonful with any visibility, and rightfully so. After all, John is one of the great American songwriters of this century. But none of us had that kind of visibility on our own. Steve and I had some skills and we got a new level of confidence when Jerry joined in with us. And now with the addition of Jerry's daughter, Lena, who also writes, we all have something to contribute. We're getting good reaction to the new stuff. Our audiences are excited about it." And he believed that's with good reason. "I'm performing better than I ever have in my life."

In doing so, he drew upon some of his earliest experiences. In 1998, the Spoonful recorded and released an unplugged set in which Joe drummed on a vinyl chair cover and on a phone book, reminiscent of the kitchen surfaces he played as an adolescent before he acquired his first drum set. "I had just those two sounds, a tambourine and some maracas, and that was one of the most charming recordings," said Joe.

Following Joe's footsteps onto the dramatic stage, his daughter Yancy has starred in several television series, including *Mann & Machine, South Beach, Brooklyn South,* and *Witchblade,* as well as the motion pictures *Hard Target, Drop Zone,* and *Zero Tolerance.* Joe expressed equal admiration for his wife, Kim, whom Joe playfully called an "obsessed" marathon runner. She became an administrator in the graduate illustration program in New York's School of Visual Arts.

Among all 128 tracks that the Spoonful recorded, Joe said he was fondest of the band's hits. "I always loved the hits. There's a reason why they're hits," asserted Joe. "They say something to a lot of people, and they're basic and open, and a lot of people can envision them like a book. When you read *The Green Leaf,* it's your green leaf. So I love 'Summer in the City,' 'Magic,' and 'You Didn't Have to Be So Nice.' And I like 'Full Measure' because I got to sing lead on it, and it's a great song. I don't ever get tired of them."

Epilogue: Steve Boone

Bassist

Steve Boone in Placerville, California, in September 1998. Photo by Amanda Domingues.

In the decades since the breakup of the Lovin' Spoonful in 1968, Steve Boone lived a life of adventure in the Caribbean, acquired a valuable business at a time when he had little cash and few assets to his name, and watched to his horror three years later as his investment sank — literally — to the floor of Baltimore's Inner Harbor.

Steve developed his affinity for the sea in his childhood. As a kid, he was shuttled from one place to another. He was born September 23, 1943, on the U.S. Marine Corps base at Camp Lejeune on the North Carolina coast, just down the road from Cherry Point Naval Air Station where his father was stationed. It was wartime, and Steve remained there with his mother when his father, Emmett Boone Jr., was shipped out for duty in the Pacific. Steve's mother, Mary, was the daughter of a coal miner from the Scranton area of Pennsylvania, and his father's family had operated a hotel in Philadelphia. Steve's mom and dad met while working in a hotel in the Pocono Mountains.

When Steve's father returned from the war, the family moved several times, first operating a resort hotel in Southern Pines, North Carolina, and managing a resort hotel in West Hampton on Long Island. Steve began taking piano lessons at age 10, but they soon ended when Steve's younger brother, Charles, accidentally tipped a pot of boiling water, burning him badly. When the family's physician recommended a moist climate to promote healing, the Boone family moved in 1954 to St. Augustine, Florida, where Steve's grandfather Emmett had retired.

"In the 1950s St. Augustine was still a very charming small Southern town and a fun place for a teenage boy who liked the outdoors and the water," recalled Steve. His mother worked as an administrator at a hospital, then later became an office manager for a newspaper before entering real estate sales. As a high school kid, Steve learned the skills of cabinetry and furniture making in the woodworking shop his father opened. During those years, Steve's older brother Emmett III — nicknamed Skip and six years his senior — formed a rock and roll band. But Steve remained focused on another goal: becoming a U.S. Navy aviator. Those plans were crushed, however, after his family moved back to eastern Long Island. There, on the last day of his junior year at Westhampton Beach High School in June 1960, Steve was involved in a serious automobile accident that fractured his collar bone, hip, and both legs, and paralyzed his right foot. He spent most of the summer in rehabilitation in the hospital and nearly a year on crutches, and began to think of what other career path he might pursue. That Christmas, his parents gave him the acoustic guitar he requested. His self-taught folk strumming eventually led him to join with Skip's band, the Kingsmen, first on rhythm, then on bass — a talent that persuaded him to abandon his pre-engineering studies in college and participate in forming the Lovin' Spoonful in January 1965.

An orthopedic brace that was fashioned for Steve carried him through the Spoonful years gracefully. Steve's injury, which disqualified him for military service, left him unable to raise his foot as he walked. His corrective brace pulled his foot back up in place and prevented it from dragging. Gradually, he learned to compensate for the foot injury and eventually shed his brace. "It's still a little awkward," said Steve, who never recovered full use of his foot.

Still, his injury never prevented him from pursuing an adventurous career. After the Spoonful dried up in 1968, he heard about a band in Virginia called the Oxpetals that had been doing some interesting experimentation with music. Steve agreed to produce their sessions, and was instrumental in landing a recording contract for them with Mercury Records.

That was in the fall of 1969, when Steve married his first wife, Patti, sold his six-room apartment on West 79th Street in Manhattan, and bought a house alongside a trout hatchery in Eastport, Long Island. Only eight months later, Steve sold nearly everything he owned, packed everything else he wanted to keep in a shipping crate, and sent it off to St. Thomas in the Virgin Islands, where the couple moved. There Steve bought a 54-foot sailboat on which they lived, and, for nearly four years, he concentrated on writing songs and thinking about what he might do next musically. Living on a tight budget, Steve inadvertently cut a few corners on tax returns. The IRS seized all of his earnings.

In search of income, Steve returned to the United States in the summer of 1973 and stopped off in Baltimore to visit members of a band that he had met in St. Thomas shortly before his divorce from Patti. At the time, the band was producing its material in Recordings Incorporated, a 24-track studio that was part of International Telecom Inc., a state-of-the-art complex encompassing three studios, an engineering department, and record-cutting equipment in an industrial park owned by McCormick & Co., the cooking spice producer. The manager of the facility, who was a fan of the Lovin' Spoonful, asked Steve if he was interested in leasing the facility because the owner wanted to get out of active management. "I don't have any pockets, much less deep pockets," Steve told him. "I'll see what I can come up with."

Steve phoned some friends, including Bob Cavallo, the former manager of the Spoonful. Cavallo asked Boone if he had ever heard of a band called Little Feat. Steve said he hadn't because the only music he heard during the previous four years in the Virgin Islands was Latin Caribbean music and Soul Train once a week. Cavallo was by then managing Little Feat and had been trying to get the group to record a new album. The problem was that Lowell George, the group's leader, would record only if working with George Massenburg — the recording engineer who had designed the studio complex, which was in Hunt Valley, about 15 miles north of Baltimore. Massenburg, engineer for albums by Linda Ronstadt, Ramsey Lewis, and Earth, Wind, and Fire, had done a session for Lowell George in Washington a year earlier.

"I learned that the engineer had done almost the same thing I had done — he got the hell out of the business and he moved to Paris to be with his girlfriend," said Boone. Before leaving, Massenburg had invited Lowell George to the Baltimore studio, and Lowell loved it. When Steve called Massenburg, he was able to persuade him to return to the states to perform session work for Little Feat. On the strength of the contract he arranged with Massenburg, Boone and a business partner leased the studio complex, where Little Feat recorded the classic 1974 album *Feats Don't Fail Me Now.*

Boone and his partner changed the name of the recording complex to Blue Seas Studio, began writing and producing commercial jingles, and developed a strong clientele in the Washington-Baltimore area. Blue Seas continued renting studio time to rock bands as well, and at the beginning of 1975 the McCormick Company issued an eviction notice to the studio owner, believing that the recording studio was incompatible with other businesses in the industrial park. When the studio owner, who was in arrears in rent payments, refused to cooperate, Baltimore county authorities and lender Maryland National Bank sanctioned a public auction of the studio's assets. Powerless and caught in the middle of the legal dispute, Boone thought he'd show up the day of the auction and spend perhaps $100 to buy a microphone. Instead, he walked away with a whole studio through a bit of financial wizardry and nimble thinking.

The auction was formatted to offer the equipment two ways: a comprehensive bid price for all of the gear in the recording complex, followed by a second, piece-by-piece auction. The company would accept the bid total of whichever process netted the highest earnings. By the day of the auction, Boone and his partner had interested a prospective investor from New York. But the investor's arrival in Baltimore that February morning was delayed by a snowstorm enroute. The auction opened with bids for the whole complex. After a long silence, Steve Boone was the first to speak. "I offer $15,000," he said. Another bidder blurted, "$18,000." Steve countered, "$18,500," and the auction room fell silent. After a few moments the auctioneer announced, "The bids are closed and now we're going to go piece by piece." But before those proceedings began, a vice president from Maryland National Bank leaned over and whispered something to the auctioneer. The auctioneer drew in a breath, then announced, "Ladies and gentlemen, the auction is over. Steve Boone is the buyer of the entire studio complex for $18,500."

At that point, Steve still didn't have any money and needed a 25 percent deposit by 3 o'clock that afternoon to hold his bid for 24 hours. "So I set up this furious sale on the floor of the auction," said Steve, who began doing what the auctioneer hadn't done — selling equipment piece by piece. "I sold an eight-track reel recorder, two echo chambers and a couple of microphones for $19,100." Steve paid the auction house and had $600 to spare. Just that minute the investor from New York came bursting into the studio and gasped, "Am I too late?" Steve replied, "You're too late for the auction, Tom, but if you want to be my partner, we already own the place."

Steve and his two partners had to move all of their remaining newly acquired gear quickly. And they knew just the place: a 130-foot long barge owned by John Armour, heir to the Armour Meat Packing Company. He had converted it into a beautiful, Danish modern houseboat for his new bride and anchored it in Baltimore's inner harbor. When she stepped onto it and became seasick, she said, "I'm not living on this thing." Steve and his partners leased it and christened the new facility Blue Seas Studio. They were back in business — for three more years anyway. Blue Seas, named after a freighter that Steve had seen stranded on the rocks at St. Thomas, may have been an unfortunate choice.

Blue Seas Studio attracted numerous pop and country music recording artists, including Emmylou Harris, Bonnie Raitt, Robert Palmer, and Ricky Skaggs. But on Christmas day in 1977, the barge sank in the harbor. "We salvaged most of our electronic gear, but the tapes all tipped over and fell into the salt water," said Steve. "We lost all of our master tapes, safeties, and backups, including stuff by Lowell George and Earth, Wind, and Fire. We weren't insured," Steve added. The partners sold the surviving electronic equipment and managed to pay off almost all of their debts.

Out of the recording studio business, Steve remained in Baltimore and re-entered music. He joined the Scott Cunningham Blues Band. "It was a pickup band, never the same cast of characters. Baltimore was so rich in talent that I played with some of the best musicians I'd ever played with. It was fun, but we didn't make a lot of money," Steve admitted. To make a few bucks, he began renovating abandoned houses in downtown Baltimore. Renting out the houses he renovated, Steve began to earn a respectable income. He married a second time, to a woman named Jonell Ryan. The couple administered the rental properties until 1987, when they divorced and Steve moved to Florida, where he had lived as a teenager.

After looking around, Steve settled in Fort Lauderdale, where he re-immersed himself in sailing. There he met Susan Peterson, with whom he formed Mermaid Productions Inc. in 1990, a year before they married. The house they bought contained a musical instrument digital interface (MIDI) computerized studio in which Steve recorded the musical compositions he was writing. Steve and Susan became actively involved in numerous public service organizations, including the Fort Lauderdale Historical Society, the Sierra Club, and the Legal Environmental Assistance Foundation. Steve, an avid boating advocate who conducted tours of local waterways, was a founding member of an organization dedicated to recreational boating access in the Broward Blueway river system, and he volunteered extensively in connection with swimming meets at the International Swimming Hall of Fame Aquatic Complex.

But as Steve's marriage to Susan faltered and then dissolved, he began writing songs in collaboration with Jerry Yester's daughter Lena, who by then was performing on the road with the new Lovin' Spoonful. "I think we've produced some real good songs," said Steve, acknowledging they're not typical Spoonful songs. "They're more in a sarcastic and humorous vein than you would expect." After Steve's divorce, his working relationship with Lena turned romantic, and the couple married in 2001 and moved to Leland, North Carolina. Florida continued to exert a strong pull on Steve, though, and in 2021 he purchased a sailboat named the Jolly Roger that he docked outside the home he purchased in Flagler Beach.

Though Steve was still on tour with the Spoonful six decades after the band's hectic heyday, the pace of appearances was much more relaxed by the mid 2020s because, as he explained, "Rock and roll music can wear you out if you let it."

Epilogue: Jerry Yester

Guitarist

Jerry Yester in Placerville, California, in September 1998. Photo by Amanda Domingues.

Jerry Yester became best known not only as a producer and arranger, but also as the musician who replaced Zal Yanovsky in the Lovin' Spoonful. But that one-year stint represented just one facet in the busy life of a guy who wore so many hats that he'd need a separate closet to store them all.

When he began touring and recording with the Spoonful on the Kama Sutra label in June 1967, Jerry was already signed as a solo artist to Dunhill Records. Racking up a track record as a song writer, producer, and musical arranger, Jerry even developed a partnership with Zal Yanovsky. And his long, varied, and distinguished music career is due in part to the plastic ukulele he received from his parents as a Christmas present when he was 14.

Although Jerome Alan Yester was born in Birmingham, Alabama, on January 9, 1943, his parents moved only six months later to Burbank, California, in the Los Angeles metropolitan area. His family included two older brothers, Ted and Jim. Jerry's father, Larry, was a professional musician who played piano, organ, and accordion. Attracted to the movie studios of Burbank and Hollywood, Larry played the part of a musician in about a dozen motion pictures, including two 1948 films, *Fort Apache* (with John Wayne and Henry Fonda) and *April Showers* (starring Jack Carson and Ann Sothern). A year after receiving the ukulele Jerry graduated to the guitar and had joined a local garage band by the summer of 1958. Playing music for enjoyment, Jerry was interested in becoming a commercial artist. But music was in his family. And in his destiny.

While attending Notre Dame High School in Sherman Oaks, a few miles from Burbank, Jerry had enrolled in glee club. His classmates in glee club included Danny Hutton, who had a brief solo career before rising to fame as a member of Three Dog Night. After Jerry graduated in 1960, his parents decided to move to the high desert town of Joshua Tree, but Jerry decided to remain with his brother Jim in Burbank, where they moved into a house. Jerry's mother, Martha, who had worked as an accountant, became a singer in the bar that she and Jerry's father bought in Joshua Tree.

Jerry enrolled at Glendale College with a major in music and art, but quickly grew bored with theory classes that discussed what he had already learned in private guitar lessons. Captivated by folk music, in particular by the songs of the Kingston Trio, Jerry bought a banjo and learned to play it. Performing as the Yester Brothers duo, Jim and Jerry played the coffee houses of Hollywood, including Terrea Lea's Garret Coffee House at 923 N. Fairfax Avenue and Theodore Bikel's Unicorn Coffee House at 8907 Sunset Boulevard. Jerry dropped out of college after a semester, enrolled the next year again, and left college for good after one more disappointing semester. When Jim joined the U.S. Army in 1961, Jerry formed a trio with singers John Forsha and Karol Dugan called the Inn Group, which became part of the original New Christy Minstrels. The Minstrels was really a collective of several individual groups, and Jerry appeared on the Minstrels' first album that yielded a late 1962 hit single: "This Land is Your Land."

In January 1963, Jerry joined the Modern Folk Quartet upon the invitation of the group's manager, Herb Cohen. The MFQ originated in Hawai'i, where it was formed by bassist Chip Douglas, who later was a producer for the Turtles, the Monkees, and Linda Ronstadt; rock photographer, banjo player and clarinetist Henry Diltz; Cyrus Faryar, who had been a member of the Whiskeyhill Singers, a group led by former Kingston Trio member Dave Guard; and Stanley White, whom Jerry replaced. During the next four years, Jerry played hundreds of college concerts with the Modern Folk Quartet. Jerry, who habitually bought music books, and studied orchestration, arranging, and composition on the tour bus, shared vocal arrangement responsibilities with Chip Douglas. Upon the addition of drummer Eddie Hoh in 1965 at the onset of the British music Invasion, the band went electric with Jerry on lead guitar, changed its name to the Modern Folk Quintet, and the following year scored a moderate-sized regional hit single called "Night Time Girl."

From 1963 to 1965 the MFQ was based in New York, where Jerry and the other MFQ members met and befriended the Lovin' Spoonful members during their formative months. "In the spring of 1965 the MFQ worked a gig at the Bitter End in the Village, and John Sebastian was our drummer. At the time, the Spoonful were together and working down at the Village Music Hall on Third Street, and John would run over to the Bitter End between the Spoonful's sets and get on stage and play a few numbers with us. We'd do our folk sets until he showed up and then we'd do folk rock songs. We worked a week that way," Jerry recalled fondly.

Yester said the Beatles' initial appearance on *The Ed Sullivan Show* in February 1964 exerted a profound effect on the Greenwich Village folk music scene. "That was the arrow through the heart of folk music," Yester told us in May 1998. "Before then, folk music was the most popular music in the country. But after that Sullivan program, folk musicians started growing long hair and buying electric guitars."

In the years following 1963, the MFQ remained a recurrent entity, periodically going on hiatus for a few years, then regenerating for a few more. When the MFQ went into hibernation for the first time in 1966, Jerry produced an album for the Association, in which his brother Jim was a member. He also was recording director for Tim Buckley's debut album, *Goodbye and Hello,* and had been signed as a solo artist with Dunhill Records at the time the Spoonful invited him to join. Jerry cherished the year he spent with the Spoonful, from June 1967 until the group's breakup in June 1968, when he and his wife, Judy Henske, moved to Los Angeles.

By that time, Judy had given birth to their daughter, Kate. Jerry welcomed the opportunity to stay closer to home, and began to concentrate more on writing. He and Judy — who had been a member of Dave Guard's Whiskeyhill Singers and recorded under her own name for Elektra — set to work on an album for Straight Records, which was owned by Herb Cohen and Frank Zappa. A potpourri of folk, jazz, and classical music that Judy and Jerry performed together, the album was called *Farewell Aldebaran,* named after a red star in the galaxy of Taurus. At that time Jerry called Zal, who participated with him in producing *Farewell Aldebaran.*

About six months after Zal left the Spoonful, he had asked Jerry to collaborate in producing his solo album, *Alive and Well in Argentina,* which Buddah released in April 1968. Their co-production of Zal's album led to an alliance between the two called Hairshirt Productions, based in Los Angeles. Under that banner, they produced recordings for Pat Boone, Tim Buckley, and a group called the Fifth Avenue Band, managed by Bob Cavallo, who later guided the careers of Prince, Savage Garden, Alanis Morissette, and other popular artists of the 1980s and 1990s. On his own, Jerry produced the last recording the Turtles made in that era, then with Judy formed a band called Rosebud. Just after completing an album for Warner Brothers in 1971, Jerry and Judy broke up.

After knocking around for six months, Jerry was asked to produce the debut Elektra album for a new duo called Aztec Two-Step in New York. There in 1972, he unexpectedly saw someone he knew — a woman named Marlene, whom he had first met eight years before. At about the same time he renewed his acquaintance with Marlene, Jerry formed a songwriting partnership with another old friend, Larry Beckett, who had been Tim Buckley's composing collaborator. Yester and Beckett continued to work together for decades.

Back in Los Angeles in 1973, Yester produced Tom Waits' moody debut Asylum album, *Closing Time,* did the orchestration and arrangements for Rob Reiner's recording of *Peter and the Wolf,* and then joined the Association, with which he remained for about a year and a half. In 1975, a particularly memorable year for Jerry, he and Marlene were married. That same year, the MFQ was reactivated, and Yester answered the call, performing with them for about three and a half years. He kept busy on the side as well, doing string arrangements for Tom Waits and Merrilee Rush, and vocal arrangements for Manhattan Transfer, America, and other performers. And during that same year, Marlene gave birth to a daughter, Lena. Five years later, Hannah was born. Jerry recorded a solo album in the early '80s and moved into session engineering at Annex Studios in Hollywood.

By 1984, Jerry and Marlene decided they needed a change in scenery, and moved to Hilo, Hawai'i. Jerry's brother Jim followed shortly, and the two brothers formed a band called Rainbow Connection with another local musician, Rainbow Page, stepson of Charles Mingus. The band used MIDI (musical instrument digital interface) technology to synthesize instrumental sounds. They began playing local hangouts — the Banyan Broiler, a popular disco called CJ's, and additional clubs, as well as for weddings and other occasions. "It was just the three of us, but we sounded like a nine-piece band if we wanted to. We had a computer on stage doing bass and drums and strings. We played guitars, flute, and conga, and we became the most popular dance band in Hilo for about five years," said Jerry. After recording *Moonlight Serenade,* an album of '40s standards in 1984 for John Stewart's Homecoming label, the MFQ reconvened four years later and signed with a Japanese label, for which the band made five albums during the next four years.

By 1990 the isolation of island living had set in, so Jerry and Marlene moved to Portland, Oregon. "Beckett lived there, and I always loved Portland." But Jerry and Marlene didn't stay there long. Not long after the MFQ finished *Wolfgang,* an album of Mozart music in 1991,

Steve Boone called Jerry to see if he'd be interested in resurrecting the Lovin' Spoonful. Jerry agreed after thinking about his previous experience in the Spoonful. "My relationship with John Sebastian wasn't as strong as the partnership he had with Zally. It just couldn't have been. One reason we decided to get back together was that feeling of unfinished business," said Jerry. Even though John and Zal declined to join them, Joe, Steve, and Jerry greatly enjoyed their reunion in 1991 — so much so that Steve Boone kept the band together well into the 2020s.

Jerry and Marlene relocated to Arkansas in 1994. That's when Bob Richards, a friend from Hawai'i, landed in Memphis, bought a motor home, and decided to drive until he found the "perfect place." That place was Marble Falls, Arkansas, in the Ozark Mountains. Unable to afford a home in Portland, Jerry and Marlene somewhat reluctantly accepted Bob's invitation to visit Arkansas. "We fell in love with the place," said Jerry. In 1994 they bought a parcel of land in a small town called Harrison. The neighbors included bears, cougars, skunks, opossums, squirrels, and groundhogs.

Although Jerry's mother died in 1998, her passing helped sweeten one of Jerry's fondest memories of his folks. A few years before the death of his father in 1977, Jerry and the MFQ played a gig at the Ice House in Pasadena, sharing the bill with a 15-piece jazz band. Engaged to write arrangements for the band's appearance, Jerry invited his father to collaborate with him. "My dad had an 18-piece band when he was 18 years old. Music was all he knew," Jerry said quietly. "He taught accordion and did gigs at night. That arrangement he did with me was actually the best arrangement for that jazz band."

The Yesters' Arkansas home permitted Jerry to fulfill his childhood dream of having his own recording studio, which he named Willow Sound. In two 15-by-15-foot rooms containing a piano, a pump organ, drums, and shelves filled with equipment, Jerry began producing sessions for local artists and leasing studio time to songwriters who needed to record demo versions of their songs.

For Jerry Yester, it was a daydream come true.

Gary Puckett and the Union Gap

Amid the loud, defiant, and sometimes violent protestations of young revolutionaries against what they called the "establishment," the military-industrial complex, and the Vietnam war, and a rapidly emerging subgenre of hard-driving rock bands such as Cream, Iron Butterfly, and Led Zeppelin, the serenades of Gary Puckett and the Union Gap brought composure to an otherwise tumultuous era. Rising above the din of protest, the band unleashed a consistent string of ballads of which five remained in the top 10 for more than 11 weeks. In 1968, San Diego-based Gary Puckett and the Union Gap delivered four consecutive million-selling singles — "Woman, Woman," "Young Girl," Lady Willpower," and "Over You" — and sold more records that year than any other recording act.

Formed in January 1967, Gary Puckett and the Union Gap began with longtime friends Gary Puckett and Dwight Bement, members of a San Diego cover band called the Outcasts. They were soon joined by Kerry Chater, Gary Withem, and drummer Peter Carrillo of another local band called Jeri and the Jeritones, members of which went on to become Iron Butterfly. The band's first road performance took them to the Pacific Northwest, an area in which Gary spent much of his childhood. Calling themselves Gary and the Remarkables, band members dressed in powder-blue, double-breasted jackets and striped pants and performed for a month each in Seattle, Washington, Portland, Oregon, and in Vallejo, California, before returning to San Diego's popular Quad Room in the Clairemont Bowl at 3093 Clairemont Drive, where they landed their first recording contract with Columbia Records.

While the band was on its first road trip, Puckett decided that Gary and the Remarkables needed a new name and image. Seeking a stronger identity for the band, Puckett drew on his interest in Civil War history and conceived the idea of wearing Union soldier uniforms. "Gary Withem insisted I got the idea while watching *F Troop* during leisure moments on the road," said Puckett. "Probably so." And having grown

Gary Puckett and the Union Gap in Civil War uniforms, in early 1968. Left to right: Gary Puckett (standing, in general's uniform); Kerry Chater (seated in foreground, corporal's uniform); Dwight Bement (sergeant's uniform); Paul Wheatbread (standing, in private's uniform); and Gary Withem (seated, private's uniform). From Photofest Archives, New York.

up in Union Gap, Washington, Puckett thought that name would be appropriate. "I remember telling the guys at this hotel in Seattle that we were going to dress in Union soldier outfits and we were going to call the band the Union Gap," recalled Puckett. "They laughed about it for days, but I wanted to be different than the tie-dyed, paisley patterned '60s flower child mode."

After the band members returned to Southern California from their Pacific Northwest tour, they began searching for Union soldier uniforms. "Western Costume in LA said they could make the uniforms for us for $400 apiece," said Puckett. Instead, Gary decided to rent a Union soldier outfit and took it to a tailor in Tijuana, who was willing to make five coats and hats for about $400 total. "We were going to debut our outfits and new name at the Quad Room in San Diego's Clairemont Bowl. So everyone met at my house and we went down there en masse. As we walked in the door, people in all 52 lanes stopped bowling, one lane at a time, and looked at us quite curiously," recalled Puckett. Quad Room patrons initially were unsure how to respond, but as word about the costumed quintet began to draw appreciative crowds to their performances, the band members relaxed and began feeling more comfortable in character, growing sideburns and mustaches to evoke a Civil War appearance.

Shortly after Gary Puckett and the Union Gap made their debut at the Quad Room, Paul Wheatbread replaced Peter Carrillo on drums. At about the same time, Gary and the band's manager, Dick Badger, presented a portfolio of the band, including song lyrics, photos, and a demo tape, to Columbia Records producer Jerry Fuller, who had written "(It's A) Young World," "Travelin' Man" and numerous other songs for Ricky Nelson, as well as "Show And Tell" for Al Wilson. "Jerry Fuller heard us and could see potential, especially in Gary's voice," said Kerry Chater. "So he came down to the Quad Room and we signed right there without any legal counseling. Lucky for us Columbia Records was a reputable organization."

The Union Gap was a multitalented group of musicians. Kerry Chater played bass and keyboards; Gary Withem played keyboards, clarinet, and sax; Dwight Bement played keyboards, clarinet, sax, guitar, and bass; Gary Puckett switched back and forth between bass, guitar, and keyboards; and everyone sang, including drummer Paul Wheatbread. "It was a very talented band," said Puckett. "During concerts, we enjoyed impressing the audience by switching instruments. We also sang a barbershop quartet number, which was a real crowd pleaser."

On August 17, 1967, the band began their first recording session, in which they laid down tracks for Puckett's "Believe Me" and "Woman, Woman" by Jim Glaser and Jim Payne, as well as a song called "Don't Make Promises," written by Tim Hardin. A month later the band's first single, "Woman, Woman" backed with "Don't Make Promises," was released. Jim Glaser and Jimmy Payne (both of whom performed with Tompall and the Glaser Brothers) wrote "Woman, Woman," which was about a man who began to see through his mate's unsuccessful attempts to conceal her cheating. Al Capps did the musical arrangement for the Gary Puckett and the Union Gap recording, and Jerry Fuller produced the session for the song, which premiered on the *Billboard* Hot 100 on November 18, 1967. The record's first regional success was in Columbus, Ohio. "Bob Harrington, a local disc jockey on WCOL, was a Civil War buff, and he thought the record jacket picture was so authentic that it might be a good record. He auditioned it, liked it, and added it to the play list. It went to No. 1," said Puckett.

"Woman, Woman" received its first major market exposure in Cleveland, which catapulted it onto the national charts. Chater recalled, "It was right in the middle of the psychedelic era and, although we looked like we fit into that mode, we didn't play that kind of music." The record sleeve portrayed the band in Union soldier uniforms in a battlefield scene, which was actually photographed at a demolished school auditorium in Beverly Hills, California. The pistol that Chater tucked into his waistband for the photo was an actual relic that his great-grandfather used during the Civil War. "Steve Popovich, the promotion man for Columbia Records in Cleveland, went to the top radio station there to get some airplay," explained Chater. "The program director looked at the cover and said, 'Oh, that's just another psychedelic group,' and he didn't want to play it. But Steve Popovich said, 'No, no, no. Just listen.' So the programmer put it on and it sounded so different from what he had expected, that he fell in love with it and played it, and played it." After rising to No. 4 on the Hot 100 and remaining on the chart for 17 weeks, "Woman, Woman" earned RIAA gold-record certification. It also reached No. 48 on the British chart. Based on the success of that initial single, Columbia released an 11-song album titled *Woman, Woman* in January 1968. It rose to No. 22 on *Billboard's* albums chart.

The band returned to the studio to record a song written by Jerry Fuller that he thought would be a good follow-up to "Woman, Woman." That second single, "Young Girl," premiered on the *Billboard* Hot 100 on

March 2, 1968, and quickly climbed the charts, but was held out of the No. 1 position by Bobby Goldsboro's "Honey," which dominated the pop and country charts in the early spring of 1968. Even so, "Young Girl" held the No. 2 slot for three weeks, remained on the chart for 15 weeks, and ultimately earned RIAA gold-record certification on April 5, 1968. It reached No. 1 in *Cash Box* and in the U.K., and also registered at No. 34 on *Billboard's* easy listening chart. "Jerry always said the hardest thing for anyone with one hit record to do is to have two," recalled Puckett. "And we were fortunate to follow a song as great as 'Woman, Woman' with its strong production qualities with another solid hit." In late April 1968, only three months after the release of the band's debut album, Columbia released their second LP, *Gary Puckett and the Union Gap Featuring "Young Girl,"* with all 11 tracks arranged and conducted by Al Capps. Gary and the Gap hit the singles chart for the third time with "Lady Willpower," which premiered on the *Billboard* Hot 100 on June 8, 1968. It was about courting and wooing a cautious young lady who had more willpower than her amorous suitor. "Lady Willpower" hit No. 1 on the *Cash Box* chart and No. 26 on the *Billboard* contemporary music chart, while on the Hot 100 it peaked at No. 2, held that position for two weeks, and remained on the chart for 13 weeks. It also hit No. 5 in the U.K. On July 18 the song earned the third RIAA gold record for the band. "Lady Willpower" was included on their third album, *Incredible,* which Jerry Fuller produced and Columbia released in October.

Gary Puckett and the Union Gap were red-hot by the time Columbia records released "Over You," the band's fourth chart single. That song also was from the *Incredible* album, which reached No. 20 on *Billboard's* album chart, making it the band's highest-ranking LP. Jerry Fuller wrote "Over You," which made its chart debut on September 21, 1968. It climbed to No. 3 on the adult contemporary chart and No. 7 on the pop chart on which it remained 11 weeks, earning RIAA gold certification on December 19. With that, Gary Puckett and the Union Gap had notched up four gold records within 1968, only a year after being the house band at a bowling alley nightspot.

For the next three years, Gary Puckett and the Union Gap rode the crest of popularity performing with acts such as the Association, the Grass Roots, the Beach Boys, Paul Revere and the Raiders, the Byrds, the Turtles, and the Mamas and the Papas. The band spent most of its years performing in the United States and Canada; however, a trip to Mexico City remained etched in the mind of Dwight Bement. The band was scheduled to fly from New Orleans to Mexico City to perform a concert at the Plaza de Toros arena with the Byrds, but flight trouble delayed their arrival by four hours. Their appearance was canceled due to a riot that broke out in the stadium when concert-goers thought the band had simply not shown up. For the next two weeks the band performed at a nightclub in Mexico City, and the obliging owners hired a young driver to take them sightseeing.

"It's 4 o'clock in the morning and this club owner wants to take us to Maximilian's castle," recalled Bement. "So we start up this hill for about a quarter of a mile and a couple of guys step out from behind trees with pistols drawn. The club owner sticks his head out the window and yells something in Spanish and then hits the driver in the back of the head and yells "*ándale.*" The driver responds and hits the gas, and further along we see another couple of guys with rifles. And when we get to the gate there are two more guys with submachine guns." Puckett recalled the group getting out of the limo, submachine guns at their backs, and walking through the gate toward the front door of the castle where they were met by the commanding officer with his guards telling them that was as far as they go. "That's when we turned around and headed back down the hill," said Bement. "You're not supposed to be going to national historic sites at 4 in the morning!"

In 1969 the band was invited by then-governor Lurleen Wallace to perform for Alabama's Shower of Stars fund-raiser — a risky proposition for a band performing in Union soldier uniforms. "We told them we didn't want to chance it," said Withem. "We could see ourselves getting up on stage in our Union soldier outfits and becoming target practice for the boys down there." After concert organizers promised to provide extra security, the band uneasily agreed to the performance, which turned out to be a huge success. Bement added, "I got hold of a stars and bars flag and after we played a couple of songs, I let it unfurl over the front of my organ, and the roof went off the place. They loved it." he said. "We were made honorary lieutenant colonels aides-de-camp in the Alabama State Militia. We went over really big in the South."

Paul Wheatbread recalled a concert for about 40,000 people that took place in New York City's Central Park. "We were really popular at the time. I remember we were driven there by limousine, and the fans were breaking the mirrors off the limousine for souvenirs," he said. "It was cold so we were dressed in scarves and turtleneck sweaters. They tore the scarf off my neck for a souvenir. The only way we could get out of the park, as I remember it, was by helicopter."

The Union Gap's fifth chart single, "Don't Give In to Him," first appeared the *Billboard* Hot 100 on March 15, 1969. Gary Usher wrote the song, and Dick Glasser produced the session. Usher had written the Beach Boys' "409" and "In My Room" with Brian Wilson, and produced recordings for the Hondells, Surfaris, Chad and Jeremy, and the Byrds. Glasser also produced recordings for the Everly Brothers, Jackie DeShannon, Andy Williams, the Ventures, and Hank Williams Jr. "Don't Give In to Him" rose to No. 15 and remained on the chart for nine weeks. On March 25, RIAA awarded gold certification for the band's *Young Girl* album, which had been released in April 1968.

The band made numerous guest appearances on a variety of popular television programs, including the *Jerry Lewis, Jonathan Winters,* and *Red Skelton* shows. But when they were invited to perform on *The Ed Sullivan Show,* Gary Withem was convinced the band had made it. "I remember the Rolling Stones performed right before us and they had to change their song lyrics to 'let's spend some time together.' It was too risqué in those days to refer to going too far, so in 'Young Girl' we had to sing, 'How can this love of ours go on,'" said Withem. "Since the Stones had to change their lyrics it was okay with us."

The Union Gap's sixth chart single, "This Girl Is a Woman Now," premiered on the *Billboard* Hot 100 on August 23, 1969. Victor Millrose and Alan Bernstein wrote the tender coming-of-age ballad. Dick Glasser produced the session, with musical arrangement by Ernie Freeman. "This Girl Is a Woman Now" rose to No. 9 and remained on the chart for 11 weeks. The B side of the single was "His Other Woman," written by Kerry Chater, who also did most of the arranging for live performances. Chater wanted to write more material for the band, but encountered resistance from producer Jerry Fuller, who wrote much of the band's material.

Gary Puckett and the Union Gap appealed to a wide spectrum of fans including teenagers and their parents, as well as college-age kids. The band recorded "Dreams of the Everyday Housewife," a song that charted for Glen Campbell in 1968. "Glen Campbell was a good friend of Jerry Fuller's," observed Withem. "In fact, Glen was the guy who showed us 'Woman, Woman,' our first record. He had brought it back from Nashville, and that's how we recorded it."

Puckett fondly recalled the time in 1970 when he worked a Las Vegas engagement at the same hotel in which Elvis was performing. "Elvis came to see my show one night. That was an exciting moment.

The maître d' brought a note backstage that said, 'Tell the boy he sure can sing.' I loved his records, especially the early ones —'Don't Be Cruel,' 'Heartbreak Hotel,' and 'I Want You, I Need You, I Love You,'" said Puckett. "Later on, in her book, Priscilla said I was one of the artists that Elvis enjoyed listening to, and he had my records in his collection."

"Let's Give Adam and Eve Another Chance" gave Gary Puckett and the Union Gap, its sole singles chart appearance of 1970, premiering on the *Billboard* Hot 100 on March 7 of that year. The tune was written by Red West and Richard Mainegra, who also collaborated in writing "Separate Ways" for Elvis Presley. Dick Glasser produced the session for "Let's Give Adam and Eve Another Chance," with music arranged and conducted by Ernie Freeman. The song rose to No. 41 and remained on the chart for seven weeks. In June 1970 Columbia released an 11-song compilation album, *Gary Puckett and the Union Gap's Greatest Hits.* While peaking at No. 50, the album sold consistently well enough to earn a gold RIAA award on March 17, 1971, and then a platinum record on November 21, 1986. But by 1970 Kerry Chater and Gary Withem had left the Union Gap to pursue careers as team songwriters for Almo/ Irving Music, the publishing company for A&M Records. A new seven-piece Gary Puckett and the Union Gap emerged, which included Paul Wheatbread and Dwight Bement as well as new members Dick Gabriel on tenor saxophone, Tom Manasian on trombone, Barry McCoy on B3 organ, and Mike Crawford on trumpet. The band re-formed once again in late 1970 to include Puckett, Bement, Wheatbread, and new members Rob DeKarr on guitar and Brian Griffin on piano, and continued performing until May 31, 1971, when Puckett decided he was ready to take a break from music for a while.

"When we broke up it was a new generation basically — a new decade at least," said Puckett. "Times were changing rapidly and much of the '60s, including the music, was mostly a memory."

But as the years rolled on, a nostalgic generation would long for the music of their youth. Now, decades later, the memories associated with songs such as those recorded by Gary Puckett and the Union Gap and other hit groups of their time seem sweeter than ever.

GARY PUCKETT AND THE UNION GAP
U.S. HIT SINGLES ON THE NATIONAL CHARTS

Debut	Peak	Gold	Title	Label
11/18/67	4	▲	Woman, Woman	Columbia
3/2/68	2	▲	Young Girl	Columbia
6/8/68	2	▲	Lady Willpower	Columbia
9/21/68	7	▲	Over You	Columbia
3/15/69	15		Don't Give In to Him	Columbia
8/23/69	9		This Girl Is a Woman Now	Columbia
3/7/70	41		Let's Give Adam and Eve Another Chance	Columbia
10/31/70	61		I Just Don't Know What to Do With Myself*	Columbia
2/6/71	71		Keep the Customer Satisfied*	Columbia

* Released as soloist Gary Puckett (without the Union Gap)

▲ symbol: RIAA certified gold record (Recording Industry Association of America)

Billboard's pop singles chart data is courtesy of Joel Whitburn's Record Research Inc., Menomonee Falls, Wisconsin.

Epilogue: Gary Puckett

Singer, guitarist, bassist, and keyboardist

A truly gifted singer and musician, Gary Puckett found meaning in music for as long as he could remember. His grandfather played banjo, sang, and danced, and both parents played instruments and were active in barbershop-style singing groups. "When I was a child, we always had a piano," recalled Gary. "My parents would rent a tape recorder a couple of months before Christmas and we would record songs and messages, which they would have transferred onto little records. My folks would send those records to my grandparents for Christmas. My mom told me one time, 'You know, I just always thought that all little boys could sing like you could sing. But that's not the case.' I inherited the qualities of their voices. They were both wonderful singers and

Gary Puckett in the 1990s. Photo by Tim Stahl.

musicians." Gary began piano lessons at 6 years of age, and played classical music for about four years. "I now wish that I had continued studying seriously," said Gary. "I still play piano but I don't have the ability that I once had because I became enamored with the guitar at some point, when rock and roll came along."

The oldest of five children, Gary Dale Puckett was born October 17, 1942, to Leona and Arlon Puckett in Hibbing, Minnesota. Shortly thereafter, Gary's father enlisted for military duty and was stationed in Germany during World War II. Within a couple of weeks of his birth, Gary and his mother went to live with his grandparents in Pelican Rapids, Minnesota. "My father was reported missing in action but returned safely after being held in a German prison camp for five months toward the end of the war." When his father returned in 1946, the family moved to Watertown, South Dakota, where Gary's sister Kathy was born.

Gary's parents wanted their children to have an appreciation of music. As a result, the whole family was musical. "Music was just a part of our everyday lives," said Gary. "Kathy, four years younger, and David, seven years younger, both studied and played the piano. Brian, who is nine years younger than I, studied clarinet but in high school took up the drums and became quite a good drummer. My youngest sister Kris joked that she had none of the 'family talents,' but she raised a beautiful family, as did the others."

Gary spent a good part of his childhood in the Yakima Valley in Washington state, as well as two years, during the fourth and fifth grades, in Tacoma. His father was in the merchandising business for the Bon Marché division of department store chain operator Allied Stores, working his way up the ranks to manager of major department stores. When Gary was about 16, the family moved to Twin Falls, Idaho, where he graduated from Twin Falls High School.

"I really didn't know what I wanted to do when I grew up," said Puckett. "My parents were hoping that I would go to school and maybe go into medicine or something at least with a college education. I was one of those kids who just didn't have a clue about what I really wanted to do with my life. Rock and roll just had a feeling about it, as opposed to what classical did for me. I grew to love classical music as an older adult and wish that I had not been such a lazy kid and continued my studies. I envy people who can play the classics."

Gary's first band was called the Redcoats, which he formed in the Yakima Valley at 15 years of age. The group consisted of piano, guitar, and drums, and Gary was the lead singer. "The guitar player was Barry Curtis. He went on as a member of the Kingsmen of 'Louie Louie' fame for many years. Now and then we got a chance to work with them, so Barry and I got together and reminisced about the good old times, like the time he tried to steal my girlfriend," laughed Puckett. "We played rock and roll! Songs by Elvis, Jerry Lee Lewis, Everly Brothers, the Platters, the Coasters, and others." Later on, in Twin Falls, Idaho, Gary joined a folk group called the Continentals. "We had three singers. I didn't even sing; I was just a guitar player."

After graduating from high school in 1960, Gary attended San Diego City College for two years. He had an interest in pursuing some aspect of psychology, but found himself becoming more and more involved in the San Diego music scene. "I was playing in a band called the Ravens while I was going to school, and eventually I just gave up on school and went to work from 9 a.m. to 5 p.m. as a delivery boy for Foreign Auto Supply. We sold basic engine parts for foreign cars. At the same time, I was working 9 p.m. to 2 a.m. in different clubs in town." Foreign Auto Supply personnel consisted of the two owners, a secretary, and two delivery boys. By the time Gary left two years later, he was given managerial duties over the parts department, machine shop, and the company's 11 employees.

Meanwhile, by 1965 Gary's band, the Outcasts, became one of the hottest bands in San Diego, performing regularly at the Quad Room nightclub. "We were just a trio but somehow we had a finger on the pulse, and were rocking hard every night," declared Puckett. The Outcasts tried unsuccessfully to launch a recording career, recording and releasing two singles, "Would You Care," and "Run Away" on Prince Records, and "I Can't Get Through to You," and "I Found Out About You" on Karate. Even though the two small labels lacked sufficient promotional punch to propel the band to stardom, their stage appearances drew good crowds.

"There was a waiting line to get in the club from about 9:30 p.m. until about midnight every night of the week." The band consisted of guitar, bass, drums, and all three handled lead singing roles. "And three, distinct personalities who were like oil and water," chuckled Gary. "Bobby Brown was a great bass player. He and I were good buddies. Tommy Kendall was an excellent drummer, but Bobby and Tommy were pretty much the oil and the water. The band was kind of volatile. We would find ourselves breaking up every week or two. But as soon as we thought it was over, we'd all realize that we had a great band and an excellent job, so we'd apologize and show up for work again."

After Tommy left the Outcasts in 1966, Bobby and Gary brought in three other members, including Dwight Bement. The five-piece band consisted of Bobby Brown on bass, Willy Kellogg on drums, Puckett on guitar and organ, Bement on tenor sax and organ, and Bob Salisbury on baritone sax. "It was a real good band, but it was another pretty unstable mix of individuals, and I finally just got tired of it all," said Puckett. "We played in Northern California for a short period of time, but it didn't take me more than about six weeks to decide that if I'm going to stay in music, I want to have a band that — one — is my own, and — two — everyone has the same desire for success in the music business. So Dwight Bement stayed with me. He was a great player and we got along well. We went looking for other players." Puckett and Bement found Kerry Chater, Gary Withem, and drummer Pete Carrillo, all of whom had been members of another San Diego group called Jeri and the Jeritones.

Gary Puckett and the Union Gap enjoyed a fruitful, but exhausting three and a half years together. But late 1970 was the beginning of the band's demise. "It was kind of like being married to four people instead of just one," Puckett told us in June 1998. "We all had different goals and were heading in different directions. Chater and Withem wanted to spend more time with their loved ones, and they had been hired at A&M Records Publishing to write songs; they're both excellent writers." Gary, too, explored other opportunities. He recorded *The Gary Puckett Album* solo, for which Richard Perry produced four tracks and Stephen Goldman produced six songs. The album yielded three singles, the first of which was a cover of Dusty Springfield's "I Just Don't Know What to Do With Myself." Gary's version of the Hal David and Burt Bacharach breakup song was more up-tempo than either the Dusty Springfield or Dionne Warwick interpretations of the song. Richard Perry produced Gary Puckett's recording, with musical arrangement by Artie Butler. Puckett's single reached No. 61 and remained on the chart for four weeks. Gary's second solo Columbia release was a rendition of Simon and Garfunkel's "Keep the Customer Satisfied," which Richard Perry produced, with musical arrangement by Gene Page. The single appeared on the *Billboard* Hot 100 on February 6, 1971, but rose no higher than No. 71 and remained on the chart for five weeks.

With the dissolution of the Union Gap in the summer of 1971, Puckett took a break from music. "I had decided at that point I was going to go on hiatus. I thought I would take some time off, maybe a year, reflect on past events, decide what I wanted to do next, and go back to work. Columbia Records had said to me, 'Gary, just re-sign the contract. We know what to do. We'll make you rich and famous.' In retrospect, that's what I should have done. The record company and I were somewhat at odds then, so I thought I'd wait a little longer to re-sign. A year later, nobody cared about the '60s. My so-called sabbatical had turned into a mandatory exile from the music business. The world had moved on with glitter rock and disco."

The '70s were difficult for Gary, who not only endured the demise of his band and the loss of his popularity, but also the breakup of a 10-year relationship and divorce from his first wife, Shannon. The divorce settlement left him with few material possessions.

It was during the late '60s that Puckett began searching for a spiritual foundation and began reading books espousing Eastern philosophies. While studying acting in 1974, Gary was introduced to transcendental meditation (T.M.). "One of the students had a book called *Tranquility*

Without Pills: All About Transcendental Meditation. I asked her if I could borrow it and found that I was somewhat impressed with what Maharishi Mahesh Yogi had to say about transcendental meditation," said Puckett. Before long, Puckett found himself being initiated into T.M., meditating morning and night, and studying books about spiritual learning and health-promoting foods.

"I found meditation to have an effect of some sort in my life at times. It gave me feelings of equanimity, but ultimately it left me feeling empty. I meditated from 1974 to 1985 and the last couple of years of meditation, I was in an emotional pit," confessed Puckett. "In the middle of meditation one day, I found myself in tears, just at the lowest that I'd ever been in my life, and I started to pray to God to fix my life. And I did that morning and night for two years. Finally, the Lord Jesus said to me, 'Stand up. Walk away from Maharishi Mahesh Yogi, and I'll show you the way.' Gradually things started happening. Christian people and situations entered my life."

Gary met Grant Goodeve, an actor from the '70s TV series *Eight Is Enough,* during a benefit he was doing for the Make-A-Wish Foundation. "Grant helped me a lot. He was very patient, and encouraged me to understand Christianity and know the Lord," said Puckett. "I also worked on the film *My Boyfriend's Back* with Sandy Duncan, Jill Eikenberry, Judith Light, and John Sanderford, who was also an inspiration to me. So I moved out of LA, bought a condominium in San Diego, and started attending Horizon Christian Fellowship, a bible-based church."

Following his return to San Diego in 1978, Gary began working in local venues. Still struggling with his spirituality, Puckett continued working quietly and writing songs in his beachfront condo. His mother, Leona, became a born-again Christian and a believer in God and the power of prayer, but Gary had distanced himself from Christianity for many years. "I was too caught up in the '60s generation 'if it feels good, do it' kind of thing, but I found myself losing all of the things that the Lord had given to me," said Gary. "I know that I'm extremely fortunate to have been blessed with the success of the Union Gap in the late '60s, but it's even more a blessing now. That's because I know it was not by my own devices, although I worked hard for it, but it was by the grace and love of the Lord Jesus. I want people to know that we are given eternal life, but only through Jesus Christ, no other way but through Him. The Lord wants me to use the celebrity he gave me in the '60s to tell others about him now. He tells us that if we stand up for him now, here on Earth, by believing he is the son of God, he will stand up for us

Jeff March, singer Gary Puckett, and Marti Smiley Childs, following Gary's performance at Cal Expo, 1600 Exposition Boulevard in Sacramento, California. Friday, July 13, 2012. Photo by Marsha March.

on judgment day and he'll give us the right to walk through the gates of heaven."

Living that message became a driving force in Gary's life during a period of introspection in which he retreated into what he called his "self-exile from the music business." One outlet in which he immersed himself was studying and practicing various forms of dance, including jazz, tap, and ballet. Although he had not at that point contemplated resumption of his singing career, he realized something when he accepted an invitation to join a Monkees reunion tour in 1986. "Studying dance made me a little more graceful on stage," he explained. The warm reception he received from music fans prompted Gary to resume an active concert schedule well into the 2020s. Gary's lifetime musical achievements were recognized in September 2023 with his induction into the California Music Hall of Fame.

Although he and his second wife, Shirley, divorced in 1998, Gary found love again. In May 2000 he married Lorrie Haimes, who had two daughters from a previous marriage. Gary and his new family settled in Clearwater, Florida.

Epilogue: Dwight Bement

Keyboardist, clarinetist, saxophonist, bassist, and guitarist

As the house lights dimmed and the curtains parted, the school principal announced the names of the two young performers and gestured to the side of the stage. No one appeared. After an uneasy pause, a young trumpet player by the name of Neil Waters shuffled hesitatingly part way across the stage. All eyes, including Neil's, gazed stage right as the curtain ruffled. Finally the bell of Dwight Bement's clarinet poked out past the edge of the curtain. Gripped by fear, the young musician began to blow the opening notes of the "Marine Hymn." That fifth grade assembly marked the performing debut of Dwight Bement, who later would overcome his stage fright enough to perform before thousands of fans throughout the country.

Fast-forward to the late 1990s when Dwight was a partner in a commercial remodeling company in Colorado Springs as well as a long-time member of Flash Cadillac and the Continental Kids. Dwight Bement successfully intertwined his identity as both a craftsman and a musician.

The construction profession is rooted in his family. "My grandfather was a carpenter who crafted his own furniture, and my father, Dwight Richard, who worked at Ryan Aeronautical in San Diego for 30 years, would pick up construction work whenever his union shop went out on strike," said Dwight. "He would take me along and let me help in any way that I could."

Born December 28, 1940, in San Diego, Dwight first became interested in music in the fifth grade when he learned to play the clarinet, an instrument his father had played in high school. Dwight wanted to play the trombone but at the age of 9 he wasn't able to reach the farther positions on that instrument. In the eighth grade his mother, Virginia, bought a piano and Dwight and his father began taking piano lessons. "Not too long after that, I was telling my mom all the things she was doing wrong," laughed Dwight. "After I learned the piano, I found it very easy to pick up just about any other instrument and play it in short order."

Dwight grew up in National City, which is just south of San Diego near the Mexico border, and attended Sweetwater High School. By the 11th grade he started playing saxophone in a band that included some of his Spanish-speaking classmates, who taught him the style of Latin-influenced music that Bement called "Chicano rock."

"When deciding on a name," recalled Bement, "we combined Medallions, a popular group at the time, and Hi-Fi, a recent technological

Dwight Bement performing in November 2013 at the Western Jubilee Recording Company's Warehouse Theater in Colorado Springs, Colorado.

wonder that preceded stereo. The end result became the Fydallions. My mom sewed that name on a square of burgundy silk and we stretched it over the bass drum head. We all went down to Penneys, bought matching burgundy corduroy jackets and we were in business."

The Fydallions performed instrumental music for car club dances and various other events. "I knew clarinet wasn't going to get it at these dances, so I chose to use the saxophone, and the first song I learned was 'Night Train,' which I continue to play to this day," Dwight told us in July 1998.

Following graduation from high school in 1958, Dwight attended San Diego State College majoring in music. He joined the Nomads, a popular band that performed at big dances and socials throughout the San Diego area.

In 1960, Dwight and some musician friends moved to Sacramento where they formed a band, once again taking the name Fydallions. "Hey! It's a good name," said Dwight. "We played night clubs and bowling alleys and stayed up all night doing stupid things." The money wasn't very good so Dwight supplemented it by working in construction. He recalls, "We would play in bars until 2 a.m., then go to an after-hours joint and play there for a couple more hours and then go to the construction site, climb up on the roof and wait for it to get light enough to see a nail head. We would hammer away until three in the afternoon doing sub-floor, framing, and roof sheeting. Afterwards, we would either go drink beer or go get some sleep, depending on which was more urgently needed. Then the whole process would start over again. I don't know how I survived it all," said Dwight. That version of the Fydallions eventually became the Spiral Starecase.

On his way back to San Diego in 1960, Bement was waylaid in Ontario, California, by his longtime friend, Ronnie Williams. Ronnie talked him into joining a band called the Blackouts. This band included Ronnie's neighbor, Frank Zappa. Bement performed with the Blackouts for a couple of years until another friend, Tommy Kendall, coaxed him into returning to San Diego to play for the next three years in a band called the Gentrys, which had no relationship to the Memphis-based band of the same name that recorded "Keep On Dancing" in 1965.

"We decided on the name by opening a dictionary, covering our eyes and placing a finger on the page," recalled Dwight. "The word was 'gentry' which means people of good birth. Perfect." Kendall left the Gentrys to form with Gary Puckett and Bobby Brown a band called the Outcasts, which Bement joined in 1964.

"The Outcasts was an excellent group, a really good band, and in 1966 we tried to take the band on the road," recalled Bement. "We went to San Francisco to play but a couple of the guys got into an argument over something and the band broke up before we had a chance to play." About a month later, Puckett and Bement formed a group specifically for recording. That group became Gary Puckett and the Union Gap.

Although Bement was justifiably proud of the success that he and the other Union Gap members achieved, he admitted, "I never particularly cared for the music of the Union Gap. It wasn't my style, and I didn't play saxophone in the band; I played organ. I never liked keyboards until four or five years ago when my level of proficiency improved to the point that I could stand to listen to myself."

Following the breakup of the Union Gap in 1971, Bement returned to San Diego and played with a local band for a few months before moving back to LA, where he became involved with Flash Cadillac and the Continental Kids. Peter Rachtman, who managed the Union Gap, also managed Flash. Rachtman recruited Bement when the band was looking for a sax player.

"Flash Cadillac was the first band to appear on *American Bandstand* without a record," said Bement. Flash, which specialized in old-time rock and roll, recorded the only original music used on the soundtrack of the motion picture *American Graffiti*. The band also appeared in the movie and received a platinum album (signifying 1 million units sold) in 1973. Bement had joined Flash Cadillac a month after the movie was finished, but appeared with the band in the 1979 movie *Apocalypse Now* and on an episode of *Happy Days* as Johnny Fish and the Fins.

"The whole band lived in this huge, three-story house on Wilton Place near Wilshire Boulevard. Every Friday night that we were in town we threw a party, *Animal House* style," said Dwight. "Everyone attended.

Dwight Bement (in checked jacket, second from left) in the 1990s with other members of Flash Cadillac: Warren Knight, Sam McFadin, and Dave Henry. Courtesy of Flash Cadillac.

Famous musicians, infamous musicians, the Fonz and other celebrities. Some of the Los Angeles Dodgers would occasionally drop in."

Bement remained with Flash Cadillac, which in 1975 moved to a 117-acre ranch in the Colorado Rockies. They built a studio, which was used for Flash recording sessions and was also leased to other bands.

About half of Flash Cadillac's engagements were performed with symphony orchestras throughout the country. The band's joyous vocal renditions of the '50s and '60s have been accompanied by orchestras in Salt Lake City, Long Beach, Reno, Atlanta, Cincinnati, Charlotte, Portland and many other cities. The band used a talented group of arrangers, including Bement, and a librarian who sent the music to the different symphonies prior to rehearsals. "The symphony players are better than we are; no one will ever deny that. We have a lot of respect for them," said Dwight. "We don't think of them as just back-up music. The orchestra members help form an 80-piece rock and roll band."

Flash Cadillac performed for many of the conventions hosted at Colorado Springs' Broadmoor, a five-star hotel set at the base of Pikes Peak on the Front Range of the Rockies, 60 miles south of Denver.

"It was nice being the house band for the Broadmoor. People called them up and asked, 'What kind of entertainment do you have in the area? We are bringing in an insurance company from Ohio for the week and we need a good dance band for the weekend', and so on," said Dwight. "We also did a lot of corporate jobs like that all over the country."

Dwight Bement in August 2024 with his daughter Gina Bement Walsh (left) and his wife Kathy Ryan at Patty Jewett Golf Course in Colorado Springs, Colorado. Courtesy of Dwight Bement.

Dwight continued to supplement his music with construction as he did in Sacramento in the early '60s. He and his two business partners in D.R. Bement Construction in Colorado Springs developed a thriving business in residential and commercial building and remodeling. Bement eventually earned licensure as a general contractor but he was quick to add, "music is numero uno."

Life on the road has fractured many relationships, but sometimes it can be the genesis for new ones. For Dwight one fleeting introduction led to a relationship that took years to germinate, but it endured over decades. It was 1968 when Dwight first met Kathy Ryan.

"I was with the Union Gap and she worked for WCFL radio in Chicago," Bement said. "We were just kind of ships passing in the night until 1983, when we hooked up permanently. We've been together ever since." Kathy ultimately became a real estate broker in Colorado Springs, where the couple settled.

By the time Dwight turned 75, he was ready to start slowing down. "We folded the construction company in 2015. And then after being together since February 1969, Flash Cadillac disbanded in 2024," Dwight told us in December 2025. He and Kathy adapted well to retirement. "I'm real easygoing. I used to be quite different. But I don't care quite as much about things as I used to, in a good way. I don't lay a lot of stress on myself. I've stayed out of trouble. I'm proud that I have good friends, and that I've cultivated good relationships with people."

Epilogue: Kerry Chater

Keyboardist, bassist, singer, arranger, and composer

August 7, 1945 – February 4, 2022

Kerry Chater with Doberman puppy Titan in the 1990s. Photo by Lynn Gillespie Chater.

Composer, arranger, keyboardist, and bassist Kerry Chater spent most of his life making other people shine — notably, Lee Greenwood, Alabama, George Strait, Reba McEntire, and numerous other country artists for whom he wrote or co-wrote numerous hits. He composed two dozen songs that climbed well into both the pop and country charts, with "You Look So Good In Love," "I.O.U.," and "If I Had You" reaching No. 1 in the country music market. In 1984, Chater received a Grammy nomination for Lee Greenwood's recording of "I.O.U.," which received BMI's 2 Million Broadcast Performances award. Chater received 16 BMI awards from the Broadcast Music Inc. licensing agency and his songs appeared on eight platinum and 20 gold albums.

Kerry's father loved to play piano and bought an upright piano when Kerry was born, hoping that he would someday want to learn how to play it. It wasn't until Kerry was 10 years old that he became interested. "I met a school friend, a kid named Doug Ingle, and we used to get together and teach each other boogie woogie piano licks," recalled Chater. In his early teens Kerry took lessons from a jazz pianist in San Diego, and by the time he was a sophomore in high school, he knew that he wanted to be a songwriter.

Kerry Michael Chater was born on August 7, 1945, in Vancouver, Canada, where he spent his first year before his family moved to Toronto. In 1951, Kerry's father, Melville Chater, who was an executive director for the YMCA, moved the family to Los Angeles. Three years later he was transferred to San Diego, where Kerry grew up with his two older sisters Elizabeth Patricia and Eve Lynn. After raising three children, Kerry's mother, Elizabeth, became an English professor at San Diego

State University, where she developed expertise in science fiction creative writing. Following retirement, she published 24 novels using Lee Chaytor as a pseudonym.

"We had music going on all the time at my house, everything from classical music — Rachmaninoff — to big band music and jazz," recalled Kerry. "My father had some albums called *Backroom Piano,* which was kind of early blues piano-only albums."

Kerry attended Helix High School in La Mesa, California, where he was in the choir and wrote songs for the girls in the choir. After high school graduation in 1964, he attended Grossmont College in El Cajon, near San Diego, for about a year, but found that performing in bands didn't leave much time for studying.

"I started working in bands when I was about 15, and I was the leader of a lot of them," said Chater. "I could get us bookings at a lot of military clubs. The only problem I had was I'd put these really good bands together, but they'd all want to play for their high school peers, and would get mad at me for booking them into service clubs. I kept telling them, 'Hey, you get one gig a month at a high school, and you get four gigs a week at these other places.' We were making lots of money."

Childhood friend Doug Ingle, a keyboardist who later founded Iron Butterfly, played with Chater in many of the same bands. "We both wanted to play piano, but I always felt he was better than I was, said Chater. "I picked up the bass so that we could be in the same band together."

Chater's first band, called the Shados, lasted for about six months. Then in 1964 he started a band called the Progressives, which included Gary Withem on saxophone, Doug Ingle (piano), and Danny Weis (guitar). The Progressives later became Jeri and the Jeritones, named after Chater's girlfriend, Jeri Martinson, who sang in the group. Kerry and Jeri began a 10-year marriage in 1966, the same year the Jeritones broke up. Ingle and Weis went on to form Iron Butterfly, and Gary Withem and Chater became members of the Union Gap.

"When I met Gary Puckett I was working in a San Diego club with a union group called the Nomads. Puckett's group had been working across town, but they had broken up and Gary was going around to the clubs to see who was playing and what they were playing," recalled Chater. "I was playing some instruments stacked on each other, which is real popular now, but it was very unheard of at the time. I had a Fender

Rhodes piano bass, which produced two and a half octaves of bass sounds, and a Fender Rhodes electric piano on top of an organ. So we saved one guy and we made a little more money. Gary and I just sat in a coffee shop and discussed the band he was putting together, and I told him about Gary Withem. So originally, the Union Gap was me playing this stack of keyboards, Puckett playing guitar, plus two saxophonists, and a drummer. And then I got tired of playing so much, and I really wanted to be playing bass because you can run around and do more stuff on stage. Since Dwight played keyboard, I went to bass."

Chater did most of the arranging for live performances of Gary Puckett and the Union Gap, and wrote a couple of album tracks and the song "His Other Woman," which appeared on the B side of "This Girl Is a Woman Now." Chater said, "Although Jerry Fuller was a great songwriter, and he was writing our hits, that was a problem for me because I couldn't get enough of my material going in there. I had to compete with our producer. So after about three years I left the group to pursue songwriting." In early 1970, Kerry felt that he had made enough money to support himself for a few months during his pursuit of a career in songwriting. The band's manager, Marty Erlichman, helped Chater and Withem get jobs as staff songwriters for April-Blackwood Music, which was the publishing arm of Columbia Records. The two wrote as a team for about a year before joining A&M Music's Almo/Irving publishing arm.

"I had publishers showing my songs, and I worked my way up. I had always wanted to write country music. That was a part of it, the biggest part of it. So finally, after I got some successes in country music, I felt I had enough impetus to move to Nashville," said Chater. After spending several years commuting back and forth between Los Angeles and Nashville, he moved to Nashville because he preferred the work ethic there in comparison to that of LA. He adapted easily to the "music city" culture of Nashville, where he soon established a reputation as a prolific songwriter — and where mutual friends introduced him to songwriter Lynn Gillespie on a blind date in 1986 — leading to a romantic relationship and marriage of the couple in 1988.

Kerry, who was working with various other songwriters, began writing with Lynn in 1991. The married couple shared song credits on recordings by numerous country artists including Mindy McCready, Paul Brandt, Lorrie Morgan, and Anne Murray. He often collaborated with other writers, a common practice in Nashville. "Quite often I'll write with two other people because in Nashville songwriters are almost like

Lynn Gillespie Chater and Kerry Chater in their home surrounded by only a portion of about 40 gold and platinum album and single record awards that their compositions earned over four decades. Photo courtesy of Lynn Gillespie Chater.

a rock group. You can have three or four of them writing together. They might work independently of each other as well, but it's not unheard of here to have three writers on a song," explained Chater.

"Songwriting here in Nashville is very 9-to-5. Even if the hours don't synch up, the attitude does. And that was one of the inspirations that got me to this town," said Chater. "I could have written country music in Los Angeles, and I had several successes out of Los Angeles that would normally be thought of as Nashville records. In LA it's not unusual for writers to get together at noon, take a lunch break at 3 and work until 9 p.m., and that isn't the way I like to work."

Most of Chater's inspiration for songs came from what he saw in people. "I guess you could categorize most songwriters in one of two categories: either they're writing about something they experienced, or they're writing about something that they're fantasizing. For example, I don't know Joni Mitchell, but I get the impression that her songs are derived from experiences that she has had. Other writers are inspired by a fabricated event such as observing people walking down the street who were obviously married and having an argument. You can build a fantasy around that situation. I write from that second scenario most of the time, because when you're continually churning out songs, you don't have time to have all of the experiences. It's like writing fiction novels. You have to invent the scenarios, and you try to pick scenarios that generally could happen to anyone."

Just as the musician continually longs for that perfect opportunity to impress the right person at the right moment, the songwriter hopes that his or her song will be heard by an artist who will then record it. Since most of Chater's songs were written on speculation, he welcomed any opportunity to present his songs to anyone of influence — whether it was the producer, the artist, the manager, or a close or romantic friend. "It's like selling anything — insurance or shoes or cars. The publisher goes to the marketplace and says, 'Here's a song that I represent.' And if the artist likes it and eventually records it, then the publisher and the writers share the royalties," explained Chater, who focused primarily on composing music, although he did write some lyrics.

Chater rarely wrote on assignment; however, after the Grammy nomination of his song "I.O.U." — co-written with Austin Roberts and recorded by Lee Greenwood in 1983 — Greenwood's producer contacted Kerry looking for more songs to record on a subsequent album. Kerry acknowledged that some of his favorite songs are the ones that have become hits, such as George Strait's 1983 recording of "You Look So Good In Love," Reba McEntire's first number one song, "You're the First Time I've Thought About Leaving" (co-written with Dickey Lee), and "I Know a Heartache When I See One," which Chater wrote collaboratively with Rory Bourke and Charlie Black. That was a hit for Jennifer Warnes in 1978, was recorded 20 years later by Jo Dee Messina, and has placed on all of the charts except R&B. The dozens of artists who have recorded songs that Kerry wrote or co-wrote include Joe Cocker, the Carpenters, Dolly Parton, the Marshall Tucker Band, Anne Murray, Glen Campbell, James Brown, Alabama, and Cass Elliot. Four of his compositions hit No. 1 on various music charts.

"The fact that they've become hits is a confirmation that I'm doing the right thing," said Chater. "And I think they're honestly good songs that deserve the recognition they're getting. In the case of 'I Know a Heartache,' I happen to like the rhythm. Even if I hadn't written it, I would have liked the song."

Kerry and Lynn settled in a home south of Nashville in a community called Brentwood. "When we bought the property, there was only one tree on it, and we had to move it because that's where we wanted to build the house. Now we have about 75 trees that my wife planted, and it's just beautiful," Kerry told us in July 1998.

Kerry's hobby was tactical pistol shooting, which he practiced at a target range. "As in any sport, there's lots of gear, and it's real expensive. We wear hearing protection gear that looks like headphones in a stereo system. You can hear actually better than your normal hearing would be until there's any loud noise, and then it shuts down automatically, so that your ears are protected," said Chater.

Lynn and her daughter, Jesse — who was born in 1981 during her first marriage — both developed love of raising, training, and riding horses during childhood. Jesse Kirchhoff became an equestrian in the Olympic sport of eventing and a horse trainer. Eventing is a competitive discipline encompassing dressage, jumping, and cross-country riding. "Jesse runs a competition barn in Columbia, Tennessee, specializing in boarding and training. When she got married, her two dads walked her down the aisle — the one who had her and the one who raised her. She is married to Drew Kirchhoff and they have four daughters: Nora, Madalene, Lynn, and Rowen," Lynn told us in February 2026. Kerry was the father of two sons from his first marriage to Jeri — Kerry Michael Chater Jr., who was born in 1968, is musical and plays guitar;

Christopher John Chater, born in 1972, became a science fiction and fantasy adventure author. Christopher has won numerous awards for his books, which include *Aquarius Rising, Out of Body*, and a series titled *Dating in the Apocalypse*.

Later in life, Kerry remained dedicated to writing music. "I know that there's no real retirement from songwriting. You can do it as long as you live. But I think the longer you go at it, the harder it gets," said Kerry. "People start to want a new generation, new voices and new ideas, and my hope is to keep going and get those new ideas to stay in the business."

Kerry, who described himself as "quiet" and "a thinker," said that performing in the Union Gap was always a vehicle for getting involved in songwriting. "It helped me in a lot of ways, because the success didn't go to my head. I realized it could be over at any moment," said Chater. He correlated his feelings to those of Clint Eastwood who said during an interview that he knew at about 6 years of age that he wanted to be an actor. Eastwood said that a 6-year-old doesn't mind getting up and doing something silly in front of everyone. And if you can remember to be that 6-year-old, then you can have a lot of fun in life. "I think that's kinda where I'm coming from, too," said Chater. "I'm trying to stay this teenager with the joy in the music and writing it."

Kerry and his wife Lynn Gillespie-Chater maintained their successful songwriting collaboration in Nashville throughout five decades. Kerry and Lynn branched out into literary writing with their thriller novels *Kill Point* (published in 2013) and *Blood Debt* (2014). Their work on a sequel, *Collusion,* came to an untimely end amid the COVID-19 pandemic. Kerry's lungs became irreparably damaged after he contracted the omicron variant of COVID-19 in December 2021, and he died at age 76 on February 4, 2022.

Epilogue: Paul Wheatbread

Drummer and singer

Paul Wheatbread loved to entertain people, and whether it was from the stage or through his consulting agency, which specialized in travel, entertainment, meeting planning, group trips, and fun, everyone was guaranteed a good time. In 1995 Paul took over the Judy Francis Agency, a hospitality consulting firm that his wife, Judy, started in 1990. As the company grew, Judy, who was then the senior sales and marketing manager for the La Jolla and San Diego Hard Rock Cafes, could no longer manage the business, so Paul took over. The agency's clients included corporations, professional associations, meeting and convention planners, lawyers, and various business organizations. Many of the firm's clients grew up listening to the music of Gary Puckett and the Union Gap.

"I consult with people who need entertainment, people who want to arrange fishing trips or group travel to destinations such as Las Vegas, San Francisco, or anywhere. I arrange for all of the accommodations, entertainment, and anything they might need," explained Wheatbread, who found himself managing all of the details that road managers once handled for Gary Puckett and the Union Gap.

"We would plan a group trip, for example to Las Vegas, and then send out flyers announcing the trip, dates, and times to our regular clients, hospitality business associates, family, and friends. We got group

Judy and Paul Wheatbread on their 1970 BSA A-65 Thunderbolt in 1999.

room rates, and discounts for flights and shows. I also took groups to the Fabulous Forum in Inglewood for Lakers games," said Paul, who worked out of his home office. "I was kinda like the old road manager, making sure that everything was happening the right way it's supposed to happen. That little travel bug stayed in me after being on the road for so many years."

Born in San Diego on February 8, 1946, Paul Wheatbread began playing the drums at 5 years of age after his parents, Leonard and Ermine, bought him a drum set for Christmas. His first interest in music was stirred by the big band sounds of Gene Krupa and Benny Goodman. Originally from Buffalo, New York, Paul's parents had moved to Southern California to work in the aircraft factories in the late '30s. During World War II his mother helped build bombers while his father put in military service. Ermine became an elementary school teacher and gave piano lessons, teaching Paul and his older brother, Mark, and younger sister, Karen, how to play. After the war, Leonard returned to the aircraft factories as a civil service worker, retiring in 1983. "My brother followed my Dad into the civil service, working on aircraft, and my sister worked for preschools — kinda followed my Mom's footsteps. I was the oddball," laughed Paul.

During his junior year at Clairemont High School in San Diego, Paul worked in a Laundromat after school for three to four hours, then played music at night. He met Gary Puckett when members of Gary's band, the Ravens, were looking for a drummer to play at the local military clubs in San Diego.

"At fifteen and a half, I wasn't quite old enough to join the musicians' union, but they made an exception for me after talking to my Dad and Gary," recalled Wheatbread. "And we'd have to go down and work in these military clubs that at the time were union."

Following his high school graduation in 1963, Paul studied music at Mesa Junior College for a couple of semesters but his love of performing lured him to the club scene full time. About six months later, the Ravens decided they would like to play at the local night clubs rather than at military clubs. Since Paul wasn't yet the legal age of 21 to play in clubs, he had to leave the band.

A few weeks later Paul joined a local group called the Hard Times. The band consisted of Wheatbread on drums and vocals, lead guitarist Bill Richardson, lead vocalist and 12-string guitar player Rudy Romero, bassist Bob Morris, and harmonica player Lee Kiefer. The band started rehearsing in Wheatbread's garage and after two months decided to go to Hollywood. The Hard Times began performing at the Sea Witch nightclub at 8514 Sunset Boulevard in Los Angeles. Dick Clark, who was looking for new talent for his teen television show *Where the Action Is,* came into the club, liked the band's sound and signed them up on the spot. The show aired five days a week on ABC-TV from 1965 to 1967. Regularly featured performers on the program included Paul Revere and the Raiders, Steve Alaimo, Keith Allison, Tina Mason, The Robbs, Tommy Roe, the Action Kids Dancers and the Hard Times.

"We recorded for a subsidiary of Liberty Records called World Pacific. We put out a song called 'Fortune Teller' about a month before the Stones put it out in 1966, but we didn't quite have the hit with it that they did," chuckled Wheatbread. "They were just trying to draw new talent, and thought the Hard Times would do the trick for that show. We had a great time, played with a lot of great rock and roll performers. Dick Clark had all the top acts on all the time — James Brown, Otis Redding."

Where The Action Is was filmed on location throughout the country and performers would travel by bus. Wheatbread recalled a particularly memorable Dick Clark tour through the South in which he performed with the Hard Times but also had the opportunity to sit in with some other acts. "Neil Diamond was the headliner and his drummer got sick, so I backed him on stage for quite a few days of that tour," said Paul. "Neil was and is a real nice guy. He'd sit there in the back of the limo with his acoustic guitar and write songs, and a couple of months later I'd hear them on the radio."

Paul lived with other members of the Hard Times in a house in Laurel Canyon in the Hollywood Hills. "The Turtles lived down around the corner, the Byrds lived down at the end of the street, and the Mamas and the Papas lived up at the other end of the street," Wheatbread told us in July 1998. "So I got to know them all pretty well. When I went back on the road again with Gary, I kept running into them, sharing bills."

After *Where The Action Is* went off the air in March 1967, Paul returned to San Diego. Gary Puckett, who was looking to replace the drummer in the new band he had assembled, heard of Wheatbread's return and asked him to join the band. "I had just turned 21 so I was finally able to play in nightclubs," said Wheatbread. "They had just changed the band's name from Gary and the Remarkables to Gary Puckett and the Union Gap, and they were getting the Civil War uniforms. About that same time Jerry Fuller, the record producer from Columbia, had heard about us and came to see us, liked us, and signed us up."

The next five years were remarkable for Wheatbread, who tasted the success he had admired in others. Paul and Judy's first son Paul II was born in San Diego in 1970, one day before the Union Gap appeared on Dick Clark's *American Bandstand*. "Because I worked with Dick on *Where the Action Is*, he was like family and he announced my son's birth live on the air," Paul said proudly.

Following the breakup of the Union Gap, Paul stopped playing music for about six months before joining a local group called Burt Torres and the Charades in which his brother-in-law Ronny Legrette was playing. "Then I got a call from Flash Cadillac and the Continental Kids' manager, asking if I wanted to play drums for them," said Wheatbread. Paul agreed, reuniting with Dwight Bement, who had begun performing with Flash Cadillac about six months prior.

Francis Ford Coppola, who used Flash Cadillac in the motion picture *American Graffiti,* contacted the band to do some location shooting and soundtrack work for his 1979 film *Apocalypse Now.* "Our role in the movie was portraying a USO band entertaining the troops in Vietnam. We played the song "Susie Q" on this floating pontoon stage on a river in the Philippines, where much of the movie was filmed. We were set up on risers on the sides of the stage so a helicopter with these Playboy bunnies on it could land between us. At the same time it was raining and windy, and we were looking up at this helicopter hoping it was going to land straight," said Wheatbread, with a nervous laugh. "They had to fly us over to the Philippines again because the first time all the roads and the set got wiped out by a typhoon."

Flash Cadillac and the Continental Kids recorded three *Billboard* Hot 100 hits in the 1970s, including "Dancin' (On a Saturday Night)," issued by Epic Records in 1974; "Good Times, Rock & Roll," released by Private Stock in 1974; and "Did You Boogie (With Your Baby)," which included spoken interludes by Wolfman Jack, produced by Private Stock in 1976. "Did You Boogie" reached No. 29, and charted for 14 weeks.

"We traveled pretty much worldwide but mainly in the states, playing the local college circuits and fairgrounds," said Paul. "We played at the Diamond Head crater in Hawaii, down in the bowl itself, a natural amphitheater, with the Turtles." In 1976 Paul and his wife, Judy, sold their house in San Diego and moved to Colorado with Flash Cadillac.

"The band had a 117-acre ranch, and we built a recording studio on it. I was the only one who had a family at the time, so rather than live at the ranch, we bought a house nearby. I could get to the ranch in about 10 minutes," said Paul. There they welcomed the birth of their second son, Andrew, in 1978. "I was with the group for two years, but the touring was kinda coming to an end, we were getting homesick, and I wanted to raise my two boys So I decided to stay home and take care of them."

With his family, Paul returned to San Diego, where he began performing locally with several bands, including Red Eye, another called Steer Crazy, and one called Haywire. "I decided to start playing country and western music because at that point in rock clubs it was disco or nuthin'," chuckled Paul. "I started playing with a group that opened for a lot of top country performers — Johnny Lee, Eddie Raven, Steve Wariner, and Gary Morris."

Paul and Judy Wheatbread in January 2026, a month before celebrating their 60th anniversary. Photo by Jon Seong.

Paul, who kept the original drum set he played with the Hard Times on *Where The Action Is,* and the original Union Gap set, as well as a newer Gretsch set, occasionally sat in with some of the local bands, including a group called the Fabulous Pelicans, in the early 2000s. "If I was playing a concert situation, I would take the Gretsch set. But if I was playing a local function I'd take the old Union Gap set and use about half of it," said Wheatbread.

While many of the best songs of the '60s and their performers are still beloved by those who lived through that era, the marriages of many of those recording artists are not nearly as durable. Among the rare exceptions is the union of Judy and Paul Wheatbread, which began in 1966. For their wedding anniversary in 1991, Paul and Judy were remarried in the same church in which they had been married 25 years earlier in a ceremony performed by the same priest and with the same wedding party in attendance. They placed their original wedding rings on their right hands and bought new ones for their left hands.

"One of the main ingredients in a good marriage is to be able to talk to one another," declared Wheatbread. "You also have to be open to each other's views on different things. I've always let Judy go after her own career and she's always let me go my own way since the beginning. We have always supported each others' careers, so our marriage has always worked out."

Paul remained most proud of his natural ability to adapt his singing and playing to all styles of music. "I've always been fortunate to be in the right place at the right time, and have my natural talents to guide me through my career," Paul told us in July 1998. "I never even knew I could sing lead vocals that well until I started performing in Flash Cadillac. I kinda surprised everybody."

Wheatbread collected antique motorcycles, and he and Judy joined the San Diego Antique Motorcycle Club. At one point they owned four motorcycles — two British BSA bikes, for which they won awards at shows, a 1961 Super Rocket, and a 1970 Thunderbolt. By the time Paul was in his late 70s he had retired from both drumming and working at the Judy Francis Agency, but Judy continued operating the agency into the mid-2020s. "Her background in hotel management makes her sought-after when corporations and large groups are at the negotiating stage, and she excels in helping them obtain better rates and concessions," Paul told us in January 2026.

Paul said that he was satisfied with the direction his life carried him. "I like staying in contact with local musicians and playing with them," he said, "but I kinda miss the stage and the touring. If that opportunity ever arises again, I'll give some serious thought about doing that before I get too old. But so far, no problems. Still healthy. Still playing."

Paul managed to keep the performing aspect of his life distinct from his other role as a group tour organizer. But every now and then, when a patron of a group tour who is escorted to a Las Vegas stage show wondered aloud about the lives of glamour that performers lead, Paul's face stretched, almost imperceptibly, into a knowing smile.

Epilogue: Gary Withem

Keyboardist, clarinetist, and saxophonist

A positive role model can make a big difference in the choices children make on their path to adulthood. If they have the inspiration to work hard toward a goal and to achieve small successes along the way, they'll likely excel. That's why Gary Withem did all he could to consistently wield a positive influence on the lives of the high school students that he taught beginning in 1975, and on the lives of his five children, because that was one of his main goals in life.

Gary Withem in the 1990s. Courtesy of Gary Withem.

In his post-Union Gap days, Withem chose to become a high school music and dramatic arts teacher because he enjoyed being around people who are trying to make the world better. "What I admired most about my high school music director is that he inspired me to go to college to pursue music," proclaimed Withem. "I think you can make a difference with kids if you can show them that there are other things to do besides drugs and partying all night long. I don't think the kids have gotten worse. I think the temptations have gotten worse. The kids are great. They just need structure, they need role models. And there are not a whole lot of role models around anymore. The athletes don't think it's worth their while. Basically it's not their job. A lot of musicians don't feel it's their problem, either. Politicians, you're not going to find many role models there. I liked to show kids that there is a way to have good, clean fun and to be proud of what they're doing in their work and to make their families proud of them. That's why I enjoyed teaching so much."

Throughout his years as an elementary, junior high, and high school student Gary Withem was involved in music. He was a member of the marching band, concert band, orchestra, and the choir. He enjoyed Stravinsky just about as much as he loved rock and roll. Withem began playing the clarinet in the fourth grade and in high school added the flute and alto saxophone to his repertoire, becoming a member of the school's stage band, which performed big band music.

"I was lucky enough to play all the old arrangements — 'In the Mood' and all those Glenn Miller tunes, and the big band styles," recalled Withem. "We had a great band director, and the pep band was also a jazz band. So when we played at basketball games, the stage band would play the traditional fight songs, and at halftime we would put on a concert of Benny Goodman tunes and all the big band sounds."

Gary Winston Withem, who was born in San Diego, California, on August 22, 1944, moved with his parents back and forth several times between San Diego and Terre Haute, Indiana, where both sets of Gary's grandparents and most of the extended family members lived. "I spent most of my early life, through the third grade, in Terre Haute, Indiana. But in the early 1950s my Dad finally he made up his mind he needed to stay in San Diego," Gary explained. That's when his father settled into a job in San Diego working with computers for an aircraft and aerospace manufacturer called Convair, which later became a part of General Dynamics. Gary began taking private woodwind lessons at a local music store in the fourth grade, and later took piano lessons.

"By the time I was in the Union Gap I had a pretty good background in writing and arranging," said Withem, who was easily recognizable as the band member who wore round spectacles. "Kerry and Dwight also studied music and were pretty good at writing music and reading rhythms, and Gary Puckett, of course, could also read music and was a good musician. And so it made rehearsals and studio work a lot easier."

Gary recalled growing up with a variety of musical talents in his family. His grandfather was the fiddler for a square dance troupe in the Midwest. Gary's father played harmonica and guitar, his mother played violin, and his only sister, GayLa, five years younger than Gary, played string instruments in high school. So on weekends and holidays, the family would perform and sing together.

Throughout high school and into college, Gary performed in bands for extra spending money. One of the early bands included Kerry Chater. "All of the members of the band could read music and we could read 'fake books,'" recalled Withem. A fake book displays the melody and the symbols for the accompanying chords for popular songs. The accompaniment is then improvised or faked by the performer. "When someone would ask for 'Blue Moon' or 'In The Mood' we could just whip out the 'fake book' and play tunes that the older people really liked. So we played just about every weekend and made more money playing two or three nights a week than most of our friends could make flipping hamburgers all week."

After graduating from Mount Miguel High School in the La Presa area of San Diego in 1963, Gary enrolled at San Diego State College to pursue music. While attending college, he performed in a band called Jeri and the Jeritones at the Moose Club, the Elks Lodge, and at military base clubs around San Diego. In 1965, the Jeritones, which included Kerry Chater, Doug Ingle, and Danny Weis, auditioned for an opening as house band for a new teen club called the Palace on Frontier Street (later renamed Arena Boulevard). The band changed its name to the Palace Pages, but that was short-lived.

"A musical group called the Friendly Stranger came down one night from San Francisco. We had been sheltered from the very basic acid rock groups that were getting off the ground. But these guys were wearing paisley outfits, and appleseed necklaces. They had hair down to their waist and they were driving a van that was decorated in seashells and pine cones and stuff. Danny and Doug really loved their sound and all of our rehearsals started getting more and more into that area and we could see that the Palace Pages were doomed."

Danny and Doug ultimately went to Los Angeles and formed Iron Butterfly. And, with only nine units left to graduate from college, Gary put his degree on hold and went on the road with Kerry Chater, Gary Puckett, and Dwight Bement, and helped evolve the sound of Gary Puckett and the Union Gap, with which he enjoyed three years of success.

In 1970 Chater and Withem joined April-Blackwood Music as team writers and later A&M Music. "We shared the office with Paul Williams, who wrote 'We've Only Just Begun' and John Bettis, who wrote a lot of the Carpenters' songs with Richard Carpenter," said Withem.

During their nearly three years together Withem wrote a couple of hundred tunes with Chater and other writers in the catalog. They wrote jingles for national commercials, soundtracks for movies and television shows, and some of their songs were recorded by Tom Jones and Bobby Vee. "It was a project writing situation. We were paid a salary and we'd just turn out the product that they wanted. We didn't really get a big movie theme, but we came close a couple of times."

In 1973, Withem decided he wanted to complete his college degree and pursue a career in teaching, so he left A&M Music to return to school, enrolling at the University of Southern California and San Diego State University. He had been dating his wife-to-be, Penny Packer, who had been working for Marty Erlichman, former Union Gap manager and

Gary Withem in December 2024.
Photo by Penny Withem.

manager for Barbra Streisand. After Withem graduated from San Diego State University and received his teaching credential, he and Penny were married on July 25, 1975, and moved to San Diego, where Gary began teaching music and serving as band director at East Lake High School, Castle Park High School, and Bonita Vista High School, all within the same district in Chula Vista, in the southern area of San Diego. In 1985 he completed his master's degree in education, while continuing to teach band, vocal music, and theater production in San Diego. The Withems also owned a florist business, Withem's Flowers at 618 Broadway in Chula Vista, which Penny managed.

Gary and Penny raised five musically inclined children: daughters Hannah (born in 1977), Abbey (1978), Tammy (1980), and Audrey (1981), and son Michael (1985).

"Whenever everybody was in the house at the same time, we would knock out some harmonies. It was fun," said Withem. "Penny is musical, too. She played strings in high school, and she has a beautiful singing voice. So we have a good girls' choir in our family."

The Sweetwater Union High School District, in which Gary taught, has very successful, well-rounded, and highly supported arts programs, which is extremely rare in public schools. "We had more musicians, more actors, and artists than any other school district in the state. We had choirs, bands, and art and photography teachers at every school in our district. And that's unusual because arts programs are usually the ones that are cut back when the budget crunch comes. So I'm real proud of what we were able to do, and I think we made a difference with some of these kids."

Some of the kids from Gary's school went on to acting careers, from Broadway to commercials, and several of his students played in major symphonies. "I've had some pretty successful kids that are making money not only in the rock and roll business, but have become road managers, worked as techs, and light people, and other functions traveling with groups."

Gary also volunteered as a musician choir director at his church. After three decades of teaching, Gary retired, and in 2007 he and Penny relocated to Sullivan, Indiana, about 25 miles south of Terre Haute.

Gary's main focus after that remained on his family. "When I had to decide whether I was going to stay in the music business, I visualized that lifestyle as one that isn't really conducive to keeping a marriage together. That lifestyle was not something that I thought was going to make me happy," Gary explained. "So I really enjoy my reclining chair on the weekends, and going out fishing. A lot of rock people love the get-up-and-go type thing — new people every night and new arenas, but it was not what I wanted to do." After retirement, he immersed himself in visits with his grown children and his grandkids — teaching them at every opportunity.

No wonder Withem always enjoyed being around people who are trying to make the world better. That's exactly the kind of person who he became.

I Feel Like I'm Fixin' to Die

Country Joe and the Fish

More a collective than a traditional band, Country Joe and the Fish coalesced as a medium of protest in late 1965 and used the San Francisco ballroom scene as a podium from which it launched a litany of antiwar political satire so potent that the band members were named on the Nixon administration's "enemies list." The formation of Country Joe and the Fish occurred a year after the initial upwelling of student protest at the University of California, Berkeley,

Country Joe and the Fish in 1967. Clockwise, from left: drummer Gary "Chicken" Hirsh, guitarist Barry "the Fish" Melton (top), guitarist-bassist Bruce Barthol, guitarist Joe McDonald (wearing necklace), and guitarist-organist-pianist David Bennett Cohen (lower left). Photo by Joel Brodsky, courtesy of Vanguard Records

that enkindled the fires of the Free Speech Movement. The arrest of UC Berkeley graduate student Jack Weinberg by campus police on October 1, 1964, precipitated the Free Speech Movement and an era of nationwide antiwar demonstrations. Weinberg had been arrested for handing out leaflets on behalf of the Congress of Racial Equality, in violation of a campus policy prohibiting political activity. During that year, civil rights demonstrations fueled by the impassioned oratory of student Mario Savio expanded in scope and channeled growing mistrust of educational, governmental, and military institutions — "the establishment." Resistance to the draft and opposition to the war in Vietnam was gaining in intensity, as students boycotted classes and engaged in ongoing teach-ins and noisy demonstrations. It was this fervent theater of protest that gave rise to Country Joe and the Fish.

The protesters began targeting the military "establishment" after the United States initiated Operation Rolling Thunder — continual bombing raids against North Vietnam. At the Oakland Induction Center near Berkeley, folksingers invigorated demonstrators as enlistees and draftees reported for military duty. The musical performers included Joe McDonald, a Navy veteran who had migrated from Southern California to Berkeley in 1964 to attend school but found participation in social causes more compelling. With a partner named Eugene "ED" Denson, who later would manage Country Joe and the Fish, McDonald had begun issuing a local social commentary publication called *Rag Baby Magazine.*

At the same time, McDonald also began composing musical satire. On an extended-play (EP), four-cut vinyl pressing that was billed as "the first talking issue of *Rag Baby Magazine,*" McDonald and a few acquaintances — guitarist Barry Melton, vocalist Mike Beardslee, Carl Schrager on washboard and bells, and Bill Steele on bass — recorded two songs: "Superbird," which skewered President Lyndon Johnson, and the first version of the satirical, stridently antiwar "I-Feel-Like-I'm-Fixin'-To-Die Rag." The two accompanying tracks by guitarist Pete Krug were "Fire in the City" and "Johnny's Gone to the War." Copies of the EP recording, on which McDonald and Melton called themselves Country Joe and the Fish, were sold at the first teach-ins against the war in Vietnam that were held in Berkeley in the fall of 1965. The popularity of the recording led to a booking by the Students for a Democratic Society (SDS), which by then was organizing antiwar protests on college campuses throughout the nation. Traveling by Greyhound bus, the duo of Country Joe and the Fish played at college campuses throughout the Pacific Northwest.

Upon their return to Berkeley, Melton and McDonald began playing regularly at a coffeehouse called the Jabberwock at 2901 Telegraph Avenue. There they were joined by several local jug band musicians, including Barry's two roommates, singer and guitarist-bassist Paul Armstrong and guitarist-bassist Bruce Barthol; and bluegrass guitarist David Cohen, with whom Melton had played briefly in a rock band. With the addition of drummer John Francis Gunning, the six-piece band started its metamorphosis.

"We became the hottest band in Berkeley," recalled Melton. "But we were no longer a jug band. We became a rock band because we could reach more people that way. We played there five nights a week and it was packed, two shows each night. It was a great time. We weren't making any money but the Jabberwock had food and we lived right next door. Joe had left his wife and moved in with me, Bruce, and Paul. We had this great landlady who lived downstairs. She was deaf, so we got to make as much noise as we wanted to, and she thought we were the most wonderful young men in the world."

In deference to the band's repertoire and motivations, manager ED Denson advised retaining the 'Country Joe and the Fish' name. The band members agreed. "When Joe and I began the band, we figured they all think we're commies for doing this stuff, so why not call it Country Joe and the Fish? Country Joe was a nickname for Joseph Stalin, and Fish is a reference to a saying of Chairman Mao's: 'The revolutionary moves through the peasantry as the fish does through water.' The reference was so obscure. It was a dumb name. Still is," asserted Melton. "We were certainly not the first people to insert political expression in music, but we were probably among the first performers to be political and popular at the same time."

The release of the second Country Joe and the Fish EP on the Rag Baby label in June 1966 attracted local radio airplay and mention in *Billboard* magazine. By autumn the band graduated to appearances presented by rock music impresario Bill Graham at San Francisco's Fillmore Auditorium at 1805 Geary Boulevard, at the intersection of Fillmore Street, sharing the bill on October 23 with the Yardbirds and on December 22 with Otis Redding, before headlining for the first time on New Year's Eve at the Avalon Ballroom, 1268 Sutter Street at Van Ness Avenue. The composition of the group solidified following the departure of Armstrong — who as a conscientious objector to military induction began a two-year alternative service obligation driving a truck for Goodwill Industries — and the replacement of Gunning with drummer

Gary "Chicken" Hirsh. At the close of 1966, Joe McDonald, Barry Melton, Bruce Barthol, David Cohen, and Chicken Hirsh signed with the distinguished folk- and blues-oriented Vanguard label, for which Joan Baez, the Weavers, Doc Watson, Ian & Sylvia, and Buffy Sainte-Marie also recorded.

As American involvement in the Vietnam conflict increased, Country Joe and the Fish assumed the mission of mobilizing opposition to the war through the powerful medium of music. In February 1967, the band members booked studio time at Sierra Sound Laboratories at 1741 Alcatraz Avenue in Berkeley to record the first of their six Vanguard albums, *Electric Music for the Mind and Body.* The LP, released in May 1967, rose to No. 39 on the *Billboard* albums chart and yielded the group's initial single, titled "Not So Sweet Martha Lorraine." Warning about a "sweet lady of death" who drives her suitors insane, the single premiered on the *Billboard* Hot 100 on August 5, 1967. Although it received light Top 40 airplay, the song became a favorite on newly emerging "underground" radio stations.

Barry Melton attributed the success of the band not so much to Vanguard Records or their association with the Family Dog and Bill Graham's Fillmore Auditorium concerts but rather to a single musical event: the Monterey Pop Festival of June 1967. As the first large rock festival, it set the stage for the American debut of the Who on a staggering bill that included the Jimi Hendrix Experience, Big Brother and the Holding Company with Janis Joplin, Otis Redding, Ravi Shankar, Hugh Masekela, the Grateful Dead, Jefferson Airplane, the Byrds, the Association, the Electric Flag, the Paul Butterfield Blues Band, Canned Heat, Laura Nyro, Booker T. and the MGs, the Mamas and the Papas, Buffalo Springfield, the Blues Project, and Quicksilver Messenger Service.

Playing colleges, ballrooms, and rock festivals across the country, Country Joe and the Fish recorded a second album, *I Feel Like I'm Fixin' To Die,* released in November 1967. For those sessions, the band members played not only their usual instruments but also embellished tracks with congas and wine bottle percussion (Chicken Hirsch), harmonica (Bruce), and harpsichord and calliope (David). The tracks on that album included the group's second single, "Janis," an ode to Janis Joplin, with whom McDonald had a romantic relationship. Country Joe and the Fish had become the spokespeople for a generation of young Americans expressing abhorrence of the horrors of war and resistance to American military policy.

But in the late summer of 1968, the peace-seeking band found itself squarely in the gunsights of danger amid one of the most disturbingly violent episodes in the nation's history. That spring, Abbie Hoffman and Jerry Rubin had called for the formation of the Youth International Party, members of which would be called Yippies. With fellow activists, they planned a "Festival of Life" to coincide with the Democratic National Convention that August at the Chicago Hilton. Rubin and Hoffman hoped to attract thousands of antiwar protesters to Chicago's Grant Park with a celebration of peace, live bands, and demonstrations against racial discrimination and the Vietnam war.

Yippie organizers Rubin and Hoffman met with Joe and Bruce to seek the participation of Country Joe and the Fish. The band, which already had a gig scheduled in Chicago a few days before the convention, was initially supportive of the festival. But as spring turned to summer, the potential for violence became increasingly apparent.

"Joe decided the festival was going to be too out of control, too dangerous, feared that our equipment would get busted up, that we might be encouraging people to get hurt. He even wanted to take out an ad in the paper announcing withdrawal of our support. I believed exactly the opposite," recalled Bruce Barthol. "I felt that if anyone could afford to get hurt and have their equipment busted, it was us. I felt we had an obligation to take part, but I was the only member of the band with that position."

Following a few weeks off in June and July, the group members traveled to Chicago for their performance at a dance hall called the Electric Theater. They arrived as convention delegates began streaming into town. "As we got off the plane at O'Hare Airport there were signs all over saying, 'Mayor Daley welcomes you' and girls in straw hats called Daley-ettes were greeting people." Their smiles did little to erase the tension gripping the city. Reacting angrily to rumors that the Yippies planned to lace the city's water system with LSD and initiate other disruptive actions, stronghanded Mayor Richard Daley dispatched an army of 12,000 police, accompanied by 7,500 Army troops, and 6,000 Illinois National Guardsmen, to confront demonstrators.

"After our performance at the Electric Theater we returned to our hotel on North Lake Shore Drive," Bruce recounted. "Chicken and I already had our room keys so we got into the elevator and pressed the button for our floor. As the doors closed I saw Barry, Joe, and David waiting for their keys, and I also noticed a guy with a crewcut hairstyle running from across the street toward the hotel door. The next morning I found out that he had run into the hotel lobby yelling, 'I'm back from Vietnam, hippies,' and punched the totally surprised Joe, Barry, and David before running out the other door."

The Democratic Convention facility was encircled with electrified barbed wire as Aretha Franklin sang the National Anthem inside. Committed to the Vietnam policies of President Johnson, Vice President Hubert Humphrey withheld support of a peace platform, triggering its defeat at the convention. In Grant Park, amid a noisy crowd of nearly 10,000 antiwar demonstrators, a young man shinnied up a flagpole to tear down the American flag. Police closed in, teargassing and clubbing demonstrators. As police rampaged in response to the taunting demonstrators, those injured in the melee included convention delegates and news reporters. The crowd chanted "the whole world is watching" as television crews broadcast images of police and national guardsmen wielding clubs and Mace against demonstrators and bystanders alike, underscoring the contention of the Yippies that the United States was increasingly becoming a police state.

Country Joe and the Fish in the late 1960s on W. 23rd Street at Sixth Avenue in Manhattan, New York City. From left: Barry "the Fish" Melton, Gary 'Chicken' Hirsh, David Bennett Cohen, Country Joe McDonald, and Bruce Barthol.

Bruce Barthol's conviction that the group should have taken a larger role in the demonstrations in Chicago precipitated his departure from the group that fall, when he moved to England.

"The first person to leave was Bruce, who was probably the conscience we should have listened to," said Barry. "He was the first person who said, 'This isn't for me. This isn't what we set out to do. We're just pop musicians.' There was a push from the business side of things not to shake the boat too much. I think Bruce had a distinct aversion to fame and money, but I also think he sensed that the mission was being lost."

Bruce was initially replaced by Mark Ryan, later a member of Quicksilver Messenger Service, then by Jack Casady, formerly the bassist for Jefferson Airplane. Following the expiration of their recording contract with Vanguard at the close of 1968, Country Joe and the Fish were undecided about how — or whether — to proceed. David Cohen remembers a conversation he had with Bill Graham at that time. "This band's not breaking up without a farewell concert," Graham said. The result was a memorable performance in January 1969 at Bill Graham's Fillmore West in San Francisco.

"Jack was playing bass with us, and a bunch of our other friends showed up and sat in with us, including Jerry Garcia, Jorma Kaukonen, Steve Miller, and Mickey Hart," Cohen recalled. The staging of the concert demonstrated how far Graham and the band members had come since they first met three years before. "The first time we ever met Bill Graham we were on stage doing a sound check. This demon came tearing across the stage yelling at us to get off the stage because he had a show to begin," Cohen laughed. At the January 1969 concert, Cohen heard Graham utter in hushed tones, "What a band!" The bittersweet concert was captured on tape, and Vanguard warehoused the audio recording for three decades until its ultimate release in 1997 on a compact disc titled *Live! Fillmore West 1969.*

McDonald's performance of "I-Feel-Like-I'm-Fixin'-To-Die Rag" prefaced by a ribald version of the celebrated "Fish cheer" at the Woodstock Music and Art Fair in Bethel, New York, in August 1969 was immortalized in the documentary concert film *Woodstock.* Bill Belmont, the group's former manager, later an executive with Fantasy Records in Berkeley, observed that "Five years after its debut at a demonstration in Oakland, it became an anthem."

Country Joe and the Fish remained together after the expiration of the Vanguard recording contract, but by the time they got to Woodstock, Joe and Barry had replaced all the other members of the band with a succession of musicians. "Joe and I stayed on and got a whole new crew of musicians," said Barry. "There's never been a Country Joe and the Fish without Joe and me. But sometime after the Woodstock festival we figured we had gone as far as we could go with each other. We shook hands, we split up the name — he took Country Joe, I took the Fish — and off we went."

On March 29, 1973, four years after President Richard Nixon began military reductions in Vietnam, the last American troops were withdrawn. During the previous 12 years, 47,369 Americans had died in combat and 153,303 had been wounded. Country Joe and the Fish, the group that had set out to end the war in Vietnam, ultimately contributed to the achievement of that goal by raising awareness of the war and encouraging a generation of young people to speak out against Washington policy.

Gary "Chicken" Hirsh opened an art supply shop in Oakland after Country Joe and the Fish disbanded. He later relocated to become a painter and T-shirt artist in Ashland, Oregon, where he died at the age of 81 on August 17, 2021.

Between 1969 and 2017 Joseph Allen "Country Joe" McDonald recorded more than 30 albums released on the Vanguard, Fantasy, and Rag Baby labels. He died at age 84 on Saturday, March 7, 2026, due to complications from Parkinson's disease, leaving behind his wife, Kathy, and five children.

ALBUMS BY COUNTRY JOE AND THE FISH

Debut	Peak	Title	Label
6/67	39	Electric Music for the Mind and Body	Vanguard
12/67	67	I feel Like I'm Fixin' To Die	Vanguard
7/68	23	Together	Vanguard
6/69	48	Here We Are Again	Vanguard
1/70	74	Greatest Hits	Vanguard
5/70	111	C.J. Fish	Vanguard

Billboard's chart data is courtesy of Joel Whitburn's Record Research Inc., Menomonee Falls, Wisconsin.

Epilogue: Barry "The Fish" Melton

Guitarist

Three decades after the formation of Country Joe and the Fish, guitarist Barry "the Fish" Melton concluded that the political potency of the band was the product of a fleeting moment in the cultural evolution of the nation, a phenomenon that emerged in shifting sands now eradicated by changing technologies.

Barry Melton performing on stage in August 2016. Photo courtesy of Barry Melton.

"We were correct in our assumption that rock and roll was the medium through which to reach young people," Melton said. "It had been just pop music before the '60s and it returned to being pop music after the '60s, but for a brief moment in time it was one of the exclusive channels of young people's expression in this country with the growth of underground radio, and it seemed to be controlled by young people rather than by adults." Such dominance by one medium is improbable today because of the vast number of social media platforms, streaming video channels, and satellite and terrestrial radio stations. "But for a moment in the '60s, music, the counterculture, and the antiwar movement became very closely identified with one another," Melton observed.

Country Joe and the Fish fused the prevailing interests in Melton's life: music, political activism, and the legal system. Melton who by the late 1990s had become a California deputy state public defender assigned to post-conviction appeals in capital litigation, worked with offenders who were under a sentence of death. He said that occupation was consistent within the continuum of his lifelong pursuit of social justice. Melton, whose days on the job were spent meeting with clients on death row, preparing legal pleadings, and searching documents and other evidence for subtle factors that could reduce a prison term or reverse a death sentence, asserted that he was in the business of saving lives. That was his principal obligation to his clients.

For people who wonder how a lifelong peace campaigner can reconcile defending capital offenders convicted of violent, gruesome crimes, Melton had a declaratory response: "My job within the framework of government was to question authority and to defend people against authority being arbitrarily and capriciously meted out. I liked being a public defender, because I was working in the only branch of government that is funded to fight the government. It's a branch of government whose job is to stop police, courts, and prosecutors from dealing with people unjustly," observed Melton. "It made sense for me. My legal career mostly was involved with defending the poor, and it served my view of what social justice is, as did my musical career to some extent. I'm not saying that's entirely why I did what I did as a public defender. It was to make a living, like anyone else. But I needed the element that I was accomplishing some greater societal purpose in my work. Being a criminal defense lawyer, working for indigent clients, in many ways is consistent with this kind of progressive political outlook I've had all my life."

Left-wing activism was inbred in Barry's family, and his parents, James G. "Jim" Melton and Terry Kuchuck Melton, encouraged him to pursue a career in music. Barry, however, was drawn to the legal profession. Born Barry Alan Melton in Brooklyn, New York, on June 14, 1947, he lived as a young child down the block from folksinger Woody Guthrie and his family.

"I went to Marge Guthrie's dance school as a young kid," Melton explained, "and I grew up in the American left wing that had arisen in New York City and resulted in Senator Joseph McCarthy's pursuit of people who had been labor organizers in the 1930s." Jim Melton, a merchant seaman, was a founder of the National Maritime Union. "In our house, I grew up listening to records by the Weavers, Pete Seeger, Woody Guthrie, and others."

With that early influence, Barry began his musical education at age 5. "I learned to read and write music from the time I could read and write English," said Melton. He took classical guitar instruction under Charles D'Aleo, who had been a violinist with the New York Philharmonic. Barry, his older brother, Mike, and their parents remained on Avenue Z near Brighton Beach in Brooklyn until 1955, when they moved to North Hollywood, California, where Barry's younger sister, Abby, was born. There Barry resumed studying guitar with Milton Norman, a jazz guitarist with the Kay Kyser Band.

At Ulysses S. Grant High School in Van Nuys, Barry played trombone and baritone horn in the school band and orchestra, but channeled his increasing interest in folk music as president of the school's folk music club. That's where Barry first met fellow student Bruce Barthol, later to join him as bass guitarist in Country Joe and the Fish. Barry, Bruce, and other friends jammed and performed together at parties and hootenannies. At fraternity parties, Barry often played in a group called the Three Prominent Bastards (inspired by a 1956 Oscar Brand folk song), dabbling in the irreverent as well as the socially relevant.

Melton began commingling his interest in music with civil rights causes. "I was a CORE [Congress of Racial Equality] volunteer doing Freedom Rider support, and I managed to get myself arrested during a sit-in at Van de Kamp's Restaurant, which wasn't integrating their lunch counters in the South."

Barry also demonstrated upon the arrival of Madame Ngo Dinh Nhu and her husband in Los Angeles. Madame Nhu was the sister-in-law of South Vietnamese President Ngo Dinh Diem, who was murdered in a 1963 coup d'état supported by the United States. Known derisively as the "Dragon Lady," Madame Nhu acted in an official capacity on behalf of Diem. She referred to self-immolation by Buddhists in Saigon and Hue protesting South Vietnamese government policies as "barbecues." Barry Melton was among the crowd that protested loudly outside the Los Angeles hotel where she was staying.

By 1963, Barry had started performing in folk music clubs in Hollywood, including the Ash Grove on Melrose Avenue. In the summer of 1964, he hitchhiked to the San Francisco Bay area, where he first met Joe McDonald during a performance by folksinger Malvina Reynolds, who wrote the song "Little Boxes" that was popularized that year by Pete Seeger.

But Melton stayed in the Bay Area only a short time before traveling on to New York to perform at the Greenwich Village "basket houses," in which young folk performers would play a set, then pass a basket among the audience for donations. All the while, though, Barry sought to coalesce his stage presence and his interest in social causes into a career in law. "Music was my parents' thing, and law was mine," said Barry, who decided at age 15 that he wanted to become a lawyer after reading a book on the life of Clarence Darrow. "I wanted to defend people, advance social justice, and all of those lofty covenants," he said.

During his senior high school year, Barry also took an interest in the writings of semanticist S.I. Hayakawa, who taught at San Francisco State College and later would become its controversial hard-line president during the height of student unrest. After graduation from Grant High in January 1965, he enrolled at San Francisco State but was unable to take classes from Hayakawa, who taught only in the upper division. After 10 weeks, Melton dropped out of college. "I was lured away by the music," he explained.

Ineligible for induction into military service because of leg injuries he had suffered in a motorcycle accident while in high school, Melton headed across San Francisco Bay to Berkeley. There he began hanging out and playing in clubs, including the Jabberwock, where he reunited with his high school pal Bruce Barthol and again ran across Joe McDonald. Melton joined McDonald in the Instant Action Jug Band, an ad-hoc group of musicians who performed at political demonstrations. Their union ultimately led to formation of Country Joe and the Fish, which, by the fall of 1966, had become a ballroom headliner.

The band, which had ignited spontaneously in the heat of protest, burned brightly for three years. When it began, the Vietnam War was barely on the radar of the national consciousness. By the time the quintet disbanded three years later, its antiwar message was seared into the American political landscape. Objection to the War in Vietnam was widespread, crossing social, philosophical, and generational lines.

The initial breakup of Country Joe and the Fish after Woodstock coincided with the breakup of Barry's first marriage. Melton dropped out of the music scene and took a six-month rest, after which he recorded a solo album titled *Bright Sun is Shining* for Vanguard Records. The 12 cuts on the album consisted largely of Barry's interpretation of bluesy standards and R&B tunes, including Smokey Robinson's "You've Really Got a Hold On Me," Otis Rush's "It's a Mean Old World," Elmore James' "The Sun Is Shining" and a song Barry wrote titled "I've Been in the Darkness." The musicians on the sessions included Donny Hathaway on piano and Phil Upchurch on bass. Barry subsequently teamed with keyboard player Jay Levy, bassist Rick Dey, and drummer Tony Dey, signed with Columbia Records, and recorded an album titled *Melton, Levy and the Dey Brothers*, produced by guitar virtuoso Mike Bloomfield. In 1971, Grateful Dead drummer Mickey Hart introduced Barry to college student Barbara Joy Langer, with whom he found a lot in common and whom he subsequently married. In 1973 Melton and McDonald paired again and toured together for the next several years. Barry continued recording, with releases that included a 1976 United Artists album titled *The Fish,* and two 1978 releases on the Music Is Medicine label titled *We Are Like the Ocean* and *Level With Me.* But as Barbara was expecting their first child in 1977, Barry had begun to ponder the wisdom of life on the road. "I wanted to prevent this relationship from going down the tubes, and I wanted to be around as my child grew up." That's when he decided to resurrect his interest in the law.

Melton enrolled in a correspondence law preparation program that had been advertised on a matchbook cover. "Matchbook U," Melton joked. Actually, the program was offered through LaSalle Extension University in Chicago. While on the road, Barry performed by night and studied law independently during the days. After studying five years under the LaSalle program and another correspondence course, he passed the California Bar exam in 1982 and opened a small law office in San Francisco's low-overhead Mission District. His clientele was "whatever walked in the door," he said.

Melton welcomed both civil and criminal cases. His first client was the owner of a health food store who was encountering difficulty with city government regulations requiring businesses with more than 10 employees to provide separate restroom facilities for men and women. "I helped keep the city at bay for like a year while the store moved to a new location with two bathrooms. The store didn't pay me money, but they gave me groceries. I was playing music at night so I had a way of making money, because I sure wasn't making anything practicing law," Melton admitted.

By night, Barry was playing with a band he had formed, the Dinosaurs, the members of which included Grateful Dead lyricist Robert Hunter, Jefferson Airplane drummer Spencer Dryden, Big Brother and the Holding Company bassist Peter Albin, and Quicksilver Messenger Service guitarist John Cipollina (pronounced chip-ohl-LEE-na). Melton and Cipollina also periodically played as a duo, under the name Fish and Chip.

After an internship at the San Francisco Public Defender's Office, Melton was able to get on the court appointment panels and handle juvenile and criminal cases by referral. A year after Melton went into partnership with two other lawyers in 1984, he was earning more money as a lawyer than as a musician. Even then, he continued playing until John Cipollina died of a lifelong respiratory ailment in May 1989. "John and I had worked a lot together for seven to eight years before he died, and we had been in three different bands together at the same time. I've got to admit, his death took the wind out of my sails."

Barry Melton in France in 2025.
Photo by Natalie Martel.

Concentrating on his practice, Melton focused on criminal law, in which he became a board-certified specialist. In 1992, he ran for judicial office. "I got only 80,000 votes, and I was mad at San Francisco," Melton laughed. "I was! I had bet my wife that if I lost we could move, because she had always wanted to move." Barry began looking for the right opportunity. In late 1993 he spotted a job opening for deputy public defender in rural Mendocino County, north of San Francisco. He wanted that job. He got it. And he quickly developed a reputation for ingenuity, intensity, and diligence.

"I've had some really great cases," said Melton. "I've never experienced a greater feeling of satisfaction from anything I've done than I have in winning a jury trial for someone who I truly believe in. There's no greater feeling even from performing before an audience. It's funny, but being a trial lawyer is a performance art in many respects. When you really believe in a client with the odds against you and yet you vindicate your client in front of a jury, there's no better feeling," said Melton, whose expertise in criminal law gained widespread recognition.

After serving as a guest lecturer in professional workshops presented by the California Public Defenders Association and the California Attorneys for Criminal Justice, Melton was offered a position as deputy state public defender for the state of California in Sacramento, which he accepted in July 1998. After a year there, he was recruited as chief public defender for Yolo County, just west of Sacramento, and remained in that position until 2009. That didn't mean he retired. He continued working in private practice as a criminal defense lawyer, working on a select number of cases. Melton has considered criminal law the most interesting and most theatrical specialty in law. "I've spent many hours of the week on my feet in court. Probably the vast majority of lawyers out there are in their office most of the time," said Melton, who chose to specialize in cases involving violent crimes because he relished the challenge of unraveling real-life "whodunnit" mysteries.

Just as the music of Country Joe and the Fish had a strong philosophical undercarriage, Melton espoused deep-seated views about crime and punishment. "A lot of what criminal lawyers do is more akin to what people think of as social work than it is lawyering skills. I believe that our society has become overly punitive, particularly with regard to nonviolent crimes, particularly drug offenses. From a humane perspective, punishment is not the right approach for crimes that concern lifestyle choices. I'm a pragmatist. I know that's the way it is. But if someone had a problem, I preferred to work hard to see that they got help rather than to see that they simply got punished, especially when there was no victim," Melton told us in April 1998.

That philosophy reflected the legacy of Barry's parents, both of whom are now deceased. Terry Melton had worked as a secretary, and Jim, who taught air conditioning and refrigeration engineering at Los Angeles City College, managed the downtown plant for the Los Angeles City Hall complex until his retirement. Barry's older brother, Mike, taught English in military dependent schools for the Department of Defense. Through the years he was stationed in various places throughout the world. Barry's younger sister, Abby, became a private investigator in Los Angeles. Barry and his wife Barbara raised two sons: Kingsley, born in 1977, and Kyle, born in 1986. Barbara, who became a licensed marriage, family, and child counselor with expertise in substance abuse, had worked for Mendocino County before signing on as head counselor with the Chemical Dependency Center for Women in Sacramento (subsequently renamed Strategies for Change). She loved to spend time in Paris, where Barry frequently performed. She rounded out her career at Yolo Hospice and the Woodland Youth Services group home but to Barry's utter despair became ill and died on February 15, 2020, at age 73.

Barry's fellow musicians and fans helped him weather this difficult period in his life, during which he took a break from music. As he entered semi-retirement from law, music resumed its place in his life as a creative outlet, through public performances. "I really find that as an adult, my life runs best if I'm doing both law and music," said Melton.

"I think I'm a better musician than I've ever been. I don't play as fast as I used to play, but I've developed a certain simplicity that in a way is more expressive than things that I used to do."

Epilogue: David Bennett Cohen

Keyboardist

The lotus flower blooms in a muddy swamp. The muddier the swamp, the more beautiful the flower. "That tells us that whatever mud exists in our lives, whatever kinds of negatives we have made, we still have the potential of the pure lotus flower in our lives," observed guitarist and pianist David Bennett Cohen, whose life was given power and purpose by this gentle Buddhist philosophy.

A disciple of folksinger Pete Seeger, grandson of anarchists, self-described revolutionary, boogie woogie enthusiast, organist with Country Joe and the Fish, published music technique instructor, grandfather, and blues piano virtuoso, Cohen always preferred to be called David rather than Dave, saying, "Don't leave out the 'id,' please" with a laugh. While Cohen once used music to ridicule the military and discredit government leaders as a means to end the war in Vietnam, his objective evolved to the spiritual: "I hope my music will show people the power of my practice."

That change occurred as Cohen became a member of the Soka Gakkai, an international Buddhist lay organization whose name is derived from a phrase meaning "value creation society" in Japanese. "We

David Bennett Cohen performing on March 18, 2024. Photo by Christine Santelli.

try to create value in everything we do. We believe that if each individual takes responsibility for his or her own life and own happiness, then world peace will occur as a natural byproduct," Cohen declared. "It's a slow process that transcends politics, but this is the only way it's going to work."

David Bennett Cohen grew up in Brooklyn, New York, where he was born August 4, 1942. He and his brother, Michael, lived with their parents, Max and Molly Cohen, on Maple Street in a neighborhood called Pigtown, between Crown Heights and East Flatbush. It was nicknamed Pigtown because of the ramshackle livestock farms that existed there in the early 1900s before urbanization occurred. "There were a few Jewish families, two black families, and everyone else was Italian," recalled David, whose father was a dentist and whose mother became a teacher.

David, who was raised without a religious background, had been taking classical piano lessons since he was a 7-year-old kid attending Public School 91. "My mother wanted me to play the piano. She thought maybe it would help round me out," he surmised. "I studied piano for about seven years and I hated it." David's eventual abandonment of piano lessons was undoubtedly influenced by a discovery he made at about age 9.

"We went to visit some friends of my parents and there was a guitar there. I couldn't stay away from it," said David. "The next thing I knew, that guitar ended up at my house. I started playing it even though I didn't know what I was doing. The summer I turned 14, I went to a camp in upstate New York called Lincoln Farm Work Camp, which was run by radicals and Communists. My parents weren't radical, but my grandparents were active anarchists, and this camp matched their political and social philosophy." There David saw Pete Seeger, with whom he was totally entranced. "I took guitar lessons from the instructor there, but I learned more from playing with people in the camp. I spent a month or two there, and it was one of the greatest experiences of my life."

As the summer of 1956 drew to a close, David returned from that camp with a driving obsession for music. His days at Brooklyn Tech High School were little more than a distraction from his pursuit of music. "I would come home from school and go to my room and play guitar for six hours. I would do homework for about 15 minutes and go to sleep. Somewhere in there I would run to the kitchen and wolf down something to eat. I had a straight C average in high school," acknowledged David, who lived for the weekends — specifically, Sundays. That's when he'd go to Washington Square, the eclectic little Greenwich Village park later immortalized in a 1963 bluegrass instrumental by the Village Stompers. Every Sunday afternoon, folk musicians would gather and play their stringed instruments in the square as artists displayed their canvases and sculptures.

"I tried not to miss a Sunday. I would take my guitar, my banjo, and sometimes my mandolin. I used to take the subway with my friend Perry Lederman and as soon as we got on the train, out would come our guitars and we'd play all the way to the park," David said. "There would be clumps of musicians strumming different types of music all around, and I would gather with my friends and play. Those years from 1956 up until about 1962 were really formative for me. When it rained on Sunday, we were real miserable."

David managed to develop an indoor interest for those rainy days. While in high school, years after quitting piano lessons, he happened to tune in to a televised performance by boogie woogie piano virtuoso Meade Lux Lewis. His interest in piano rekindled, David bought a record album by Lewis and two other leading boogie pianists, Albert Ammons and Pete Johnson. "They used to tour together back in the '30s and '40s, and that record they made was unbelievably wonderful. It was recorded with just their three pianos, and it just cooks." The album inspired Cohen to resume playing piano. He learned to play piano as he learned to play guitar and banjo — by immersing himself in music, studying the techniques of others, eventually crafting his own style.

After graduating from high school in 1960, David enrolled in The George Washington University in Washington, D.C., but his grades suffered as he longed for the New York music scene. A year later, he moved back in with his folks and enrolled in classes at Brooklyn College, eventually managing to move out on his own by teaching private guitar lessons. "My parents helped support me, because I was barely supporting myself," said Cohen. He frequented a Greenwich Village hangout called the Folklore Center, a MacDougal Street institution where books, records, and musical instruments were sold and folk music performances were staged.

One day in 1962, David brought a girl named Sherry to one of the folk music concerts hosted by the Folklore Center, run by Israel Young. As he paid for his tickets at the door, David announced, "Izzy, this is my wife" to the startled owner. "It was a joke, but the rumors started that David Cohen got married. So we went and got married. We didn't do it just to give a truth to the lie. We really cared for each other. The first year was total rapture and after that it was hell," said Cohen, who gave up music during his marriage. "I was 19 years old — definitely too young. We never had any kids, but all through the marriage some voice was calling to me that I was stuck and I needed to get out of it. I felt I had a mission and that I was being stifled." The marriage lasted a little more than three years, until 1965. "That's when I split," said David, who dropped out of college, hitchhiked, and rode by bus to Berkeley, California, where Burt Soloman, a friend from the Washington Square days, had moved to attend UC Berkeley.

Although David intended to visit only briefly, he was electrified when he arrived in Berkeley in May 1965. "The Free Speech Movement was still percolating. You could feel the music in the air. I would go hang out in the music stores, like the Campus Music Shop run by a fellow named Campbell Coe, and Jon Lundberg's Fretted Instruments guitar store." That summer, word reached him that Sherry had found someone else. "I was ecstatic," said David, who returned to New York, where he and Sherry divorced. Cohen once again immersed himself in the New York folk scene. "I didn't like electric music, I didn't like jazz, I didn't like rock and roll. I liked blues and folk music. I was pretty arrogant."

David's admittedly narrow view broadened considerably that fall when he and a friend, Joan Silverberg, went to see a Beatles double feature at a theater in the Village. "We sat in the back and she brought wine and chicken and joints. Other people brought food and we were passing it around, and we had so much fun. We sat through *A Hard Day's Night, Help!* and *A Hard Day's Night* again. We would have stayed longer, but the theater closed. At that point I decided I wanted to play rock and roll," Cohen told us in March 1998.

He returned to California, bought an electric guitar, started hanging out at music stores and clubs, and was soon playing with a couple of bands. The members of one of those bands, called Blackburn and Snow, included drummer Gary "Chicken" Hirsh, later to join Country Joe and the Fish along with Cohen. They and the other group members hung out together at a Berkeley club called the Jabberwock, where Country Joe and the Fish would come together.

One day after a Blackburn and Snow rehearsal, Jeff Blackburn asked Cohen if he'd like to go see the Grateful Dead, who were playing at

UC Berkeley. "When we got there I was blown away. I had never heard anyone play guitar like that. After the set, I introduced myself to Jerry Garcia, and we became friends," Cohen said.

Shortly afterward, Cohen left Blackburn and Snow to concentrate on playing with another band in which Barry Melton was a member. Melton had already been playing with Joe McDonald, who was looking for an organ player. "I had banged on the piano at the Jabberwock every now and then. I'd do some boogie woogie stuff and played tunes like 'St. Louis Blues,' but I wasn't serious. I wanted to play guitar. But Barry told Joe, 'Oh, David can play the organ.' I had never even seen an organ up close," David told us in March 1998. "But I joined the band anyway and played guitar because they didn't even have an organ. The first gig we played was on campus in early 1966. Then the band bought this Farfisa Compact organ, and that's what I started playing. The only person that I had ever heard play organ like I wanted to play was Al Kooper. So I took all of my guitar licks and applied them on the organ. It worked fine. We were playing so much that I didn't have much time to listen to other people playing."

Cohen said that from the outset the band had two missions: to stop the war in Vietnam, and to legalize drugs. "Basically we were iconoclasts. We were not mainstream and we were proud of it. We were trying to revolutionize society." In that, Cohen believed that the group succeeded. "Look at all the long hair on Wall Street. Part of our mission was to raise the consciousness of people. Joe's songs were very intelligent. They never were written for the lowest common denominator. I also think that through the music, the band had a sense of humor — a satirical sense of humor. There was a very beautiful side of Country Joe and the Fish," said Cohen, pointing to "Bass Strings," "Pat's Song," "Section 43," and "Janis" as representative examples.

The latter song was written in tribute to Janis Joplin, with whom Joe McDonald had developed a brief, incendiary relationship. "Our band hung out together with Big Brother and the Holding Company. We were all friends, but one day Joe and Janis were an item. Janis and the band had lived together in Lagunitas in Marin County until Janis bought a house in Larkspur. She threw a party when she bought the house and we came, and I told her, 'Janis, this is great.' She took me by the hand and took me outside and she throws her hands up and said, 'One record. One [expletive] record.' She meant that the album *Cheap Thrills* enabled her to afford to buy the house. She was really something," smiled Cohen.

"I remember Joe telling me that they were sitting in Joe's car in front of her house when she was living on Lyon Street at Oak near the Panhandle in San Francisco. They had the windows rolled up and they were having a screaming fight. People would come up and knock at the window and say, 'Hi. Where are you playing next?' I know that Janis said to Joe, 'Why don't you write me a song before we split up?' So he wrote 'Janis' with the notion that it would be recorded by Big Brother and the Holding Company." When Big Brother decided against recording it, Country Joe and the Fish took it into the studio, releasing it on their second album and ultimately as a single in 1967.

Cohen last performed with Country Joe and the Fish during the album recording sessions for *Here We Are Again* in the spring of 1969, leaving the group just before its appearance at Woodstock that summer. His departure stemmed from what he perceived as a loss of direction and integrity. "The band became perverted. We shifted from being serious to being clowns," he said, referring to the group's performances of "Rock and Soul Music" accompanied by a baseball game pantomime. It wasn't satire, it wasn't even funny. It was just dumb." Cohen was newly married at the time to his second wife, Marjorie, with whom he had a daughter, Sara. The marriage lasted only three years.

After that, Cohen played with or opened for numerous bands and musicians, including the Blues Project, the Luther Tucker Blues Band, Huey Lewis, Bonnie Raitt, Jerry Garcia, the Mick Taylor Blues Band, Johnny Winter, Rufus Thomas, Kenny Rankin, Michael Bloomfield, Melvin Van Peebles, Leo Kottke, Meatloaf, Booker T. Jones, Elvin Bishop, Tim Hardin, Eric Andersen, The Roches, Norton Buffalo, and Happy and Artie Traum, as well as several bands he formed.

But Cohen also found a new interest. Folk music guitarist Harry "Happy" Traum had started a business called Homespun Tapes, offering audio guitar instruction lessons. By 1975 Traum decided to expand the Homespun instructional catalog beyond stringed instrument lessons. He asked David to record a piano instruction lesson. Cohen did that and more with Homespun Music Instruction, completing seven videos on blues, rock, and ragtime piano as well as *Blues and Rock Techniques for Hammond Organ,* instructional audio series on blues and rock piano, and he wrote four instructional books, including *David Bennett Cohen Teaches Blues Piano,* and *David Bennett Cohen Teaches Rock and Roll Piano.* He also completed two guitar instruction albums for Kicking Mule Records, as he continued to compose music. In the 1990s, David performed as a substitute in the band of the hit musical *Rent,* on Broadway and on tour. He also continued teaching private piano and guitar lessons well into the 2020s.

In the important decisions of his life, David always followed his instincts. Doing so took him to Greenwich Village, and then to Berkeley, which led to his involvement with Country Joe and the

David Bennett Cohen and Maureen in January 2026. Self-portrait by David Bennett Cohen.

Fish. However, David initially resisted the path that would prove to be the most cathartic in his life. In 1985, a friend of his in San Francisco introduced him to Buddhism. Cohen, who had received no religious instruction in his youth and who subscribed to no religion as an adult, rebuffed his friend's initial invitation to attend a meeting. "But as soon as I started chanting and meeting people who had been practicing for awhile, I felt an immediate attraction. It's the best thing I've ever done," he proclaimed.

Unlike many ritualistic Western religions, Buddhism imposes relatively little formal structure and places emphasis upon introspection. "We chant Nam Myoho Renge Kyo, the mystic law of the universe, in the morning and evening. We also read two chapters from the Lotus Sutra, which says that anybody can attain enlightenment to become absolutely happy. Judaism and Catholicism are both steeped in superstition. We don't worship a God that is more important than we are. We have the same potential within our own lives," Cohen asserted. "Through chanting I've developed the wisdom to help me influence people in a positive way. That's my mission now. I'm still a revolutionary but I'm going through a human revolution now."

Buddhism brought order and tranquility to David's life. He married his third wife, Maureen, on October 21, 1989, and the couple settled in Forest Hills, Queens, New York. Their daughter, Sara Cherokee Sutler-Cohen, born December 30, 1969, has a son Devin, who was born in 1994.

While resurrecting his musical passion for the blues, David remained fond of his rock and roll years. "Monterey Pop was a fabulous gig," said Cohen. "And I'll never forget traveling up and down the West Coast after Monterey Pop with the Jimi Hendrix Experience. Sitting in dressing rooms with him playing guitar made for great moments. He was an exceptional musician."

Cohen offered a disarmingly honest appraisal of Country Joe and the Fish. "Judging from today's standards, the group wouldn't even have a chance to succeed. The musicianship wasn't all that great, and the material was very controversial," said Cohen. He attributed the success of the group to what he called "a combination of fortune" — the result of being at the right place at the right time. While critical of the band's execution, he praised the group's musical repertoire. "Every now and then I'll go back and listen to the first two albums, and I really believe that Joe wrote some masterpieces."

To David, music has been a parable for life itself. "The violinist plays the violin, the trombonist plays the horn, the cellist plays the cello, the harpist plays the harp, but the conductor plays the orchestra. Even if you have a four-piece band there's a fifth piece — the band itself. When you're hearing yourself play within the band, it just overwhelms you. That's the best high I've ever experienced," said David. "One of the most important things that I teach is the concept of the ensemble. It's not enough to show somebody how to play something on the guitar or on the piano, but you need to demonstrate how that fits with other instruments, and how to create unity, which is so powerful. And that's the Buddhist philosophy as well — the concept of unity. We keep our individuality with a common goal."

Epilogue: Bruce Barthol

Guitarist and bassist

November 11, 1947 – February 20, 2023

Awaiting his flight to London, Bruce Barthol sank disconsolately into a chair in the passenger waiting area at New York's Kennedy International Airport as a television set flickered results in the November 1968 election that would send Richard Nixon to the White House. Although Democratic candidate Hubert Humphrey nearly equaled Republican Nixon in the popular vote, Nixon handily captured the electoral vote as Barthol left America behind.

Only five years earlier, as a high school student in Southern California, Bruce imagined joining the Army, attending Officers' Candidate School with a specialty in a foreign language, and entering the foreign service. "That was my plan, but Vietnam made some career alterations," said Bruce, whose aspirations were abruptly shattered during a conversation that left him incredulous and disillusioned. One day in 1962, a friend of Bruce's brother asked him, "Do you know what we're doing in Vietnam? We drop this stuff on people that's like flaming jelly and it adheres to human flesh." Bruce, then 14, indignantly rejected that notion. But the military lost all appeal for him when he learned the truth about American use of napalm, a sinister chemical compound of gasoline

Bruce Barthol in the 1990s. Photo by Tina Quirino.

suspended in a gelatinous thickener which, when set ablaze, sticks to the skin of people upon whom it is fired. "That reality was very distressing because I had always considered my country in the right. Vietnam turned into a series of gut-wrenching horrific surprises."

His initial disbelief subsumed by outrage, Barthol joined his high school friend Barry Melton in protesting a visit to Los Angeles by Madame Ngo Dinh Nhu, the "Dragon Lady" of South Vietnam who endorsed atrocities committed against antiwar protesters in her country. From then until 1975, when Bruce participated in his last march protesting the Vietnam War, he committed himself to dissenting actions by the military that he had once hoped to join.

Seventeen years before it became the flashpoint for the youth protest movement, Berkeley was the birthplace of Bruce Barthol on November 11, 1947. Bruce's grandparents were from the San Francisco Bay area, and even from the first few years of his life, Bruce remembers that Berkeley tilted toward eccentricity. As Bruce approached school age, his family moved to State College, Pennsylvania, when his father, Richard, was appointed to the psychology teaching faculty at Penn State. A social worker by profession but an activist in spirit, Bruce's mother, Esther, demonstrated the power of personal conviction. "My mom was active politically and worked to repeal some of the 'blue laws' that had not only kept the county 'dry' but also prohibited movies on Sundays," recalled Bruce. He attended school in Pennsylvania during his first three grades before his family moved to Los Angeles in 1956, when his father began teaching at UCLA.

In early 1959, Bruce and his family relocated to Spain, which at that time was under the dictatorship of General Francisco Franco. There, at age 11, Bruce attended Air Force Dependent School in Madrid, where his family lived in an off-base apartment. Bruce enjoyed the adventure. "There were new foods, some of which were really good and some were really weird," Bruce laughed. "On my first day of school I found myself in a huge complex that contained the enlisted men's family housing building and all of the schools, first grade through high school."

Bruce, whose family enjoyed absorbing local culture, said he ran into the narrow-minded attitudes common among military personnel overseas. "I pulled out my lunch my mom had made — a sandwich on a Spanish roll with Spanish ham. And these four boys in my class came over, stood around my desk and said, 'You eat spic food?' Most of the kids in that school wanted nothing more than to get home."

Returning to Los Angeles, Bruce's family settled in the Sherman Oaks section of the San Fernando Valley. There Bruce enrolled in Robert A. Millikan Junior High (since renamed Louis Armstrong Middle School) in the fall of 1960, against the backdrop of a presidential election year in which Sen. John Kennedy defeated Vice President Richard Nixon. (After Nixon won election to the White House eight years later, Barthol and the other members of Country Joe and the Fish found themselves on the presidential "enemies list" for their outspoken criticism of the administration's military policies in Vietnam.) Following his graduation from junior high, Bruce went on with other neighborhood kids to Ulysses S. Grant High School in Van Nuys, where he met and befriended Barry Melton and cultivated an interest in music that had been inspired by his family. Bruce's father, Richard, played piano, his older brother, Clark, played upright bass, and his mother, Esther, enjoyed singing. As college students, both of Bruce's parents had performed in theater, a pursuit that Esther continued in New York after her graduation, studying with the Group Theatre. Unable to eke out a living in theater during the Great Depression, Esther returned to California to pursue a career in social work.

So it was with the encouragement of his parents that Bruce took up music in school when he was 12. Inspired by Benny Goodman's playing, he chose clarinet but quickly became disappointed that playing in the school orchestra was not as much fun as he had imagined it would be. "You played either first, second, or third clarinet on 'Song of the Volga Boatmen.' That was fun to a degree, but it wasn't as much fun as playing 'When the Saints Go Marching In.' All I wanted to do was jam."

It wasn't surprising, then, that Bruce began to fool around with the guitar that his family had purchased while in Spain. His interest in the guitar at about age 14 coincided with the rise of the folk music scene. Initially interested in traditional folk music, Bruce was particularly captivated by a singer he heard for the first time on a folk music radio program. He went to the record section in the local White Front department store. "I asked if they had the *Freewheelin'* album by Bob Dylan, spelled D-I-L-L-O-N. What the heck did I know? I heard the name on the radio," he laughed.

As Bruce became proficient in his guitar playing, he picked up harmonica and Autoharp and began to play music with friends, including Barry Melton. "Barry and I were in the Young Democrats as well as in the folk music club at high school. We were the youngest members of a private beatnik coffeehouse in Hollywood called the Thirsty Ear, and we would see each other not only at the UCLA Folk Festival, but also on picket lines," said Barthol, who was also a member of the Los Angeles chapter of the Congress of Racial Equality (CORE). As a result of skipping ahead halfway through fifth grade and accelerating through high school by taking summer classes, Bruce graduated from Grant High in the summer of 1964 and enrolled at UC Berkeley that September at the age of 16.

The Free Speech Movement erupted on the Berkeley campus as he turned 17 two months later. Studying Spanish and history, Barthol quickly became involved in protesting the university's prohibition of political expression, which he called "a collusion of authorities engaging in idiotic and unconstitutional behavior." Bruce heard and was persuaded by protester Mario Savio's impassioned cries for resistance. "The university forced many people to become active members of the Free Speech Movement," said Bruce, who joined protesters on campus and at other locations including Jack London Square in neighboring Oakland, where demonstrators targeted discriminatory hiring practices at restaurants. "We would picket every Friday night, and we just hoped we wouldn't get pulled over by the Oakland cops on our way back to the Berkeley line. People were busted on concealed weapons charges if the cops found picket signs in their car trunks. It was pure harassment." After boycotting classes during a student strike, his grade-point average fell to 1.98 and he was placed on academic probation for a semester.

On his 18th birthday Bruce filed for conscientious objector status with the military Selective Service. After completing that third semester, he decided to step away from his academic studies for perhaps a year. "I was tired of going to school. I was getting Cs and Bs and just wasn't feeling engaged," Bruce told us in April 1998. "I wanted to go to the Bahamas and listen to the legendary guitarist Joseph Spence. I no longer wanted to be bound by the interminable tyranny of studying." Instead, Bruce found himself bound by the tyranny of work, after taking a job as a lineman with the telephone company in March 1966 to earn the money to travel. Assigned as an installer and repairman, Bruce climbed telephone poles to connect and disconnect lines. At that time, he lived with some friends: guitar player Barry Melton, and guitarist and percussionist Paul Armstrong, joined soon afterwards by singer-guitarist Joe McDonald. While working weekdays for the phone company, Barthol spent his evenings and weekends next door to his apartment building, in a folk club called the Jabberwock where Country Joe and the Fish were evolving. "My time with the phone company was the longest three months of my life," said Barthol, who began performing with the band. "When I quit the phone company in June, the Fish had already begun happening." The band went electric with Bruce on bass guitar.

As the band developed a following, Barthol found playing in the increasingly larger rooms both exciting and challenging. "Country Joe and the Fish had an adventurous artistic impulse, and an intelligent consciousness of what songs might accomplish." Still, Barthol believed that the band could have been more aggressive in pursuit of its goal. "Throughout our time together, that war remained a constant irritant. I wish we had been a little braver. We should have gone to Vietnam, but we were too scared to contemplate it. We actually could have played Saigon and we wouldn't have been killed. We would have had a real appreciative audience of GIs. I guess for me the sum of the good things about the band were in contradiction to the very success the band was enjoying. And those pressures of success and that changed world eventually spiraled the band apart." Evidently the other band members perceived Bruce's diminished sense of satisfaction, and decided it would be best for him to go his own way.

Three months after the band's appearance in Chicago in August 1968, Bruce boarded a plane for England with no plans other than leaving the United States. "I was so relieved to get away from the psychotic, tense, 'soon-you'll-be-dead' feeling I had at the time. What a year 1968 was! Hardly anybody who started out that year ended up where they thought they'd be."

Bruce moved to London, where he formed a country rock band called Formerly Fat Harry, consisting of two friends from Berkeley — guitarist and keyboard player Gary Peterson and guitarist Phil Greenberg— and a Briton, drummer Laurie Allen. The band played throughout England and toured in Europe before recording a self-titled album at the EMI Studios on Abbey Road, released on EMI in Europe and Capitol in the United States. The engineering team included Alan Parsons (later of the Alan Parsons project.) The breakup of Formerly Fat Harry three years later wasn't particularly disturbing to Bruce. "I guess by then I was tired of being an expatriate and wanted to come back to the United States and re-engage." Bruce moved back to Berkeley in 1972, quickly involved himself with the campaign of Democratic presidential candidate George McGovern, and joined a local satirical theater group called the East Bay Sharks. Passing the hat, the East Bay Sharks performed for the McGovern campaign and in support of ballot measures for rent control, legalization of marijuana, and other sociopolitical issues.

In 1974, Barthol formed a band called the Energy Crisis, which briefly served as Joe McDonald's backup band. But the lure of musical theater proved stronger than Bruce's diminished interest in rock and roll. In 1976, through his involvement with the East Bay Sharks, he began his enduring association with the Tony Award-winning San Francisco Mime Troupe, a socialist-inspired musical theater collective specializing in political satire. Bruce was intrigued not only by the troupe's somewhat rambunctious history but also saw an opportunity through which he could combine music and politics. "I remember the epiphany I experienced just before I was invited to join the mime troupe. At the time I was playing with a rock group called Delicia and the Darvons at the

Bruce Barthol (third from left) performing at a Lincoln Brigade event May 27, 2012, at the Freight and Salvage performance venue, 2020 Addison Street in Berkeley, California. He was accompanying Mime Troupe actors and musicians Velina Brown, Tony Marcus, and Barrett Nelson. Photo by Richard Bermack.

Long Branch Saloon at 2504 San Pablo Avenue in Berkeley, where the audience was mostly high on beer and Seconal. I wanted both sides of the brain engaged. The chance to work with material with some meat on it drew me to the troupe," said Barthol.

The troupe's audacious character also held strong appeal for him. "The park commission had busted the mime troupe in 1964 on an obscenity charge and the troupe beat it in court, opening up Golden Gate Park for free performances. Bill Graham was the business manager for the mime troupe, and it was his first famous benefit dance that led to the creation of the Fillmore Auditorium and the Avalon Ballroom dance halls," said Barthol. "The troupe's history snakes in and out of the whole San Francisco scene in the '60s and since."

Bruce, whose composing credits date to songs recorded on the first Country Joe and the Fish album, *Electric Music for the Mind and Body*, signed on as a composer-lyricist and musician for the San Francisco Mime Troupe, with which he remained for more than three decades. During that time he amassed an impressive succession of critical and artistic successes, writing more than 100 compositions for more than two dozen shows performed in San Francisco and on tour. His credits include music for 1981's "Factwino Meets the Moral Majority" and 1988's "Ripped Van Winkle," both of which won Original Score honors presented by the Bay Area Drama Critics Circle. The Factwino character, who appeared in several productions, was cast as an alcoholic who had a lucid command of facts with which to contradict fallacious arguments.

Although most people associate the term "mime" with pantomime, the San Francisco Mime Troupe has been anything but silent. "The term 'mime' actually means to mimic," observed Barthol. "That name has been a pain in the ass for 20 years. Every year or two there's been an effort to change the name, but it's always fizzled." The group's website explained, "We use the term *mime* in its classical and original definition, 'The exaggeration of daily life in story and song.'" Barthol was one of 10 collective members who together operated the mime troupe, based in San Francisco's Mission District. In his time with the mime troupe, he participated in numerous European tours, as well as performances in Mexico, Cuba, Nicaragua, Israel, the Philippines, and Hong Kong.

Barthol supplemented his modest income from the mime troupe not only by composing for other theatrical groups, but also through academic assignments since his appearance as a lecturer at Freie Universität in Berlin in 1982, when he discussed the cultural history of San Francisco. Bruce

This is a 2013 performance by the Former Members, a band composed of musicians from high-profile bands, consisted of David Bennett Cohen, drummer Roy Blumenfeld, Bruce Barthol (at right) and guitarist Greg Douglass (not shown). Courtesy of David Bennett Cohen.

split his time between San Francisco and West Berlin from 1981 to 1983. In subsequent years, he lectured about American musical history, political theater, and the contributions of the San Francisco Mime Troupe in appearances at other institutions, including the University of Connecticut, Fordham University, New York University, and Golden Gate University in San Francisco. He served as artist-in-residence at both California State University, Long Beach, and at San Francisco State University where, in 1988, he drew upon his own experiences living in Franco's Spain for a student production of *Spain '36,* about the Spanish Civil War.

Barthol's involvement in academia influenced his decision to return to school 25 years after he had dropped out. In 1993, he was awarded a master of fine arts degree in musical theater from New York University's Tisch School of the Arts. The following year, he served as an instructor for the summer arts program at Humboldt State University in Arcata, California (since renamed California State Polytechnic University, Humboldt).

Bruce's musical theater compositions are not limited to the San Francisco Mime Troupe. In 1990, he collaborated on the score for the Oscar-nominated documentary film *Forever Activists.* Since 1990, musical compositions by Bruce have been performed in the Working Theater presentation of *The Windowman* in New York City, in the Intersection Of The Arts production of *Cages* in San Francisco, and in a production of *They Are So Sweet, Sir* in the Philippines. In 1998 he wrote the score for a bilingual version of 16th-century Spanish playwright Lope de Vega's *Fuente Ovejuna,* produced at Borderlands Theater in Tucson, Arizona. Bruce served as musical director and conductor for that production. He also continued to play bass with an old friend, folksinger Rosalie Sorrels, and occasionally with Midnight Rodeo, a band formed by Big Brother and the Holding Company drummer David Getz.

Spurred by his passion for radical history, and likely influenced by his time living in Madrid, Bruce composed two songs about the Spanish Civil War for the Troupe. The play was never completed, but his two songs became part of the lexicon of the traditional Spanish Civil War songs and Bruce began performing at events of the Veterans of the Abraham Lincoln Brigade (VALB), the organization of American volunteers who fought for the Spanish Republic against the fascist forces of General Francisco Franco in the prelude to World War II. "For more than three decades Bruce continued working with VALB and that organization's successor, the Abraham Lincoln Brigade Archives (ALBA), co-producing and performing in numerous shows for their annual reunions with the help of other Mime Troupe members. He was known as the musical conscience of the Mime Troupe and the Bard of the Lincoln Brigade," observed Richard Bermack, a writer and documentary photographer based in Berkeley, California, who wrote the 2005 book *The Front Lines of Social Change: The Veterans of the Abraham Lincoln Brigade.*

Bruce also worked on his own project, notably his darkly satirical commentary on contemporary society in his 2008 solo album, *The Decline and Fall of Everything.* After 33 years, Bruce retired from the San Francisco Mime Troupe in 2009 and enjoyed life in the cabin that his uncle built on two acres of redwood forest in Sonoma County about 50 miles north of San Francisco. During that period, he joined with friends David Bennett Cohen, Roy Blumenfeld of the Blues Project, and Greg Douglass of the Steve Miller Band in forming a band called the Former Members.

While he mellowed in some respects, he remained driven by the same sense of outrage that propelled him into public view decades earlier. "I've always been motivated by a certain social political consciousness, mostly because some things are so annoying, you can't ignore them. In any era there are myths and assumptions that serve the forces of greed, hate, and reaction. As a former supporter of the cultural revolution in China, and I do have to confess that really didn't work out too well, you learn to look at things clearly.

After falling ill, Bruce died February 20, 2023, four weeks after entering hospice care in Santa Rosa, California. He was 75 years old.

In-A-Gadda-Da-Vida

Iron Butterfly

The mid-'60s emergence of free-form rock and roll reflected the revolutionary attitudes of youths searching for their own musical style and means of expression. American bands such as Jefferson Airplane, the Grateful Dead, and the Doors performed lengthy instrumentals that relied upon improvisation. This new counterculture gave rise to freeform progressive, underground FM radio, such as that originated in April 1967 by former Top 40 DJ "Big Daddy" Tom Donahue at San Francisco's KMPX. The success of Donahue's album-oriented format in California and at underground stations evolving throughout the United States, in turn, contributed to the emergence of psychedelic rock exemplified by Iron Butterfly.

About the same time, a whole new counterculture was evolving that included freedom of expression through underground newspapers, including the *Los Angeles Free Press,* the *Village Voice* in New York, and the *Berkeley Barb,* whose mission was philosophical and deviated from traditional papers' daily dose of violence, sports, and business. Long hair, love beads, sex, drugs, and radical political expression became the symbols of psychedelia, and music became a principal means through which the emerging hippie culture communicated its dissatisfaction with the "establishment."

Heavy, loud, and improvisational acid rock evolved from psychedelic rock. This short-lived music style gained widespread popularity with the distorted lyrics and long jams of Iron Butterfly's monumental ATCO Records LP *In-A-Gadda-Da-Vida,* featuring the title track that filled one entire side of the vinyl record and remained on the charts for 140 weeks, more than half of that time in the top 10. From the gossamer opening organ chords to the closing pronouncement 17 minutes later, "In-A-Gadda-Da-Vida" is a work of surprising complexity that musically conveys the stark contrast of delicacy and power that the group's name symbolizes. The melodramatic baroque organ and guitar signature that periodically seep in and intertwine themselves amid searing solos lend

Iron Butterfly in 1969. From left: guitarist Erik Braunn, drummer Ron Bushy, bassist Lee Dorman, and organist Doug Ingle. From Photofest Archives, New York.

cadence to the song's freeform expressiveness. And not since Sandy Nelson recorded "Let There Be Drums" in 1961, or the Surfaris' "Wipe Out" in 1963, was drumming given such prominence in a record. Iron Butterfly popularized drum solos, which became a staple of many late '60s and early '70s bands. Within the first year of its release, ATCO indicated that the album sold nearly 8 million copies, 16 times the Recording Industry Association of America (RIAA) standard for a Gold Album. Ahmet Ertegun, president of ATCO parent Atlantic Records, conceived a platinum album award (denoting $2 million in sales), which he first presented for Cream's 1968 double album *Wheels of Fire*, followed by one for Iron Butterfly. In 1993, RIAA conferred a quadruple-platinum award certifying sales of 4 million copies of *In-A-Gadda-Da-Vida*, which first earned a gold record in December 1968.

The name Iron Butterfly is a contradiction in terms deliberately chosen by keyboardist Doug Ingle to suggest a fabric of delicacy and intricacy interwoven among a superstructure of raw amplified power. Ingle, who referred to himself as a ballad writer, asserted, "I've never written anything but ballads. My songs always turned into something quite different once the group got their hands on them. We call it the Butterfly filtering system. It always comes out distorted from its original format."

Launched in San Diego by Doug Ingle in August 1966, Iron Butterfly began its musical metamorphosis at Bido Lito's, a family-owned, underground club at 1608 Cosmo Street, a couple of blocks west of Vine Street between Sunset and Hollywood boulevards. "Bido" was short for "Bill and Dorothy," and "Lito" named for their kids, "Linda and Tom." The band initially consisted of keyboardist Ingle, guitarist Danny Weis, singer Darryl DeLoach, bassist Jerry Penrod, and drummer Jack Pinney. In early autumn Pinney was replaced by San Diego drummer Bruce Morse — who in turn was soon superseded by Ron Bushy. Leading off for weekend headline acts such as the Seeds and Love, Iron Butterfly played three to four shows a night, six nights a week at Bido Lito's — the club was closed one night — and was earning $20 to $25 a week per musician. Doug Ingle recalled, "We slept on the office floor above the club. Jerry Penrod, our bass player at the time, was a big guy. They called him 'mountain.' He was like a Mongolian warrior. If you didn't know him you'd think, 'Oh my God, let's cross the street now before we have to make eye contact.' But to actually know him, you couldn't have asked for a nicer guy. At any rate, I woke up one night in this Ma and Pa Kettle sleeping arrangement with my arm across his chest. And I opened my eyes and his eyes were just kind of glaring at me like, 'What's this?' I quietly went downstairs and took one of the reclining chaises longues and dragged it upstairs and took over the ladies' restroom. I had hot and cold running water, a private stall, and for the first time, I had my own room," he laughed.

The police would frequently raid Bido Lito's after hours, looking for drugs. "Like SWAT teams they'd come flying across from the other businesses, on the rooftops," Ingle said. "They were looking for illegal stuff — marijuana — and that was the kind of club where they might find it. They were crazy times."

Over a period of about a year, the band found itself leaving the underground and gradually moving up Sunset Strip in West Hollywood to Pandora's Box at Sunset and Crescent Heights Boulevard and then to the Galaxy, which was on the north side of Sunset Boulevard, three doors west of the trendy Whisky à Go-Go.

As the band's following continued to grow, the weekend lines to get into the Galaxy were surpassing the lines for the Whisky à Go-Go. "The Whisky would have a headliner, and our line would pass their line, go up the street, around the corner, down the alley, back down to Sunset and past itself. So this attracted attention," said Ingle. "By that point the Whisky à Go-Go didn't look good, so they brought us on. That had never happened before." As house band for the Whisky for a two-month run beginning in November 1966, Iron Butterfly began opening for Buffalo Springfield, the Doors, the Turtles, Jefferson Airplane, Big Brother and the Holding Company, and Smokey Robinson and the Miracles. In the ensuing months the band's renown grew as it was booked for performances not only in numerous venues around the LA area — including the Hullaballoo, the Cheetah, the Valley Music Theatre, and the Santa Monica Civic Auditorium — but also the Avalon Ballroom in San Francisco.

The Butterfly's quotient of cover songs had begun yielding to increasing amounts of original material when they inked a deal in the spring of 1967 with independent producers and songwriters Charlie Greene and Brian Stone, who worked closely with Atlantic Records. "Buffalo Springfield and Sonny and Cher had signed with them," said Ron Bushy, "and so did we." In late summer at Gold Star Recording Studios at 6252 Santa Monica Boulevard and at Nashville West studio at 5505 Melrose Avenue in Hollywood, the group recorded its first ATCO Records album, *Heavy,* with Greene and Stone. But the label delayed its release as the band underwent substantial personnel and management changes. During the interim, Danny Weis left the group and joined Rhinoceros, an LA-based rock group. "The guy was a great guitar player," said Bushy.-

During the band's brief hiatus, Ron came home one night to find Ingle working on a new song. "Doug had a little too much red wine and he sang this song for me that came out in-a-gadda-da-vida, but he was trying to sing 'in the Garden of Eden,'" said Bushy. "I liked it, so I wrote it down on a piece of paper phonetically. The next morning we looked at it and liked it, so we kept the name."

When lead singer Darryl DeLoach and bassist Jerry Penrod also decided in early September 1967 to leave the band, Ingle and Bushy began casting around for musicians to replace them. They soon auditioned and hired guitarist Erik Brann, who had just turned 17 years old and who later changed his last name to the original Danish spelling: Braunn. Bassist Douglas Lee Dorman auditioned and joined the band on his 25th birthday, September 15, 1967. To avoid confusion with Doug Ingle, Dorman agreed to go by Lee. The band's lineup stabilized with keyboardist and singer Doug Ingle, lead guitarist Erik Braunn, bassist Lee Dorman, and drummer Ron Bushy.

With Atlantic Records holding release of *Heavy,* the Butterfly was struggling to stay afloat in Hollywood. "We lived on the streets for a long time," said Bushy. "I got hooked up with Bonney Ward, the ex-wife of Burt Ward of *Batman.* She had a huge mansion in Brentwood, so half the guys would come over and stay there, too."

Following performances in 1967 at Notre Dame High School, a private Catholic school in Sherman Oaks, and a teen center in Van Nuys, the Butterfly performed their first big concert on Saturday, December 23, as the second of five bands opening for the Doors at the Shrine Exposition Hall at 700 West 32nd Street at Figueroa Street in Los Angeles. From there, the Butterfly opened on short notice for Jefferson Airplane at Pauley Pavilion at UCLA because the Airplane's intended opening act didn't show up. The Butterfly turned in such a crowd-pleasing performance that the Airplane invited them on a two-and-a-half-month tour of the United States.

"We were doing colleges with the Airplane," recalled Braunn, "and Marty Balin comes into our dressing room while I was practicing, and he said, 'You know, Gracie Slick really has a crush on you.' And I said, 'Really?' because when *Surrealistic Pillow* came out I thought they were a great band, and I thought she was really neat. So I said, 'I don't know what to do about that.' He looked at me perplexed and asked, 'How old are you?" And I said, '17.' Knowing that Gracie was 28 at the time, Marty went back to their dressing room and I just heard this enormous amount of laughter, and I never saw Gracie again on tour. She always stayed away from me."

On January 22, 1968, ATCO finally released the *Heavy* album, the 10 songs of which included the Butterfly's first ATCO single, "Unconscious Power." The pioneering heavy metal album encompassed 30 minutes of searing acid rock, trippy psychedelic jams, and rock blues riffs — all tame by 21st-century standards but outrageous and trend-setting at the time of release. Written by Doug Ingle, Danny Weis, and Ron Bushy, the "Unconscious Power" 45 rpm record was released in April 1968, but did not produce activity on the national charts. The Butterfly generated attention that summer, however, with the debut of the *In-A-Gadda-Da-Vida* album, featuring its celebrated 17-minute title track containing one of the longest and most explosive drum solos in the history of rock. The band members had been in the midst of a West Coast concert schedule in late May when they took a detour to Hempstead, Long Island, New York to Ultra-Sonic Recording Studios at 149 N. Franklin Street, to record *In-A-Gadda-Da-Vida*. Atlantic Records had used Ultra-Sonic to record Vanilla Fudge and the Rascals. The four-day studio booking began on Monday, May 27, at Ultra-Sonic, which had eight-track recording equipment that was technologically advanced for that time. The assigned producer, Jim Hilton, had not yet arrived as the band began setting up. Recording engineer Don Casale told the band members to do a run-through so he could check sound levels on the various microphones. The band members relaxed and settled into a 17-minute jam as they improvised "In-A-Gadda-Da-Vida." What they didn't know was that Casale already had hit the "record" button, and the entire song was captured on tape.

After the band hit the resounding final notes of the song, Casale summoned them into the recording booth to hear the playback. Everyone in that room recognized that a second take would have been unnecessary. After overdubbing a guitar solo and vocals, recording was done. With all six of the album's songs completed by May 30, Jim Hilton packed the master tapes in his suitcase and flew to Los Angeles the next day to begin the process of mixing the eight discrete channels down to two-track stereo at Gold Star Recording Studios, 6252 Santa Monica Boulevard, in Hollywood. "When we recorded 'In-A-Gadda-Da-Vida,' a guy named

Brian Ross, who is deceased now, mixed the drums. He had conceived the idea of what they call flange phasing to get that whooshy sound, only it was done manually by mixing the simultaneous playback of two identical recordings that are slightly out of synchronization. Now they have machines," explained Dorman. The flanging technique is achieved by playing identical audio on two tape machines simultaneously, but then deliberately slowing the playback of one a fraction of a second by gently lowering a finger against the rotating metal flange of the reel on one machine. "The cost of that album to Atlantic was about $17,000." In contrast, the recording and production work for an album today typically costs about $200,000, more than 10 times the amount it cost Atlantic to produce "Vida." Its June 1968 release triggered volcanic sales activity.

The popularity of the band's recordings propelled them on the touring circuit. They headlined at ballrooms, auditoriums, stadiums, and at numerous rock festivals, including on August 4, 1968, at the two-day Newport Pop Festival in Costa Mesa, California. That event featured an extensive entourage including Sonny and Cher, Steppenwolf, Country Joe and the Fish, Jefferson Airplane, the Grateful Dead, Eric Burdon and the Animals, the Byrds, Tiny Tim, Quicksilver Messenger Service, and the Chambers Brothers.

Iron Butterfly's single version of "In-A-Gadda-Da-Vida" burst onto the *Billboard* Hot 100 chart on August 24, 1968. The 45 rpm record, 2 minutes 52 seconds long, was edited from the 17-minute album track. It peaked at No. 30 and remained on the chart for 12 weeks. That was the band's highest ranking release on the singles chart, overshadowing the follow-up release, "Soul Experience." Written by Doug Ingle, Ron Bushy, Erik Braunn, and Lee Dorman, "Soul Experience" made its premiere on the *Billboard* Hot 100 on February 22, 1969, peaked at No. 75, and remained on the chart for five weeks. But the robust sales of the *In-A-Gadda-Da-Vida* LP, which reached No. 4 on *Billboard's* album chart, demonstrated that the Butterfly was primarily an album and concert band. On January 17, 1969, ATCO released the band's third album, titled *Ball,* which rolled to No. 3 on the *Billboard* album chart. Its nine songs included "Soul Experience" and the band's follow-up single, "In the Time of Our Lives," a Bushy and Ingle composition that reached only No. 96 after its July 12 chart debut. Disappointment was short-lived, however. On July 22, 1969, the band earned a second gold record, this time for the *Ball* album. Increased airplay of "In-A-Gadda-Da-Vida" stimulated its re-entry on the *Billboard* Hot 100 on May 17, 1969. During this second romp on the chart it peaked at No. 68 and remained on the chart for five weeks.

On August 15, 1969, the day the Woodstock Music and Art Fair opened, Iron Butterfly's equipment truck was stuck in traffic about 20 miles from the festival site. The group, which had been on tour for the entire summer, was waiting at their hotel in Manhattan, New York, for word from their manager on how to get to Woodstock, and once they arrived, what equipment they'd be using.

"We were told that the Who was going to let us use their amps and drums, and that Sly Stone would let us use his Hammond organ, so that was solved," recalled Dorman. "Our manager told us to go to the Port Authority Building at 10:15 a.m. to catch a helicopter, but it never showed up. So the entire weekend we went back and forth from our hotel to the heliport until our manager finally called back at 7 or 8 o'clock Sunday evening and said, 'Come home. It's over with.' It's just too bad that we weren't there because we, along with so many of the bands that were there, were part of an era, and I don't think anybody knew that was the end. That was, for some reason, the changing of the guard. We had no idea of its significance at the time."

Iron Butterfly went on to play many pop festivals throughout the country. Doug Ingle recalled an August 1969 festival in which Iron Butterfly shared the bill with Janis Joplin following the breakup of Big Brother and the Holding Company. "We were flown in via military helicopter — big Hueys — which was an experience in and of itself. Janis was on stage just prior to our going on, and after the show, she ran up to me, threw her arms around me, crying, saying, 'Doug, what am I going to do? They don't like me.' Up to this point I didn't know if she knew me from Adam. I was flabbergasted. But the best I could come up with was, 'Janis, you know, they're slow to respond. They absolutely love you. I saw the twinkle in their eyes and you triggered their imagination. You gave them everything you've got. Bottom line is they're waiting to hear 'Piece of My Heart' the way they heard it on the record. And until they have a little bit more time, they're not going to know how to respond to the new material until it's more familiar, until they've heard it a few more times on the radio.' And that was the last time I saw her." Janis was found dead on October 4, 1970.

Erik Braunn had an opportunity to play with Jimi Hendrix before Hendrix's death in September 1970. "The Butterfly was playing at the Spectrum in the summer of 1969, and I got a call from my manager saying, 'Jimi Hendrix just called me and he has sent a limo and wants to know if you'll come up to Manhattan to play guitar for him on a project he's producing.' For me it was a great honor to have Jimi Hendrix want me to play guitar," said Braunn. "I played with Hendrix, Mitch Mitchell, my longtime friend Harvey Brooks, who was the bass player on all of the great early Dylan stuff, and Keith Emerson, before the formation of Emerson, Lake, and Palmer. It turned out to be just a jam, and it was recorded, but never released."

The Butterfly began to splinter in 1969, when Erik became disillusioned about an impending shift in musical direction. "I was upset because Doug Ingle had started writing folk music on a guitar, and the songs that he was writing were nothing like the kind of music that I wanted to play," Braunn told us in April 1998. "I wanted to go out and play some stuff that really was intense, and strong, and loud, and rock and roll. And in a meeting among the four of us I said, 'Well, if we're going to go down this path and all of a sudden start sounding like some folk group, I'm not interested.'" After a concert at the San Diego International Sports Arena on December 13, 1969, Braunn departed the Butterfly, which then expanded to five members with the addition of guitarists Mike Pinera and Larry Reinhardt.

"Easy Rider (Let the Wind Pay the Way)," the fourth and final chart single by Iron Butterfly, made its premiere on the ATCO Records label on the *Billboard* Hot 100 on October 24, 1970. The record label credited the composition to Iron Butterfly and Robert Woods Edmonson. Iron Butterfly and Richard Podolor arranged music for the session, for which Podolor was producer. "Easy Rider (Let the Wind Pay the Way)" reached No. 66 and remained on the chart for six weeks.

The deaths of Janis Joplin, Jimi Hendrix, Jim Morrison of the Doors, and Brian Jones of the Rolling Stones collectively brought to a staggering conclusion many of the musical excesses associated with the late '60s, and helped precipitate a return-to-the-land musical movement advanced by the gentle country-rock ballads of John Denver, Linda Ronstadt, Jackson Browne, James Taylor, Carly Simon, the Eagles, Pure Prairie League, and the Allman Brothers Band.

The Butterfly quietly fluttered to a halt amid the shifting sands of musical tastes and dissolved in May 1971. Several short-lived reunions occurred over the years with fluctuating rosters, in 1974, in '78, in '87, and in 2012. The Butterfly's original lead singer, Darryl DeLoach, died at age 55 of liver cancer in October 2002. Guitarist Larry Reinhart died of liver disease at age 63 in January 2012. Early Butterfly bassist Greg Willis died at age 67 in November 2016, four years after suffering a stroke. Guitarist Mike Pinera died of liver cancer in November 2024.

IRON BUTTERFLY
U.S. HIT SINGLES ON THE NATIONAL CHARTS

Debut	Peak	Title	Label
8/24/68	30	In-A-Gadda-Da-Vida*	ATCO
2/22/69	75	Soul Experience	ATCO
7/12/69	96	In the Time of Our Lives	ATCO
10/24/70	66	Easy Rider (Let the Wind Pay the Way)	ATCO

* Edited from the multi-platinum album of the same name

Billboard's pop singles chart data is courtesy of Joel Whitburn's Record Research Inc., Menomonee Falls, Wisconsin.

Epilogue: Doug Ingle

Keyboardist, lead singer, and composer

September 9, 1945 – May 24, 2024

Fulfilling his father's dream of becoming a professional musician, Doug Ingle entered into his musical career quite unexpectedly. When Ingle decided to move to Los Angeles to pursue a career in writing theme music for the motion picture industry, the band he had taken with him in order to pay the bills unexpectedly became one of the hottest bands on the Sunset Strip.

Doug Ingle during a performance in a bill with the Taj Mahal band and the Blues Image at the Anaheim Convention Center in Anaheim, California. Saturday, May 24, 1969. Photo by Jeff March.

Doug's father, Lloyd Ingle, was a music major at Drake University in Des Moines, Iowa. "My dad was a first-string classical pianist who could not provide for a family of four on a symphony salary, so he became a church pianist and leaned on his backup, which was accounting, and that's what he did throughout his professional life," said Ingle.

Born in Omaha, Nebraska, on September 9, 1945, Douglas Lloyd Ingle moved with his family into a one-bedroom cottage in Evergreen, Colorado, when he was 2 months old. He and his sister, Pat, six years his senior, spent several years in a cabin with no indoor plumbing and a coal-burning stove for heat. Although the population of Evergreen grew to more than 8,000 residents by 2020, it was an isolated village in the mountains above Denver with only 350 residents when Doug was a child.

"My dad was my inspiration. He introduced me to such a wide gamut of musical references from gospel to classical music, to boogie-woogie, and the standards such as 'Peg O' My Heart,'" said Doug. "We had an upright Boston Everett piano, which was a wedding gift to my parents, and when I was about 5 years old, my father would slip me between the sound board and the wall of the cabin and he would rock out with the boogie-woogie." Doug still owned the piano as an adult.

Small though it was, Evergreen had a nondenominational community church, for which Doug's father was the piano player. "Every Sunday after church in the spring and summer we had parades through town that just constituted the kids pulling their favorite pet in their red wagons," recalled Ingle. "And then we'd go to the park for the spring and summer rodeo circuit."

While vacationing in San Diego in 1954, Doug's mother, Virginia, decided she'd had enough cold, snowy Colorado winters and wanted to stay. She took a job with San Diego County, and over a period of two years the family joined her. "My sister, Pat, and I came out first on the Union Pacific train. My dad came later, taking a job as an accountant at a local music store."

Doug Ingle began his music career performing in cover groups in high school. One of the early bands in which he performed was called the Progressives. The band's leader, Kerry Chater, who played bass, and Gary Withem, a sax player, later became members of Gary Puckett and the Union Gap.

"We played Mancini and 'Louie, Louie' and everything in between. We found a lot of work in the military enlisted men's clubs and petty officers' clubs. If you could play a variety of music, then you had a real good opportunity to work," said Ingle. The Progressives later became Jeri and the Jeritones. "Kerry Chater's girlfriend was Jeri, and although she was no Barbra Streisand, she was cute," chuckled Ingle.

In 1965 the Jeritones auditioned for and became the house band for a new club in San Diego called the Palace and changed their name to the Palace Pages. The band included Doug Ingle, Danny Weis, Kerry Chater, and Gary Withem. Following the breakup of the Palace Pages, Doug and Danny moved to Los Angeles and a new band evolved with a new sound and new members. Doug called the band Iron Butterfly.

Although Doug had not formally met Ron Bushy, he knew of him. Ron was a member of a cover group called the Voxmen, named after the brand of amplifiers that the Beatles used. "We were archrivals," confessed Ingle. "The Jeritones and the Voxmen were not on speaking terms. We were top competitors in the same market. At the battle of the bands, we'd often glare at each other across from the wings of the stage. One year the Voxmen would come in first, and the next year we would come in first. It was a real rivalry."

Doug graduated from Hoover High School in San Diego in 1964 and attended UCLA Extension in San Diego for one semester, taking a course on musical counterpoint. "I don't know how, but I got an A-plus-plus, and I decided I wanted to write theme songs for motion pictures. I wasn't interested in the actual scoring," said Doug. "I actually wanted to write the theme music and then they could do with it as they pleased." Ingle decided to take the Iron Butterfly to LA so that he would have a source of income while pursuing a new career. "Then the darn thing took off. It wasn't supposed to do that," he laughed.

A bit too naive and caught up in the limelight, Ingle paid little attention to the fruits of his labor. "I was just so happy to be doing what I enjoyed doing that I never really paid too much attention to the money," confessed Ingle. "And quite frankly, it all came so fast and so unexpectedly, and the emphasis was never placed on monetary subsistence. I'm afraid that I became somewhat agnostic in the sense that, gosh, all my life I've been told, 'you really need to get some kind of a backup system because the likelihood of succeeding in music is slim to none.' I just thought, 'gee, these people don't know what they're talking about. Making a living and a good one at that is a piece of cake.' But I was a child among men. The management back in LA was getting extremely wealthy, and my wife at the time was having quite a good time, I guess."

Tickled by the initial success of the Butterfly, Doug lost his focus on theatrical scoring and concentrated on the band, which began traveling to club dates out of the area. Doug recalled the time the Butterfly played at a nightclub called the Phantasmagoria at 3220 Knox Street in Dallas. "When we'd finish for the night, the cowboys would drive by in their pickup trucks throwing empty quart beer bottles at us for target practice," laughed Ingle. The band also experienced bomb threats. In Phoenix an entire auditorium had to be evacuated after an anonymous telephone caller reported planting a bomb in the building. A bomb was later found under the stage. Another unnerving incident occurred at the Kinetic Playground in Chicago. "This guy opened a club and a competitor, which presumably had an interest in a rival club, sent a message saying, 'Don't open your doors or your club's going down the same night.' Sure enough, he opened the doors, and that night after hours our equipment was in a blaze with the rest of the club."

The enormous popularity the band enjoyed on stage and on the *Billboard* charts between 1968 and 1970 was a wondrous blur. But the group's decline after that was precipitous. In 1969 Erik Braunn left the band and Mike Pinera, formerly of Blues Image and co-writer of the song "Ride, Captain, Ride," and Larry "Rhino" Reinhardt came on board. "Pinera, who was of Cuban descent, had a Latino R&B influence on his guitar playing, and Rhino, who we picked up out of Macon, Georgia, was a blues-oriented slide guitar player," said Ingle. Almost overnight, the Butterfly transformed from a keyboard-oriented, rock group to a guitar-oriented rhythm and blues band. Ingle wasn't happy with the direction in which the group was heading and gave notice halfway through a European tour in 1971 that he intended to leave the band at the conclusion of that tour but that he would be willing to perform a farewell tour of the United States.

"At first I was elated to be off the road. I had a nice home in Calabasas, which is in the foothills between Malibu and the San Fernando Valley," recalled Ingle. "But then I started leaning more heavily on drugs. I started drinking more and smoking marijuana, and when that got boring I was smoking primo hash regularly, to the point that I actually lost track of two and a half years of my life. Then I got levied by the Internal Revenue Service." Ingle owed $185,000 in back taxes and lost his house but was able to hold on to $10,000, which he used to buy a mobile home.

In 1975 Doug and his wife, Alice, and their four children moved into a mobile home park for which Doug became manager, which entitled him to a free parking space and utilities. He began training as an apprentice house painter, becoming an independent subcontractor in 1977. By then he and his family had moved to a duplex in Sierra Madre, near Pasadena, and Doug was painting houses. When forced busing came into effect to desegregate schools in Los Angeles, and their children weren't coming home until well after dark because they had been bused to the far side of Los Angeles, Doug said to Alice, "Let's just get out of here and put the kids in a place where they can get a grasp on life, a good start."

They decided to move to Port Angeles, Washington, "the farthest northwest tip of the continental United States, up by Victoria, Canada," said Ingle. "It was as beautiful as you could get with somewhat mild winters." But the timing was bad. It was raining, and no one was hiring painters. "I ended up bartering my services in exchange for furniture because we didn't have any," recalled Doug. He then sought a job through the state of Washington's employment services, taking tests to determine an occupation for which he was best suited.

"The results indicated that I should be dealing directly with the public in the field of entertainment, more specifically, in the field of music," said Doug. "When I told my wife, she said, 'Does that mean that if you got a call from somebody in LA and they weren't willing to pay you but they would give you studio time, for instance, for a spec-type recording, you would go?' I said, 'You're damn right I would.' And the next thing I knew she was seeing another guy."

In 1979 Doug returned to Southern California on a Greyhound bus and took up residence in a warehouse in the Northridge neighborhood in the San Fernando Valley. Ron Bushy and Taylor Kramer had built a studio and had been living in the facility they called Bushwack Studios until Ron and his wife to be, Nancy, had moved into her home in West Los Angeles. "During Ron's absence, a rather undesirable lot of individuals began to frequent the place," confessed Ingle. "It was often referred to by the neighboring businesses as the 'bottomless pit,' a flop house." Ingle cleaned up the place, living in it and allowing local bands to use it as a rehearsal facility. Since he didn't have any equipment of his own, Ingle gave bands cut rates on rehearsal time for the opportunity to use their equipment during their absence, while Bushy paid the rent.

From there Doug became a landscape foreman and ranch hand for the Smoke Tree Ranch Studios at 9752 Baden Avenue in Chatsworth, California, which was built and owned by longtime friend Doug Parry. Gino Vannelli, Dolly Parton, and a few other acts had recorded at the ranch.

"I made $50 per week, had a free place to stay and if there was any down time with the clients, I had access to the studio for my own projects, which worked out fairly well," he said. "But after a year of doing that, I found that the downtime was precious little, if any, at which time I moved to Beaverton, Oregon, a suburb of Portland, and continued painting houses."

In September 1983, Doug returned to California to re-establish Iron Butterfly with Lee Dorman and Larry Reinhardt. "We toured all over the country but never made any money," explained Ingle. "We called them our Western Union tours. We had to go 120 miles out of our way to get a line of credit via Western Union just to continue, and we kept getting

Doug Ingle in 1997, during an Iron Butterfly European Tour.

involved with scavengers of the industry, just cleaning up what's left as opposed to supporting something new." After two years, Ingle called it quits and moved to San Diego, where he took a job with Lifestyle Music Network, selling adult contemporary music via satellite to businesses to provide as background music.

Meanwhile, Lee, Mike, and other musicians had kept the Butterfly active and asked Doug to join them on a tour leading up to Atlantic Records' 40th anniversary concert, "It's Only Rock 'n' Roll," on May 14, 1988, at Madison Square Garden in New York City. About that same time, Doug had met his wife-to-be, Cheri, who was a friend of Ron Bushy's wife, Nancy.

"During one of the dates we shared the marquee with Spirit at the John Ford Amphitheatre in Hollywood. Nancy brought Cheri, and from that point forward, Ron played Cupid," laughed Doug. "I called Cheri from Philadelphia at the end of the New York anniversary concert, and she sounded so thrilled to hear from me that I asked her if she could pick me up at the airport. I've never heard anybody sound so happy to hear from me, and from that time on, it just got better and better."

Doug and Cheri were married in 1992, and between them they have nine children — Doug had six and Cheri had three — along with grandchildren. Doug spoke warmly about his children, most of whom lived in the Pacific Northwest. One of his proudest achievements was his ability to openly communicate with his children. "That suggests a level of mutual trust and respect," said Doug. There was a time when alcohol prohibited him from communicating clearly with them.

Although pleased with the direction in which his life was going and his involvement in the rekindled Iron Butterfly in the late 1990s, Doug said he remained committed to "a genuine sense of inner peace." He hoped that through his experiences, others will be encouraged to become independent of destructive vices that nearly destroyed his life, and that his music could in some way enlighten people's lives.

Doug Ingle died at age 78 on May 24, 2024. He had been the last surviving member among the 1968–69 configuration of the band who recorded the 17-minute rock anthem "In-A-Gadda-Da-Vida."

Epilogue: Ron Bushy

Drummer

December 23, 1941 – August 29, 2021

Ron Bushy's childhood passion was to become an orchestra conductor. He loved classical music and opera. In the sixth grade he would sit in his bedroom conducting to the *1812 Overture* and *Marche Slave* by Tchaikovsky, or he would sing along with Mario Lanza. Born in Washington, D.C., on December 23, 1941, Ronald Edgar Bushy had decided at an early age that he wanted to play drums. His parents, Willard and Alice Bushy, were opposed to it and urged him instead to take accordion lessons, which he hated.

Ron Bushy at a 1997 benefit performance on behalf of Wildlife Waystation, an exotic animal sanctuary in Little Tujunga Canyon northeast of Sylmar, California. Courtesy of Ron Bushy.

After his parents divorced in 1951, Ron and his sister, Karon, three years younger, went to live with their grandparents in Clinton, Connecticut, for three years. His grandfather, a retired Connecticut state police officer and commissioner of the Clinton Police Department, taught him how to whittle. With his newfound skill, Ron went to the local hardware store, bought himself a dowel and proceeded to whittle a couple of drum sticks. He picked up an old tire inner tube from the local gas station, cut the rubber in two sections, stretched it across a board and fashioned himself a practice pad.

"I used to go out in the garage, where I taught myself how to play drums on my practice pad with the drumsticks I made. No one even knew what I was up to in the garage," Bushy confessed. When Ron's father, then a Navy Lieutenant working for the Bureau of Naval Personnel and the Pentagon, remarried in 1953, the family moved to Alexandria, Virginia. After demonstrating his recently acquired skills to his father, Ron joined the Alexandria Police Boys' Band as a drummer. He attended

Thomas Jefferson Junior High and George Washington High schools in Alexandria, moving during his sophomore year with his family to San Diego, where his father served as a commander and executive officer of the USS Henderson. There, at Mission Bay High School, Ron joined the school band.

"I didn't know how to read music, I just faked it," chuckled Bushy. "I remember Mr. Freeburn, the conductor of the band, used to get really upset with me, because I would always be playing parts that weren't written in the score. He even threw the baton at me a few times."

After graduating from high school in 1959, Ron attended San Diego City College, where he received his AA degree in science. He then went on to San Diego State College, majoring in zoology and psychology. "I changed my major several times," he said. "I actually wanted to become a marine biologist and later attended Scripps Institution of Oceanography, but I never did get my four-year degree."

While in college taking 15 units per semester, Ron worked the graveyard shift as a GFP (government-furnished parts) analyst at General Dynamics Astronautics for the Atlas missile project for three years. He then joined Turquoise Animal Hospital in San Diego assisting the resident veterinarian, Dr. Millwood Custer, in surgery for another two years while still attending San Diego State. "I drove a Vespa scooter and Austin Healey 3000 while living at Pacific Beach, Mission Beach, and La Jolla commuting to and from college."

Ron enjoyed playing bongos on the beach, where he met a guy named Frank, a steel pedal guitar player who had a band that needed a drummer and asked Ron if he'd like to join them. When Ron told him that he'd never played a drum set before, Frank replied, "We can go to Ace Music and rent one for 15 bucks a month." And they did. Ron recalled, "I took the drum set back to my apartment and learned how to play drums to 'Green Onions' by Booker T. and the MGs. I caught on real fast."

After performing a few gigs at the Naval Training Center in San Diego, Ron formed another rock and roll band called the Bushmen in 1965. "We played a lot of Yardbirds, Turtles, Byrds, stuff like that," explained Ron. "That band was together for about a year, and just kind of part-time." At the same time, Bushy was working as an automobile repossession investigator for Pacific Finance, a job he took to support his first wife, Marion Carr, who was working on her master's degree in English at San Diego State College.

"One time I was repo-ing a car because this guy hadn't made payments for over a year. As I was hooking up his car to my tow bar the guy came out and pushed me, and I was arrested for assault and battery. It was his word against mine," he asserted. "The county sheriffs showed up and handcuffed me and the whole bit. The guy said, 'tell him to give me my car back.' And they said, 'no, he's got it hooked up. It's his.' But they took me off to jail. I went to court, and I got summary probation. That, along with my deferment from college and being married, put me over the hump from going to Vietnam. So, in some respects, I was lucky. My roommate from college and my best friend, David Rose, became a paratrooper and was shipped off to Vietnam. On his first jump he was shot in mid-air and died."

Tired of dealing with all of the "flakes and deadbeats" associated with the repo business, Bushy quit Pacific Finance in 1965 and took a job at Ace Music, where he met members of a band called the Voxmen. After sitting in with the Voxmen for one night at Art's Roaring 20s in El Cajon, the band members asked Ron to join them, which he did. "I didn't make enough money with the Voxmen in San Diego to support myself and my wife, so at the same time I took a part-time job driving a Good Humor ice cream truck for almost a year. It was wild. I didn't make much money, and I ate up all of my profits," he laughed.

When the Voxmen decided to go to Hollywood, they got a job playing at the Sea Witch at 8514 Sunset Boulevard, a half mile east of the Whisky à Go-Go. There Ron discovered that his San Diego acquaintances with Iron Butterfly were playing at a club just down the street. "We started hanging out together and then Bruce Morse's mother got sick, he had to go back to San Diego and the Butterfly was without a drummer so I sat in and played with them for a week," recalled Bushy, whose marriage by then had dissolved. "In essence what happened was we switched drummers. Bruce liked the Voxmen's music better, and I liked the Butterfly." Ron remained with the Butterfly for the next six years, throughout the era of their most triumphant successes.

During that time, Ron met and married dancer Constance Accurso, and in January 1970 the couple welcomed a daughter, Jessica. The marriage didn't last, however — a casualty of the hard touring life of a rock musician.

During the Butterfly's European tour in 1971, Doug Ingle announced that he wanted to call it quits. The group, by then consisting of Larry Reinhart, Mike Pinera, Doug Ingle, Lee Dorman and Bushy, had agreed that they would fulfill one last obligation to perform a farewell bus tour of the United States with Black Oak Arkansas, whose newly released debut album Lee Dorman and Mike Pinera had produced. "I never got to play that tour," lamented Ron. "While I was getting off the plane at 4 a.m. in Nashville, I was carrying two Halliburton camera cases, and as I threw one over my left shoulder, it ripped my arm right out of the shoulder socket. They drove me to a hospital, which seemed 100 miles away." The band completed the tour with former Blues Image drummer Manny Bertematti. Ron rented a car and tagged along to seven or eight concerts. "I remember this one gig. I was out in the audience with my arm in a sling. I just couldn't take it anymore, so I ran up on stage, got on the drums and played the solo," said Bushy. "I paid dearly for that in pain," Ron told us in April 1998.

In 1972, following the breakup of Iron Butterfly, Bushy built a recording and rehearsal studio he called Bushwack and formed a group called Gold. "We recorded an album at Doug Parry's Smoke Tree recording studio in Chatsworth but it never went anywhere," said Bushy. Iron Butterfly was reincarnated in 1974 with bassist Philip Taylor Kramer, Howard Reitzes on keyboard, Braunn, and Bushy to record an album called *Scorching Beauty*. During recording of a subsequent album, *Sun and Steel,* in 1975 Bill DeMartines replaced Reitzes on keyboard. The next few years Bushy played with Iron Butterfly and other bands, until 1979, when he went to work for Fisher Lumber, a hardware store on 14th Street and Colorado Avenue in Santa Monica, where he struck up a friendship with a Makita power tools sales representative.

"I started bugging him, saying, 'Hey, I'd like to drive around in a company car and travel, go see all the different buyers and sell them tools.'" His persistence eventually paid off. Bushy joined Makita in 1981, selling power tools and accessories for five years and becoming one of the company's top salesmen. He was awarded "Salesman of the Year" in 1984, "Salesman of the Month" honors six times, and trained all new sales personnel from 1983 to 1986. He was made a member of the company's research and development committee for new products and designed the company's ML700, a 7.2-volt NiCad flashlight along with its own successful marketing program. Bushy convinced the company that if they'd package the flashlight as a kit with the cordless grinder, it would appeal to heating and air conditioning professionals and plumbers, who often have to work in dark spaces. The kit quickly became a popular-selling item.

During his time with Makita, he met and fell in love with Nancy Braverman, whom he married on Valentine's day — February 14, 1982. Ron helped raise Nancy's two daughters, Brooke and Nicole, who were 5 and 7 years of age at the time. "Meeting and marrying Nancy is the best thing that ever happened to me," said Bushy with a smile.

Bushy then served a brief stint in 1986 as a sales representative for GTE Directories Corporation in Culver City, responsible for selling Yellow Pages advertising, before joining Bosch, a German manufacturer of automotive parts and power tools. "When I hired on at Bosch, they promised to give me the same sales territory I had with Makita [all of Los Angeles County, Ventura County, Santa Barbara County, and San Luis Obispo County] but they reneged on it and instead gave me a geographically sprawling region that included part of eastern San Fernando Valley, San Bernardino County and all of Riverside County, including Palm Springs," said Bushy. "Sometimes I wouldn't get home until 10 or 11 p.m."

In 1988, Ron, Erik, Lee, and Doug got back together to perform for Atlantic Records' 40th anniversary concert at Madison Square Garden. "I quit Bosch, and we re-formed the original 'Vida' band. The band did a two-month tour leading up to Atlantic's 40th in New York, but it was just impossible. Atlantic even offered us a record deal, but the band just didn't see eye-to-eye musically," recalled Bushy.

After contemplating what to do next, Bushy re-joined Makita in August 1988, working for another three years until he suffered a back injury while loading a Makita generator into the back of his company minivan. He ended up in therapy and while on disability, Bushy attended Platt College in Alhambra, in the Los Angeles area, where he received diplomas in computer graphics and graphic design. A longtime artist and photographer, Bushy had designed Iron Butterfly's *Live* album cover, worked on the *Metamorphosis* album cover and etched the gorilla with wings on the *Evolution* hits compilation album cover.

After graduating from Platt in 1994, Bushy got the itch to get back into music. "Mike Pinera and I got back together and started playing and then he kinda bowed out, so Lee and I got together. We went through several guitar players and keyboard players until Doug returned in 1996."

Bushy began using his computer graphic skills to design Iron Butterfly T-shirts and merchandise to sell at concerts and through the group's website, for which he designed the graphics. "We're incorporated now, Iron Butterfly Music Inc. The art and merchandise company is called Mariposa Art and our booking agency is Papillon Ltd. *Mariposa* is Spanish for 'butterfly' and *papillon* is French for 'butterfly,'" explained Bushy. "This time, we're trying to do everything right."

Ron became a grandfather in 1997, when his daughter, Jessica, gave birth to a baby girl named Sierra Stone, followed by Olivia and Mica.

A self-proclaimed perfectionist, Bushy said, "If I can't do something right I won't do it. I usually figure out everything myself, without asking anyone for help. I'm also resourceful and adaptable. If I was stranded on an island I could probably survive, I'm sure. I can make do with anything. I have a real inventive mind, and I'm very curious about everything."

Bushy continued writing songs and composed the lyrics for many songs including "Unconscious Power," which is on the Butterfly's first album, *Heavy.* He also wrote the lyrics for "Soul Experience," and "In the Time of Our Lives," from the *Ball* album. "I wrote 'Pearly Gates' on the Scorching Beauty album together with Jon Anderson from Yes while we were on tour in Europe in 1971. You can hear the Yes and Jon Anderson influence in it," observed Ron.

Bushy, who continued to perform intermittently with the Butterfly as late as 2018, especially enjoyed talking with the fans and signing autographs. He observed, "What's amazing is that we're playing for audiences of all ages, from 9 years old to 90. It's unbelievable. These young kids who weren't even born know our songs."

Nine years old. Just about the age Ron was when he whittled his first set of drumsticks.

Ron Bushy, revered for his explosive drum solo on the band's emblematic 1968 hit "In-A-Gadda-Da-Vida," died at age 79 due to esophageal cancer shortly after midnight the morning of August 29, 2021. His wife, Nancy, and his daughters, Jessica, Nicole, and Brooke, were with him at UCLA Santa Monica Medical Center in California during his last hours.

Epilogue: Lee Dorman

Bassist

September 15, 1942 – December 21, 2012

Lee Dorman in the 1990s. Photo by Ron Bushy.

In his mind, Lee Dorman could journey back to the misty mornings in the late '40s and early '50s when, as a child growing up in Hermosa Beach, California, he would go with his father to watch the fishing vessels chug in and out of the harbor near his home. And he would imagine what it must be like to be the captain of one of those vessels. That vision must have remained indelibly in his mind through the years, for he became a captain musically as well as literally.

Not more than six months after the breakup of the Butterfly in 1971, bassist Dorman became involved in the formation of a group called Captain Beyond in Los Angeles. The group consisted of Dorman, guitarist Larry Reinhardt, former Deep Purple lead singer Rod Evans, and drummer Bobby Caldwell, who performed with Johnny Winter. "The four of us got together, made a demo album on a four-track machine and took it to Phil Walden (Capricorn Records co-founder), who was just signing his Capricorn-Warner deal at the time and was about ready to unleash the Allman Brothers album *Eat a Peach* on the world. He agreed to sign the band," said Dorman, whose first name is Douglas but he agreed in 1967 to go by his middle name, Lee, to avoid confusion with the Butterfly's Doug Ingle.

Southern rock label Capricorn released the self-titled *Captain Beyond* album in 1972, and the following year the group recorded a second album called *Sufficiently Breathless,* with Marty Rodriguez replacing Caldwell on drums. Captain Beyond toured Europe for a while, then broke up in 1974 for lack of work.

"We kept drawing a salary even though we weren't working," Dorman said. "The president of the record label, who was the manager of the band, was so tied up with other acts that he unfortunately just kind of put us on a shelf rather than turning us over to somebody who might have had us touring with Black Sabbath or a more related band. But to put a jazz-rock band opening for the Allman Brothers doesn't make sense. So ergo, the band just kind of wasted away." The band's demise was particularly frustrating to Dorman, whose commanding bass lines gave the power and presence to Captain Beyond, just as he had provided the substructure for the Butterfly. It's little known that the genesis of that throbbing energy was a ukulele.

Lee was born in St. Louis, Missouri, on September 15, 1942. That same year his family moved to Hermosa Beach, California, when his father took a job for Lockheed Aircraft Company. Lee, an only child, was introduced to music at the age of 5 when his grandmother, a former vaudeville performer who lived in Berkeley, taught him how to play the piano and the ukulele. When Lee was 8 years old his parents signed him up for accordion lessons, a short-lived experience that he disliked, but one that gave him a foundation for his later interest in music.

"Most everything musically I've picked up I was able to learn because of my training on the ukulele. Later I switched to bass when a friend of mine, who was a bass player, asked if I wanted to learn. And I said 'sure.' So he showed me and I just picked it up. I taught myself how to play guitar, and on some albums I played vibes."

In 1952 Lee's father got a job with the Weyerhaeuser Company and moved his family to Tacoma, Washington, where Lee peeked in on backyard rehearsals of a teenage band that would become the Kingsmen, best known for their 1963 hit "Louie Louie" and a 1965 hit called "The Jolly Green Giant." His father had bought him a 1940s drum kit for $100 from a pawn shop, and Lee taught himself how to play.

"It was a huge bass drum with a big tropical scene painted on the front and it had straps on it so you could carry it down the street," said Dorman. "Some of the Kingsmen were rehearsing in my neighborhood one day, and I walked over to listen," recalled Dorman. "I got to know them pretty well, and a couple of times I actually kept a beat for them during rehearsal when the drummer wasn't there."

In 1955 Lee's father took a job in Washington, D.C., and the family moved to Kensington, Maryland, where in high school Lee began playing drums for a band called the Dukes, performing top 40 rock and roll at sock hops and school dances.

After initially attending Walter Johnson High School in adjacent Bethesda and then graduating from the private college prep school McDonogh School for Boys in Owings Mills, Maryland, Lee traveled across the country to attend Monterey Peninsula College, where he took general education courses. "Then fate steered me down the music highway," he said.

Learning that a robust music scene was developing in San Diego, Lee relocated there in the summer of 1964, and soon joined a foursome called the Prophets. "We played around San Diego about the same time Gary Puckett was playing the Quad Room in one of the biggest bands in the area called the Outcasts," said Dorman. "There were a lot of really good musicians in San Diego, who were coming up like I was, and that's where I first met Ron Bushy."

In 1965, the Prophets decided to add topless girls to their act and put together a show to take to Las Vegas. "We opened a lounge show at Caesars Palace," said Dorman. "They called the show Buddha Belly's Purple Veil Review, or something like that. We all wore tuxes and did our thing, and then the girls came out and did their thing."

Dorman's group spent two months at Caesars, then went on to play the Riviera and the Thunderbird. "The money was good and the band received free room and board," said Dorman. "Even today when you play casinos, that's part of the deal. If you stay away from the tables, you don't have to spend any money." When the girls decided to leave the act, Dorman and the other band members found a Vegas agent, who put them on the road performing at supper clubs. "We worked what I call the West Coast chitlins circuit, which is all of the little one-stop hoppers from San Diego as far east as El Centro, and then Vegas, Reno, Tahoe, and all the way up to Billings, Montana. And that was pretty good bread," said Dorman.

During their travels, the band ended up in Los Angeles, alternating two-week stints between two popular clubs both called the Mirage. One was on Van Nuys Boulevard at the Ventura Freeway in the San Fernando Valley, and the other on Santa Monica Boulevard near 10th Street in Santa Monica, where Lee renewed acquaintances with Ron Bushy.

"The Butterfly was going to audition a guy from the Spoonful. And I happened to be there," recalled Dorman. On his 25th birthday in 1967, Dorman auditioned for the Iron Butterfly and was hired as the band's bass player that night.

"Here I was on my way back to school, and music kept pulling me. I just never thought about it as a career, it just always seemed something for fun," Dorman told us in May 1998. "I think being part of a band that made a record was special, and then, of course, my gosh, I had the opportunity to be part of a band that was successful. There are so many good bands that never reach that level."

Dorman's father was always behind him in anything he wanted to pursue. "Back when I was going to college I told him, 'I'm not sure what I want to do.' And he said, 'It doesn't make any difference. Try something. If you don't like it, then change. But whatever you do, try to be the best at it. If you learn to be a dentist, then wind up owning a bowling alley, so what? If somebody has a problem with their teeth there, you'll have that knowledge and you might be able to help them out. You don't lose any knowledge." Lee always cherished the support and advice of his father, who died in 1979.

Like the pilot of a vessel, Lee weathered the demise of both the Butterfly and Captain Beyond, and remained when each band resurfaced. Lee was there when Captain Beyond was resurrected in 1976, when Warner Brothers called Dorman's attorney and said, "We'd like to have a third Captain Beyond album." So original drummer Bobby Caldwell returned and Willy Daffern joined the band as lead vocalist. Captain Beyond recorded its third and final album, *Dawn Explosion,* under the Warner Brothers label before breaking up again in 1978.

Although none of the songs charted for Captain Beyond, Dorman said in later years he discovered a Captain Beyond CD in Europe. "Many musicians have come up to me and said, 'Now that was a band's band.' It was jazz rock, and we opened in Europe and never went back. We played very little in the states, which probably contributed to the demise of the band."

Following the 1978 breakup of Captain Beyond, Dorman decided to take a break from music. "Occasionally I would get a phone call from a booking agent who wanted to know if we could get the Iron Butterfly together, and sometimes two or three of us would get together and go out and play the songs. It was maybe 30 days out of a year."

Throughout the years, several incarnations of Iron Butterfly performed with different members. "Occasionally I worked with Mike Pinera and Erik Braunn. We would just go for a couple of weeks here and there." Ron and Lee performed as Iron Butterfly, Featuring Lee Dorman and Ron Bushy. "We had been trying to get Doug involved, and he was not ready at the time," said Dorman. "Finally all of a sudden he called up and said, "You know, I think it's time." That was in July of 1994. "Of course it's always nice when you have the real lead singer," Dorman said with a hearty laugh.

While the Butterfly was touring Europe in 1997, a video production company documented the band's performances. "They were at all of our jobs with cinematic cameras and they were backstage, they were on the tour bus, they were at the whole thing," said Dorman. The DVD, titled *Concert and Documentary: Europe 1997,* drew the praise of fans.

Lee resided during the latter portion of his life in the Southern California beach community of Dana Point and also shared an apartment in Burbank with his girlfriend, Linda Zimmerman, a James Beard-honored cookbook writer and a real estate agent. "Linda and I met in Chicago in 1968 and were around each other a total of 10 days at different times, but we didn't see each other again until 1996," said Dorman. Linda moved to Los Angeles in 1969 to work in the film industry, becoming an associate producer for the movie Grease and for other films. "Since we've been back together, she'll introduce me to somebody or I'll introduce her to somebody, and it turns out that we'd met that person a long time ago. For a long time we were within 20 miles of each other, but we didn't know it."

Lee described himself as easygoing. He said, "I'm real laid-back until I get pushed real hard. Some people say that I'm too laid back, that I could be doing more, and maybe they're right. But it just takes a lot for me to be self-lit." But Lee took pride in his ability to organize, and on his production and audio values. "I really like organizing things and seeing that they come off," proclaimed Dorman. "There's always gonna be a slight margin for error, but I pride myself on keeping it as low as possible."

Following the third Captain Beyond album, Dorman sold everything, moved to the beach and started doing a lot of sailing. He took some courses, got his Coast Guard license to operate 100-ton sailing vessels, and served as captain of a lightweight charter business for three years. "I took people to Santa Barbara and Catalina. And I brought a couple of boats down from San Francisco. My presence was known by all of the record companies. Here were all of these people I knew who had money and loved to go sailing," said Dorman. He skippered bay cruises and sunset cruises offering choice of cuisine, from hot dogs to lobster and caviar. "It was fun. I got to run around in shorts and a T-shirt and get paid for it," he laughed. Lee didn't own a boat, but would make arrangements to rent other people's boats, depending on the size of the parties, whether it be 30-foot vessels or a 100-foot yacht.

Lee continued to tour with Iron Butterfly into 2012. "I like going places," Lee acknowledged. "Some of it [the demands of touring] can get a little long in the tooth, but those that are long in the tooth are when you go on at 11 p.m., you have to get up at 4 in the morning to leave on a 6 o'clock plane. That's the only time. And I really like good food, so when I have the opportunity I take my little Zagat guide with me and go to a good restaurant, because believe me, I've had all the burgers there are, and I don't want to do any more," he laughed.

Dorman conceded that he probably could have done more in his career had he moved more quickly on opportunities. But what better feeling is there than to know that every project in which he was involved ended up with a record deal. "If I just sat in a rocking chair and reflected, I would say to myself, 'Hey, I was part of something that put a notch somewhere. And it's a miracle that I was able to be in my lifetime part of something that made a difference," he reflected. "And Iron Butterfly and 'In-A-Gadda-Da-Vida' made a difference to a lot of people."

Lee, who began having cardiac problems, was found dead in a vehicle on December 21, 2012, in the beach town of Laguna Niguel, California, where he had resided at the time. The Orange County coroner's office determined that his death was due to natural causes. The Orange County Sheriff's Office surmised that he may have been on the way to a medical appointment when he died. Lee Dorman was 70 years old.

Epilogue: Erik Braunn

Guitarist

August 11, 1950 – July 25, 2003

Success can be measured not only in professional achievements but also in the ability to attain inner peace, whether through creative expression or the mental strength and well-being derived from studying philosophy or religion. Erik Braunn attained success in many ways, including a spiritual strength obtained through his involvement beginning in the late 1960s in four different forms of martial arts — tae kwon do, kuk sool won, shotokan, and jeet kune do. Preferring to practice independently, Braunn achieved his personal goals through daily training regimens. Fame came and went for Braunn at a very early age, but he managed to make a comfortable living for himself by keeping music a vital part of his existence.

Erik Braunn in the 1990s. Photo courtesy of Erik Braunn.

For as far back as he could remember, Erik Braunn wanted to become a professional musician. When he was 4 years old his mother bought him a violin and enrolled him in lessons at a Boston music store. "I studied violin with the chairperson of the Boston Symphony," recalled Braunn, who rode the train once a week from the suburbs to Boston to take his lessons. After a year and a half, Braunn was excelling but his mother couldn't afford to continue paying for lessons, so the symphony accepted him into its prodigy program and taught him at no charge. He made his first recording at 6 years of age, a piece by Paganini called *Moto Perpetuo.*

Born Richard Davis on August 11, 1950, in Pekin, Illinois, Braunn lived at various times in Anchorage and Fairbanks, Alaska, on the edge of the Everglades in Florida, and in Boston, Chicago, LA, San Francisco, and New York. After his mother married a major in the Air Force, sometimes the family would move as frequently as once a year. By the time he reached high school, his mother, a registered nurse, had settled in the San Fernando Valley where Braunn attended Cleveland and Reseda High Schools. "I pretty much raised my two younger brothers, until the time I joined Iron Butterfly at age 17 and moved away from home." As a youngster he had spelled his name Erik, but as a student at Reseda High School he was known as Rick Davis. When his father, Jim Davis, and his mother, June, divorced, he assumed June's birth surname, Braunn (credited during his early Butterfly years as "Brann"), and reverted to Erik as his given name.

Braunn, who began playing guitar at the age of 13, studied classical guitar in the late 1980s at Los Angeles Pierce College under the professorship of John Schneider, a Grammy-winning classical guitarist. But Braunn claimed that most of his knowledge came from spending hours in libraries and studying music with some great teachers. "I studied jazz with Barney Kessel, Joe Pass, and my first teacher, Milt Norman, who was a genius, and known for his incredibly fast chord progressions," said Braunn. "I also studied with Ted Greene, who is still recognized as one of the geniuses in the guitar world."

Braunn owned his own publishing company he playfully named Zen Du Jour, which means "enlightenment of the day." He wrote or co-wrote 19 Iron Butterfly songs, including one on the *In-A-Gadda-Da Vida* album called "Termination," and three on the third album, *Ball*.

In 1974 and '75, Braunn and Ron Bushy recorded the albums *Scorching Beauty* and *Sun and Steel* with MCA Records. Braunn recalled, "I had just left Iron Butterfly, and I made a tape with the LA Jazz All Stars, a wonderful group of jazz musicians, and I recorded with a studio band that went on to work with Linda Ronstadt." Braunn presented his tapes as a solo artist to Mike Maitland of MCA Records, which agreed to produce an album. "*Scorching Beauty* was kind of a disaster," admitted Braunn, "However, I think the *Sun and Steel* album was the best produced and best engineered album Iron Butterfly ever made." The name was based on a book by Yukio Mishima, a novelist, actor, and film director who became a prominent force in a paramilitary organization. "Mishima was a full-blown samurai warrior. He had his own army and tried to overthrow the government. His ideals in [his book] *Sun and Steel* were about the refinement of the soul and spirit."

When Braunn first joined Iron Butterfly in 1967 he had turned down a scholarship to UCLA for arts and drama. In high school he had won several acting awards during competitions at the University of Southern California and UCLA. "I had a drama class the last period of every day, and we had a brilliant teacher who actually taught Val Kilmer and Connie Sellecca," recalled Braunn. "We had elaborate productions. One department built the sets, another department made all of the costumes and, of course, there were the actors. So I was used to being on stage when I joined the band."

Following his departure from Iron Butterfly in December 1969, Braunn bought a house in Tarzana from Neil Diamond, who had built a studio in a barn on the property. "I put together a band called Flintwhistle back in 1970-'71." The band included Darryl DeLoach and Steve Weis, brother of former Iron Butterfly guitar player Danny Weis. "We rehearsed in the studio and played around a little bit, but I decided to start recording on my own and learned production. I made about 40 or 50 recordings of songs I wrote. I'd perform with Richie Hayward, the drummer from Little Feat, and a guy named Craig Cole, who was living in my guest house at the time. He played saxophone and he was really good," said Braunn. "I would invite these guys up and we recorded a song called 'Am I Down' and a few other songs that helped me get the MCA deal." Braunn sold the house to John Sebastian in 1973.

Like many recording artists of the 1960s, Iron Butterfly had a string of bad luck with managers. "One of our managers withheld tax forms from the IRS for the one year that the band made the most money, and the IRS came and cleaned everybody out. I probably lost $3 million in property. I was 20 at the time," Braunn said. "The best management I've ever had has been myself, and that's when I re-formed all the original members for the 40th anniversary of Atlantic Records. I managed that, and I hired the agents."

Braunn, who began writing songs at the age of 13, amassed more than 300 songs in his catalog. A Doors fan, Braunn knew Jim Morrison and, for a brief time, shared the same girlfriend. Braunn recalled, "Jim and I started talking backstage at a college date in Berkeley and our conversation turned to girlfriends. He had a girlfriend named Pam and I had a girl named Sheri. He started talking about seeing this other girl who was a waitress. And I said, 'I've been seeing another girl, and she's a waitress, too. She works down at Thee Experience,' which was a club on Sunset Boulevard. And he said, 'So does my girlfriend. Her name is Raggy. We were both seeing the same girl, and we both just started laughing. Neither of us ended up with her."

Erik fathered one child, whom he did not get to know. "The one child was with my girlfriend, who put the baby up for adoption," Erik told us in April 1998. He did marry another woman briefly at age 20 but soon divorced. He ultimately met the love of his life, Gail, in 1981 and the couple married in 1989.

Erik, who wrote in a variety of musical styles including rock and roll, hard rock, country, jazz, and folk, said he enjoyed entertaining. "I like touring and performing. I still work at my guitar playing, and I think I'm up there with the good boys, but to me there was a point when I realized that you've got to write songs, and you've got to be able to write good songs. The lyrics and the melody have to be strong," proclaimed Braunn. "I'd like to be known as a good guitar player, a good writer, a good singer, and I'd like to have my music inspire people."

Braunn found some of the misperceptions about Iron Butterfly amusing. "Somebody once commented that they thought it was strange that I was alive because they thought I was a heroin addict, which I never have been. In fact, I don't do any drugs at all," he declared.

Braunn was quick to identify his two proudest achievements: being part of a band that recorded a historic quadruple platinum album, and resurrecting the original band for Atlantic Records' 40th anniversary celebration at Madison Square Garden

More than 30 stellar singers and groups comprising a Who's Who in Atlantic's history performed for the 40th anniversary concert, including Sam Moore (of Sam and Dave), Phil Collins, Led Zeppelin, Yes, and the Bee Gees. Iron Butterfly had 12 minutes to play and was the 12th act. "When we came on, we got an instant standing ovation — the first of the day — and we got one in the middle, and we got one at the end," recalled Braunn. "I remember being backstage and crying afterwards, because it was such an emotional thing."

Erik enjoyed motorcycles and motorcycle road racing. He owned a Honda CBR 900 RR, which signifies "race replica." In addition to his martial arts prowess, Braunn was a Golden Gloves-certified boxer, enjoyed target shooting (but didn't hunt), gardening, and nature. Erik and Gail had more than 24 different species of roses on their property. "Gail orders bulbs from Holland so one thing comes up and dies down and another pops up. We have a lot of birds in our neighborhood and we like to feed them."

Erik also enjoyed practicing guitar and spending a couple of hours a day in the library. "I've read practically everything in the library on philosophy, psychology, novels, autobiographies, biographies, and poetry. I'm a big Edgar Allan Poe fan," he said. "I think as a songwriter all of the mistakes I've made make me who I am today. I'm concentrating mostly now on putting together the songs that I want to play and putting a band together."

Many individuals influenced Braunn. "I have always looked for inspiration, and I've never had any trouble finding it," said Braunn. "People who have touched my life include my first guitar teacher, Milt Norman, and my first drama teacher, Robert Carrelli, as well as Jimi Hendrix and Jim Morrison."

Tim Buckley was also an inspiration to Braunn. "I had seen Buckley at the Troubadour and he sang like an angel." said Braunn. "And I used to go down for the concerts and watch him before we went on every night that he played. He was just exceptional."

Despite the many interests that competed for his attention over the years, Erik was unequivocal about defining the driving force in his life. "Everything's always been about the music to me," said Erik. "Music is most important for me. Music has determined how I've lived my life, and I imagine it always will."

Erik Keith Braunn died of cardiac arrest at age 52 on July 25, 2003. In addition to his wife, Gail, he left behind three brothers: Gary, Jeff, and Ron Davis.

Index

Westminster School,
London, 123, 125, 140,
141
WHBQ, Memphis, 221, 233
Wheatbread, Paul, 274,
275, 278, 280, 300–305
Where the Action Is, 143,
155, 302, 303
Whisky à Go Go, 155, 346,
361
White, Stanley, 269
Wichita, Kansas, 28, 43, 44
Wienstroer, Norman, 3
Williams, Paul, 308
Wilson, Carl, 225
Wilson, Jackie, 53, 59
Wilson, Sonny, 196, 222,
228, 229
WINS, New York, 74, 107

Withem, Gary, 273–275,
278–280, 284, 285, 294,
295, 306–310, 354
WLAC, Nashville, 233
WMGM, New York, 114, 118
WNEW, New York, 74
Wolfman Jack, 303
Woodstock Music and Art
Fair, 100, 252, 256, 317,
322, 331, 350
Woodstock, New York, 256

X

XL Records, 196, 199, 205

Y

Yakima Valley, Washington,
283
Yankee Dance Hall,
Yankee, New Mexico, 12,
13, 17

Yanovsky, Zal, 240–243,
245, 246, 248, 268, 270,
272
Yarrow, Peter, 242
Yes (band), 364, 374
Yester, Jerry, 241, 246–248,
260, 266, 268–272
Yester, Jim, 268–271
Yolo County California, 324,
325
Ysleta, Texas, 36

Now that you've finished reading *For the Record, Volume 1,* we hope you're interested in learning what other hit-making recording artists confided in us. Complete your set and gain more insights from our other three volumes.

For The Record, Volume 2

- The Association, the six-man band whose polished blend of folk-rock and shimmering harmonies led to three gold records — "Windy," "Never My Love," "and Cherish"

- Herman's Hermits, whose string of hits includes three gold records — "Mrs. Brown, You've Got a Lovely Daughter," "I'm Henry VIII, I Am," and "There's a Kind of Hush"

- The Kingston Trio, who triggered the early '60s folk music craze, and whose hits included "Where Have All the Flowers Gone," "Greenback Dollar," and million-seller "Tom Dooley"

- Chris Montez, whose musical career was inspired by Ritchie Valens and whose hit tunes included "Let's Dance," "Call Me," and "The More I See You"

- The Spiral Starecase, who recorded "She's Ready," "No One for Me to Turn To," and the smash hit "More Today Than Yesterday"

- Bobby Vee, whose 30 hit records included "Take Good Care of My Baby," "The Night Has a Thousand Eyes," and the million-selling "Come Back When You Grow Up"

- The Zombies, known for the gold record "Time of the Season" and for being the first British band after the Beatles whose own songwriting yielded a No. 1 U.S. hit — "She's Not There"

For The Record, Volume 3

- The Buckinghams, the Chicago pop-rock horn quintet whose songs include the chart-topping hit "Kind of a Drag" and the top-10 songs "Don't You Care" and "Mercy, Mercy, Mercy"

- Bobby Goldsboro, best known for his gold record "Honey," along with "Little Things," "It's Too Late," and "Summer (The First Time)" and also for creating children's TV programs

- The Moody Blues, who took rock music to unprecedented levels of sophistication with groundbreaking concept albums and hits including "Nights in White Satin" and "Tuesday Afternoon"

- Donnie Brooks, whose three chart singles included the top-10 hit "Mission Bell," and whose work as a promoter into the early 2000s kept numerous '60s performers working on stage
- Sam and Dave, the electrifying duo whose top-selling gospel-inspired soul music hits included "I Thank You" and "Soothe Me," and gold records "Hold On, I'm Comin'" and "Soul Man"
- Ray Stevens, prolific composer, singer, producer, and TV program host whose novelty tunes and ballads include gold-certified "Gitarzan," "Everything Is Beautiful," and "The Streak"
- The Grass Roots, whose 21 folk-rock and bright pop chart singles included the top-10 hits "Let's Live for Today" and "Sooner or Later," and the gold record "Midnight Confessions"

For The Record, Volume 4

- The Atlanta Rhythm Section, the top-notch session musicians too good to remain just a backing band, whose hits included "So In To You," "Imaginary Lover," and "Do It Or Die"
- The band Love, remembered for hits "My Little Red Book," "7 And 7 Is," and "Alone Again Or," and for *Forever Changes*, widely regarded among the best rock albums ever recorded
- Anne Murray, who topped the pop, country, and adult contemporary charts with many of her 80 singles, including "Snowbird," "You Needed Me," and the Beatles' "You Won't See Me"
- Billy Joe Royal, who recorded pop smashes "Down in the Boondocks" and "Cherry Hill Park," along with country music hits "Burned Like a Rocket" and "Out of Sight and On My Mind"
- The Standells, known for the Boston pride rallying cry "Dirty Water," and "Try It," the mildly titillating song that unintentionally provoked a nationwide controversy about lewd lyrics
- B.J. Thomas, whose hits included "Hooked On a Feeling," "(Hey Won't You Play) Another Somebody Done Somebody Wrong Song" and "Raindrops Keep Fallin' On My Head"
- Three Dog Night, which during a nine-year span attained 21 consecutive top 40 hits, including the No. 1 hits "Mama Told Me (Not to Come)," "Joy to the World," and "Black and White"